Inequalities in Health

Population-Level Bioethics

Volumes in the Series

Inequalities in Health
Concepts, Measures, and Ethics
Edited by Nir Eyal, Samia Hurst, Ole F. Norheim, and Daniel Wikler

Inequalities in Health

CONCEPTS, MEASURES, AND ETHICS

Edited by Nir Eyal, Samia Hurst,
Ole F. Norheim, and Daniel Wikler

OXFORD
UNIVERSITY PRESS

OXFORD
UNIVERSITY PRESS

Oxford University Press is a department of the University of Oxford.
It furthers the University's objective of excellence in research, scholarship, and education by publishing worldwide.

Oxford New York
Auckland Cape Town Dar es Salaam Hong Kong Karachi
Kuala Lumpur Madrid Melbourne Mexico City Nairobi
New Delhi Shanghai Taipei Toronto

With offices in
Argentina Austria Brazil Chile Czech Republic France Greece
Guatemala Hungary Italy Japan Poland Portugal Singapore
South Korea Switzerland Thailand Turkey Ukraine Vietnam

Published in the United States of America by
Oxford University Press
198 Madison Avenue, New York, NY 10016

Library of Congress Cataloging-in-Publication Data
Inequalities in health : concepts, measures, and ethics/edited by Nir Eyal . . . [et al.].
p. ; cm.—(Population-level bioethics series)
Includes bibliographical references.
ISBN 978-0-19-993139-2 (hardcover : alk. paper)
I. Eyal, Nir M. (Nir Morechay), 1970– II. Series: Population-level bioethics series.
[DNLM: 1. Health Status Disparities—Congresses. 2. Bioethical Issues—Congresses.
3. Healthcare Disparities—economics—Congresses. 4. Healthcare Disparities—ethics—Congresses. 5. Socioeconomic Factors—Congresses. 6. World Health—Congresses. WA 300.1]
LC Classification not assigned
362.1—dc23
2012039177

9 8 7 6 5 4 3 2 1
Printed in the United States of America
on acid-free paper

CONTENTS

CONTRIBUTORS

Anthony B. Atkinson is research professor at the department of economics, University of Oxford, Kt., FBA, fellow of the Econometric Society, fellow of the European Economic Association, foreign honorary member of the American Academy of Arts and Sciences, and foreign honorary member of the American Economic Association. His research interests include public economics, economics of income distribution, and poverty and security.

Gustaf Arrhenius is professor of practical philosophy at Stockholm University, Torgny Segerstedt Pro Futura Scientia Fellow at Swedish Collegium of Advanced Study (SCAS), and co-chair of the Franco-Swedish program in economics and philosophy at Collège d'études mondiales and SCAS. His research interests are primarily in moral and political philosophy, especially issues pertaining to the intersection between moral and political philosophy and the medical and social sciences. He is the author of *Population Ethics* (Oxford University Press, forthcoming), and his papers have appeared in journal such as *Economics & Philosophy, Philosophical Studies*, and *Utilitas*.

Yukiko Asada is associate professor in the department of community health and epidemiology at Dalhousie University. Her work investigates ethical assumptions underlying quantitative methods used in population health. Her published work includes *Health Inequality: Morality and Measurement* (University of Toronto Press, 2007).

Nick Beckstead is a Ph.D. candidate in philosophy at Rutgers University. His primary research interests include normative ethics, applied ethics, and decision theory.

Norman Daniels, Ph.D., is Mary B. Saltonstall Professor of ethics and population health in the department of global health and population at Harvard School of Public Health. Formerly chair of the philosophy department at Tufts University, where he taught from 1969 to 2002, his most recent books include *Just Health: Meeting Health Needs Fairly* (Cambridge, 2008); *Setting Limits Fairly: Learning to Share Resources for Health*, 2nd edition (Oxford, 2008); *From Chance to Choice: Genetics and Justice* (2000); and *Is Inequality Bad for Our Health?* (2000). His research is on justice and health policy, including priority setting in health systems, fairness and health systems reform, health inequalities, and intergenerational justice. He directs the ethics concentration of the Health Policy Ph.D., recently won the Everett Mendelsohn Award for mentoring graduate students, and teaches courses on ethics and health inequalities and justice and resource allocation.

Angus Deaton is Dwight D. Eisenhower Professor of Economics and International Affairs at Princeton's Woodrow Wilson School and economics department. He is the author of five books and many papers including, most recently, The great escape: health, wealth, and the origins of inequality, his interests include health, development, poverty, inequality, and well-being. He is a long-time consultant to the World Bank on poverty measurement and on international comparisons, and to the Gallup Organization, exploring global and national links between life evaluation, hedonic well-being, income, and health. He was the first recipient of the Econometric Society's Frisch Medal and was Editor of *Econometrica* from 1984 to 1988. He is a fellow of the British Academy, of the Royal Society of Edinburgh, of the Econometric Society, and of the American Academy of Arts and Sciences. He was president of the American Economic Association in 2009. He holds honorary degrees from the Universities of Rome, London, St. Andrews, Edinburgh, and Cyprus and is an honorary fellow of Fitzwilliam College, Cambridge.

Nir Eyal is associate professor in global health and social medicine (Medical Ethics) at the Harvard Medical School. His primary appointment is at Harvard University's campus-wide Program in Ethics and Health. He is writing, among other things, on fair health resource rationing, on ethical care delivery in resource-poor settings, and on philosophical issues in bioethics and political theory.

Marc Fleurbaey is Robert E. Kuenne Professor of Economics and Humanistic Studies at Princeton University. He is the author of *Fairness, Responsibility, and Welfare* (Oxford University Press, 2008) and the co-author of *A Theory of Fairness and Social Welfare* (Cambridge University Press, 2011).

Johann Frick is an instructor in the Department of Philosophy and the Center For Human Values at Princeton University. His current work focuses on population ethics, the concept of interpersonal justification, and the ethics of risk imposition.

Daniel M. Hausman is the Herbert A. Simon and Hilldale Professor of Philosophy at the University of Wisconsin-Madison. His research has centered on epistemological, metaphysical, and ethical issues lying at the boundaries between economics and philosophy. His most recent book is *Preference, Value, Choice and Welfare*, published by Cambridge University Press in 2011.

Samia Hurst, M.D., is Swiss National Science Foundation professor of bioethics at Geneva University's medical school in Switzerland, a member of the Swiss Academy of Medical Sciences' Central Ethics Commission, and chief editor of the journal *Bioethica Forum*. Her research focuses on fairness in clinical practice and the protection of vulnerable persons.

F. M. Kamm, Ph.D., is Lucius Littauer Professor of Philosophy and Public Policy, Harvard Kennedy School, and Professor of Philosophy, Harvard University. She has authored *Creation and Abortion; Morality, Mortality,* vols. 1 and 2; *Intricate Ethics; Ethics for Enemies: Terror, Torture and War, The Moral Target: Aiming at Right Conduct in War and Other Conflicts* (all from Oxford University Press), and numerous articles. She serves on the editorial board of *Philosophy & Public Affairs* and on the Faculty Advisory Committee of the Edmond J. Safra Ethics Center. She has held Guggenheim and NEH Fellowships and is a fellow of the American Academy of Arts and Sciences.

Julian Le Grand is the Richard Titmuss Professor of Social Policy at the London School of Economics. From 2003 to 2005, he was seconded to No. 10 Downing St. as senior policy adviser to the Prime Minister. He has also acted as an adviser to the World Health Organization, the World Bank, the U.K. Department of Health, and the President of the European Commission. He is the author, co-author, or editor of more than nineteen books and over ninety articles on economics, philosophy, and public policy. In 2012, he was awarded the Eupolis Prize by the government of Lombardy, was a runner up in the Wolfson Prize, and was elected a Fellow of the British Academy.

Kasper Lippert-Rasmussen (D.Phil., Oxford) is professor of political theory at the University of Aarhus, Denmark. He works primarily in political and moral philosophy and has published in journals such as *Journal of Political Philosophy, Ethics, Philosophy and Public Affairs, Philosophical Studies, Economics and Philosophy*, and *The Journal of Ethics*. Presently he is working on a book-length manuscript on discrimination. He is an associate editor of *Ethics* and chair of Society for Applied Philosophy.

Michael Marmot is an MRC research professor of epidemiology, knighted for his research into the social determinants of health and the social gradient of health. He is the director of the UCL Institute of Health Equity, and the research teams he chairs have produced a number of key reports and policy recommendations on health inequalities, including *Closing the Gap in a Generation: Health Equity Through Action on the Social Determinants of Health* and *Fair Society, Healthy Lives: Strategic Review of Health Inequalities in England post-2010*. (The Marmot Review). He is currently chairing a review of health inequalities and the health divide in Europe.

Sarah Marchand is a philosopher whose work focuses on measures of well-being in the context of theories of distributive justice and on the ethics of health resource allocation. Her paper, "Class, Health, and Justice" (Milbank

Quarterly/Health and Society, 1998, with D. Wikler and B. Landsman) was one of the first papers on health inequalities to appear in the bioethics literature.

Erik Nord has a Ph.D. in health economics from the University of Oslo. Since 1985, he has been at the Norwegian Institute of Public Health, where he is now a senior researcher. He is also a part-time professor in health economics at the University of Oslo, Department of Pharmacy. His research has mainly been in studying principles and population preferences for priority setting in health care and developing methods for incorporating such preferences in economic evaluation of health programs. He has been an advisor on methods for economic evaluation of health care to the World Health Organization, the Organization of Economic Cooperation and Development, the U.S. Department of Health, IQWIG in Germany, and NICE in the UK. His publications include numerous articles in health economics journals and the book *Cost-Value Analysis in Health Care: Making Sense Out of QALYs* (Cambridge University Press 1999).

Ole F. Norheim is a physician and professor in medical ethics, University of Bergen. He is currently heading the research project Priority Setting in Global Health, funded by a grant from the Ministry of Foreign Affairs in Norway. His articles have appeared in the *British Medical Journal, Journal of Medical Ethics, Bioethics, American Journal of Bioethics, Politics, Philosophy & Economics*, and *Social Science & Medicine*, among others.

Toby Ord is a research fellow in philosophy at the University of Oxford. He works on many topics in theoretical and practical ethics, including moral uncertainty, global poverty, and the impacts of future technologies.

Wlodek Rabinowicz is professor of practical philosophy at Lund University, Centennial Professor at the London School of Economics and Political Science, and a long-term fellow of the Swedish Collegium of Advanced Studies. He is a former president of the European Society of Analytic Philosophy. He is one of the editors of *Theoria* and a former editor of *Economics and Philosophy*. He has extensively published in value theory, decision theory, and philosophical logic.

Ritu Sadana is lead specialist at the World Health Organization in Geneva, Switzerland. She recently set up a collaborative project to support national policy makers to consider and improve health equity while expanding universal health coverage. As part of WHO's contribution to the Commission on Social Determinants of Health, she coordinated activities to reanalyze national data from a health equity perspective and to synthesize evidence on what works to reduce health inequities in several areas. She has contributed to many WHO flagship publications, most recently as editor-in-chief of *The European Health Report 2012*. She serves as an editorial advisor for *The Bulletin of the World Health Organization* and has published in *Science*,

Public Health Reports, *British Medical Journal*, and *The Lancet*, *Social Science & Medicine*, among others.

Shlomi Segall is the head of the Joint Program in Politics, Philosophy, and Economics (PPE) at the Hebrew University of Jerusalem. He is the author of *Health, Luck, and Justice* (Princeton University Press, 2010).

Larry S. Temkin is distinguished professor of philosophy at Rutgers University. He has published on equality, justice, health inequality, enhancements, obligations to the needy, aggregation, practical reasoning, intransitivity, and the good. His individualistic approach to inequality has been adopted by the World Health Organization and the Gates Foundation in their measurements of the Global Burden of Disease, and his work on the Leveling Down Objection helped spawn the debate about prioritarianism (in fact, the word prioritarianism was coined by him). He is the author of *Rethinking the Good: Moral Ideals and the Nature of Practical Reasoning* (Oxford University Press, 2012) and *Inequality* (Oxford University Press, 1993). Temkin has received fellowships from the Danforth Foundation, the National Humanities Center, Harvard University's Safra Foundation Center for Ethics, All Souls College Oxford, the National Institutes of Health, the Australian National University, and Princeton University's Center for Human Values, where he was the Laurance S. Rockefeller Visiting Professor for Distinguished Teaching. He is also the recipient of eight major teaching awards.

Alex Voorhoeve is reader in philosophy at the London School of Economics. He works on egalitarianism, responsibility, and the theory of rational choice. His articles have appeared in *Philosophy & Public Affairs, Economics & Philosophy,* and the *Journal of Political Philosophy*, among others. He is the author of *Conversations on Ethics* (Oxford University Press, 2009).

Daniel Wikler is Mary B. Saltonstall Professor of Population Ethics and professor of ethics and population health in the Department of Global Health and Population of the Harvard School of Public Health. He was the first "staff ethicist" for the World Health Organization. His publications address ethical issues in population health measurement, resource allocation, the assignment of responsibility for health, and the use of human subjects in health research.

Introduction

WHAT'S WRONG WITH HEALTH INEQUALITIES?

Nir Eyal, Samia Hurst, Sara H. Marchand,
Ole F. Norheim, and Daniel Wikler

Travel from the Southeast of downtown Washington to Montgomery County, Maryland. For each mile travelled life expectancy [LE] rises about a year and a half. There is a twenty-year gap between poor blacks at one end of the journey (LE 57) and rich whites at the other (LE 76.7).[1]

Differences in health and longevity across societies and (as Michael Marmot's observation indicates) within societies, are large and ethically disturbing. Several decades' research in epidemiology and social and biomedical sciences in many countries confirms that inequalities in health co-vary with inequalities in income, education, and other social attributes. Barriers to health care access are only one contributing factor. Although the literature on health disparities can be traced back to the work of Engels and Virchow in the mid-nineteenth century, the field has expanded rapidly in recent decades. Some key publications, beginning in the 1970s stimulated a vigorous research effort involving scientists from many disciplines and countries. Marmot's "Whitehall" studies, for example, showed that the health prospects of British civil servants correlate with their rank.

A series of reports by governmental and international agencies have proposed broad programs of remediation.[2,3] Notable among these is report of The World Health Organization's Commission on the Social Determinants of Health, discussed in both Marmot's and Sadana's contributions to this

The editors would like to thank the Brocher Foundation, Hermance, Switzerland, for its generous financial support of the Summer Academy 2010 in Global Population Health, for which earlier drafts of most of the essays in this volume were written. They are also grateful to the Otto and Marie Neurath Isotype Collection at the University of Reading, and to Rob Banham, Diane Billbey and graphic design society RU-CMYK (especially Craig Melvin and Emma Saunders), for help in accessing the archive. Carol Maglitta went far and beyond in supporting graphic design for this volume and the series. Sarah Marchand helped create the index.

[1] Marmot, M. (2004). *The status syndrome: How social standing affects our health and longevity.* New York: Henry Holt and Company.

[2] Pelican Series. (1982). *Inequalities in health: Black Report.* New York: Penguin Books.

[3] World Health Organization Commission on the Social Determinants of Health. (2008). *Closing the gap in a generation: Health equity through action on the social determinants of health.* Geneva: World Health Organization.

volume. The volume of empirical findings (and policy initiatives) on health inequalities continues to grow. Marmot's and Deaton's chapters offer contrasting interpretations of these findings.

The literature assumes that many of these inequalities constitute "inequities" that fairness requires us to demands reduce or eliminate. But what makes (some) inequalities inequities? Margaret Whitehead's formulation is often cited: inequities are inequalities that they are unnecessary, avoidable, unfair, and unjust.[4] But which differences in health are unfair and unjust? In extreme cases, such as Marmot's example of Washington DC, the lack of fairness is obvious, but our intuitions may be less firm when the inequalities are narrower, or do not coincide with other social fault lines, have complex causes. These intuitions may peter out entirely in the face of more complex judgments, such as deciding which of two patterns of inequality is more unfair—a question that several contributors to this volume address. When our immediate, intuitive response to specific inequalities is closer to moral puzzlement than to confident certainty (or when observers disagree), we will need to rely on a more systematic theory of distributive fairness and health.

Despite widespread concern with the unfairness of inequalities in health, there has been relatively little sustained and critical attention paid to underlying conceptual and basic ethical questions: Which inequalities are unjust? What precisely is the nature and import of that injustice? What criteria should be used to evaluate efforts to mitigate that injustice? We hope that the chapters in this book, which address such questions, will be of interest to epidemiologists, economists, philosophers, physicians, activists, and others with an interest in understanding distributive justice as it focuses on health or in identifying, explaining, and correcting inequalities in health.

Until recently, articles and books whose titles included the words "inequalities" (or "disparities") and "health" typically addressed disparities in access to care caused by barriers affecting underserved groups, such as African Americans in the United States. These very important injustices are noted by a number of the authors in this book (including Daniels, Deaton, Hausman, Kamm, Marmot, Ord and Beckstead, Lippert-Rasmussen, and Segall). But these chapters address them as one of several sources of inequality in health. Since health has many determinants, these essays focus on inequalities in health rather than only on disparities in access to health services. Their subject is who is healthy and who is not, rather than whether doctors and hospitals are treating patients equitably, or whether some groups lack health insurance. What the chapters in this book do address is a wide range of ethical issues that bear on health inequalities. We devote the balance of this introduction to identifying some of these issues.

---

[4] Whitehead, Margaret. (1992). The concepts and principles of equity in health. *International Journal of Health Services*, 22, 429–445. The WHO Commission's definition eliminates three of these: "Health inequities are avoidable inequalities in health between groups of people within countries and between countries." World Health Organization Commission on the Social Determinants of Health, 2008.

Concepts and Measures of Health Inequality

As Temkin's contribution argues, inequality is a multidimensional concept. It might designate, for example, the gap between those doing worst and those doing best or the gap between those doing worst and the median or average. Atkinson observes that it might also designate the relative gap multiplied by how badly the worse off are doing, if the worst off are very badly off in absolute terms. And, as Nord shows, the relevant inequalities may pertain to lifetime health, to health at a specific point in time, or to health prospects from a point in time into the future.

To voice a concern over "inequality in health" in a society does not specify which of these inequalities concerns us. Perhaps it is one, or another, or still another inequality, or some combination. Any attempt to gauge a society's progress in reducing health inequalities over time, or to compare and rank different societies with respect to health inequalities at a given moment, requires choosing particular inequality measurements. For these purposes, we need to specify, for example, how much of an individual's lifetime experience of health is being used as the interval for comparison, how to weight differences in severity or deprivation, and whether the inequality in question is one between individuals or between groups. Rankings by one measure might differ from rankings by others. Inequalities may narrow over time by one measure and widen according to others.

Comparisons of societies according to their level of inequality of health are particularly difficult when the populations are of different sizes. Gustaf Arrhenius's chapter demonstrates that such comparisons require attention to more than the overall inequality-based unfairness to worse-off individuals. What he calls the egalitarian value of a population turns out to be a strictly decreasing function of pairwise relations of inequality *and* a strictly increasing function of pairwise relations of equality.

Some of these conceptual questions about inequality apply to income just as much as they apply to health. But Asada, Atkinson, and Ole Norheim, who assess the adequacy of adapting the Gini coefficient and other measures of income inequality to health, point to some key differences between health and income. For example, the biological upper limit of longevity that has no counterpart in money earned.

DO ALL INEQUALITIES IN HEALTH MATTER?

Need we be concerned about *all* inequalities in health?

Among the contributors to this volume, Deaton points to health inequalities resulting from the unequal diffusion of new medical information or technology within a society as one exception. Although it may be regretted that not all will benefit at first, the prospect of improved population health may be a compensating good from a moral point of view, especially if all will catch up over time.

One interpretation of Deaton's point links it to a philosophical debate between egalitarians and so-called prioritarians, who favor giving higher priority to the worse off. Doing the best we can for the worst-off usually reduces their deficit relative to those doing better, but sometimes it increases it. For example, in a given instance it may be that the intervention that would result in the greatest improvement in the health of the worst off would be to curtail air pollution but that the benefit this would confer on the better off would be greater still. The widening of the gap in this case would not be a step away from justice, according to prioritarians. Moreover, any effort to reduce the gap by trying to limit the health improvement enjoyed by the better off would be morally wrong, for surely we should curtail air pollution when there is no cost to anyone. Nir Eyal, expanding on earlier work by Temkin, defends egalitarianism against this prioritarian challenge.

Are inequalities in health stemming from patterns of imprudent personal choices another exception? Or are these inequalities of moral concern as well? Contributors to this volume differ in the weight they attach to personal responsibility for health and in their reasons for doing so. Some, such as Segall, Julian Le Grand, and Temkin, endorse versions of a theory of justice according to which it is unfair when someone is worse off than others through no fault of his own, whereas inequalities that result from avoidable choices might be judged to be fair. A different kind of egalitarian theory attracts other contributors, including Hausman and Daniels. Their conception of justice emphasizes treatment of everyone as equals, emphasizing equality of opportunity and freedom from disenfranchisement, exclusion, and humiliation. Personal responsibility plays a less central role.

Their different perspectives on justice notwithstanding, these contributors are united in holding that in practice, health inequalities usually remain of great concern even when they result from personal choice. Notably, that consensus includes Le Grand, an early champion of personal responsibility in health policy. Marmot and Deaton add that policy should look beyond an individual's imprudent choices to conditions—presumably beyond the individual's control—that resulted in the individual's making these choices, at least where these choices follow social patterns.

And what about so-called natural inequalities in health that are of purely biological origin? Do these inequalities matter? And can they be said to be unjust? Here, we should distinguish between inequalities that we can do nothing about and those that could be remedied by appropriate preventive or therapeutic intervention. In both cases, the sources of the inequality may be biological rather than social, but the failure to provide therapy is always a social choice. For some authors, such as Marmot, inequalities in health are unjust only when they are social in origin. For others, such as Hausman, they are unjust regardless of their source when we could ameliorate them by intervening. And for Lippert-Rasmussen, some inequalities in health are unjust or unfair even if they are natural in origin and irremediable. He points to natural genetic differences that lead to vast differences in life prospects. For him, natural injustices are often as bad as similar social injustices.

The much-discussed gap in life expectancy between men and women is a good test case for whether natural inequalities (and personal responsibility for health) matter. Although the number of years of difference varies over time and between societies, women tend to live longer than men nearly everywhere. Presumably, we could reduce this gap by targeting life-prolonging health resources toward men. If so, would justice require us to do so, in order to narrow health disparities? Or, would justice require us *not* to do so, as the following passage may suggest:

> Not all health inequalities are unjust or inequitable. If good health were simply unattainable, this would be unfortunate but not unjust. Where inequalities in health are avoidable, yet are not avoided, they are inequitable. This distinction can be illustrated by the difference in men's and women's health. Women, in general, live longer than men. This difference is likely due to biological sex differences, and is not, therefore, inequitable. However, in cases where women have the same or lower life expectancy as men—that is, where social conditions act to reduce their apparently natural longevity advantage—inequality is a mark of inequity.[5]

INEQUALITIES BETWEEN INDIVIDUALS AND BETWEEN GROUPS

If we are concerned about inequalities in health, should our attention focus on inequalities between individuals, as is customary in economics and political philosophy, or on inequalities between certain groups? In particular, when we are concerned with health inequalities in a particular country, should we focus on differences in health across the social boundaries that are significant in that society? In the United States, this might be race; in another, that between urban dwellers and those living in the countryside. Some take this approach:

> Equity is not the absence of all disparities; it is the absence of systematic disparities between social groups that have greater and lesser degrees of underlying social advantage because of such factors as wealth, sex, race and ethnicity, or urban and rural residence, for example. Policy makers need information on health inequalities between different social groups.[6]

---

[5] Michael Marmot, on behalf of the Commission on Social Determinants of Health. (2007). Achieving health equity: from root causes to fair outcomes. *Lancet*, 370, 1153–1163. Published Online September 6, 2007. doi:10.1016/S0140-6736(07)61385-3

[6] Celia Almeida et al. (2001). Methodological concerns and recommendations on policy consequences of the World Health Report 2000. *Lancet*, 357 (May 26), 1692–1697. Marmot's endorses the same approach: "By common usage in Britain, when we use the term 'health inequalities', we mean differences among social groups; in economics, the term inequality is commonly used to apply to differences among individuals—this is interesting but not what I mean by health inequalities."

Attention to health inequalities between individuals has been defended on a number of grounds. Some are methodological. The World Health Organization (WHO) team whose individual-based health inequality measure was the target of the critique in the preceding paragraph responded that important information may be lost if researchers ignore individual health inequalities.[7] To be sure, information about groups defined by wealth, sex, race, and so forth can be useful, in part because these inequalities tend to have large causal impacts on health in many domains. Racial minorities, for instance, tend to be worse off in terms of a variety of health outcomes, as well as in access to health resources. But individual differences can transcend racial, ethnic, gender, wealth, and geographic differences. Indeed, differences in terms of working conditions, environmental sanitation, water supply, access to health services, social norms about risk factors, type of housing, or birth spacing can define at-risk "groups" (for example, those living with poor sanitation). It is useful to focus interventions on such groups—not necessarily less useful than to focus on social groups such as females.[8] Differences between individuals can also redefine which social boundaries matter the most. Subsequent research by many of the scientists who created the WHO individual-based measure (after having relocated to the Gates-sponsored Institute for Health Metrics and Evaluation) partitioned the U.S. population into eight "Americas" based on factors like race, but also on ones like population density, each of which shows distinctive patterns with distinctive trends over time.[9] Asada's and Norheim's contributions to this volume call for attention to individual differences primarily on methodological grounds. For Asada, more than for Norheim, group inequalities should be investigated as well. She recommends using both "univariate" measures that assess only inequality in health and "bivariate" measures that assess how much health co-varies with factors such as income.

Other arguments for attention to health inequalities between individuals interpret the debate a little differently, as concerning not (only) methodology and causal explanation, but (also) what matters intrinsically: whether what is unfair in itself (as opposed to being only a fruitful proxy or the major cause of unfairness) is group differences or individual differences in health. This is how Lippert-Rasmussen's chapter seems to cast the debate, and it proposes a thought experiment to show that individual differences matter intrinsically:

> Suppose we have a population consisting of two men and two women and that one man and one woman have 10 units of the relevant health value and

---

[7] See Emmanuela Gakidou and Gary King. (2002). Measuring total health inequality: adding individual variation to group-level differences. *International Journal for Equity in Health*, 1(3), 1–12.

[8] Christopher J. L. Murray. (2001). World Health Report 2000: Commentary: comprehensive approaches are needed for full understanding. *BMJ*, 323(7314), 680–681. Further contributions to the debate over the WHO inequality measure, for which Temkin served as an adviser, can be found at http://www.who.int/health-systems-performance/docs/overallframework_docs.htm. (accessed August 21, 2012).

[9] Christopher J. L. Murray, S. C. Kulkarni, C. Michaud, N. Tomijima, M. T. Bulzacchelli, et al. (2006). Eight Americas: investigating mortality disparities across races, counties, and race-counties in the United States. *PLoS Medicine*, 3(9), e260. doi: 10.1371/journal.pmed.0030260.

> that the remaining two persons have 5. On a group-based view focusing only on men and women, there is no regrettable health inequality, while there is...on an individualistic view. If intuitively this example involves a regrettable health inequality, then inequality between individuals should be further explored.

It seems important to distinguish between these different functions of focusing on group inequality or, alternatively, on individual inequality. Focus on a given intergroup difference may be methodologically helpful without capturing inequalities that are intrinsically bad or wrong and vice versa.

INEQUALITY AND DISCRIMINATION

As previously mentioned, these essays address inequalities in *health* more than inequalities in *health care,* where conscious or unconscious bias—discrimination by health workers and facilities—may obstruct access to care. But concerns about inequality and discrimination in health and health care sometimes go beyond personal bias and partiality. The standard cost-effectiveness calculation, which is prevalent in health economics and certainly isn't aimed at discriminating against any group, is often accused of so-called disability discrimination—of systematically deciding against the disabled in some key areas. A cost-effective allocation of lifesaving resources during a pandemic, for example, would normally take into account the chances that the recipient would have a very good or healthy and long life if saved. That is, it would consider the likelihood of her survival to translate into a lot of health or health-related quality of life—say, into many quality-adjusted life years (QALYs). As a direct result, maximizing cost-effectiveness gives people with untreatable disabilities a lesser chance of receiving scarce lifesaving resources. Saving *their* lives generates a smaller health bang for the buck. Initially at least, that seems unfair toward them.[10]

Kamm's contribution to this volume elaborates and expands on this worry. For Kamm, the disabled can legitimately complain of invidious discrimination when they are denied resources on cost-effectiveness grounds. Her intricate position takes into account additional factors, such as whether lifesaving treatment is being denied to the disabled through action or mere omission.

Beckstead and Ord's chapter defends the cost-effectiveness approach. It argues that this side effect of using the cost-effectiveness calculation must be deemed fair or appropriate lest we accept some absurd positions. We must choose, in particular, between accepting disability discrimination or else accepting at least one of three unappealing alternatives: preference for early death, a pointless violation of autonomy, or cyclic preference.

---

[10] John Harris. (1995). Double jeopardy and the veil of ignorance—a reply. *Journal of Medical Ethics,* 21, 151–157.

EQUITY AND UNCERTAINTY

Those seeking to reduce wrongful inequalities in health must, like all of us, peer into the future through a crystal ball that is often cloudy. Uncertainty over the consequences of our interventions presents a host of questions, including ones of ethical principle. A relatively simple question of principle is how much weight to give "risk" of unequal health outcomes. A more complicated set of questions asks whether, in view of uncertainty, what matters is *risk of unequal health outcomes* or, alternatively, *unequal health risk*—that is, the distribution of prospects/risk between persons (as opposed to the distribution of good/bad health outcomes between them).

Suppose, for example, that a population of equally healthy persons are each offered an opportunity to benefit greatly that is accompanied by a small risk of lesser harm—not unusual in population health. They might consider themselves fortunate. The predictable result, however, will be an increase in outcome inequality. Most will gain a lot and some will lose. Would it be more egalitarian therefore to refrain from offering the intervention? Would it be fairer, more in the spirit of equality at least, to offer an alternate intervention that is sure to benefit everyone very moderately? To do so would offer each a lower increase in expected utility than under the first intervention, but it would prevent these unequal outcomes and perhaps count as egalitarian. On the other hand, the first intervention, although it is certain to produce winners, losers, and inequality in health outcomes, may claim to treat all with equal concern. Under the first intervention, the gamble was identical for each person, and each would rationally prefer that gamble and its high expected utility to the certain moderate benefit offered by the second alternative.

Marc Fleurbaey and Alex Voorhoeve insist that an egalitarian must favor the second intervention—prioritizing equal outcomes over equal chances. Their surprising result relies on the idea that moral calculations based on full information are preferable to ones based on partial information. Johann Frick responds that, in one important way, the first intervention is not unfair at all: those who turn out to be losers cannot reasonably complain of unfairness when that intervention represented higher expected utility for them. He adds, however, that uncertainty over who the losers will be does not guarantee full egalitarian fairness when it is known in advance that outcomes will be strongly unequal.

Finally, Wlodek Rabinowicz presents an argument in favor of equality when information that would distinguish the individuals in question is lacking. He proceeds from a presumption of equality that directs us to treat different individuals equally when we cannot discriminate between them on the basis of available information. This may occur, for example, when we must allocate health resources with little or no information about the potential recipients' different needs. Rabinowicz argues that in such situations equal treatment should be chosen because it minimizes *expected* injustice in outcome. Rabinowicz defines the "moral cost of error" as the "expected injustice in outcomes," and he shows that, absent information, equal distribution will minimize that moral cost.

Conclusion

Research in population health is increasingly focused on health inequalities and on the social determinants of health. That research has highlighted causal factors whose influence on health had scarcely been imagined before. As such, it suggests new directions for intervention both within the field of health as traditionally defined and in other domains.

The great strides that scientists from many disciplines have made in identifying, explaining, and devising strategies to fight inequalities in health have rarely been matched by sustained efforts to pose and answer a host of fundamental questions about concepts, measures, and ethics. We hope that the chapters in this book will stimulate interest in addressing these questions.

PART } I

Defining and Measuring Health Inequality

1 }

Inequality and Health

Larry S. Temkin

Let me begin this chapter with two vignettes.

> First vignette. My children were born in Houston's Methodist Hospital, in the heart of the Texas Medical Center. The entryway resembled a five-star hotel, where "customer service representatives" stood behind a long marble counter and there was a huge open foyer, which included an escalator several stories high, a gorgeous fountain, large arrangements of fresh flowers, statues, marble floor and columns, and an incredibly high, vaulted ceiling. The hospital's new birthing suites were opulent, with large private rooms, mosaic tiling, a spacious private bathroom with a Jacuzzi tub, lots of seating for visitors, a comfortable couch that could be turned into an extra bed, a TV, sound system, telephone, and soft lighting. An expectant mother never had to leave her room before, during, or after her delivery. Children born in those rooms were, quite literally, born into the lap of luxury. Unsurprisingly, Methodist Hospital was a private hospital, where only the well-to-do—or the well-insured—could afford to stay. Suffice it to say, the conditions were a little different at Houston's main public hospital, where the poor and uninsured gave birth.
>
> Dickens's famous novel, *A Tale of Two Cities*, chillingly resonates with modern day Houston. In the very shadows of the city's glorious skyscrapers lie barrios and ghettos within which the infant mortality rate exceeds that of many developing nations. Moreover, many of Houston's poor often do without needed medical care, even as, just a few miles from them, the Texas Medical Center provides world-class treatment to oil-rich sheiks and other incredibly wealthy patients from around the globe.
>
> Second vignette. My cousin's third child was born severely premature. Fortunately, he spent his first three weeks in a critical care unit for premature infants at Los Angeles's Cedar-Sinai Hospital. The bill for those three weeks exceeded half a million dollars and, surely, that bill and the services it bought far surpassed the reach of most of LA's uninsured or underinsured residents whose children, born with similar problems, may well have died. And, of

course, even as extreme and costly measures were taken to keep my cousin's child alive, countless children around the globe died because they had not received a simple vaccine, package of oral rehydration salts, dose of vitamin A, or antibiotics.

If, for the sake of a simple and conservative calculation, we assume that the full cost of providing lifesaving medications to certain children in the developing world might be $500, then for the same amount that it cost to save my cousin's son, one might have saved more than 1,000 children in the developing world.

Surely, those who die due to a lack of basic medical care that is widely and cheaply available in much of the world are no less deserving of life or assistance than their counterparts in the developed world. It is just their bad luck that they were born in the wrong place and the wrong time, or in the wrong class and to the wrong parents.

For many, the preceding vignettes highlight the appeal and importance of equality in our considerations about health and health care. We don't merely recognize the sad but inevitable truth that some people are in poor health or receive little or substandard health care and see the pressing need to address the situation; we rankle at the further fact that there is so much undeserved inequality in the distribution of health states and health care. For many, the situation is not merely unfortunate: it is terribly unfair, and this provides significant additional force to the legitimate claims of many living in poor health. Of course, such vignettes do not provide an argument for equality's normative significance, nor are they intended to. But they help highlight a value and concern that many share.

In this chapter, I begin by distinguishing and clarifying the particular version of egalitarianism with which I am concerned, a view I call *equality as comparative fairness*. I then briefly illuminate the complexity and difficulty of measuring inequality by considering the question: "When is one situation worse than another regarding inequality?" I conclude by addressing the importance of health from an egalitarian perspective.

My discussion here is, per force, cursory and oversimplified. Interested readers might wish to read some of my other writings on these topics, where each of these issues is dealt with in greater detail and depth.[1]

---

[1] See, for example, *Inequality* (Oxford University Press, 1993); "Equality and the Human Condition" (*Theoria* [South Africa] 92, December 1998, pp. 15–45); "Equality, Priority, and the Levelling Down Objection," in *The Ideal of Equality*, edited by Matthew Clayton and Andrew Williams, pp. 126–161 (Macmillan and St. Martin's Press, 2000); "Egalitarianism: A Complex, Individualistic, and Comparative Notion," in *Philosophical Issues*, vol. 11, edited by Ernie Sosa and Enriquea Villanueva, pp. 327–352 (Blackwell Publishers, 2001); "Egalitarianism Defended" (*Ethics* 113 (4), 2003, pp. 764–782); "Equality, Priority, or What?" (*Economics and Philosophy* 19(1), 2003, pp. 61–88); "Illuminating Egalitarianism," in *Contemporary Debates in Political Philosophy*, edited by Thomas Christiano and John Christman, pp. 155–178 (Wiley-Blackwell Publishing, 2009); "Justice, Equality, Fairness, Desert, Rights, Free Will, Responsibility, and Luck," in *Distributive Justice and Responsibility*, edited by Carl Knight and Zofia Stemplowska, pp. 51–76 (Oxford University Press, 2011).

Equality as Comparative Fairness

Egalitarians come in many stripes. Too many, I'm afraid. Correspondingly, in discussing equality, it is extremely important that one be clear about the sense in which one is using the term.

I call the conception of egalitarianism with which I am concerned here *equality as comparative fairness*. On this view, there is an intimate connection between the concern for equality and a concern about fairness; so, equality is a subtopic of the more general—and even more complex—topic of fairness. Specifically, concern about inequality is that portion of our concern about fairness that focuses on how people fare *relative to others*. So, our concern for equality is not separable from our concern for a certain aspect of fairness; they are part and parcel of a single concern. Thus, egalitarians in my sense are not motivated by a sense of *envy*, but by a sense of *fairness*. They believe that undeserved inequality is bad precisely when and because it is unfair. The preceding vignettes were intended to provoke the sense of comparative fairness with which egalitarians, in my sense, are concerned.

Many contemporary egalitarians have been identified as so-called luck egalitarians.[2] Acknowledging the importance of personal responsibility, luck egalitarianism supposedly aims to rectify the influence of luck in people's lives. Correspondingly, a canonical formulation of luck egalitarianism is that it is bad when one person is worse off than another through no fault or choice of his or her own.[3] So, luck egalitarians object when equally deserving people are unequally well off but not when one person is worse off than another due to his or her own responsible choices, say, to pursue a life of leisure or crime.

---

[2] These include Richard Arneson, G. A. Cohen, and Ronald Dworkin. See, for example, Arneson's "Equality and Equal Opportunity for Welfare" (*Philosophical Studies* 56, 1989, pp. 77–93); Cohen's "On the Currency of Egalitarian Justice" (*Ethics* 99, 1989, pp. 906–944); and Dworkin's "What Is Equality? Part 1: Equality of Welfare," and "Part 2: Equality of Resources" (*Philosophy and Public Affairs* 10, 1981, pp. 185–246 and 283–345). Dworkin famously defends the view that egalitarians should seek to rectify *brute* luck, but need not be concerned about *option* luck. Kasper Lippert-Rasmussen challenges Dworkin's distinction in "Egalitarianism, Option Luck, and Responsibility" (*Ethics* 111, 2001, pp. 548–579), as do I in "Justice, Equality, Fairness, Desert, Rights, Free Will, Responsibility, and Luck." I believe the term "luck egalitarianism" was first introduced, pejoratively, by Elizabeth Anderson in "What Is the Point of Equality?" (*Ethics* 109, 1999, pp. 287–337).

[3] See Cohen's "On the Currency of Egalitarian Justice" and my *Inequality*. In my 1983 Princeton Ph.D. thesis, *Inequality*, I originally claimed that egalitarians thought that "it is a bad thing (unjust or unfair) for them [some people] to be worse off than the other members of their world through no fault of their own (p. 6)." Cohen told me in conversation that he derived his classic formulation of the egalitarian's position from mine, but that since he thought of "fault" as involving a moral shortcoming, he believed it crucial to add the "no choice" clause to my original formulation. As I later spelled out in my book, *Inequality* (p. 13, note 21), I always intended the expression "through no fault of their own" to be shorthand for the expression "through no fault or choice of their own." I assumed that if someone freely chose to do x and was not under duress when doing so, then the doing of x was his "fault" in the sense of his being *responsible* for it, not necessarily in the sense that his doing x reflected a moral shortcoming. To avoid unnecessary confusion, I later adopted Cohen's reformulation of my position as my own.

In fact, I think luck egalitarianism has been misunderstood by most of its proponents as well as its opponents. I believe that the so-called luck egalitarian's fundamental concern isn't with luck, per se, or even with whether someone is worse off than another through no fault or choice of his or her own, it is with *comparative fairness*. But this has been obscured by the fact that, in most paradigmatic cases where inequality involves comparative unfairness, it also involves luck or someone being worse off than another through no fault or choice of his or her own.

Thus, on close examination, the intimate connection between equality and fairness illuminates the ultimate role that luck plays in the egalitarian's thinking, as well as the relevance and limitations of the well-known "through no fault or choice of her own" clause. Among equally deserving people, it *is* bad because it is unfair for some to be worse off than others through no fault or choice of their own. But among unequally deserving people, it *isn't* bad because it isn't unfair for someone less deserving to be worse off than someone more deserving, even if the former is worse off through no fault or choice of his or her own. For example, egalitarians needn't object if criminal John is worse off than law-abiding Mary, even if John craftily avoided capture and so is only worse off because, through no fault or choice of his own, a falling tree injured him.

Additionally, in some cases, inequality is bad because unfair even though the worse off *are* responsible for their plight, as when the worse off are so because they chose to do their duty or perhaps acted supererogatorily in adverse circumstances not of their making. So, for example, if I'm unlucky enough to walk by a drowning child, and I injure myself saving her, the egalitarian might think it unfair that I end up worse off than others, even though I am so as a result of my own responsible free choice to do my duty to aid the drowning child.

Correspondingly, on reflection, luck itself is neither good nor bad from the egalitarian standpoint. Egalitarians object to luck that leaves equally deserving people unequally well off. But they can accept luck that makes equally deserving people equally well off or unequally deserving people unequally well off proportional to their deserts. Thus, luck will be approved or opposed only to the extent that it promotes or undermines *comparative fairness*.

Before proceeding, let me emphasize that I am not claiming that comparative fairness egalitarianism is the sole position deserving of the name egalitarianism. Many other positions also have a claim to be egalitarian in spirit, some of which are compatible with comparative fairness egalitarianism and others of which are not. But I believe that comparative fairness egalitarianism represents a distinct, substantive version of egalitarianism that is particularly central and relevant to concerns about health and health care inequalities.

Similarly, let me emphasize that any reasonable person who is an egalitarian in my sense will be a pluralist. Equality is not the only thing that matters to the comparative fairness egalitarian. It may not even be the ideal that matters most, but it is *one* ideal, among others, that has independent normative significance. This is worth bearing in mind because, despite the discussion in the later section "The Importance of Health" and this volume's other chapters, I think it is a serious and open question how much we should allow considerations of equality to influence the development and distribution of health care.

Suppose, then, that we accept comparative fairness egalitarianism. We believe that undeserved inequality is bad when and because it is unfair and that the unfairness typically involves some being worse off than others through no fault or choice of their own. How do we compare societies, or outcomes, in terms of inequality? How, for example, do we measure the extent of a situation's inequality regarding comparative fairness? Unfortunately, it is no easy matter to answer such questions because, as we shall see next, it is one thing to know that we hold such a position, quite another to unpack all that it involves.

Comparing Outcomes Regarding Inequality

When is one outcome worse than another regarding inequality? In some cases, the answer to this question can be easily given. Consider, for example, Figure 1.1, where the heights of the columns represent people's quality of life, and the widths represent the number of people in an outcome. This diagram, and the others, are greatly oversimplified, but they serve to illustrate my points.

We know that among equally deserving people, an outcome like *B*, where some are worse off than others, is worse than one like *A*, where everyone is equal, in terms of inequality. We also know that, among equally deserving people, the inequality in an outcome like *D*, where the gaps between the better and worse off are large, would be worse than the inequality in an outcome like *C*, where the gaps are small.

In many other cases, however, it is extremely difficult to decide how two outcomes compare. Consider, for example, the set of 999 outcomes that I call the *Sequence*. In the Sequence's first outcome, there are 999 people better off and one person worse off, in the Sequence's second outcome there are 998 people better off and two people worse off, in the third outcome there are 997 better off and three worse off, and so on. The Sequence's first, middle, and last outcomes are represented in Figure 1.2.

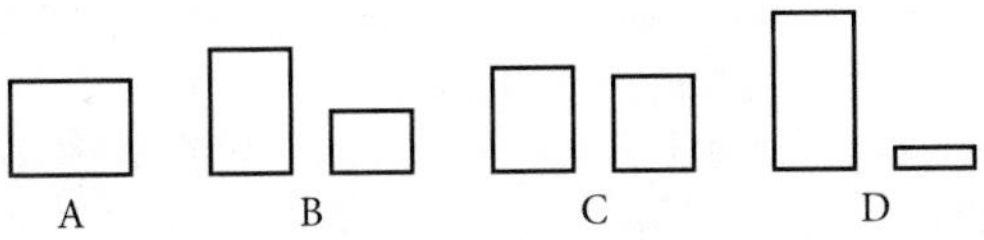

FIGURE 1.1 The Sequence (A).

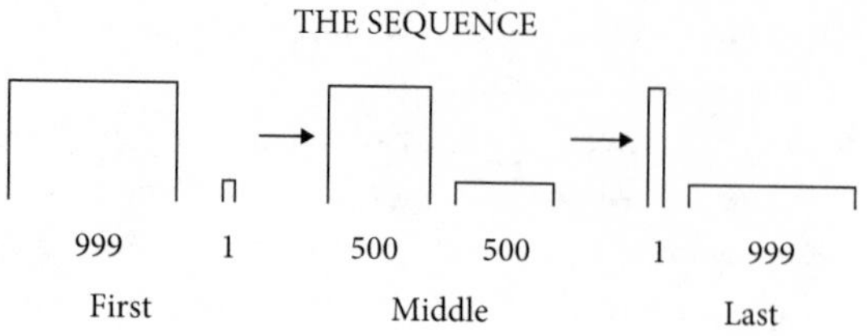

FIGURE 1.2 The Sequence (B).

How do the Sequence's outcomes compare—*not all things considered*—where it may seem clear that the first outcome is best and the last worst—but *regarding inequality*? On reflection, I think many plausible answers can be given to this question.

For example, one way we may judge inequality is in terms of how "gratuitous" the inequality seems. In the Sequence's early outcomes, for example, the inequality may seem "pointless and unnecessary." If direct redistribution were possible to bring about equality, the better off would hardly lose anything and the worse off would gain tremendously. Hence, the inequality in the early outcomes may seem particularly offensive because there seems to be virtually nothing gained by it.

In the middle outcomes, however, redistribution would "cost" a lot. A large number would have to sacrifice a great deal to achieve equality. In such outcomes, we could understand the reluctance of the better off to redistribute and, although we might think it would be good if they were to voluntarily do this, we might not think they were morally required to. In those outcomes, then, the inequality might strike us as more excusable, and hence less disturbing, than the inequality in the earlier outcomes.

In the later outcomes, direct redistribution from better to worse off would involve tremendous loss for some with virtually no gain for those thus "benefited." Therefore, the inequality might seem least offensive in the later outcomes, where the "cost" of the inequality might seem smallest and the "gain" highest.

This position might be summed up as follows. Egalitarians will think it unfair if, through no fault or choice of their own, some are badly off—for example, struggling to survive—while others are well off—for example, living lives of ease and comfort. But from one perspective, at least, egalitarians may be most offended if just a few are badly off while the vast majority are well off because the inequality then seems particularly gratuitous. Thus, in accordance with this way of thinking, it will seem that the Sequence is getting *better and better* regarding inequality.

Another reason egalitarians may think the Sequence is getting better and better is that it appears to be less and less the case that those who are worse off are being especially victimized by the situation. In the earlier outcomes, for instance, it is as if the entire burden of the inequality is borne by those few who are unfortunate enough to be among the worse off. Given that those few people are much worse off than everyone else, it may seem that they have a very large complaint regarding inequality and, correspondingly, that the inequality is especially offensive. By contrast, the later outcomes' inequality may seem relatively inoffensive. In those outcomes, each member of the worse off group is as well off as all but a few of the others. Hence, in those outcomes, it may seem as if nobody has much to complain about regarding inequality.

This view is plausible, and it expresses itself in the way we react to the actions of bullies or tyrants. If a bully or tyrant decides to humiliate certain people, from a utilitarian standpoint, we may well hope that it is a small portion of the population that is so mistreated. Nevertheless, from an egalitarian standpoint, we may well find the mistreatment most offensive if it applies to only a small segment of the population. Thus, it may seem particularly unfair for a few people to bear the brunt of their world's injustice, and it may seem especially galling that the vast majority should be leading normal happy lives while one small segment of it gets crushed beneath the heel of oppression.

One way of putting this point is that certain egalitarian intuitions are especially attuned to instances of invidious or capricious discrimination in which a particular person or small number of people is singled out for discriminatory treatment. In fact, I think it is the singling out in this way of an individual or small number that is the paradigmatic case of when we judge a harmful discrimination to be grossly unjust or unfair.

There are, then, several ways of thinking that might lead one to think that the Sequence is getting better and better regarding inequality. But there are also ways of thinking that might lead one to judge that the Sequence *first get worse, then better*.

It is easy to be drawn to such an ordering by reasoning as follows. In the early outcomes, everyone is perfectly equal except, regrettably, for a few, isolated individuals. In those outcomes, then, the worse off represent an ever-so-slight perturbation in an otherwise perfectly homogeneous system. Therefore, because in the early outcomes there is just a slight deviation from absolute equality, those outcomes may seem nearly perfect regarding inequality. In the middle outcomes, the deviation from absolute equality is much larger. Half the population is much better off than the other half. In the later outcomes, there is once again just an ever-so-slight deviation from absolute equality. Everyone is perfectly equal except, regrettably, for a few isolated individuals. Like the early outcomes, therefore, those outcomes may appear almost perfect regarding inequality. In sum, it seems there is a natural and plausible way of looking at the Sequence's outcomes such that we would judge that the outcomes first get worse and then get better.

Another line of thought also supports the "worse, then better" ordering. In the early outcomes, only a few people have a complaint regarding inequality, so, as large as their complaints may be, those outcomes' inequality may not seem too bad. However, in the middle outcomes, it may seem both that a large number have a complaint—half of the population—*and* that the magnitude of their complaints will be large—they are, after all, worse off than half the population through no fault of their own. In the later outcomes, on the other hand, the situation may seem analogous to, although the reverse of, the one obtaining in the earlier outcomes. Although almost everyone has something to complain about, it may seem that the size of their complaints will be virtually negligible because they are as well off as almost every other person in their outcome. Hence, as with the early outcomes, the inequality may not seem too bad.

It seems, then, that there are egalitarian reasons to rank the Sequence's outcomes as getting worse, then better, as well as reasons to rank them as just getting better.

Still other reasons seem to support ranking the Sequence's outcomes as getting *worse and worse.*

In the early outcomes, only a few people are worse off than the better off. In the middle outcomes, half the population is worse off than the better off. In the later outcomes, virtually everybody is worse off than the better off. Since the size of the gap between better and worse off is the same in each outcome, we may conclude that the early outcomes are the best regarding inequality, and the later outcomes are the worst.

Let me note just one of several examples in which such reasoning is involved. If I ask audiences to think of the worst periods of inequality in human history—as I have many times over the years—one of the most common responses is that of medieval Europe. But the common conception of medieval Europe involves a few—kings, queens, and noblemen—living in the lap of luxury while the vast majority—peasants and serfs—struggle to survive. Such an outcome resembles the Sequence's later outcomes, rather than its early or middle ones. And whereas here, as elsewhere, I think people's intuitive responses may be partly influenced by many different factors, I think one reason so many think of medieval Europe as among the worst periods of inequality is that the number of worse off is so large relative to the fortunate few who are well off. This way of thinking is compatible with the judgment that the Sequence is getting worse and worse, but not with the judgments previously discussed.

This discussion has been vastly oversimplified. But I hope to have conveyed some sense for why I claim inequality is complex. There are many different positions or aspects capable of underlying and influencing our egalitarian judgments. In fact, in my book, *Inequality*, I argued that there are at least three plausible and distinct ways of measuring the size of an individual's complaint with respect to inequality—the *relative-to-the-best-off-person view of complaints*, the *relative-to-the-average view of complaints*, and the *relative-to-all-those-better-off view of complaints*—and I argued that each of these views could be plausibly combined with any of three plausible and distinct ways of aggregating individual complaints—corresponding to a *maximin* principle of equality, an *additive* principle of equality, and a *weighted additive* principle of equality—in order to arrive at a ranking of how good an outcome is regarding inequality. In addition, as my brief discussion suggests, I argued that we might assess how bad an outcome is regarding inequality in virtue of how gratuitous the inequality is or in terms of how much total deviation there is from the closest state of equality. Finally, I also noted that we have a conception of social justice or fairness according to which we would assess a situation's inequality in terms of the nature of a group's or a society's principles and institutions that are responsible for the kind of inequality obtaining among its members.

So, in *Inequality*, I argued that there were at least twelve different aspects of inequality underlying and influencing our egalitarian judgments. I did not claim that each of these aspects was equally appealing. But I did contend, and continue to believe, that each represents elements of the egalitarian's thinking that are not easily dismissed.

Since the publication of *Inequality*, Wlodek Rabinowitz has argued that there is yet another plausible way of thinking about inequality that is distinct from the ways I considered, one that would generate a different answer than my aspects to the question of how, if at all, proportional increases in a population would affect its inequality.[4] And Shelly Kagan once suggested that he thought that each of my aspects might be interpreted in at least two or three different but plausible ways so that, in fact, there might be as many as twenty-four or thirty-six different ways of thinking about inequality, in addition to any further ways, independent of mine, such as the one suggested by Rabinowitz. And I hasten to add that all of these different aspects or ways of plausibly thinking about inequality arise within the single approach to equality I am concerned with here; namely, the approach of equality as comparative fairness. Recognizing that other approaches to inequality are also plausible only adds further layers of complexity to the topic.

Little wonder then, as I have contended over the years, that so many discussions of equality have been shrouded in error and confusion. Before one can decide how to measure inequality or, for that matter, whether and how much one should even care about equality, one first has to be clear about what one really cares about insofar as one cares about inequality. Unfortunately, this is no easy task.

---

[4] See Wlodek Rabinowicz's "The Size of Inequality and Its Badness. Some Reflections Around Temkin's Inequality" and my response to his paper "Measuring Inequality's Badness: Does Size Matter? If So, How, If Not, What Does?" in *Theoria* 69 (1–2), pp. 60–108.

The Importance of Health

Many egalitarians have debated the following question: insofar as we are egalitarians, what kind of equality should we seek? A host of candidates have been championed, including, among others, income, resources, primary goods, wealth, power, welfare, opportunity, needs satisfaction, capabilities, functionings, rights, and liberties.[5] This topic is extremely important because equality of one kind often requires inequality of another.

What role should a concern about health or access to healthcare play in the egalitarian's thinking? To answer this question, we must think hard about the human condition and what really matters most about human existence. I can't pretend to do an adequate job of this here, but let me at least briefly illustrate the importance of taking up this issue.

Aristotle claimed that the highest form of human existence was the life of contemplation.[6] Bentham championed a life of pleasure with an absence of pain.[7] Aristotle and Bentham had radically different views about what mattered most about human existence, but both would have agreed that a valuable human existence depends, in fact, on certain basic, fundamental necessities. Minimally, it depends on physical and psychological preservation, which in turn depends on minimum levels of food, shelter, security, freedom from pain, and good health.

Let us focus on health. Some years back, I had a brief bout of food poisoning. It lasted a scant three hours, but during that time I was violently ill. Never do I recall feeling so wretched. I shook with fever and chills, moaned unceasingly, and literally writhed in pain. I counted the seconds, fervently hoping that the pain would pass and the waves of nausea would subside. Every five to ten minutes, I would force myself to throw up, and this would bring with it a few moments of respite; but, within a minute, the bile would again begin to build up in my stomach and the cycle of misery would start anew.

---

[5] See, for example, Richard Arneson's "Equality and Equal Opportunity for Welfare" (*Philosophical Studies* 56, 1989, pp. 77–93); Richard Arneson's "Welfare Should Be the Currency of Justice" (*Canadian Journal of Philosophy* 30, 2000, pp. 497–524); G. A. Cohen's "On the Currency of Egalitarian Justice" (*Ethics* 99, 1989, pp. 906–944); Ronald Dworkin's "What Is Equality? Part 1: Equality of Welfare" and "Part 2: Equality of Resources"; Ronald Dworkin's *Sovereign Virtue* (Harvard University Press, 2000); Amartya Sen's "Well-being, Agency, and Freedom: The Dewey Lectures 1984" (*Journal of Philosophy* 82, 1985, pp. 169–220); Amartya Sen's "Equality of What?" (in *Tanner Lectures on Human Values*, vol. I, University of Utah Press and Cambridge University Press, 1980); John Roemer's *Equality of Opportunity* (Harvard University Press, 1998) and "Defending Equality of Opportunity" (*The Monist* 86, 2003, pp. 1–32); John Rawls's *A Theory of Justice* (Harvard University Press, 1971) and "Social Unity and Primary Goods," in *Utilitarianism and Beyond*, edited by Amartya Sen and Bernard Williams, pp. 159–186 (Cambridge University Press, 1982); and Erik Rakowski's *Equal Justice* (Clarendon Press, 1991).

[6] See book X chapter VII of Aristotle's *Nicomachean Ethics*, translated by J. A. K. Thompson (George Allen & Unwin Ltd., 1953).

[7] See Jeremy Benthan's *An Introduction to the Principles of Morals and Legislation*, 1789, reprinted as *The Principles of Morals and Legislation* (Prometheus Books, 1988).

While sick, I self-consciously reflected on my state—as perhaps only a philosopher foolishly would. During that time, I was acutely aware of the kernel of truth in the old bromide that "if you don't have your health, you don't have anything." I have a wonderful family, good friends, a rewarding job, and interesting, long-term, projects, but for three hours they were of *no* benefit to me. I knew that my state was temporary, but wondered how long such a state would have to go on before one would simply want to die. I couldn't imagine living in such a state for even a week, let alone a month, a year, or many years. Moreover, I was perfectly aware that my state was surely much better than that faced by the truly desperately ill. Then, and later, I was filled with admiration and compassion for those who courageously face and somehow endure a lifetime of chronic pain or illness.

Good health isn't *everything*, but it is a *lot*. Freedom from debilitating illness is more than a necessary precondition to a worthwhile human existence. Arguably, good physical and psychological health constitute a large part of what makes a human life worth living.

The preceding considerations are oversimplified and hardly conclusive, but they are suggestive. Many discussions of inequality focus on the gaps between the rich and the poor but, as large and important as those may be, the gaps between the well and the sick may be even more important.

Consider Figure 1.3, which conveys the fact that far more people are poor than rich, that most who are ill are poor, and that a smaller proportion of the rich are ill relative to the proportion of poor who are ill. It also conveys the view that whether one is healthy or ill, it is better to be rich than poor, but that it is better to be healthy than ill. Indeed, as drawn, Figure 1.3 suggests that, whereas the gaps between rich and poor may be significant, the gaps between healthy and ill are even more significant.

Figure 1.3 is vastly oversimplified. It is not drawn to scale and is merely intended to illustrate a general pattern for which exceptions clearly abound. Still, if one interprets "ill" in Figure 1.3 as "seriously or desperately ill," our preceding considerations suggest that the figure may accurately represent the relative positions of the world's better and worse off.

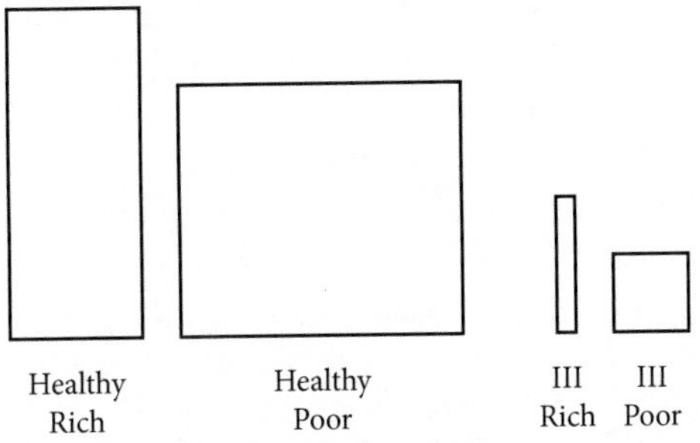

FIGURE 1.3 The relative positions of the world's better and worse off.

Suppose, on reflection, we think the world should be represented somewhat along the lines of Figure 1.3. This, of course, would have important egalitarian implications. Instead of focusing on improving the lot of the poor, there would be strong reason to focus on improving the lot of the ill. To be sure, there would be reason to focus on the ill poor before the ill rich, but there would also be reason to focus on the ill rich before the healthy poor.

Indeed, if Figure 1.3 accurately represented how people fared relative to each other, then increasing the income or wealth of the healthy poor would *reduce* the gap between the healthy poor and the healthy rich, but, in doing this, it would *increase* the gap between the healthy poor and the ill. This would be akin to improving the lot of some who were, in fact, already among the world's better off in terms of what matters most and, depending on what we ultimately say about the kinds of considerations presented in the section "Comparing Outcomes Regarding Inequality," this might, in fact, *worsen* the situation's overall inequality.[8]

I have focused on health as a large and necessary component of human well-being. But, obviously, health alone is not a sufficient component of human well-being, and there may be other components that play similarly central roles in our lives. As touched on earlier, these may include minimal levels of food, shelter, security, and freedom from pain. Moreover, there are other, less tangible goods like freedom, autonomy, or love, without which human lives may be significantly lacking in value.

Unfortunately, here, as elsewhere, there is no substitute for deep and substantial thinking about the nature of the human condition and the good. What are most necessary, central, and valuable for human beings? How are these components of well-being related and distributed? Until such questions are answered, it is impossible to determine to what, exactly, egalitarians are committed.

Let me be clear: I am not arguing that we have reason to be complacent about the extraordinary gaps in economic inequality that pervade our world. Indeed, as is well-known, there are important correlations between economic success and the other components of well-being that I have been emphasizing.[9] Still, our results may have important implications regarding the aims and focus of egalitarianism. To a large extent, the current battleground of egalitarianism is an economic one. Egalitarians rely heavily on economists to meaningfully measure disparities in income and wealth, and political programs are developed and advocated with the goal of reducing economic disparities. But if the

[8] I present considerations in support of this position in "Equality and the Human Condition." See, also, part E of "Egalitarianism: A Complex, Individualistic, and Comparative Notion."

[9] See, for example, the classic work by Sir Michael Marmot on one aspect of this issue, the social determinants of disease. A representative publication is his "Economic and Social Determinants of Disease" (*Bulletin of the World Health Organization*, 79, 2001, pp. 906–1004).

inequalities that matter most are actually inequalities of food, health, safety, and the like, then a profound shift may be required in the tools, approach, and policies of egalitarianism.

Perhaps egalitarians need to consult doctors, nutritionists, agronomists, or political scientists. Perhaps they require meaningful measures of serious illness, nutritional deprivation, human rights realization, or political stability at least as much as measures of economic inequality. Similarly, perhaps the focus of egalitarianism needs to change from efforts to shift the wage scale, alter people's savings habits, or redistribute wealth to altering the focus and distribution of medical care, increasing crop yields, changing patterns of nutritional consumption, or promoting political stability or human rights.

In sum, once one gets clear about what really is most important for the living of a valuable human life, how that is distributed among people, and how variations in distribution would actually affect inequality, the assumptions and policies of contemporary egalitarianism may require revision.

Conclusion

The preceding discussion raises a host of worries. I suspect that many doctors confronted with the foregoing considerations will want to side with antiegalitarians and contend that all this is completely beside the point. Where questions like basic health are concerned, many will claim that all that matters are factors like need, urgency, immediacy, and availability of appropriate care. This is one area, many will claim, where questions of equality just don't, and shouldn't, come into play. Whether you are rich or poor, black or white, male or female, what determines whether you should receive treatment is your current condition of health, availability of appropriate care, long-term prospects, and little or nothing else.

I'm not sure what to say about such a response. One might simply contend that here, as elsewhere, the ideal of equality is relevant—but not overriding—and that, in the case of medical emergencies, other important ideals come into play that may play a greater role in our all-things-considered judgments. Then again, perhaps we actually *should* be paying more attention to issues of equality in the distribution of health prospects, medical conditions, or medical care than we, in fact, typically do. Regardless of the ultimate answer to such questions, I think it is extremely important for people to accurately recognize the nature, scope, and implications of equality. The common tendency for people to argue about virtually every major social and political issue in egalitarian terms—without anything remotely resembling a clear conception of that notion—does a disservice to both many pressing issues and the ideal of equality.

Acknowledgements

This chapter is based on a talk given at the Brocher Summer Academy in Global Population Health, *Measurement and Ethical Evaluation of Health Inequalities*, in Geneva, July 2010. I am grateful to the sponsors of that Summer Academy: the Brocher Foundation, the Harvard University Program in Ethics and Health, and the University of Geneva. I am also grateful to the organizers of that conference and the editors of this volume, Nir Eyal, Dan Wikler, Samia Hurst, and Ole Frithjof Norheim. Finally, I owe a special debt to Derek Parfit, who first prompted me to think about these topics many years ago, and whose influence and support have been invaluable.

2 }

Health Inequality, Health Inequity, and Health Spending

Anthony B. Atkinson

In the summer of 2010, the BBC *Today Programme* had a major radio story on health inequalities and how they had increased. This story is relevant here in two ways. First, it is evidence of the popular interest in the topic: the *Today Programme* is described by the BBC as one of their flagship programs, with an audience of approximately 6 million. Second, the radio program covered, in a few minutes, all three major points of this chapter: health inequality, health inequity, and health spending.

In the first section, I approach the subject of health inequality from the standpoint of the measurement of income inequality. This parallel is often drawn. For example, Smits and Monden (2009) have recent published an interesting article on the "length of life inequality around the globe," in which they examine inequality in the distribution of age at death using measures of inequality taken over from the study of income distributions: the Gini coefficient and the Theil index. In a study of the health of the U.S. population, Asada (2005) also used the Gini coefficient, stating that "the Gini coefficient has most frequently been applied to income distribution, but it is possible to apply to health distribution" (2005, p. 4). It is possible, but I shall argue—as others have before me—that different dimensions of inequality need different measures. These different measures weight differently the differences among people, but their structure also implies differences in the weighting of different dimensions. This in turn leads me to consider the issue of the priority attached to these different dimensions as societies get richer.

The second section takes up the issue of the health gradient, or the fact that health outcomes tend to be positively correlated with socioeconomic status. This is different from health inequality Health inequality is about health; the gradient concerns the relation between health and another variable: socioeconomic

Revised version of the Brocher Lecture given in July 2010. I am grateful to the participants in the Workshop for their remarks and to Angus Deaton for sending me most helpful comments.

status. For this reason, I refer to the gradient as "health inequity." It is the gradient that particularly concerned the BBC's *Today Programme*. But, before drawing conclusions, one has to examine the underlying mechanism that may lead to a causal relationship between low income and poor health. In particular, it is necessary to distinguish between *position* in the distribution and the *income* or other advantage that attaches to positions. This in turn leads to a more general consideration of the linkages between health and socioeconomic status, including the reverse causation from health to income and redistributive policies such as health-related transfers.

The third section of this chapter is concerned with public spending on health and the implications of the fiscal crisis that is preoccupying all governments. In the public debate, the political rhetoric is that "there is no alternative" to major cuts in public spending. But there are evidently choices to be made, both about the extent of spending cuts and the programs that should be scaled back. This is a classic example of a situation in which public reasoning, espoused by Amartya Sen (e.g., 2009), is an essential underpinning of the democratic process.

Is There a Parallel with Income?

Can we apply to health the same methods of measurement as used for income and earnings? The simple answer, in my view, is "no," but it is useful to see why. Suppose that we begin with age at death—the variable used by Smits and Monden to examine global health inequality. Like income, age at death is a continuous variable. But, unlike income, it has a fairly evident upper bound. If the median lifespan is around 70 years, then the maximum ever achieved to date, by Jeanne Calment (122 years) is 75 percent higher than the median. Yet, when we consider income, 10 percent of Swiss workers earn more than 75 percent of the median (Atkinson 2008), and within this top decile group there are people earnings many multiples of median earnings.

The scales are quite different. Indeed, it is not even clear that a continuous scale is appropriate for health. Many studies of health make use of an ordinal scale of self-reported health status: for example, from 1 (very good) down to 4 (poor) and 5 (very poor). Not only is there an upper limit (we cannot do better than 1), but, also, we cannot be sure that a move from 5 to 4 is commensurate with a move from 4 to 3. In that case, as has been spelled out by Allison and Foster (2004), we have to go back to first principles. It may be possible to identify an improvement: for example, a health distribution is better when there are fewer in "very poor" health and more with "very good" health. But we cannot attach a numerical value to the extent of health inequality.

But, returning to a continuous variable such as age at death, we can see that it is not just the scale that is different; it is also how we think about the scale. The summary of the Swiss earnings distribution was a relative one, in the sense that I compared the earnings of a person at the top decile with those of the median. Swiss francs do not appear as such in the statistic quoted. This is an evident convenience, but it also conceals an assumption about our distributional values. We are implicitly assuming a constant degree of *inequality aversion*. What does this mean? Suppose that all earnings are multiplied by a constant amount. If it is simply a matter of inflation, or of moving from a monthly to an annual basis, then this is fine. But if these are real changes, we may not regard the new situation as having the same degree of inequality. This has been challenged in the case of income, notably by Kolm (1976), but it seems even more debatable in the case of health status. It does not seem plausible to suppose that health inequality indicators should be invariant with respect to equal proportionate changes. For example, suppose that there has been a rise in the age at death at the bottom decile from age 50 to 55 and that the rise at the top decile has been from 80 to 80 + X. What value of X would indicate that there had been no change in health inequality? A proportionate measure would indicate X = 8, but invariance with respect to equal *absolute* changes might seem more appropriate, indicating X = 5.

Does this matter? One of the conclusions reached by Smits and Munden was that "length of life is more unequally distributed among men than among women" (2009, p. 1118). Support is provided by the global Gini coefficient, which they calculate as 18.9 percent for men but 17.7 percent for women. The Gini coefficient is a *relative* summary measure of inequality: it is half the mean difference divided by the mean. In other words, if we were to take two women at random from the world population (from anywhere from Afghanistan to Zimbabwe), then the expected difference in their achieved age at death would be twice 17.7 percent or approximately 35 percent of the mean. However, if we were, following the argument that I have just made, to take the absolute Gini coefficient, not dividing by the mean, then the values for men and women would be virtually the same: 12.1 for men and 12.0 for women. For both men and women, the expected difference between the achieved age at death would be essentially 24 years.

It is not just that health is a different variable from income, with a limited scale, but that our values with regard to the distribution of health are likely to be different. This is the essential point. To pursue it, let us suppose that the scaling issue has been resolved and that health and income can be placed on a commensurate scale. Should we be more or less concerned about inequality in health than about inequality in income? On one side, it can be argued that irremediable and incompensable inequalities, to use the terms of Hausman (2007), are not unjust and that these are larger in the case of health than in the case of income. In the case of income, we could, arguably, approach equality, even if at the cost of large reductions in mean income. In the case of health, differences in achieved length of life or in health status are never going to be eradicated. The Gini coefficient is then being compared, not with zero, but with a positive number associated with the residual irremediable and incompensable inequalities. As Hausman puts it, "when inequalities in QALYs (Quality Adjusted Life Years) are very large, their implications for overall inequality are unambiguous" (2007, p. 65), but this is less evident for smaller values.

On the opposite side, it has been forcefully argued in the health inequality literature that "we should be more averse to, or less tolerant of, inequalities in health than inequalities in income" (Anand 2004, p. 16). He goes on to give the following reasons: "the status of health is a special good, which has both intrinsic and instrumental value. Income, on the other hand, has only instrumental value. [Health] directly affects a person's well-being" (Anand 2004, p. 16). The implications of the Anand position are that we should not use the same measure of inequality. If the Gini coefficient is the right index of inequality to apply to income, then it is not the right one to apply to health.

Put another way, the Smits and Munden study produced global Gini coefficients of less than 20 percent, whereas studies of global income inequality typically produce values in excess of 60 percent. The study by Asada for the United States produced values for the Gini coefficient of 10 percent or less, whereas the Luxembourg Income Study (2010) Key Statistics show a Gini for disposable income in the United States of 37 percent. But no meaning can be attached to these differences between the values for health and the values for income. The variables are not necessarily commensurate, and we may wish to apply a higher degree of inequality aversion in the case of health.

Much of what I have said so far is far from new. For example, Gakidou, Murray, and Frenk state clearly that the "literature on measuring income inequality... is very helpful in the design of health inequality measures, but... health has some fundamental differences from income that require special consideration" (2000, p. 47).[1] But I now want to move on to a further set of issues that are less discussed. The choice of a measure of inequality involves balancing the different claims of people with differing levels of health, say the person at the bottom decile (with a life expectancy of 20 percent below the mean) and the person at the top decile (with a life expectancy of 20 percent higher than the mean). In saying that health inequality aversion is greater, we are saying that the relative claim falls more sharply as we move up the distribution. Suppose now that we consider the claims of a person at the bottom decile today compared with those of the bottom person in the distribution at some date in the future, when everyone is enjoying a longer life expectancy (and larger income)? Applying the same set of values, we would conclude that the claim would fall more rapidly over time for the health dimension

[1] They propose an inequality index that allows both for differences in inequality aversion and for differing degrees of relativity (dividing by the mean to the power of β, where β can vary between 0 and 1).

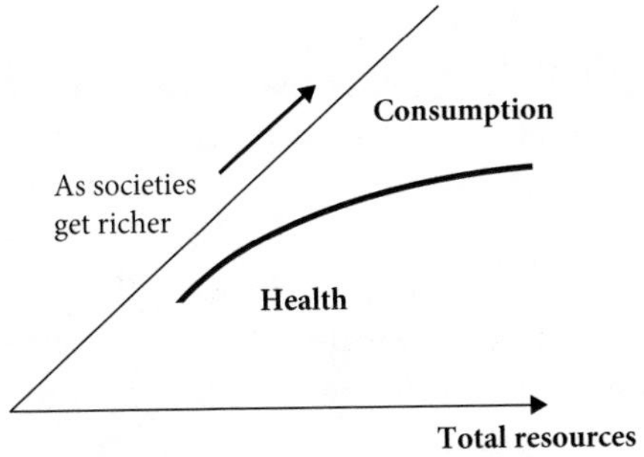

FIGURE 2.1 Health has initial priority.

than for that of income (measured commensurately). Returning again to the article by Anand, we see that he quotes Descartes: "the preservation of health is…without doubt the first good" (Anand 2004, p. 17). If that is the case, then we have a lexicographic evaluation: first health and then consumption (of other goods). In a less extreme form, initially, health has priority but, as we become better off, the balance shifts toward consumption. The expansion path, showing the allocation of resources as we get richer, is illustrated schematically in Figure 2.1.

This view of the relative priority of different dimensions is open to debate. Indeed, a quite different set of priorities is embodied in the Human Development Index (HDI) produced by the United Nations Development Program. The HDI has done a most valuable job in drawing attention to the importance of nonincome dimensions of social and economic performance; at the same time, it embodies implicit judgments about priorities. These take two forms. The first is that, in its original form, the HDI combined the health (and education) variables with the *logarithm* of income. It is, however, the second judgment on which I want to concentrate, which is that the index is a uniformly weighted sum of the three variables. Countries are judged at all levels of development according to the same mix of health, education, and (log) income. This makes no allowance for changing priorities as societies become richer. In particular, it seems quite possible that societies, as they grow richer, may place an increased, rather than a decreased, emphasis on health and health spending.

HEALTH INEQUITY AND THE HEALTH GRADIENT

To this point, I have discussed the distributions of health and income in parallel. Inequality in health has referred simply to the distribution of that variable: that is, the fact that people achieve different lengths of life. A related but different issue, to which I turn in this section, is that these two distributions may be associated. Health outcomes may be correlated with income (or other measures of economic status): there is a health "gradient." In statistical terms, if, in the previous section, we were concerned with the *variances* of health and income, we are now, in this section, concerned with the *covariance* of health and income. It is important to keep these separate. Both are important, but they are different. Although the academic literature has been clear on this, many official documents continue to use the term "health inequalities" quite indiscriminately. For example, the European Union (EU) Commission's October 2009 document on "Solidarity in Health: Reducing Health Inequalities in the EU" opens by expressing its concern about "the extent of the health inequalities between people living in different parts of the EU and between socially advantaged and disadvantaged EU citizens" (2009, p. 2). The first of these refers to differences in country means; the second refers to the covariance; neither refers to overall health inequality.

Here, I now focus on the health gradient, and I take the empirical finding of a positive correlation as given, not examining the underlying evidence. The gradient is important both as a measure of social performance and as a guide to possible policy action. The health gradient has received prominent attention in the reports of the 2008 World Health Organization (WHO) Commission on Social Determinants of Health, and of the 2010 Strategic Review of Health Inequalities in England, both chaired by Sir Michael Marmot. The latter concludes that "health inequalities result from social inequalities. Action on health inequalities requires action across all the social determinants of health" (Marmot 2008, p. 15). The message is an attractive one: there is a kind of "double dividend." Action to reduce social inequality has benefits not only in itself but also in terms of reducing health inequality. As income is redistributed toward the lower income groups, for instance through transfers financed by progressive taxation, so the differences in health outcomes are narrowed. There is a double advantage in terms of social justice. This line of approach is particularly appealing if one believes that little can be done through health policy to change the health income relation. Responsibility is shifted from the Department of Health to the Department of Social Security and the tax authorities.

The policy implications do, however, depend crucially on the interpretation, as has been brought out clearly in the work of Deaton (2003) and others. This leads some policy makers to be skeptical. In the United Kingdom, a recent House of Commons Select Committee report concluded that "we did not see any conclusive evidence that suggested changing tax and benefit policies to reduce income inequalities would lead to a reduction in health inequalities" (House of Commons, Health Committee 2009, p. 26). The impact of income redistribution does indeed depend crucially on how we interpret the health gradient. There are two major issues. To begin with, causality may run both ways. The positive association may arise because health status affects earning power (and possibly the ability to organize finances). I do not attempt here to explore the ways in which such a simultaneous relationship between health and income could be disentangled. Instead, I want to point to the need to distinguish between market income (earnings + income from savings) and disposable income after taxes and transfers. Transfers (and to some degree taxes) depend on health status, particularly via benefits paid under sickness insurance, long-term disability programs, and benefits for care.

The second issue concerns the nature of the causal link between socioeconomic status to income. If the gradient arises because there is a link between health and the *amount of income*, then redistribution is effective. Conversely, if the gradient arises on account of a person's *relative position* in the income distribution, then the Select Committee is right to say that income redistribution has no effect: it narrows the income gap but does not change the relative rankings. The bottom decile will still be the bottom decile, even if this household has a higher income. There will, on this interpretation, be no double dividend.

The major contribution of the WHO Commission (Marmot 2008) was to enlarge the scope of the policy debate: we have to move beyond the medical care/health status link to consider the wider social and economic determinants of health. We have to consider tax policy as well as health spending, and this means income tax and not just health-related taxes such as those on cigarettes. Individual doctors should be concerned not only with prescriptions and hospital referrals, but also with employment services and help with family relationships. In the *Today* radio program, they interviewed a doctor from London's East End. He kept referring to these wider services, and the interviewer kept saying "but these are not medicine," to which the doctor replied: "they may be just as important for health."

Here, I want to highlight two elements that seem to me of particular importance for present policy. The first is the provision of health-related social transfers, to which I have already drawn attention. These have grown to be important (see Lonsdale and Seddon 1994), but have not always been important. In the United Kingdom, the 1942 Beveridge Plan made little provision for the disabled, apart from those who were injured at work or in the armed forces: "carers do not feature" (Timmins 1995, p. 57). It was not until the 1970s that there "came a fresh batch of new and improved non-means-tested and essentially bipartisan disability benefits: mobility allowance, invalid care allowance, and a new non-contributory invalidity pension for those who had been unable to earn insurance benefits" (Timmins 1995, p. 345). Health-related cash transfers, such as invalidity, disability, and caregivers' benefits, have grown substantially in recent decades (see Barr and Coulter 1990). To these transfers must be added the spending in kind, both state and mandated private spending, which is required by equality legislation (such as the legal duty of U.K. public organizations to promote equality of opportunity for disabled people). In the formulation of health policy, we must take a broad definition of the relevant interventions.

The second element concerns the allocation of public health care. This is an issue relevant to considering the effectiveness of public health systems, such as the U.K. National Health Service (NHS). The performance of the NHS has to be judged in the light of its objectives, and these include tackling health inequity. The productivity of the NHS cannot be measured solely in terms of the total benefit; we have to consider the distribution of the benefits. This does indeed apply to all aspects of public expenditure: in the United Kingdom, the official guidance on the evaluation of spending projects (HM Treasury 2003) states that benefits should be weighted according to the relative prosperity of those receiving the benefit. If policy makers are concerned that those in the bottom 20 percent suffer poorer health than do those in the top 20 percent, then this could be recognized by giving a larger weight to those parts of health output that benefit those in the bottom 20 percent. This would be parallel to "distributionally-adjusted national income." Following the particular version proposed by Sen (1976), the health outputs could be weighted according to the recipient's rank in the distribution. For example, distinguishing five income groups, the top 20 percent would get a weight of 1, the next 20 percent from the top would get a weight of 2, the middle 20 percent would get a weight of 3, the next 20 percent a weight of 4, and the bottom 20 percent would get a weight of 5. In this way, if policy has shifted resources toward services or areas benefiting the more deprived, then this would be reflected in a faster growth of adjusted output. In fact, estimates of the social wage, based on survey data, by Sefton (2002, table 7) showed that in 2000/1 the bottom 40 percent in terms of income received 50 percent of the benefits from the NHS, a figure that had increased since 1996/7. Applying the rank order weights just described, over this 4-year period distributionally adjusted NHS output would have increased by approximately 1 percentage point more than output measured without such an adjustment.

I stress these two elements—health-related transfers and distributional adjustments—because they are relevant to the final section, which is concerned with health and the economic crisis.

HEALTH SPENDING AND THE FISCAL CRISIS

To this point, this chapter may have had an air of unreality. I have been discussing the desirability of tackling health inequality and inequality more widely without any reference to the problems that are preoccupying most governments: the economic crisis and the rebalancing of public finances.

As I said at the outset, public debate is being stifled by the assertion that "there is no alternative" to the cuts in public spending being pursued. Yet there are clearly questions that have to be asked about the extent of spending cuts and about their allocation between different programs. In a sense, it is the reverse of the question that I asked earlier. How should societies adjust to rising levels of resources? The question is now put simply in reverse. What should be the shape of the contraction path? In the case in which health was given initial priority, then the expansion path has a modest slope, and putting this into reverse means that the cuts should also be modest, with most falling on reduced consumption (in other words, tax increases) or on other forms of spending, such as education. Conversely, there are other possible views about relative priorities. The HDI approach implicitly involves equal proportionate expansion and, hence, contraction. Or, it may be that people see health as receiving increasing weight as we get richer, giving a substantial part of marginal resources to health. Such a view would imply that, if we have to contract, then the cuts should fall heavily on health.

At first sight, it may seem that the first scenario—modest cuts—is the more probable. In the United Kingdom, the Coalition Government elected in 2010 promised to ring-fence spending on the NHS; in the United States, the new health care reform expands coverage. However, there are reasons for concern. The first reason is that the ring-fence applies to total spending but not to the objectives, particularly concerning health equity. One of the criticisms made of the NHS in the United Kingdom is that the large increase in inputs in the past 10 years has not led to a corresponding increase in outputs: there has been a marked decline in productivity. But this refers to productivity measured in a national accounts fashion, ignoring the health equity objective. As I have just noted, when distributional weights are applied, the adjusted output has grown faster. There is a risk that this equity concern will be lost from sight.

The second reason is that the ring-fencing applies to medical care and not to the other health-related spending. The other services provided by the East End doctor may well be subject to public sending cuts. At particular risk is social protection spending, and this is why I have highlighted the importance of this expansion.

Conclusion

In this chapter, I have highlighted a number of issues that I believe to be central to public debate but that are of some subtlety. I have suggested that one cannot just borrow measures of health inequality from the literature on income inequality. One cannot just look at the health gradient and draw policy conclusions. I have suggested that there are questions that have been neglected but that need to be addressed, such as changing priorities as societies get richer. And, at a time when recession rather than progress dominates the political agenda, there is a need for a clear statement of the principles underlying public policy.

References

Allison, R. A., and Foster, J. E. (2004). Measuring health inequality using qualitative data. *Journal of Health Economics, 23*, 505–524.

Anand, S. (2004). The concern for equity in health. In S. Anand, F. Peter, and A. Sen (Eds.), *Public health, ethics, and equity*. Oxford: Oxford University Press.

Asada, Y. (2005). Assessment of the health of Americans: the average health-related quality of life and its inequality across individuals and groups. *Population Health Metrics, 3*, 7.

Atkinson, A. B. (2008). *The changing distribution of earnings in OECD countries*. Oxford: Oxford University Press.

Barr, N., and Coulter, F. (1990). Social security: solution or problem? In N. Barr et al. (Eds.), *The state of welfare*. Oxford: Clarendon Press.

Deaton, A. S. (2003), Health, inequality and economic development, *Journal of Economic Literature, 41*(1), 113–158.

European Commission. (2009). *Solidarity in health: Reducing health inequalities in the EU*. Brussels: Communication from the European Commission.

Gakidou, E. E., Murray, C. J. L., and Frenk, J. (2000). Defining and measuring health inequality: an approach based on the distribution of health expectancy, *Bulletin of the World Health Organization, 78*, 42,54.

Hausman, D. M. (2007). Are health inequalities unjust? *Journal of Political Philosophy, 15*, 46–66.

HM Treasury. (2003). *The Green Book: appraisal and evaluation in central government*. London: TSO.

House of Commons, Health Committee. (2009). *Health inequalities*. Third report of the session 2008-09, HC 286-1. London: Stationery Office.

Kolm, S.-Ch. (1976). Unequal inequalities I. *Journal of Economic Theory, 12*, 416–442.

Lonsdale, S., and Seddon, J. (1994). The growth of disability benefits: An international comparison. In S. Baldwin and J. Falkingham (Eds.), *Social security and social change*. Hemel Hempstead: Harvester Wheatsheaf.

Luxembourg Income Study. (2010). *Key statistics*. Available at http://www.lisdatacenter.org/.

Marmot, M., chair. (2008). *Closing the gap in a generation*. Report of the Commission on Social Determinants of Health. Geneva: World Health Organization.

Sefton, T. (2002). Recent changes in the distribution of the social wage. CASEpaper 62, Centre for Analysis of Social Exclusion. London: London School of Economics.

Sen, A. (1976). Real national income. *Review of Economic Studies, 43*, 19–39.

———. (2009). *The idea of justice*. Cambridge, MA: Harvard University Press.

Smits, J., and Monden, C. W. S. (2009). Length of life inequality around the globe. *Social Science and Medicine, 68*, 1114–1123.

Timmins, N. (1995). *The five giants: A biography of the welfare state*. London: HarperCollins.

3 }

A Summary Measure of Health Inequalities

INCORPORATING GROUP AND INDIVIDUAL INEQUALITIES

Yukiko Asada

Recent decades have witnessed substantial research and policy efforts made to address health inequalities. Epidemiological studies have described numerous health inequalities in various populations (e.g., Braveman and Tarimo 2002; Mackenbach et al. 2003). Critical philosophical investigations have begun to identify unfair health inequalities (e.g., Daniels 2008; Hausman 2009; Segall 2010), which epidemiologists refer to as health *inequities* (Kawachi, Subramanian, and Almeida-Filho 2002), although what exactly "unfair" means is still vigorously debated. Concerted policy initiatives have made health equity a policy priority, most notably, the World Health Organization (WHO)'s Commission on Social Determinants of Health (2008).

Measurement of health inequalities—*unfair* health inequalities or health *inequities,* to be more precise—is central to any of these efforts. Health inequality information presented to us is of value only if we measure health inequalities reflecting our moral considerations and in a way useful for policy making. Among the many important issues related to the measurement of health inequalities, the choice of group or individual inequalities is fundamental. Should we measure and compare the average health of groups, such as the poor versus the rich (group inequality), or the health of each individual in the population (individual inequality)?

To date, the health inequality research and policy community has predominantly favored group inequality.[1] Much was said about its main attractions when Chris Murray, Emmanuela Gakidou, and Julio Frenk, then at the WHO,

---

In addition to the comments and intellectual stimulation I received from the organizers and participants of the Brocher Summer Academy in Global Population Health: Measurement and Ethical Evaluation of Health Inequalities, in Geneva, July 2010, I am grateful for helpful exchanges I have had over the years regarding the idea of a summary measure of health inequalities with Jeremiah Hurley, Mira Johri, David Kindig, and Ole Frithjof Norheim.

[1] For example, the predominant focus on group inequality is evident in empirical studies pertaining to health inequalities and inequities by race and gender introduced and examined by Daniels (Chapter 12, this volume).

proposed individual inequality as a superior alternative to group inequality (Murray, Gakidou, and Frenk 1999; Gakidou, Murray, and Frenk 2000). The continuing dominance of group inequality, even after the heated debate prompted by the Murray et al. proposal, may give a mistaken impression that nothing is left to discuss on this subject. In this chapter, I argue that the predominant use of group inequality is a missed opportunity for the advancement of the measurement of health inequalities. Careful examination of choices that underlie these two measurement approaches suggests neither group nor individual inequality fully captures what we wish to measure. A hybrid approach combining the strengths of both approaches, which I call a *summary measure of health inequalities* (Asada 2010), may be a viable alternative.

The plan of this chapter is as follows. In the first section, I explain the two measurement approaches, group and individual inequalities. In the next, I clarify choices that underlie these two approaches. Then, I argue for the development of an alternative, general analytical approach, a summary measure of health inequalities, and specify key characteristics that a summary measure of health inequalities should satisfy. In the next section, I sketch out a research agenda for the development of a summary measure of health inequalities, before concluding the chapter.

Group and Individual Health Inequalities

Studies describing health inequalities differ in many aspects, but the vast majority of them share one characteristic: they measure health inequality in a bivariate fashion, as a joint distribution of health and another attribute such as income, education, gender, or race/ethnicity. As Figure 3.1 shows, this measurement approach typically reports one attribute at a time, for example, as different levels of health across income groups. The degree of health inequality across these groups can be quantified by an index. An index can be simple (e.g., a range measure) or complex (e.g., the Concentration Index).[2] Rather than the average level of health of each group, one can also look at the level of health and the level of income (or another attribute) of each individual (e.g., by applying the Concentration Index to the individual-level data). Regardless of the unit of analysis (group or individual) or the index used, this approach always measures health inequality in relation to one other attribute. For this reason, "bivariate" (Wolfson and Rowe 2001) is a more appropriate characterization of this approach than "group," hence, from here on I call this the "bivariate approach." Measured in a bivariate fashion, health inequalities have been extensively described in relation to, for example,

[2] See Asada (2007) and Harper and Lynch (2005) for surveys of health inequality and inequity indices.

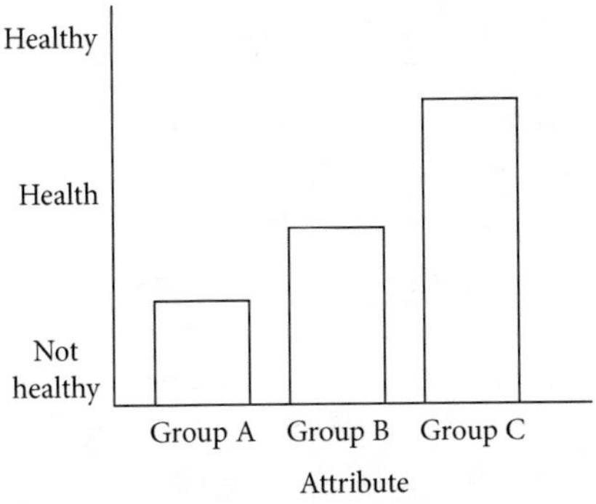

FIGURE 3.1 The group or bivariate approach to measuring health inequalities.

socioeconomic status (Braveman and Tarimo 2002; Mackenbach et al. 2003) or race/ethnicity (Harper et al. 2007). This measurement approach has also influenced policy making, including *Healthy People 2020* (a decennial national road map for health policy in the United States) (U.S. Department of Health and Human Services 2010) and the WHO's Commission on Social Determinants of Health (2008).

Another approach examines the distribution of health across individuals in the population regardless of its association with other attributes (Figure 3.2). It simply quantifies the extent of health inequality. This approach is often referred to as "individual inequality" (Asada and Hedemann 2002; Gakidou and King 2002) since the unit of analysis is always the individual. It is also called the "univariate approach" (Wolfson and Rowe 2001) since the focus is only on health—one variable. As I discuss in detail later, however, each of these terms points to a distinct characteristic of this approach. From here on I shall, for brevity, refer to this approach as the "univariate approach" (not because "univariate" is a better characterization of this approach but simply to contrast with the bivariate approach).

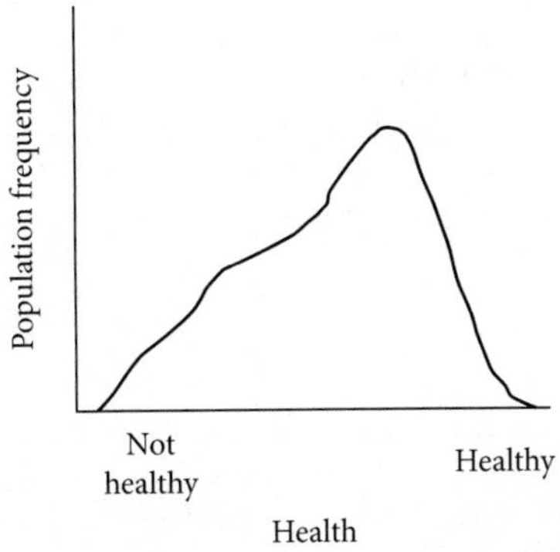

FIGURE 3.2 The individual or univariate approach to measuring health inequalities.

Choices That Underlie the Two Approaches

Heated debate was sparked around 2000 when Chris Murray, Emmanuela Gakidou, and Julio Frenk proposed the univariate approach as a superior alternative to the bivariate approach (Gakidou, Murray, and Frenk 2000; Murray, Gakidou, and Frenk 1999; and, for the debate, see, e.g., Almeida et al. 2001; Asada and Hedemann 2002; Braveman, Krieger, and Lynch 2000). The univariate approach is common in other fields (most notably in the measurement of income inequality), and a few researchers had measured health inequalities in a univariate fashion (e.g., Le Grand 1987). No researcher before them, however, had argued that considerations of policy and ethics pointed to the univariate approach as superior to the bivariate approach.

Here, I critically synthesize this debate by considering the heart of the choice between the bivariate and univariate approaches as the question: is it meaningful to examine the distribution of health per se across individuals? I examine this question both from policy and moral perspectives.[3]

POLICY DEBATE

The policy debating points are around comparability, overall picture, and intervention targets that the two approaches offer (Table 3.1). Murray and his colleagues argued that the univariate approach has better policy applicability than the bivariate approach because it uses the individual as the unit of analysis, thus avoiding the issue of comparability and complexity of the measurement of attributes (Gakidou, Murray, and Frenk 2000; Murray, Gakidou, and Frenk 1999). The individual is the ultimate unit of analysis, invariable across time and populations. Comparability is a challenging criterion for the bivariate

TABLE 3.1 } **A summary of the policy debate between the bivariate and univariate approaches**

	Bivariate/group Approach	Univariate/individual Approach
Comparability	Many attributes, different importance of and measures for each attribute	Individual is the ultimate unit of analysis; invariable across time and populations
Overall picture	Gives many pieces of information without an overall picture	Gives an overall picture
Intervention target	Indicates intervention target groups	Suggests no intervention target groups—one step removed from policy

[3] My classification of policy and moral debate loosely corresponds to that of principles of regulation and fundamental principles of justice, respectively, used by Lippert-Rasmussen in Chapter 4 of this volume, which primarily focuses on the bivariate (group) versus univariate (individual) debate in the measurement of health inequalities.

approach simply because the bivariate approach, by definition, involves the measurement of other attributes in addition to health. Furthermore, the importance of attributes varies across populations. For example, race/ethnicity is one of the most frequently and routinely measured attributes in health inequity studies in the United States, although it is rarely measured in Canada. Even the same attribute is often measured differently across populations. The most frequently used indicator of socioeconomic status, for example, is social class in the United Kingdom and income or education in many other industrialized countries.

A multiplicity of health inequality information produced by the bivariate approach leads to another shortcoming. Although the bivariate approach has created a wealth of information useful for many purposes and contexts, the vast array of information obscures the overall picture of health inequalities. It is, for example, difficult to answer the seemingly straightforward question of which country has the worst health inequalities. Such a question presumes a systematic mechanism to compare multiple bivariate health inequality relationships (e.g., health-income, health-education, and health-gender) across countries, which is an ambitious task given the current state of the literature. The univariate approach, on the other hand, by producing one type of health inequality information in each population, readily offers an overall picture of health inequality.[4]

Supporters of the bivariate approach, however, had a strong rebuttal point. They argued that, to develop policy, it is useful to identify who is sick (Braveman, Krieger, and Lynch 2000). The bivariate approach, by nature of measuring the attributes that are associated with ill health, always indicates intervention target groups, whereas the univariate approach only gives information on the distribution of health. Of course, researchers and policy makers can examine appropriate intervention targets after obtaining information on univariate health inequality. Nonetheless, the supporters of the bivariate approach maintain that the univariate approach is one step removed from policy.

MORAL DEBATE

To understand the moral choices that underlie the bivariate and univariate approaches, it is useful to distinguish the moral significance of *univariate* health inequality from that of *individual* inequality. The former asks whether it is morally meaningful to examine health distribution only, whereas the latter inquires about the unit of analysis: whether we should be concerned about health inequality between groups or across individuals. Moral arguments

[4] For this very reason, for example, Smits and Monden (2009) (also cited in Chapter 2, by Atkinson, in this volume) use the univariate approach for international comparison of health inequalities.

provided by the debate between Murray et al. and the supporters of the bivariate approach mostly concentrated on the moral significance of univariate health inequality.

Figure 3.3A examines the question of the moral significance of univariate health inequality (Asada and Hedemann 2002). Figure 3.3A shows that Country A has a narrower distribution of life years than Country B, suggesting health inequality is *smaller* in Country A than in B. Can one make further ethical interpretations from these distributions and say that Country B has a more *unfair* or *inequitable* health distribution than Country A? Murray and his colleagues argued that health has intrinsic value, and these univariate health inequalities are not merely variations but are ethically significant variations, thus, Country B is more inequitable than Country A (Gakidou, Murray, and Frenk 2000; Murray, Gakidou, and Frenk 1999). Supporters of the bivariate approach instead argued that what is morally significant in health inequality is the systematic associations between health and other attributes; thus, there is nothing morally significant about the univariate health inequalities in Figure 3.3A (for example, Braveman, Krieger, and Lynch 2000).

This moral debate proceeded as a choice between clear-cut opposing views, but a more nuanced assessment is necessary for understanding the core issues of this debate. I argue that it is not too difficult to accept moral significance of univariate health inequality if one accepts *some* value of health.[5] In the most extreme case, one might argue that health is special above everything else

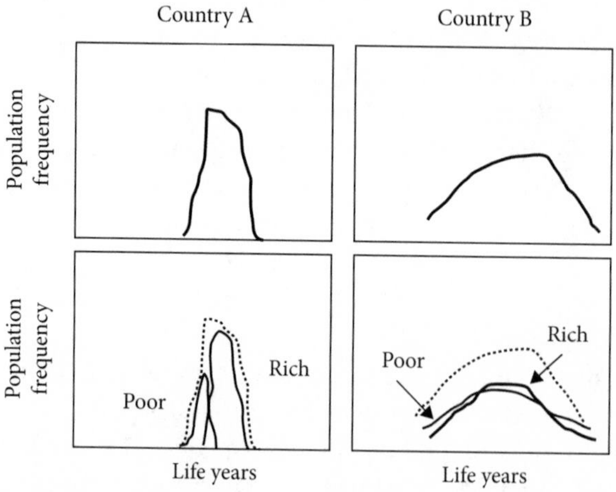

FIGURE 3.3 (A) Univariate health inequality in two populations (*top*) and (B) bivariate health inequalities in two populations (*bottom*).

[5] Lippert-Rasmussen, whose chapter in this volume also focuses on the bivariate (group) vs. univariate (individual) debate (Chapter 4), is in agreement on this point. He reviews two arguments used to cast doubt on the moral significance of univariate health inequality: that health inequalities caused by social factors (as opposed to natural factors) or health inequalities that are neither remedial nor compensable

(Anand 2002) simply because everything we value in our lives is conditional on our being alive. To put it bluntly, the dead have nothing. According to this view, univariate health inequalities carry very important information pertaining to ethics. This is obviously a coarse argument, because, first of all, health is not only life or death, and, moreover, among the living, it is unclear how important health is relative to other goods (e.g., political liberty, self-respect, and basic shelter and food). To accept the moral significance of univariate health inequalities however, it is not necessary to take this extreme view. One only needs to accept health as one of the things we value in our lives, whatever the reason may be (e.g., as a resource, component of welfare, or component of capabilities).[6] The moral significance of univariate health inequality can then be justified if one supports that either (a) the distribution of health serves is a good indicator of distributions of other things we value, or (b) each of what we value has moral significance of its own and should be examined separately. Following these views, one could argue that the distributions of life years in Country A and B in Figure 3.3A do not only suggest the degree of inequality but also that of inequity, at least to some extent.

A harder question, for which relevant literatures do not seem to have a clear answer, is that of the *relative* moral significance of univariate and bivariate health inequalities. Which is morally more important, univariate or bivariate health inequalities? An extension of Figure 3.3A would be helpful to articulate this question (Asada and Hedemann 2002). Suppose that we had enough data to look into the association between health and income in each of Country A and B and found the situations illustrated in Figure 3.3B. In Country A, health is strongly correlated with income: the poor tend to be sick and the rich healthy. In Country B, however, health and income are not strongly correlated; just knowing the income level of a person would not give a clue to how sick or healthy that person might be. With information on univariate and bivariate health inequalities, both of which can be considered unfair or inequitable, it is now challenging to judge which country, on the whole, has worse health inequity. The univariate approach suggests, in terms of health inequity, that Country B is worse than Country A, whereas the bivariate approach suggests

---

are of moral concern. He argues against them and concludes "In my view, individual inequalities in health matter, at least in part, because such inequalities can be no less unfair, no less unjust, than group inequalities. However, some of the reasons why we should be concerned with individual inequalities motivate an indirect concern for group health inequalities." Hausman, however, disagrees (Chapter 7, this volume). He argues against the moral significance of univariate health inequality from a perspective of justice and suggests that, if the moral significance of univariate health inequality exists, it comes from benevolence.

[6] One view, arguably the most developed, to articulate the value of health is Daniels's account (1985, 2008) as discussed in many chapters of this volume. Daniels considers that health as normal species functioning is critical to satisfy the principle of "fair equality of opportunity" in John Rawls's theory of justice as fairness (1971).

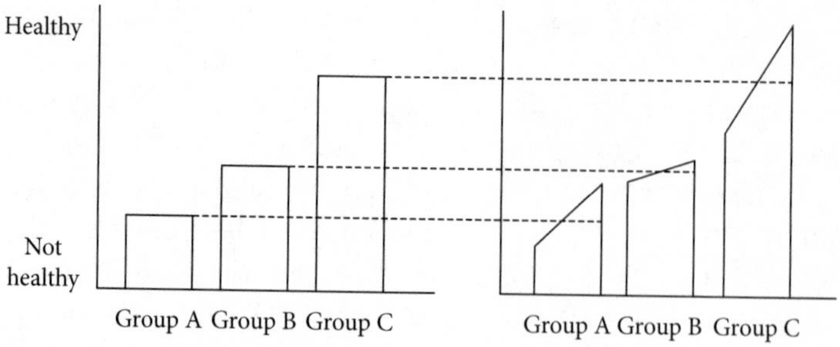

FIGURE 3.4 (A) Typical reporting of bivariate health inequality (*left*) and (B) within-group inequality (*right*).

the opposite, that Country A is worse than Country B. The current literature unfortunately does not clearly guide us as to whether univariate or bivariate health inequalities should override one another and for what reasons. As some of the chapters of this volume suggests,[7] the literature is developing, and this is one of the areas in which rigorous normative work is much needed for the development of the measurement of health inequalities.

The bivariate versus univariate debate largely overlooked the question of the moral significance of individual health inequality. This is ironic because, as I mentioned in the section on group and individual inequalities, this debate is often referred to as the "group versus individual debate." This lack of attention was unfortunate because the philosophical literature (most notably, Larry Temkin's work [1993]) offers an important insight and, in contrast to the unresolved question of the moral significance of univariate health inequality, there seems to be a clear answer to this question: the primary focus of the analysis of health inequality should be the individual rather than the group.

Comparison of groups typically means comparison of group averages (more precisely, group means or medians). But, as Temkin painstakingly points out, the moral significance of group averages is unclear when we consider within-group variations (1993). Figure 3.4A is a typical reporting of health inequalities using the bivariate approach. It is, however, unlikely that all members in each group have the same level of health, and their actual health level may actually resemble Figure 3.4B. One should then rightly ask why we should be concerned about between-group inequalities while ignoring within-group inequalities.

[7] For example, Atkinson (2013, Chapter 2, this volume) frames the issue of relative moral significance of univariate and bivariate health inequalities as the question of whether we care about health inequalities more than inequalities in others, such as income. Bivariate health inequalities discussed in this chapter correspond to covariance of health and other attributes in Atkinson's chapter. Temkin (2013, Chapter 1, this volume) introduces a schematic case (Figure 1.3), hypothetical, but informed by real world, which helps us think hard about the relative moral significance of univariate and bivariate health inequalities. He asks among whom we wish to reduce inequalities, the healthy rich, healthy poor, ill rich, or ill poor, and for what reason: to reduce health inequity or inequity in well-being?

The moral significance of group averages becomes even more ambiguous when we acknowledge group-overlapping variations that we typically observe in health inequalities. For example, using a stratified random sample of the American population in 1996–1997 from the Community Tracking Study, Ferrer and Palmer described inequalities in health status measured by SF-12 across income quintiles (2004). In addition to the typical comparison of average health of income quintiles (in the Ferrer and Palmer study, median health of each group), they examined the distribution of health status within each income quintile group. The medians of income quintiles showed a familiar graded relationship: the higher the income, the better the health. However, in every income quintile group, there were healthy people. What made the median levels of the lower income quintile groups sicker than others were their larger within-group variations toward the sicker end. In short, health status was badly overlapping across groups. Within-group and group-overlapping health inequalities suggest that group averages are at most a conceptually and empirically convenient shortcut, and, even when we are concerned about the moral significance of bivariate health inequalities (i.e., associations between health and other goods, such as income, education, or race/ethnicity), we should be cognizant of health inequalities within groups as well as between groups.[8]

In summary, the careful examination of the choices that underlie the bivariate versus univariate approaches suggests several important lessons for the future development of the measurement of health inequalities. First, we have now clarified some of the attractive features that we wish to bring to the measurement of health inequalities from policy and moral perspectives. To be relevant to policy, we wish to measure health inequalities in a way that is comparable across populations and time, offering an overall picture of health inequalities in a given population and suggesting intervention target groups. From moral perspectives, there appears to be some moral significance in univariate health inequality, but, at the same time, we seem to be morally concerned about bivariate associations between health and other attributes. In addition, the primary unit of analysis of health inequalities should be the individual, and within-group inequality carries important information even when one is interested in comparing groups' average health.

---

[8] Lippert-Rasmussen (2013, Chapter 4, this volume) discusses the group identification challenge in addition to the within-group and group-overlapping health inequalities discussed here, which he calls *intragroup inequality*. He asks which group characteristic we should focus on for what reasons, given that each person can be described with multiple group characteristics. This is a difficult question for anyone who accepts the importance of bivariate health inequalities (including those who accept the importance of both univariate and bivariate health inequalities). It is possible to stratify groups by many relevant characteristics, for example, rich-female-urban residents, rich-female-rural residents, poor-female-urban residents, and so forth. However, it is not at all clear among whom we wish to reduce inequalities for what reasons. Temkin's Figure 1.3 in Chapter 1 of this volume gives a flavor of the challenges we will face in comparing multiple group characteristics at once.

TABLE 3.2 } **Attractive features of the bivariate and univariate approaches**

	Bivariate/group Approach	Univariate/individual Approach
POLICY USEFULNESS		
Comparability		X
Overall picture		X
Intervention target	X	
MORAL SIGNIFICANCE		
Univariate health inequality	Unresolved	
Individual health inequality		X

X suggests attractive feature

Second, although both bivariate and univariate approaches bring some of these features that we find appealing, neither approach offers all of them, as summarized in Table 3.2. The bivariate approach has been missing an opportunity by acting as the winner of the debate without taking seriously its criticized shortcomings. Third, there is a critical, unresolved moral issue: the relative importance of bivariate and univariate health inequalities. As Sen argues, a good measurement is a candid reflection of our conceptions, and the lack of a clear answer, without presupposition, should be expressed as it is in the measurement of health inequalities (1997). Finally, this debate sparked an intersection of ethics, methods, and policy that the field of health inequality measurement has rarely enjoyed but can greatly benefit from for future development.

An Alternative Approach: A Summary Measure of Health Inequalities

Based on the close examination of the choices that underlie the bivariate and univariate approaches, I propose an alternative, general analytical approach, a summary measure of health inequalities that consolidates these two approaches.[9] A summary measure should satisfy the following three features: (1) comprehensiveness—offering three types of policy-relevant information (overall health inequality, overall health inequity, and bivariate health inequities) at once; (2) transparency—clearly separate descriptive (inequality) and normative (inequity) steps; and (3) flexibility—enabling users to choose and incorporate different definitions of health inequity.

Calculation of a summary measure requires individual-level data, and analysts first need to identify the individual-level measure of health to

[9] Note that my approach is different from the one suggested by Wagstaff and van Doorslaer (2004). Their approach gives information on univariate health inequality and *one* bivariate health inequality (e.g., income-related health inequality), whereas my approach offers information on univariate health inequality and *many* bivariate health inequalities (e.g., income-, education-, gender-, race/ethnicity-related health inequalities).

be used and a suitable index to quantify the extent of inequality in the distribution. Overall health inequality is the distribution of the observed health across individuals in the population. Overall health inequity is the distribution of the *unfair* health across individuals in the population. Although the critical assessment of the choices that underlie the bivariate and univariate approaches indicated that it is reasonable to accept some moral significance in overall health inequality, it is unclear what exactly this moral significance is. Reporting overall health inequality and overall health inequity side by side makes ethical judgments explicit. Each analyst needs to decide the definition of health inequity he or she wishes to adopt and incorporate it clearly by distinguishing inequity (the distribution of unfair health) from inequality (the distribution of observed health).

Methodologically, to estimate unfair health, analysts can standardize fairness in a manner similar to standardize age in epidemiological studies comparing mortality or morbidity rates across populations by removing the effect of age. Specifically, fairness standardization proceeds with the following three steps. Step 1, by applying regression models to individual-level data, explain the variation in health as much as possible with the data at hand. Step 2, classify the explanatory factors used in step 1 into "legitimate" (or ethically justifiable or unproblematic) and "illegitimate" (or ethically unjustifiable or problematic) factors that influence a person's health (Fleurbaey and Schokkaert 2009). Step 3, estimate unfair health for each person by removing the influence of the legitimate factors on health. Distribution of unfair health is what the analysts are after: health inequity. Fairness standardization is more complicated than age standardization because, unlike age, fairness involves ethical judgments. Classification of the legitimate and illegitimate factors is challenging. Data are rarely available that offer variables that perfectly operationalize these categories, and many variables represent both legitimate and illegitimate influences on health (e.g., from a perspective of health inequalities beyond individual control as inequitable, the variable "smoking" is partially legitimate, representing personal choice, and partially illegitimate, showing social circumstances). Still, a general analytic framework is present to connect normative and empirical work.

Bivariate health inequities offer information on how much overall health inequity can be explained by each policy-relevant attribute (such as income, education, gender, or race/ethnicity). For this, analysts can use the regression-based inequality decomposition method (Shorrocks 1982). Information on bivariate health inequities is valuable both for ethical and policy considerations. Overall health inequity is the part of the inequality that we will wish to eliminate, and it is reasonable to argue that associations with other attributes may make health inequity even more ethically problematic. The size of attribute contribution should not be the sole consideration in determining which attribute is the most problematic and, thus, requires the most urgent policy intervention. Other considerations, such as historical importance of the attribute, should factor in. Nonetheless, reporting multiple attributes in this way offers an insight that is otherwise hard to obtain.

Future Research Agenda for a Summary Measure of Health Inequalities

Apart from the obvious next step of empirical application of the skeleton of the summary measure idea sketched in the previous section, the following two considerations are important for the future research agenda for a summary measure of health inequalities. First, for a summary measure to be useful for the real world, its development should go hand in hand with considerations for policy application. The more complex the methods used, the stronger the communication strategy needs to be. Exploration of effective communication is critical for the conceptually and methodologically sophisticated approach that the summary measure takes. Other relevant considerations include the sensitivity of a summary measure to changes in health inequality and inequity and issues of data availability and sample sizes in jurisdictions of various sizes (e.g., country, state, province, county, etc.).

Second, exploration of values will be essential. A summary measure of health inequalities, as sketched here, reflects ambiguities to some moral questions that the field of health inequality currently faces. Because there is no agreed upon single definition of health inequity, a summary measure is designed to be flexible so users can introduce different definitions of health inequities. In addition, given the lack of clear answers, a summary measure is intentionally silent about (a) relative importance of overall health inequity (i.e., univariate health inequity) and bivariate health inequities and (b) relative importance of bivariate health inequities associated with different attributes (i.e., which bivariate health inequity is more important; e.g., income, education, gender, or race/ethnicity-related health inequity). As we clarify these moral issues, a summary measure can reflect our values more explicitly.

Two approaches are possible to address difficult moral questions: analytical ethics (investigating the answers through logic and rational thinking) and empirical ethics (asking people what they think about these questions). Neither alone could inform policy satisfactorily because analytical ethics almost never offers the single answer to the question (e.g., philosophers have offered many theories of justice but have never reached a consensus view), and empirical ethics, even when a consensus view emerges, may still be morally wrong (e.g., slavery was largely accepted but was wrong). Although some inquiries in the health field, such as priority setting (e.g., Nord et al. 1999) and the measurement of health (e.g., Fryback 1998), have advanced balancing these two approaches, empirical ethics has mostly been silent in the inquiry of health inequality. Filling this void might be informative for further exploration and possible clarification of difficult moral issues regarding health inequalities.

Conclusion

Important policy and moral choices underlie the bivariate (group) and univariate (individual) approaches to measuring health inequalities. Although the debate between these approaches appeared to be settled, in this chapter, I argue that there is more to learn. Careful examination of these choices suggested that neither approach allows us to measure everything that we wish to measure in health inequalities. Accordingly, I proposed a summary measure of health inequalities, a hybrid approach combining the strengths of both of these approaches, as a possibly viable alternative analytical framework. Examination of value questions will be key for the development of a summary measure, particularly the elicitation of people's values on health inequalities.

References

Almeida, C., Braveman, P., Gold, M. R., Szwarcwald, C. L., Ribeiro, J. M., and Miglionico, A. (2001). Methodological concerns and recommendations on policy consequences of the World Health Report 2000. *Lancet, 357,* 1692–1697.

Anand, S. (2002). The concern for equity in health. *Journal of Epidemiology and Community Health, 56,* 485–487.

Asada, Y. (2007). *Health inequality: Morality and measurement.* Toronto: University of Toronto Press.

———. (2010). A summary measure of health inequalities for a pay-for-population health performance system. *Prevention of Chronic Disease, 7,* A72. http://www.cdc.gov/pcd/issues/2010/jul/09_0250.htm, accessed October 11, 2011.

Asada, Y., and Hedemann, T. (2002). A problem with the individual approach in the WHO health inequality measurement. *International Journal of Equity Health, 1,* 2. http://www.equityhealthj.com/content/1/1/2, accessed October 11, 2011.

Atkinson, A. (2013). Health inequality, health inequity, and health spending. In N. Eyal, S. A. Hurst, O. F. Norheim, and D. Wikler (Eds.), *Inequalities in health: Concepts, measures, and ethics* (Chapter 2). New York: Oxford University Press.

Braveman, P., Krieger, N., and Lynch, J. (2000). Health inequalities and social inequalities in health. *Bulletin of the World Health Organization, 78,* 232–233.

Braveman, P., and Tarimo, E. (2002). Social inequalities in health within countries: Not only an issue for affluent nations. *Social Science & Medicine, 54,* 1621–1635.

Daniels, N. (1985). *Just health care.* Cambridge: Cambridge University Press.

———. (2008). *Just health: Meeting health needs fairly.* Cambridge: Cambridge University Press.

———. (2013). Reducing health disparities: No simple matter. In N. Eyal, S. A. Hurst, O. F. Norheim, and D. Wikler (Eds.), *Inequalities in health: Concepts, measures, and ethics* (Chapter 12). New York: Oxford University Press.

Ferrer, R. L., and Palmer, R. (2004). Variations in health status within and between socioeconomic strat. *Journal of Epidemiology and Community Health, 58*, 381–387.

Fleurbaey, M., and Schokkaert, E. (2009). Unfair inequalities in health and health care. *Journal of Health Economics, 28*, 73–90.

Fryback, D, G. (1998). Summarizing population health: Directions for the development and application of population metrics. In M. J. Field, and M. R. Gold (Eds.), *Summarizing population health: Directions for the development and application of population metrics* (Chapter C). Washington, D.C.: National Academy Press.

Gakidou, E. E., and King, G. (2002). Measuring total health inequality: Adding individual variation to group-level differences. *International Journal for Equity in Health, 1*, 1–12. www.equityhealthj.com/content/1/1/3, accessed October 11, 2011.

Gakidou, E. E., Murray, C. J. L., and Frenk, J. (2000). Defining and measuring health inequality: an approach based on the distribution of health expectancy. *Bulletin of the World Health Organization, 78*, 42–54.

Harper, S., and Lynch, J. (2005). Methods for measuring cancer disparities: using data relevant to Healthy People 2010 cancer-related objectives. *NCI Cancer Surveillance Monograph Series, 6*, 05-5777. http://seer.cancer.gov/publications/disparities/, accessed October 11, 2011.

Harper, S., Lynch, J., Burris, S., and Smith, G.D. (2007). Trends in the black-white life expectancy gap in the United States, 1983–2003. *JAMA, 297*, 1224–1232.

Hausman, D. M. (2009). Benevolence, justice, well-being and the health gradient. *Public Health Ethics, 2*, 235–243.

———. (2013). Egalitarian critiques of health inequalities. In N. Eyal, S. A. Hurst, O. F. Norheim, and D. Wikler (Eds.), *Inequalities in health: Concepts, measures, and ethics* (Chapter 7). New York: Oxford University Press.

Kawachi, I., Subramanian, S. V., and Almeida-Filho, N. (2002). A glossary for health inequalities. *Journal of Epidemiology and Community Health, 56*, 647–652.

Le Grand, J. (1987). Inequality in health: Some international comparison. *European Economic Review, 31*, 182–191.

Lippert-Rasmussen, K. (2013). When group measures of health should matter. In N. Eyal, S. A. Hurst, O. F. Norheim, and D. Wikler (Eds.), *Inequalities in health: Concepts, measures, and ethics* (Chapter 4). New York: Oxford University Press.

Mackenbach, J. P., Bos, V., Andersen, O., Cardano, M., Costa, G., and Harding, S. (2003). Widening socioeconomic inequalities in mortality in six Western European countries. *International Journal of Epidemiology, 21*, 830–837.

Murray, C. J. L., Gakidou, E. E., and Frenk, J. (1999). Health inequalities and social group differences: what should we measure? *Bulletin of the World Health Organization, 77*, 537–543.

Nord, E., Pinto, J. L., Richardson, J., Menzel, P., and Ubel, P. (1999). Incorporating societal concerns for fairness in numerical valuations of health programmes. *Health Economics, 8*, 25–39.

Rawls, J. (1971). *A theory of justice.* Cambridge, MA: Belknap Press of Harvard University Press.

Segall, S. (2010). *Health, luck, and justice.* Princeton, NJ: Princeton University Press.

Sen, A. (1997). *On economic inequality.* Oxford: Oxford University Press.

Shorrocks, A. F. (1982). Inequality decomposition by factor components. *Econometrica: Journal of the Econometric Society, 50,* 193–211.

Smits, J., and Monden, C. (2009). Length of life inequality around the globe. *Social Science and Medicine, 68,* 1114–1123.

Temkin, L. (1993). *Inequality.* Oxford: Oxford University Press.

———. (2013). Inequality and health. In N. Eyal, S. A. Hurst, O. F. Norheim, and D. Wikler (Eds.), *Inequalities in health: Concepts, measures, and ethics* (Chapter 1). New York: Oxford University Press.

U.S. Department of Health and Human Services. (2010). *Healthy People 2020.* Washington, DC. http://healthypeople.gov/2020/default.aspx, accessed October 11, 2011.

Wagstaff, A., and van Doorslaer, E. (2004). Overall versus socioeconomic health inequality: a measurement framework and two empirical illustrations. *Health Economics, 13,* 297–301.

WHO Commission on Social Determinants of Health. (2008). *Closing the gap in a generation Health equity through action on the social determinants of health.* Geneva: World Health Organization. http://www.who.int/social_determinants/thecommission/final report/en/index.html, accessed October 11, 2011.

Wolfson, M., and Rowe, G. (2001). On measuring inequalities in health. *Bulletin of the World Health Organization, 79,* 553–560.

4 }

When Group Measures of Health Should Matter

Kasper Lippert-Rasmussen

The Issue

Discussions of inequality in health generally focus on health inequalities obtaining between social groups: for example, on "health disparities between population groups defined by social characteristics such as wealth, education, occupation, racial or ethnic group, sex, rural or urban residence, and social conditions of the places where people live and work" (Braveman, Starfield, and Geiger 2001, p. 678; Daniels 2013, Chapter 12, this volume). But in 2000, the World Health Organization (WHO) published a report seeking to compare the extent of health inequalities between individuals in different countries (Murray, Gadikou, and Frenk 1999). I refer to the view underlying that report as *the individualistic view of health inequalities* because it implies that a concern for health equality should (also) address inequalities between individuals. This view contrasts with the more conventional *group-based view,* according to which the measurement of health inequalities should concern itself *only* with social groups.

The difference between the two views can be brought out as follows. Imagine a population of just two men and two women. One man and one woman have 10 units each of the relevant health value. The other man and woman have 5 units each. On a group-based view focusing on gender alone, there is no health inequality, but there is on an individualistic view. Indeed, on the relevant group-based view, there would be more health inequality if the two women had 8 units and the two men 7. By contrast, if we were to measure the degree of inequality between individuals by the sum of all health score differences for all possible pairs of individuals divided by the number of such pairs, there would be less health inequality.

The *World Health Report 2000* ignited an intense debate. Defenders of the individualistic view have argued that group-based measures overlook the significance of morally relevant "factors other than income, social class, and race." Such measures, they complain, disregard information that is relevant from the perspective of the health egalitarian planner aiming to reduce health inequalities: for example, they ignore systematic causes of inequality of health between individuals, such as variation in "environmental sanitation, water supply, health services, and social norms about risk factors" (Murray 2001, p. 680).

Friends of the group-based view respond that data relying on individualistic measures of health inequality are irrelevant to egalitarian health planners; that an individualist measure such as the one used in the *World Health Report 2000* "effectively removes equity and human rights from the public health monitoring agenda" (Braveman et al. 2001, p. 679); and that the measure falsely implies that any health inequality—whether it results from natural causes (as opposed to an "unfair social system") or is neither remediable nor compensable—is an unjust health inequality (Asada and Hedemann 2002, p. 2; Hausman 2007, p. 50).[1]

In my view, individual inequalities in health matter, at least in part because they are no less unfair, no less unjust, per se, than group inequalities.[2] However, some of the reasons why we should be concerned about individual inequalities motivate an indirect concern about group-health inequalities. The next section sets aside some issues that might otherwise blur the focus on the individualist versus group-health inequality measures issue. I then introduce a distinction between levels at which this issue arises. The fourth section introduces two basic conditions that any group-based measure must satisfy: the measure must be sensitive to intragroup differences, and it must explain which group inequalities are unjust. Next, I critically assess the claim that group-based measures are preferable because justice only corrects health inequalities with social causes. The next section evaluates a similar claim to the effect that only deficiencies in health that can be mitigated are unjust. The last section addresses and rejects the claim that data on health inequalities between individuals are irrelevant to an egalitarian health planner.

Assumptions

Four issues need to be set aside if we are to focus exclusively on the individualist versus group-based health inequality issue. First, claims about inequality of health presuppose a metric of health that allows us to rank the health levels of distinct individuals or groups. Any metric is bound to be controversial, but, fortunately for present purposes, we need only assume that there

---

[1] Health inequalities are remediable if it is possible to eliminate them; they are compensable if it is possible to eliminate the overall inequality to which the health inequality contributes through means other than by eliminating the health inequality.

[2] For present purposes, I can remain neutral on whether all individual (or group) health inequalities are unjust. It suffices that some are.

is *some* metric of health that allows individuals and groups to be ranked in terms of health.

Second, inequalities can obtain in dimensions other than health. Presumably, although inequalities tend to cluster in a way ensuring that people who are worse off in terms of income or education are also worse off in terms of health, inequalities in different dimensions can and do diverge. On some views, there is one fundamental dimension, such as welfare, in terms of which people should be equal. To the extent that health is an important component or causal determinant of this dimension, it might be reasonable to be concerned with health inequalities even if "a concern to lessen inequalities in welfare does not imply any concern to equalize separately different components of welfare" because health inequality is an indicator of likely overall inequality (Hausman, Asada, and Hedemann 2002, p. 182). On other views, in addition to this fundamental dimension (or even instead of it), there are several different spheres of justice within which people should ideally be equal, and health is just one of these spheres (Lauridsen and Lippert-Rasmussen 2010). On the whole, I bracket these issues and focus on inequalities of health in isolation from other inequalities.

Some will object, arguing that whether health inequalities between individuals are morally significant depends, at least in part, on whether health is special. Yukiko Asada writes that if, on the one hand, "we are concerned about health equity independently from inequities in other important goods" (i.e., if health is special), then "we should measure health inequality irrespective of its relation to other important goods, that is, across individuals" (Asada 2006, p. 28). If, on the other hand, "health distribution would always need to be measured with distribution of other goods," then "the traditional practice of measuring health inequality across groups" gains support (Asada 2006, p. 29). Neither of these claims seems true. Suppose the distribution of health should be considered in its own right and is special in that sense. It remains an open question whether justice is concerned with health inequalities separating individuals or groups. One might hold that many inequalities between individuals have natural causes and that inequalities so caused are not unjust, whereas inequalities between social groups reflect inequalities with social causes, in which case one might want to focus on inequalities between groups despite one's belief that health is special.

Conversely, one might want to measure health inequalities between individuals even if one thinks that health is just one component in, or cause of, the relevant equalisandum. Thus, one might want to do this if one thinks that health involves inequalities that are unrelated to most other inequalities—for example, because they reflect defective genes. And one might want to do it even if the health inequalities correlate with most other inequalities, as a result of which the health inequalities can serve as a proxy for inequalities between individuals.

Third, plain *equality* is not the only concern we might have about the distribution of health. From a prioritarian perspective, the badness of one additional unit of bad health has greater moral disvalue the worse off the relevant person (or group) is healthwise. On a sufficientarian view, there is some minimum level of health such that it is particularly bad when someone (or some group) falls below this level. Like egalitarianism, strictly understood, these views have both group-focused and individualistic variants. My discussion is neutral on the issue of whether plain egalitarianism or some kind of restructured egalitarian position like those just mentioned is correct.

Fourth, some commentators would deny that a situation in which some people have poorer health than others as a result of their own faults, or choices, is unjust. Insofar as inequalities between individuals can reflect differential choices, whereas inequalities between groups cannot, this is one reason why egalitarians should be concerned with group-health inequalities. But, first, not all inequalities between individuals reflect choice or fault; and second, because social groups are not defined on a choice-insensitive basis, it seems group inequalities can reflect differential choice after all.[3] Suppose that people have a genuine choice as to whether to attend higher education. Group-health inequalities between those with higher education and those without may, in part, result from differential choice. Accordingly, choice is orthogonal to my concern in this paper.

Principles of Regulation Versus Fundamental Principles of Justice

Concerns about health inequality arise at various levels, in various forms. A crucial distinction needs to be made between fundamental issues of justice and principles of regulation. The former do not reflect any facts about which states of affairs we can bring about or can bring about without sacrificing values other than justice. The latter guide us toward the realization of fundamental ideals, including the ideal of justice, as effectively as possible—or, as G. A. Cohen, from whom I borrow this distinction, puts it: "if rules for social living [i.e., rules of regulation] are soundly based, they will reflect both values other than justice and practical constraints that restrict the extent to which justice can be applied. That being so, justice itself could not be what is specified by such rules" (Cohen 2008, p. 3).

Principles of regulation and fundamental principles of justice might well differ strikingly, and the two may require quite different informational input. The information available at reasonable cost places constraints on the appropriate rules of regulation. First, one might have fundamental aims other than

---

[3] When groups are small it can also just happen that group inequalities are correlated with group differences in patterns of injustice-defeating choice.

justice-related ones, such as maximizing aggregate health. Second, one's fundamental aims might be too complicated to serve as a means of regulating one's conduct on a daily basis. To take a simple example, it might be exceedingly costly to reliably compute health inequalities between individuals, in which case the principles of regulation should be formulated in group terms. Finally, one's principles of regulation must take into account potentially unjust refusals to cooperate. For example, if there is a limit to how extensively one can promote health equality through scheme S before resourceful people with the luxury of cutting a better deal for themselves opt out of S (thereby harming those worst-off people who, in the absence of unjust opting out, would have benefited from S), rules of regulation might effectively veto S *even if* S is what justice requires.

One reason not to be concerned about individual health inequalities is that such inequalities are not *fundamentally* unjust. In principle, this leaves open the possibility that a regulatory regime referring to inequalities between individuals could be justified as a body of rules of regulation because, say, observance of these rules promotes the achievement of other relevant aims, such as equality between relevant social groups, better than alternative principles of regulation.

However, it is more likely that, although health inequalities between individuals are all that matter, fundamentally speaking, in justice in health, the best principles of regulation are those that also refer to group inequalities—perhaps because the best way to reduce health inequalities between individuals is by concentrating on the reduction of health inequalities obtaining between certain socially salient groups. A view of this kind might be what Dan Hausman is recommending. He believes that, with a few exceptions, data on the inequalities obtaining between individuals, as opposed to data on health inequalities "between well-studied social groups" (Hausman 2007, p. 50), are inferentially irrelevant as regards justice in health. This does not settle whether Hausman holds that, ultimately, inequalities between individuals are what matter from the point of view of justice (Hausman 2013, Chapter 7, this volume).

In any case, the main point here is that what counts as an objection to a concern about health inequalities between individuals depends crucially on whether this concern is located at the level of a fundamental principle of justice or at the level of regulation. Some objections to individualist measures of health inequality fuse objections at both levels. The (somewhat speculative) objection, mentioned earlier, that generating data on the health inequalities obtaining between individuals removes "equity and human rights from the public health monitoring agenda" illustrates this. It operates at the level of a fundamental principle because it contends that many individual health inequalities are not unjust. It also operates at the level of regulation, however, because it appeals to the harmful effects of a focus on individual health inequalities—something which, from a Cohenite perspective, is irrelevant to whether, ultimately, justice is concerned with individual health inequalities. The fact that a focus on a particular concern has unwelcome effects does not imply that this concern fails to articulate what justice is ultimately all about.

Two Individualist Arguments

Any view according to which, fundamentally, group-based health inequality is what matters must address the intragroup inequality challenge and the group-identification challenge. The first challenge is this: for any selection of groups such that inequalities between these two groups matter, intragroup inequalities may exist. If intergroup inequalities are unjust, there seems to be no good reason to deny that intragroup inequalities are so as well. A particularly powerful version of the intragroup challenge is one in which intergroup inequality exists between two groups and we eliminate it by lowering the average well-being of the best-off group while, at the same time, drastically increasing intragroup inequalities within the two groups. Thus, suppose men are better off health-wise than women. This reflects the fact that, on a points scale, half the men are at 12 (excellent health) and the other half at 4 (very bad health), whereas all women are at 7 (good health). If all we care about is intergroup inequalities between men and women, we are committed, implausibly, to considering a new state of affairs, one in which the health of the worst-off men is reduced to 2 better. This would represent an improvement on the initial situation because now perfect intergroup equality between men and women obtains. Those with leanings to the group-based approach tend to highlight certain kinds of group, such as high and low income groups. With these groups, we cannot plausibly answer the challenge by contending that whereas intragroup inequalities are due to differential choice or fault, intergroup inequalities are not.

Consider next the group-identification challenge. Any given population can be divided into a very large number of different groups, and any selection among these must explain why some group inequalities are relevant to justice whereas others are not. This challenge is particularly acute because, for any division of a population into different groups generating inequality, there will be an alternative division ensuring that less, or even no, inequality obtains. Suppose we have a four-person population consisting of two men, at 15 and 20 points, and two women, at 5 and 10 points. Here, group inequality exists between men and women. But if, instead, we compare the group consisting of the best-off man and the worst-off woman with the group consisting of the worse-off man and the best-off woman, then, if the group average (i.e., mean) is the relevant measure of inequality, there is no group inequality at all because this is 12.5 points in both groups. Why is the first comparison the one that matters?

One possible answer is that the individuation of groups should echo the major social causes of health equality. We distinguish between blacks and whites because racial discrimination is a major social causal factor behind health inequalities. In my view, it is unlikely that the selection of groups will neatly fit the contours of the social causes of health inequalities (which is not to say that *no* group division fits the shape of social causes of health inequality). Ethnic groups might still count as socially significant groups even if they do not differ on health parameters. Again, various occupational groups may differ significantly healthwise—say, waiters working in bars versus waiters working in nonsmoking "eco" coffee shops—even if they are not seen as forming different social groups. Also, it is unclear that relative positions of artificial-looking groups, such as the worst-off woman and the best-off man in my simple example, may not also in some sense fit the contours of the structures that determine the distribution of health. Finally, I reject the view that social causes of health inequality merit the concern, from the point of view of justice, whereas nonsocial causes of health inequalities do not (see next section).

Another possible answer to the question why some, but not other, group inequalities matter from the point of view of justice is that the individuation of groups should be in keeping with people's self-conception because we care about living in a society in which people can relate to one another as equals. The opportunity to relate as equals is eroded by inequalities in group health which, unlike those in my artificial example, matter to people's self-conception because they undermine equal respect and self-respect—especially when the inequalities in question are apparent to anyone who cares to consider the matter.

Although this concern is important, it represents a departure from the issue I am engaged with here (see Hausman 2013, Chapter 7, this volume). That is, the ideal of equal social relations and the ideal of an egalitarian distribution of health are distinct. Note also that a preoccupation with equal social relations would motivate concern about a certain group measure only insofar as that measure matters to social standing. So, for example, this preoccupation would not justify group-based views' familiar focus on health inequalities between groups defined by rural and urban residence in a society in which rural versus urban residence makes no difference to one's social standing.

Natural Versus Social Health Inequalities

One reason for believing that measurements of health inequality should disregard individual health inequalities is the following: only health inequalities that are the causal result of social factors are unjust, and only group-based measures of health inequality fit unjust health inequalities. More than one line of thought is at work here. One is the idea that inequalities in health reflecting genetic differences are not unjust and that health inequalities between whites and blacks reflect unjust patterns of discrimination and are tainted for that reason (Anand 2002, p. 487; Fabienne 2001, p. 163). Notice that this concern seems to be more readily formulated if one is concerned with fundamental principles of justice in health, not regulation: the idea that we should be more concerned with discrimination-induced health inequalities than with health inequalities caused by genetic variation alone is not based solely on the notion that we must accommodate other values or observe practical constraints.

Several prominent writers have, in effect, indicated that they are inclined to favor a group-based measure at least partly on this ground. Asada and Thomas Hedemann, for instance, compare two populations with identical variation in individual health. The first has experienced systematic discrimination; in it, there is a large health inequality between social groups. The second population, in which there has been no systematic discrimination, is free of the group inequality that characterizes the first but contains the same level of health inequality between individuals. Asada and Hedemann submit that since the individualistic WHO measure would deem these two populations identical in terms of health inequality, and since most would consider the first population to contain greater health-inequality injustice, the WHO measure "is bound to miss some important inequities" (Asada and Hedemann 2002, pp. 2, 4).[4]

Similarly, Paula Braveman and her colleagues say that equity "concerns a special subset of health disparities that are particularly unfair because they are associated with underlying social characteristics, such as wealth, that systematically put some groups of people at a disadvantage with respect to opportunities to be healthy. Equity is linked to human rights as it calls for reductions in discrimination in the conditions required for people to have equal opportunity to be healthy" (Braveman et al. 2001, p. 679).

Again, Hausman has said that he finds the following principle plausible: "states of affairs that [i] do not derive from social arrangements or the actions of people and [ii] are not subject to control or remediation by human action are neither just nor unjust" (Hausman 2007, p. 53; cf. Hausman 2009, pp. 236, 237; Hausman et al. 2002, p. 178).

In my view, there is such a thing as natural injustice, and social injustice is not worse per se than natural injustice (Lippert-Rasmussen 2004). However, even if one judges social inequalities to be worse than natural inequalities, it does not follow that one should disregard inequalities between individuals and become exercised about any group inequality. First, conceptually

[4] In her contribution to the present volume (Chapter 3), Asada favors a hybrid measure of health inequality combining the strengths of individual and group-based measures.

speaking, the social causes of inequality may determine the level of inequality between individuals. The design of the education system does not merely make certain children with certain social backgrounds end up with better results than others. It also determines total variation in educational attainment. Hence, if we are concerned with inequalities with social causes, there is, conceptually speaking, no reason why we should take different views of health inequalities obtaining between groups and health inequalities obtaining between individuals.

Second, inequalities tend to cluster: if an individual is worse off as the result of one characteristic, she is likely to have other characteristics that tend to render people worse off and not many characteristics that render people better off. But sometimes such characteristics counteract one another. In principle, the effects of discrimination against and discrimination in favor may cancel one another out altogether. Although this might never happen in practice, the conceptual possibility that it can do so still bears on whether social inequalities differ noninstrumentally from natural inequalities in their implications for justice. Suppose that there is sex discrimination against women *and* discrimination in favor of people with a higher education; and suppose that more women than men have undertaken higher education. Here, a group-based measure of inequality might show that there is no difference between men and women (because although men enjoy discrimination in favor of them in virtue of their sex, a higher proportion of them are being discriminated against because they have not undertaken higher education) and no difference between people with a higher education and people without (because although people with a higher education enjoy discrimination in their favor, the effects thereof are neutralized by the fact that the majority of people with a higher education are women who suffer sex discrimination). What we have here are inequalities with social causes that would not be registered with a coarse-grained, group-based approach operating with two independent groupings: men/women, higher education/no higher education. However, the inequalities *would* be registered with individual health measures.

Third, even if we are concerned with inequalities with social causes, it does not follow that we should be concerned with the sorts of group that normally appear in measurements of health inequality. "Men" and "women" are groups of this kind. Yet inequalities between these two groups may reflect causes other than (the relevant) social causes. Take a country recovering from a war in which a lot of its young men were killed. Men, considered as a group, may have a worse health status than women in this country because, as a result of the war, men are on average older than women, and age affects health largely irrespectively of social factors. Hence, if one thinks that we should be concerned with inequalities between men and women because such inequalities reflect unjust discrimination in favor of women, one should not compare women and men as such.

Remediable or Compensable Health Deficiencies

Hausman has presented an argument against individualist measures of health inequalities that differs subtly from arguments appealing to the distinction between natural and social causes of health inequality. Like proponents of the argument explored in the previous section, he does not think that all health inequalities are unjust. However, he does not separate those that are and those that are not simply in terms of the distinction between social and natural causes. Instead, he separates the just and the unjust on the basis of a distinction between inequalities that are remediable or compensable and those that are neither, contending that the latter are not unjust. Presumably, health inequalities with natural causes could be remediable and compensable, whereas health inequalities with social causes might be neither. Moreover, he specifies that, in the sense of "remediable or compensable," he has in mind those relevant health inequalities that "could be addressed by public health measures," where this includes policies that are not health policies in a narrow sense—for example, improved education in primary schools (Hausman 2007, pp. 49, 51).

I want to register two kinds of disagreement with this restrictive view of what counts as an unjust inequality in health. First, suppose there are health inequalities reflecting the "idiosyncrasies" of individual people, and suppose these inequalities cannot be countered with public health measures because, with the technologies available, it would be too costly or intrusive to collect the information necessary to do so. Health inequalities of this sort may be unjust even if our rules of regulation should disregard them. Imagine, then, that we can fund a research program in data collection technologies that will enable us to neutralize such idiosyncratic inequalities using public health measures at reasonable cost and without excessive intrusion into people's lives. One argument favoring the funding of this program is that it would allow public health measures to be used to address various idiosyncratic injustices in the future which, presently, we must live with. This argument would not be available to someone who believes that it is only those health inequalities that can be neutralized through public policy that are unjust.

Hausman's view might be modified to meet this first expression of disagreement. It might be said that, for any present health inequality, if an accessible future exists in which this inequality can be neutralized through public health policy, then this health inequality is unjust at any time it obtains. This is a possible view, but it puts pressure on those who adopt it to go even further. If a health inequality can be unjust now, even though right now it cannot be neutralized, why cannot a health inequality be unjust even though there is *no* time at which it can be neutralized?

The second disagreement I wanted to register is this. Why should it be only those possibilities of addressing health inequalities through public health measures that count toward the injustice of health inequalities?

The worry I have in mind here is an analogue of one G. A. Cohen has expressed about incentives-induced inequalities. According to a standard Rawlsian view, the difference principle sanctions a specific kind of inequality: the kind reflecting the fact that, for the state or a basic structure, to make the worst off as well off as possible there must be generous incentives for talented people who will otherwise choose not to make these extra, incentivized efforts, even though their doing so would benefit the worst even more. According to Cohen, the kind of inequality just mentioned is relevant to the question of whether state taxation policies are just. However, it is irrelevant to the separate question of whether the resulting inequality is just. Because the pattern of human effort and talent to which this argument appeals reflects the decisions of talented people not to act as productively as they could to the benefit of the worst off, and these because decisions are unjust, the resulting inequality is unjust.

A similar line of argument applies to health inequalities. Consider drinking culture. We serve wine and beer to friends during meals. Many of us allow our teenage children to drink alcohol. Much of the time, we expect to go out for a drink when we socialize. In moderation, a great deal of this is pure pleasure, but we also know that some of us find it hard to limit our drinking and develop alcohol-related problems. Suppose there is a limit to how far we can neutralize alcohol-related health inequalities through public health measures and that we could get much further if we changed our ways with regard to alcohol consumption in our daily lives. In my view, in failing to change our ways, we would be acting unjustly toward those people who, for various reasons and quite involuntarily, face a greater risk of becoming alcoholics.

This point is analogous to Cohen's contention that talented people are behaving unjustly in insisting on incentives—a point that is, in fact, easily extended and applied specifically to eating habits, norms about exercise, and so forth. In all of these cases, it may be the case both that we can only get so far in our efforts to minimize health inequalities through public health policies and that we could make further progress by changing our behavior in our daily lives. Such inequalities could be unjust even if they could not be addressed at the level of public policy.[5] Accordingly, insofar as individualist measures of health inequality are shaped by the existence of such inequalities, they might be relevant to an informed public that is willing to revise its ways in the light of what justice requires.

---

[5] Recall that, for Hausman, the relevant sense of "remediable or compensable" is one such that the relevant health inequalities "could be addressed by public health measures," for example, state policies, laws, and state-funded incentives. The sort of drinking culture reform I imagine here is not a case of change through public health measure even though public health measures may, and sometimes seek to, affect drinking culture.

Irrelevant for Egalitarian Health Planners

Another reason why there is no need to collect information about individual health inequalities is that such statistics do not show which kinds of public health policy one could implement to reduce unjust health inequality (Asada 2013, Chapter 3, this volume; Hausman 2013, Chapter 7, this volume). Note that one might combine an individualist view of health inequalities with the fundamental principles of justice and still deny that individualist measures of inequality are of use to the egalitarian planner.

Suppose health inequalities between individuals are unjust. Can we now say that data on these inequalities are nevertheless irrelevant to egalitarian health planners? I think not. Note, first, how strong that claim actually is. It is much stronger than the claim that the data in question are *less* relevant than those derived using alternative measures. To be relevant, the statistics need not be the single-best indicator of the relevant inequality to be measured. Several indicators together may give more relevant information than the best of these indicators alone.

Second, even if the data gave a minister of health "no idea where to begin to look to tackle disparities," they might be useful to egalitarian health planners as an indicator that one should start looking for such causes, as is suggested by the example in the next paragraph (Braveman et al. 2001, p. 678). And there is no direct inference from group-based data on health inequalities to remedies either. Reducing social inequality to improve justice in health is not always a policy option.

Third, suppose the health inequalities that are egalitarian justice concerns are inequalities of health over a lifetime. Suppose, moreover, that it is bad if some people are worse off than others in their lifetime health through no choice or fault of their own, and assume that health planners must allocate a fixed quantity of resources between two contrasting health programs: one seeking primarily to prevent a disease striking mainly at the age of 50 or above (like Alzheimer's disease, supposing such a prevention program would become feasible) and one seeking primarily to prevent a disease mainly affecting children (measles). Suppose, finally, that the frequency of these two diseases and (implausibly, of course) their consequences do not interact with nonhealth inequalities. I believe that justice in health requires health planners to give priority to the second program. This speaks against the group-based view.

One response is to say that it is a "don't care" issue—from the point of view of justice—which of the two policies mentioned is pursued (Hausman 2007, p. 49). Justice is indifferent here. What matters is equality in "moral status" and "life prospects," and this can be realized in both situations provided everyone (at birth) has the same risk of getting Alzheimer's disease in the first scenario and the same risk of getting measles in the second. Hausman writes: "Whole-life outcomes are bound to be quite unequal no matter how equally society distributes those social factors that contribute to health. Equalizing whole-life health is not a sensible moral objective" (Hausman 2007, p. 61). But, to my mind, the scenario I have described shows that Hausman's "much outcome inequality whatever aim pursued" argument is unconvincing. This scenario suggests that the aim of reducing whole-life health outcome inequalities is a sensible, moral objective. The reduction of aggregate differences in whole-life outcomes might still matter a great deal, from the point of view of justice, even if we cannot achieve complete outcome equality, and justice favors the measles program over the Alzheimer's program.

Conclusion

I have defended the position that justice in health is sensitive to individual inequalities. I have argued that group-focused views are hard pressed to offer persuasive responses to the intragroup inequality challenge and the group-identification challenge. Moreover, some considerations normally thought to motivate exclusive concern about group inequalities—that is, that health is not special relative to other goods and that only socially caused or remediable health inequalities are unjust—fail to motivate that concern. Finally, we need to be clear whether arguments about the moral relevance of individual health inequalities concern the fundamental principles of justice or principles of regulation. Where regulation is concerned, data on individual health inequalities may be of use even to the egalitarian health planner.

References

Anand, S. (2002). The concern for equity in health. *Journal of Epidemiological Community Health, 56*, 485–487.

———. (2006). Is health inequality across individuals of moral concern? *Health Care Analysis, 14*, 25–36.

Asada, Y. (2013). A Summary measure of health inequalities: Incorporating group and individual inequalities. In N. Eyal, S. A. Hurst, O. F. Norheim, and D. Wikler (Eds.), *Inequalities in health: Concepts, measures, and ethics* (Chapter 3). New York: Oxford University Press.

Asada, Y., and Hedemann, T. (2002). A problem with the individual approach in the WHO health inequality measurement. *International Journal for Equity in Health, 1*, 2, 1–5.

Braveman, P., Starfield, B., and Geiger, H. J. (2001). World Health Report 2000: How it removes equity from the agenda for public health monitoring and policy. *BMJ, 323*, 678–680.

Cohen, G. A. (2008). *Rescuing justice and equality.* Cambridge, MA: Harvard University Press.

Daniels, N. (2013). Reducing health disparities: No simple matter. In N. Eyal, S. A. Hurst, O. F. Norheim, and D. Wikler (Eds.), *Inequalities in health: Concepts, measures, and ethics* (Chapter 12). New York: Oxford University Press.

Fabienne, P. (2001). Health equity and social justice. *Journal of Applied Philosophy, 18*(2), 159–170.

Hausman, D. (2007). What's wrong with health inequalities? *Journal of Political Philosophy, 15*(1), 46–66.

———. (2009). Benevolence, justice, well-being and the health gradient. *Public Health Ethics,* 2(3), 235–243.

———. Egalitarian critiques of health inequalities. In N. Eyal, S. A. Hurst, O. F. Norheim, and D. Wikler (Eds.), *Inequalities in health: Concepts, measures, and ethics* (Chapter 7). New York: Oxford University Press.

Hausman, D., Asada, Y., and Hedemann, T. (2002). Health inequalities and why they matter. *Health Care Analysis, 10,* 177–191.

Lauridsen, S. and Lippert-Rasmussen, K. (2010). Just medicine and indirect, non-health effects. *Medicine, Health Care, and Philosophy,* 2, 59–69.

Lippert-Rasmussen, K. (2004). Are some inequalities more unequal than others? Nature, nurture, and equality. *Utilitas, 16,* 193–219.

Murray, C. J. L. (2001). Commentary: Comprehensive studies are needed for full understanding. *BMJ,* 323, 680–681.

Murray, C. J. L., Gadikou, E. E., and Frenk, J. (1999). Health inequalities and social group differences: What should we measure? *Bulletin of the World Health Organization,* 77(7), 537–543.

5 }

Priority to the Worse Off

SEVERITY OF CURRENT AND FUTURE ILLNESS VERSUS SHORTFALL IN LIFETIME HEALTH

Erik Nord

A common feature of ethical theories of fairness in resource allocation and of the thinking of ordinary people about fairness in health care is that benefits are considered to have greater value if those who are worse off receive them (Daniels 1993; Nord 1999; Rawls 1971). Concerns for the worse off run counter to the utilitarian idea that resources should be allocated simply with a view to maximizing overall health benefits. Concerns for the worse off are commonly referred to as "the priority view" (Parfit 1991). Brock (2001) offers a number of possible justifications for the view, including the argument that the worse off suffer undeserved relative deprivation and/or that the worse off have more urgent needs.

If priority in health care is to be given to the worse off, there is first a question of whether one should be concerned about those worse off in health or those worse off overall (i.e., in their global life situation). Although some would argue in favor of the latter (see, e.g., Hausman 2012), there is probably less agreement about this than about giving priority to those who are worse off in terms of health. In this chapter, I focus on worse-offness in terms of health. Given this focus, I address a question that has been raised regarding the time perspective of "worse-offness": is being worse off a matter of being in a bad state at a given point in time, of having a bad prognosis, of having had a poor history of health, or perhaps all of these i.e., of having large health losses as judged over a whole lifetime?

The late British economist Alan Williams strongly advocated the latter view. He related the notion of being worse off to the idea that resources should be allocated to ensure everybody a "fair innings" of health over their lifetime (Williams 1997). According to Williams, one is worse off as determined by the less quality adjusted life years (QALYs) one is expected to enjoy from birth until death. Norheim and Asada (2009) argue similarly.

Amartya Sen (2001) regards Williams' approach as an interesting and potentially powerful one, particularly since it seems to deal with social class inequality in a fulsome way. But he also stresses its limitations for policy making. For example, Williams claims that men are not getting their fair innings, insofar as their health-adjusted life expectancy is significantly lower than that of women. Although acknowledging the latter fact, Sen suggests that giving preference to male patients "cannot but lack some quality that we would tend to associate with the *process* [emphasis added] of health equity" (2001, p. 21). Sen thus warns against approaches that insist on taking a single-dimensional view of health equity, stating that "it is possible to accept the significance of a perspective, without taking that perspective to be ground enough for rejecting other ways of looking at health equity, which too can be important."

My own position is similar to that of Sen. I hold that health can be defined and measured in several meaningful and policy-relevant ways, including "current," "future," "past," and "lifetime" health. Individuals' scores on these different measures are correlated, partly because illness early in life is empirically correlated with illness later in life and partly because the concept of lifetime health subsumes past, current, and future health. But the correlations are not necessarily high. A person may be worse off than another person by all measures, but he can also be worse off on one measure and, at the same time, better off on another one. For some allocation problems, decision makers may thus find it helpful to have *descriptive* information on worse-offness on several or all of the possible health measures. At the same time, ethicists and policy makers may have *normative* views with respect to the relative *weights* that should be assigned to different aspects of worse-offness in priority setting between patients and patient groups.

In my own previous work on worse-offness, I have focused on so-called "severity of illness" (Nord 1993; Nord et al. 1999). This includes current impairments and symptoms and expected future loss of quality of life and/or length of life due to the illness. The main reason for this focus is that official Norwegian guidelines for priority setting in health care, proposed by the Ministry of Health and endorsed by Parliament, since 1987 place great emphasis on severity of illness thus understood (Norwegian Commission for Prioritising Health Care 1987). By contrast, health losses in the past or aggregate health losses over the whole lifetime have never since been mentioned as relevant—let alone salient—factors for priority setting in Norwegian policy documents. The same focus on the severity of current and future illness, rather than on past health losses or lifetime health, is to be found in official guidelines for priority setting in the early 1990s in the Netherlands, New Zealand, and Sweden (Campbell and Gillett 1993; Dutch Committee on Choices in Health Care 1992; Swedish Health Care and Medical Priorities Commission 1993), and in the medical ethics literature (Daniels 1993). Lately, the Dutch position has been reinforced by a government guideline saying that willingness to spend public money to gain a QALY will range from 10,000 euros for conditions of little severity to 80,000 euros for conditions of great severity (College voor zorgverzekeringen 2009).

So what do I then think of proposals—put forward, for instance, by Williams (2001)—to focus more on shortfalls in health over the whole lifetime and less on the severity of a person's current and future health problem?

My first answer is that the younger the person or group in question, the less difference is there between focusing on current and future severity and focusing on expected lifetime health. At birth there is no difference (future severity equals expected lifetime shortfall).

However, in older intervention groups, focusing on lifetime health rather than on severity can make a big difference for the valuation of a given health benefit. For instance, pain acquired at the age of 70 may be more unpleasant than the symptoms of a pollen allergy acquired at the age of 10. But the aggregate QALY loss over the whole lifetime may be greater in the latter case than in the former. So, whom is it more important to treat with a new medicine—the 70-year-old with the new pain or the 70-year-old with the old allergy?

I return to this question later, but first I want to make a general point. I believe that the relevance of different measures of worse-offness for societal priority setting and willingness to pay for health benefits probably depends on the nature of the decision problem. To see this, consider the two following examples. In problem A, a national medical administration is to determine its willingness to spend public money on reimbursement for a new and better drug for people with a given chronic illness X, compared to its willingness to pay for reimbursement for a new and better drug for people with a given chronic illness Y. Assume that those with conditions X and Y are of all ages and that the two drugs yield the same health benefit (measured, for instance, in QALYs). It then seems ethically plausible that public willingness to pay be strongly influenced by the degree of *need* in the two patient groups—defined as the current and expected future health losses associated with the two illnesses. In problem B, on the other hand, a regional health authority is to determine its willingness to pay for a health education program targeting adults living in an area where life expectancy at birth is 70 years, compared to its willingness to pay for such a program in an area where life expectancy at birth is 80 years. In this case, it seems ethically plausible that the regional health authority's willingness to pay be higher in the former area on account of that area's poorer performance on lifetime health.

Many more examples could be given. But I think these two suffice to demonstrate that more than one measure of health and worse-offness in health deserves a place in the economic evaluation and priority-setting tool box. So, basically, I am a pluralist. However, I do feel that the idea of using lifetime health as a statistic for expressing worse-offness is relatively new in health policy making compared to focusing on current and future severity. In the following sections, I therefore point out some theoretical and practical challenges facing the use of lifetime health as a statistic for expressing worse-offness.

First, as already touched on, focusing on lifetime health losses may de facto disadvantage elderly people who have lived most of their life in good health but in old age come to need relief of—perhaps severe—discomfort. Particularly if the fair innings argument is allowed to prevail, relief of discomfort in the elderly will—all else equal—be given less priority than similar relief in younger people (Nord 2005). I find this difficult to justify ethically. In publications following his initial 1997 paper, Alan Williams never commented on this objection.

Second, there is in priority setting in national health services a de facto focus on current suffering and expected future health losses. There is, thus, in a sense, an ethical and political burden of proof resting on those who argue in favor of a larger role for the lifetime health approach in priority setting. I believe they need to consider carefully in which specific types of comparisons and decisions it might be useful to supplement current evaluation practice with lifetime health considerations. As indicated, the relevance of lifetime health considerations is probably greater in the comparison of preventive programs for different social groups than in the comparison of treatment programs for different diagnostic groups.

Third, in specific decision problems in which lifetime health considerations are deemed salient, there are measurement issues. One concerns level of measurement. In decisions about priority setting between technologies and interventions for different diagnostic groups, representation of population values in cardinal (numerical) terms has proved interesting and useful for decision makers, as in the National Institute for Health Care and Excellence's (NICE) heavy reliance on utility measurements and QALYs in the United Kingdom and the recent Dutch introduction of varying limits to willingness to pay for a QALY depending on the severity of the targeted condition. The Norwegian Medicine Agency, in its continuous dealing with applications from the pharmaceutical industry to have new drugs listed for reimbursement, has expressed interest in numerical guidance similar to that recently introduced in the Netherlands. On the other hand, there is in Norway, for instance, no government body that regularly evaluates health programs for different social or geographical groups. It does not seem plausible that in making ad hoc decisions about such programs, decision makers would feel a need for data at a cardinal level on population preferences regarding equity in lifetime health. It seems more likely that choices in such decision contexts will be the result of deliberations based on general epidemiological data combined with a wide political consensus that large social inequalities in health are undesirable.

If—in decisions about programs for specific social or geographical groups—one nonetheless should wish to replace ad hoc judgment with more systematic procedures and incorporate concerns for equity in lifetime health in numerical evaluations, how should one go about establishing the *strength* of social preferences for giving priority to groups who are disadvantaged?

TABLE 5.1 } **Using the time tradeoff (TTO) and the person tradeoff (PTO) to determine weights for life years gained in different social groups**

Social group	Life expectancy	TTO	PTO	Weights
1	80	5	30,000	1.0
2	76	2	15,000	1.5
3	72	1	10,000	2.5

On this account, research in the past on the strength of concerns for severity may have something to offer.

Consider Table 5.1. Assume three different social groups (socioeconomic, geographical, ethnic or other) with life expectancies at birth of 80, 76, and 72 years, respectively. Appropriate groups of reasonable people could be asked to deliberate about a time tradeoff (TTO) question: how many years of increased life expectancy in group 1 and 2 would they deem as equally worthy of funding as an increase by 1 year of life expectancy in group 3? Median (or mean) answers, or consensus answers, might, for example, be 5 and 2 years, respectively. Similarly, they could be asked to deliberate about a person tradeoff (PTO) question: how many persons in group 1 and 2 would have to gain a year of life expectancy for that to be deemed as valuable as 10,000 people in group 3 obtaining such a 1-year gain? Median answers (or the consensus answer) might for example be 30,000 and 15,000 persons, respectively. The ratios expressed in the two sets of responses (TTO and PTO) would most likely not be mathematically consistent with each other because different framings of problems are known to lead to different answers (Kahneman and Tversky 1979). But policy makers could take both sets of responses into account and make a rough overall judgment. They might thus decide that, in formal economic evaluation of programs that reduce mortality risks in different social groups, a set of weights for life years similar to those in the righthand column of Table 5.1 might be used to roughly capture societal concerns for social group equity in life expectancy. In principle, concerns for social group inequalities in *quality adjusted* life expectancy, as measured in terms of QALYs or disability-adjusted life years (DALYs), can be accommodated in the same way.

Weighting life years or QALYs or DALYs gained in different social groups is a rather simple way to incorporate concerns for equity in lifetime health in formal program evaluation. A more sophisticated approach is to use a societal valuation function of the form $SV = Q^a \times E^b$, where Q is the total number of QALYs gained by a program and E is the resulting degree of equality in lifetime health across individuals (Norheim 2010, 2013, Chapter 14, this volume; Wagstaff 1991). The values of the parameters "a" and "b" are set such as to reflect the importance that societal decision makers place on total QALY gains relative to equality in lifetime health. The parameters thus express a tradeoff between these two concerns.

One challenge in this latter approach is to decide who should be included in the measurement of equality. For instance, if a program targets a population subgroup A, what is the total population in which the resulting degree of equality in lifetime QALYs should be measured? It can hardly be the whole population because few programs are big enough to have a noticeable effect on equality in the whole population. Should it therefore be subgroup A plus another subgroup B, which is targeted by a competing program? But then, why particularly program B rather than C or D or E? Presumably, one would want to look at a set of programs and value each of them in turn, in the light of resulting QALY gains and effects on equality measured across all the target groups in question. The measurement of such equality effects is no small task.

Another challenge is to estimate the parameters "a" and "b," from the formula, through preference elicitations. This can be complicated. For instance, in a study for NICE in the United Kingdom with a view to estimating "the social value of a QALY," Dolan et al. (2008) used a format as shown in Figure 5.1. As one can see, there is much information to be processed in the comparison of the two scenarios X and Y. Respondents were asked to consider a large number of such paired scenarios. The reliability and validity of responses to such complex preference measurements is not clear (Slovic 1995). The results of the study were eventually not used by NICE.

I conclude that, in evaluating treatment programs for different diagnostic groups, there is clear evidence that decision makers and the population at large in a number of countries wish to give priority to those with more severe current suffering and/or greater expected future health losses. I personally consider this to be a plausible ethical view. In practical decision making invoking concerns for severity, representation of population values in cardinal (numerical) terms may, in my opinion, be helpful. Such numerical information also seems to be wanted by government bodies working on a regular basis with technology assessment and priority setting across diagnostic groups. By contrast, concerns for equity in *lifetime health* are mostly expressed in comparisons of health in different socioeconomic or geographical groups. Data on the strength of societal preferences for group equity in lifetime health are at present almost nonexistent. To collect such data is an interesting challenge for future research. However, as indicated earlier, it is not clear that decision makers will find it helpful to have such preference data at a cardinal level of measurement.

Scenario X	Group 1:	60 years in full health, 8 years in poor health.
	Group 2:	56 years in full health, 8 years in poor health.
Scenario Y	Group 1:	72 years in full health, 16 years in poor health.
	Group 2:	48 years in full health, 16 years in poor health.

FIGURE 5.1 Example of question about the tradeoff between aggregate health and its distribution.

Acknowledgements

I am grateful to Lars Granum and Morten Aaserud at the Norwegian Medicine Agency for earlier exchanges on which I have drawn in this chapter and to Einar Anders Torkilseng at the Norwegian Directorate for Health for having provided useful comments to a draft version of the paper.

References

Brock, D. (2001). Priority to the worst off in health care resource prioritisation. In M. Battin, R. Rhodes, and A. Silvers (Eds.), *Health care and social justice*. New York: Oxford University Press.

Campbell, A., and Gillett, G. (1993). Justice and the right to health care. In *Ethical issues in defining core services*. Wellington, New Zealand: The National Advisory Committee on Core Health and Disability Support Services.

College voor zorgverzekeringen. (2009). Pakketbeheer in de Praktijk 2. The Hague: Ministry of Health, Welfare and Sports.

Daniels, N. (1993). Rationing fairly: Programmatic considerations. *Bioethics, 7*(2–3) 224–233.

Dolan, P, Edlin R., Tsuchyia A. (2008). The relative societal value of health gains to different beneficiaries. http://www.haps.bham.ac.uk/publichealth/methodology/projects/RM03_JH11_PD.shtml

Dutch Committee on Choices in Health Care. (1992). *Choices in health care*. Rijswijk: Ministry of Welfare, Health and Cultural Affairs.

Hausman, D. (2012). *Egalitarian critiques of health inequalities*. New York: Oxford University Press.

Kahneman, D., and Tversky, A. (1979). Prospect theory: An analysis of decision under risk. *Econometric, 47*, 501–512.

Nord, E. (1993). The trade-off between severity of illness and treatment effect in cost-value analysis of health care. *Health Policy, 24*, 227–238.

———. (1999). *Cost-Value analysis in health care. Making sense out of QALYs*. New York: Cambridge University Press.

———. (2005). Concerns for the worse off: fair innings versus severity. *Social Science & Medicine, 60*, 257–263.

Nord, E., Pinto, J. L., Richardson, J., Menzel, P., and Ubel, P. (1999). Incorporating societal concerns for fairness in numerical valuations of health programs. *Health Economics, 8*, 25–39.

Norheim, O. F. (2010). Gini impact analysis: Measuring pure health inequity before and after interventions. *Public Health Ethics*, doi: 10.1093/phe/phq017.

———. (2013). Atkinson's index applied to health: Can measures of economic inequality help us understand trade-offs in health care priority setting? In N. Eyal, S. A. Hurst, O. F. Norheim, and D. Wikler (Eds.), *Inequalities in health: Concepts, measures, and ethics* (Chapter 14). New York: Oxford University Press.

Norheim, O. F., and Asada, Y. (2009). The ideal of equal health revisited: definitions and measures of inequity in health should be better integrated with theories of distributive justice. *International Journal for Equity in Health, 8*, 40. doi:10.1186/1475-9276-8-40.

Norwegian Commission for Prioritising in Health Care. (1987). *Retningslinjer for prioritering innen helsevesenet* [Guidelines for prioritising in health care]. *NOU 1987*:23. Oslo: Universitetsforlaget, 1987.

Parfit, D. (1991). Equality or priority. In *The Lindley lecture*. Levenworth: Department of Philosophy, University of Kansas.

Rawls, J. (1971). *A theory of justice*. Cambridge, MA: Harvard University Press.

Sen, A. (2001). *Why health equity*. Keynote address to IHEA conference, York, July.

Slovic, P. (1995). The construction of preference. *American Psychologist, 50*, 364–371.

Swedish Health Care and Medical Priorities Commission. (1993). No easy choices—the difficulties of health care. *SOU*, 1993, *93*. Stockholm: The Ministry of Health and Social Affairs.

Wagstaff, A. (1991). QALYs and the efficiency-equity trade-off. *Journal of Health Economics, 10*, 21–41.

Williams, A. (1997). Intergenerational equity: an exploration of the fair innings argument. *Health Economics, 6*, 117–132.

———. (2001). The 'Fair Innings Argument' deserves a fairer hearing. Comments by Alan Williams on Nord and Johannesson. *Health Economics, 10*, 583–585.

6 }

Egalitarian Concerns and Population Change

Gustaf Arrhenius

We usually examine our considered intuitions regarding inequality, including health inequality, by comparing populations of the same size. Likewise, the different measures of inequality and its badness have been developed on the basis of only such comparisons. Real-world policies regarding health inequalities, however, will most often also affect the size of a population. For example, many interventions with regard to social determinants of health are very likely to prevent deaths and affect procreation decisions. In addition, population control policies, such as China's one-child policy, affect both health and inequality. So, we need to consider how to extend measures of inequality to different number cases; that is, how to take into account the complication that population numbers are often not equal between the different alternatives open to us. Moreover, examining different number case is a fruitful way of probing our ideas about egalitarian concerns and will reveal as yet unnoticed complexities and problems in our current conceptualization of the value of equality, or so I'll argue. Considering such cases will reveal that the notion of equality is even more complex than Larry Temkin has already shown in his influential work on the value of inequality.[1]

Consider the example show in Figure 6.1:

Figure 6.1 shows three populations: A, B, and C. The width of each block represents the number of people, and the height represents their lifetime

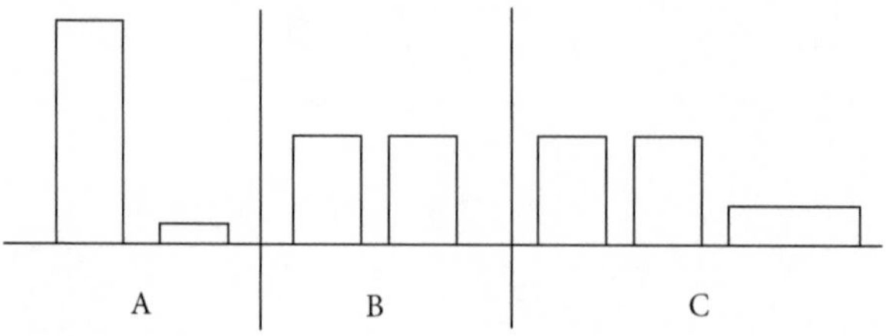

FIGURE 6.1 Three populations.

[1] See Temkin (1993, 2012) and his chapter (Chapter 1) in the present volume.

welfare. These populations could consist of all the past, present, and future lives, or all the present and future lives, or all the lives during some shorter time span in the future such as the next generation, or all the lives that are causally affected by, or consequences of a certain action or series of actions, and so forth. All the lives in the diagram have positive welfare, or, as we also could put it, have lives worth living.[2] We shall also assume that all the people in the diagrams equally deserve their welfare.

Population A consists of one group of people with very high welfare and a same-sized group with very low positive welfare. B is a perfectly equal population with the same number of people, total, and average welfare as A. C consists of the B people and an extra group of people with lower positive welfare than the B people.

One might ask how we should we rank these populations in terms of moral goodness or desirability; that is, how these populations are ordered by the relation "is at least as good as, all things considered." I take it that most of us would agree that B is better than A.[3] These two populations are equally large and have the same total and average welfare. The only difference is that there is inequality in A whereas B is perfectly equal. Hence, A is worse than B since it is worse in regards to equality, or so one might reasonably argue.[4]

It might not be as clear how we should rank population B and C. The number of best-off people is the same in these two populations. The only difference between these two populations is that, in C, there are a number of "extra" people whose lives are of poor quality but worth living. Could the existence

---

[2] We shall say that a life has *neutral welfare* if and only if it is equally good for the person living it as a neutral welfare component, and that a life has *positive* (*negative*) welfare if and only if it has higher (lower) welfare than a life with neutral welfare. A welfare component is neutral relative to a certain life *x* iff *x* with this component has the same welfare as *x* without this component. A hedonist, for example, would typically say that an experience which is neither pleasurable nor painful is neutral in value for a person and as such doesn't increase or decrease the person's welfare. The above definition can of course be combined with other welfarist axiologies, such as desire and objective list theories (see below for a discussion of the "currency" of egalitarian justice). For a discussion of alternative definitions of a neutral life, many of which would also work fine in the present context, see Arrhenius (2000*a*, 2013, chapters 2 and 9). See also Broome (1999, 2004), and Parfit (1991/1984, pp. 357–358 and appendix G). Notice that we actually don't need an analysis of a neutral welfare in the present context but rather just a criterion, and the criterion can vary with different theories of welfare.

[3] I'm assuming here that we can compare populations such as A and B without any further information. Some theorists would deny this because they think an outcome can only be better or worse if it is better or worse for somebody, which might not be the case if A and B consist of different people. To apply these so-called "person affecting views," we also need to know the identities of the individuals in the compared populations. I've discussed these approaches at length elsewhere (Arrhenius 2000*a*, 2003, 2009*b*, 2013) and showed that, at best, they don't help much in solving problems in different number cases, so I won't dwell on them further here. For the purpose of the present chapter, I'll assume that we can compare the value of populations without knowledge of the specific identities of the individuals in the compared populations (this approach is sometimes called, misleadingly in my view, the "impersonal view").

[4] Prioritarians would agree that B is better than A but for a reason that doesn't turn on equality: rather, the gain for the worst off outweighs the loss for the best off.

of these extra lives that are worth living make C worse than B? Some would say yes since the C population is worse in regards to equality: there is perfect equality in B but inequality in C, and this inequality counts against C.[5] Others would deny this. As Derek Parfit puts it in a discussion of a similar case, "[s]ince the inequality in [C] is produced by Mere Addition [as is the case in Figure 6.1], this inequality does not make [C] worse than B."[6] Moreover, there is a higher total of welfare in C, so even if we grant that C is worse with respect to equality, could this really outweigh the goodness of the extra welfare in C?

I've discussed the role of equality in the evaluation of populations of different sizes with respect to their all things considered goodness elsewhere, and this is not the main topic of the present chapter.[7] Rather, following in the tracks of Larry Temkin's influential work on inequality, I'm interested in the more limited topic of rankings of populations with regard to the value of equality alone; that is, how they can be ordered by the relation "is at least as good as with respect to egalitarian concerns."[8] It is then a further question how such a ranking would play into the all-things-considered rankings of populations in which we also have to consider other aspects, such as the total well-being in a population. For example, whereas it seems clear that population B is better than A since B is better as regards both equality and welfare, it is, as we pointed out, unclear whether the badness of the inequality in C outweigh the goodness of the extra welfare so as to make C worse than B.

One should also distinguish the current project with the project of ranking populations in terms of the primarily descriptive relation "is at least as (un) equal as."[9] This is a very worthwhile project if we are, for instance, interested in investigating causal relationships between inequality and, say, health, crime, social cohesion, people's sense of self-respect, economic growth, and the like.[10] Again, this is not the subject we are pursuing in the present chapter, although some of the issues we are going to discuss are of relevance for this topic too. As we shall see, descriptive and evaluative measures of inequality are likely to come apart. For example, whereas a reasonable evaluative measure is likely to give greater weight to differences of welfare at low levels as compared to differences at high levels (i.e., a population of two people at level <95, 100> is

---

[5] C is also worse than B with respect to average well-being. However, *average utilitarianism* has a number of very counterintuitive implications in different number cases, so we can safely put it aside. See, e.g., Arrhenius (2000*a*, 2000*b*, 2013), and Parfit (1991/1984), section 143.

[6] Parfit (1991/1984, p. 425).

[7] Arrhenius (2009*a*; 2013).

[8] See Temkin (1993, 2012) and his chapter (Chapter 1) in the present volume.

[9] I say "primarily" because, as pointed out by Sven Danielsson (see Rabinowicz 2003, fn. 7), depending on the currency of inequality, this relation might be partly evaluative because the currency might involve an evaluation. For example, to say that Nir has higher welfare than Ole in outcome X is an evaluation to the effect that Nir is *better off* than Ole in X.

[10] See Wilkinson and Pickett (2009) for an impressive study of the strong correlation between a country's level of economic inequality and its bad social outcomes.

better than a population of two people at level <5, 10> with respect to egalitarian concerns), this might be harder to justify in a descriptive measure (albeit not impossible).[11] I also would like to point out that some of the measures of inequality that we shall discuss have been primarily proposed as descriptive measures, or so it appears, whereas we shall investigate them as measures of the value of inequality.

One might be skeptical about our ability to rank populations by the relation "is at least as good as with respect to egalitarian concerns" rather than by the relation "is at least as good as all things considered." One might suspect that other value considerations will distort our judgments or that we cannot really make sense of the former ordering in contrast to the latter (compare with the discussion of the ranking of B and C earlier). This is a fair worry, but I think we can make sense of such an ordering and bracket other value considerations. For example, we can ask ourselves what we would prefer or choose from a moral perspective if we only cared about equality (of some sort).

More importantly, one might object that to understand the relation "is at least as good as with respect to egalitarian concerns", we already need to have a grip on the descriptive relation "is at least as (un)equal as." Since egalitarian concerns must supervene on some kind of relations of inequality among people, we need to know about them to be able to know what an egalitarian should be concerned about. This I think is a valid point which I do worry about but I think one can grant the point and still claim that we don't need to develop complete ranking of populations in terms of "is at least as (un)equal as" before we undertake the project of ranking populations in terms of the relation "is at least as good as with respect to egalitarian concerns." What we do need to consider is which objects are the basic building stones in such a ranking, and these might very well overlap with those involved in a descriptive ranking but we might put them together in different ways and give them different weights. Actually, I think this also holds for different descriptive relations of inequality of interest. Depending on the purpose for which we would like to use a descriptive measure, different ways of weighing together different egalitarian aspects will be fitting.

Still, one might ask what the point is of considering population change and different number cases from an egalitarian perspective. I think there are at least two reasons to consider such cases. First, as the discussion above indicates, it

---

[11] For further cases illustrating the difference between descriptive and evaluative measures, see Rabinowicz (2003), p. 63–6. Rabinowicz writes that "[m]aking larger distances weigh more might be justified as an expression of an evaluative standpoint, but hardly otherwise." However, even from a descriptive standpoint one could claim, I surmise, that the same difference contributes less to inequality at high levels as compared to low levels. One could claim, for example, that proportions matter: it matters whether I have only half or 95% of your wellbeing. This could be captured by measuring inequality by the difference in welfare divided with the average welfare of the compared lives. Hence, when individual welfare increases, the inequality diminishes even with a fixed welfare difference.

might shed new light on the vexed topic of population ethics and our duties to future generations. Second, it might be a fruitful way of probing our ideas about egalitarian concerns and might reveal as yet unnoticed complexities and problems in our current conceptualization of the value of equality and suggest new ways of formulating it. This is indeed what I believe, and it will be the main thrust of this chapter. An apt comparison is with average and total utilitarianism before population ethics took off. In respect to populations of the same size, average and total utilitarianism are extensionally equivalent. Since the former only presupposes measurement of welfare on an interval scale whereas the latter presupposes a ratio scale, most utilitarians (at least in economics) were of the former kind. However, in respect to populations of different size, these two theories have very different implications and those of average utilitarianism are so counterintuitive that the average utilitarian is close to extinct these days. Likewise, I think that considering population change and different number cases will reveal that the notion of equality is even more complex than Larry Temkin has already shown in his influential work on inequality.[12] Moreover, it will show that there are good reasons to reconsider what an egalitarian should be concerned about, or so I'll suggest.

Before turning to these questions, let me say a bit more about what kind of equality we shall discuss in this chapter. Equality clearly plays a fundamental role in moral and political reasoning. Views about equality can differ immensely, however, depending on a number of factors: what kind of equality one is seeking (political, legal, moral, and so forth), the "currency" of equality (welfare, opportunity, rights, and so forth), and among what kind of objects equality is supposed to hold (citizens, human beings, sentient beings, possible beings, groups, and so forth). It goes without saying that a full treatment of this subject is far beyond the reach of the present chapter. We shall only consider one kind of equality: equality of welfare among people. However, the concept of welfare used here is a broad one. For the present discussion, it doesn't matter whether welfare is understood along the lines of experientialist, desire, or objective list theories.[13] Hence, many of the views presented in the debate on the currency of egalitarian justice as alternatives to welfare—for example Rawls' influential list of primary goods—will fall under the heading of welfare as the term is used in this chapter.[14] Moreover, which is worth stressing in context of this anthology, health, either as source of welfare or as a component of welfare, is of course not excluded from our concept

---

[12] See Temkin (1993, 2012) and his chapter (Chapter 1) in the present volume.

[13] For experientialist theories, see, e.g., Sumner (1996), Feldman (1997, 2004), and Tännsjö (1998). For desire theories, see, e.g., Barry (1989), Bykvist (1998), Griffin (1990/1986), and Hare (1981). For objective list theories, see e.g., Braybrooke (1987), Hurka (1993), Rawls (1971), and Sen (1980, 1992, 1993).

[14] For this debate, see Rawls (1971), Sen (1980, 1992, 1993), Dworkin (1981*a*, 1981*b*, 2000), Cohen (1989, 1993), Arneson (1989), and Nielsen (1996). Rawls developed his list of primary goods as a part of his theory of justice, however, and not as a theory of welfare. He also claims that "good is the satisfaction of rational desire" (1971, p. 93; cf. Sumner [1996], 57.

of welfare. Indeed, if one so likes, all the inequalities we consider next could be supposed to consist in or be caused by inequalities in health.

Total and Average Pairwise Welfare Differences

Here's an intuitive measure of the inequality in a population:

> *Total Pairwise Welfare Difference (TD)*: The measure of a population X's inequality equals the sum of the absolute value of all welfare differences for all distinct pairs of individuals in the population.

Consider, for example, a population A consisting of three person p_1, p_2, p_3 with welfare 10, 20, and 20, respectively; that is A = <10, 20, 20>. According to TD, we shall consider the absolute value of the welfare differences of all distinctive pairs of individuals in the population; that is, (p_1, p_2), (p_1, p_3), and (p_2, p_3), The measure of the inequality in A is thus:

$$TD(\text{A}) = |10 - 20| + |10 - 20| + |20 - 20| = 20$$

TD is an intuitive starting point since it seems appropriate that both the number and the size of inequalities matter. TD also seems to capture what Temkin has in mind when he describes his *individual complaint theory* (ICT) as the combination of his *additive principle of equality* (AP) and *relative to all those better off view of complaints* (ATBO) principle:[15]

> [T]he ultimate intuition underlying egalitarianism is that it is bad…for some to be worse off than others through no fault of their own.…[T]he additive principle reflects the view that if it is really bad for one person to be worse off through no fault of his own, it should be even worse for two people to be in such a position. Similarly, the relative to all those better off view of complaints reflects the view that if it is bad to be worse off than one person through no fault of your own, it should be even worse to be worse of than two.…After all, to paraphrase the basic insight of the utilitarians, more of the bad is worse than less of the bad.[16]

Similarly, Wlodek Rabinowicz has proposed a measure of the "amount of inequality" in a population that is exactly along the lines of TD, although he only sees it as a descriptive nonevaluative measure of the amount of inequality in a population.[17]

Clearly, TD is quite a simple theory, and we might reasonably want to adjust it so as to take into account that, for example, differences at low levels matter

---

[15] For more on these principles, see Temkin (1993, ch. 2).

[16] Temkin (1993, pp. 200, 201).

[17] Rabinowicz (2003, p. 62).

more than differences at high levels. However, let's instead turn to another simple measure proposed by Rabinowicz:[18]

> *Average Pairwise Welfare Difference (AD)*: The measure of a population X's inequality equals the sum of the absolute value of all welfare differences for all distinct pairs of individuals in the population divided with the number of such pairs.

AD is simply TD divided by the number of distinct pairs of individuals in the population $\frac{1}{2}n(n\text{-}1)$, that is $AD = TD/\frac{1}{2}n(n\text{-}1)$. Consider again population A = $\langle 10, 20, 20 \rangle$. Since the number of distinct pairs of individuals in this population is three, we get the following measure of the inequality in A:

$$AD(\mathrm{A}) = (|\,10 - 20\,| + |\,10 - 20\,| + |\,20 - 20\,|)/3 = 20/3.$$

So, here we have two competing measures of the value of inequality. Let's try out these two measures on a number of cases to see how they differ. Let's first start with a case made famous by Temkin (see Figure 6.2):

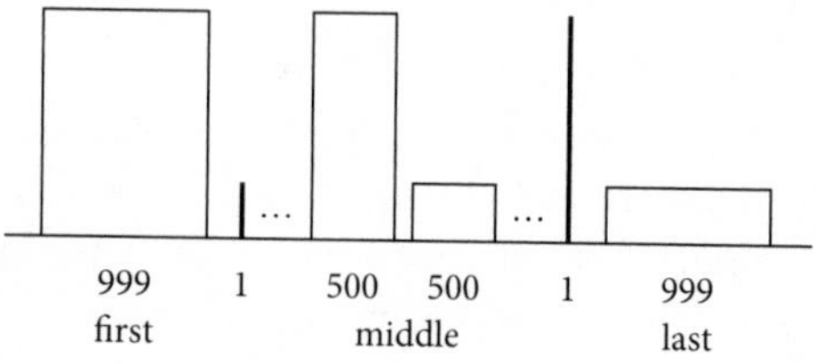

FIGURE 6.2 Temkin's Sequence.

In the Sequence, we have a thousand populations, each consisting of a thousand persons. In the first one, we have 999 best-off people and one worst-off person. The level of welfare of the best-off people is the same in all populations and likewise for the worst-off people. As we go down the sequence, however, the number of best-off people decrease and the number of worst-off people increase. In the middle population, there is an even split between the number of worst- and best-off people. In the last population, there is one best-off person and 999 worst-off people.

In terms of Temkin's complaints theory, we can describe the Sequence as first involving one individual with 999 complaints, then 500 individuals with 500 complaints each, and, last, 999 individuals with one complaint. Hence, the badness of the inequality first increases, peaks at middle population, then decreases.

What is the verdict of TD and AD? Well, we first have 999 pairs involving an inequality, then 500 × 500 such pairs, and, finally, again 999 such pairs. Hence, TD also implies that the badness of the inequality first increases, peaks at the middle population, and then decreases so that we have the same situation in

[18] Rabinowicz (2003, pp. 61–62).

regards to inequality in the last population as in the first population. Likewise, AD yields the same result since the number of distinct pairs is constant in same number cases.

As pointed out by Rabinowicz, TD and AD yields the same ordering in terms of inequality in same number cases since the number of distinct pairs is constant.[19] In other words, these two views are extensionally equivalent in same number cases. To distinguish these views, we thus have to turn to different number cases.

III. Proportional Variations in Population Size

Consider the case shown in Figure 6.3:

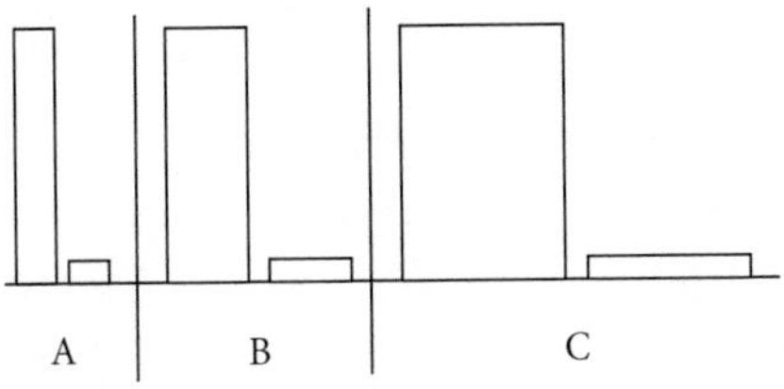

FIGURE 6.3 Proportional variations.

In Figure 6.3, the best-off people have the same level of welfare in the three populations A, B, and C, and likewise for the worst-off people. There is, however, a doubling of the population size of the worst- and best-off groups in B as compared to A, and in C as compared to B. According to what Temkin calls "the Standard View," which is also called "the Population Principle," the above populations do not differ with regards to inequality:

> *The Standard View (SV)*: Proportional population size variations do not affect (the badness of) inequality.[20]

All standard economic measures of inequality, such as the Gini coefficient, imply SV. According to TD and Temkin's ICT, however, proportional increases in population size increase the badness of inequality since the number of pairs

---

[19] Rabinowicz (2003, p. 74).

[20] See Temkin (1993, p. 191). Temkin's statement of this principle is, however, a bit different from mine: "Proportional variations in the number of better- and worse-off do not affect inequality." My statement is similar to Rabinowicz (2003, p. 75). Dalton (1920, p. 357), might have been the first to formulate this principle (although in terms of income) under the name "the principle of proportionate additions to persons." Foster (1985, pp. 42, 45) calls it "the population principle," and this seems to have become the received label in the economic literature. Rabinowicz (2003, fn. 19), claims that Foster "refers to this view as the requirement of population homogeneity" but Foster doesn't use this label (he uses the label "homogeneity" for a different requirement, see p. 42). He does, however, write that "condition PP [the population principle] also acts as a 'population homogeneity' property" (p. 46).

consisting of unequal individuals increases. In other words, with a proportional increase, there are more worst-off people and thus a greater number of complaints.

Intriguingly, AD has the opposite implication: proportional increases in population size decrease the badness of inequality since the number of pairs of equal individuals increases faster than the number of pairs of unequal individuals. For example, consider population A1 = <10, 20, 20> and A2 = <10, 10, 20, 20, 20, 20>, the latter population being a proportional increase in population size (a doubling) relative to the former. According to AD, the measures of inequality in these two populations are as follows:

$$AD(\mathrm{A1}) = (2\,|\,10 - 20\,| + |\,20 - 20\,|)/3 = 20/3 = 200/30.$$

$$AD(\mathrm{A2}) = (8\,|\,10 - 20\,| + |\,10 - 10\,| + 6\,|\,20 - 20\,|)/15 = 80/15 = 160/30.$$

Hence, AD ranks A1 as worse in regards to inequality as compared to A2. The reason is that AD not only takes into account the number of unequal pairs but, in difference from TD, is also sensitive to the number of equal pairs in a population since they figure in the denominator. In the change from A1 to A2, the number of unequal pairs increases from 2 to 8, a fourfold increase, whereas the number of equal pairs increases from 1 to 7, a sevenfold increase. Consequently, the fraction of equal pairs relative to all pairs goes up in the move from A1 to A2. The equal pairs are 1/3 of all pairs in A1 but 7/15 (close to half) of all pairs in A2.[21]

So, an interesting aspect of AD is that the number of equal pairs affects the measure of inequality in a situation. As I'll explain later, I think this is a move in the right direction, although I think AD gives too much weight to increases in equal pairs, as its implication in this case illustrates.

What is then the right answer to these two cases of proportional variation? Well, I think SV is false and I also think AD gets it wrong in this case. Here, the verdict of TD and Temkin's ICT is intuitively compelling: A2 is worse than A1 with respect to egalitarian concerns since there is a greater number of worst-off people and thus a greater number of complaints in A2 as compared to A1. For the same reason, B and C in Figure 6.3 are worse than A regarding egalitarian concerns.

As we shall show, however, there are other versions of proportional population variations in which our intuitions lean toward AD's verdict rather than TD's. To demonstrate this, we have to first consider a reconceptualization of the value of equality, the need of which will be better brought out by a another type of case, to which we now turn.

---

[21] For the same point regarding TD, AD, and proportional increases in population size, see Rabinowicz (2003, p. 75–76). There are other measures that violate the Standard View in the same manner as AD, see Foster (1985, p. 63); Rabinowicz (2003, fn. 21).

Mere Additions of Better-Off People

In population A in Figure 6.4 below, we have two persons, one with half of the welfare of the other. In Z, we have added another 998 best-off people. Z seems intuitively to be better with respect to egalitarian concerns since Z is very close to perfect equality. A, on the other hand, is a straightforwardly unequal population.

Here's how we can analyze this intuition. In A, there are no relations of equality but one relation of inequality. In Z, on the other hand, there is a staggering 498,501 relations of equality, which in comparison dwarfs the puny 999 relations of inequality.[22] Hence, I surmise, one might reasonably judge Z as better than A in regard to egalitarian concerns, and a natural way to account for this intuition is to claim that, from an egalitarian perspective, we should care not only about relations of inequality but also about relations of equality. Moreover, contrary to the received view, I suggest that equal relations are not just of neutral value because of absence of inequality but have a positive value that sometimes can outweigh the negative value of unequal relations. Egalitarians should thus not only be concerned with the badness of unequal relations but also with the goodness of equal relations.[23]

Interestingly, that Z is better than A in regards to egalitarian concern is implied by the Gini coefficient (and some other standard economic measures, e.g., relative mean deviation).[24] The Gini coefficient is approximately 0.17 for A and only 0.0005 for Z.

Likewise, AD ranks Z as better than A with respect to inequality since $AD(\text{A}) = (|\ 10 - 20\ |)/2(2 - 1)/2 = 10$ whereas $AD(\text{Z}) = (999\ |\ 10 - 20\ |)/(1{,}000 \times 999)/2 = 0.02$. The reason for this ranking is the same as we have seen before: the number of pairs of equal individuals increases faster than the number of pairs of unequal individuals.

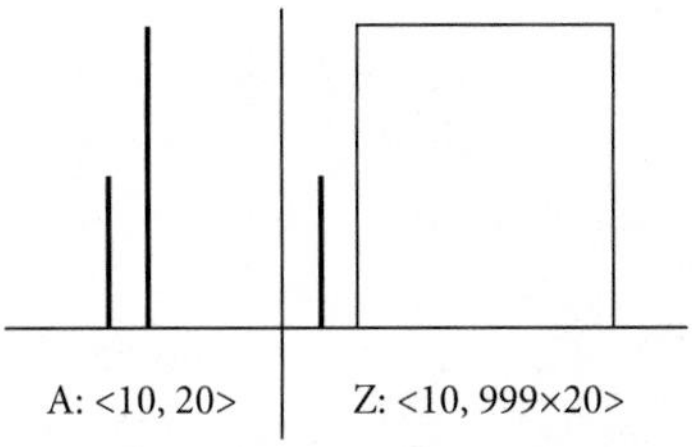

FIGURE 6.4 Mere additions of better-off people.

---

[22] Since the number of pairwise relations in a population of size n is $\frac{1}{2}n(n - 1)$, we get that the number of equal relations in Z is $999(999 - 1)/2 = 498{,}501$.

[23] Kawchuk (1996) makes a similar proposal in her excellent M.Phil. thesis, to which I owe much of the inspiration for the current chapter.

[24] See Kawchuk (1996, p. 159).

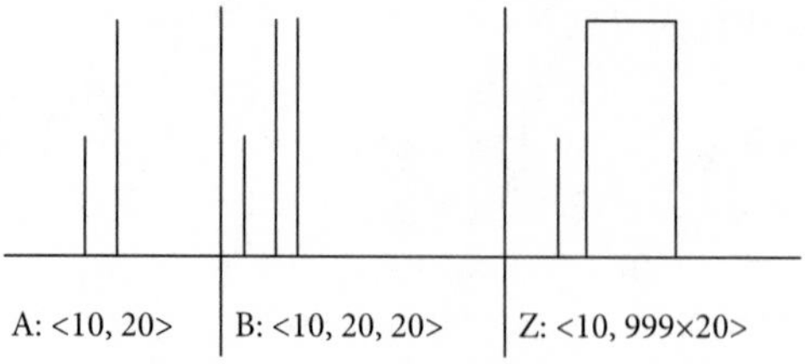

FIGURE 6.5 Mere additions of better-off people sequence.

TD, on the other hand, implies that Z is worse than A with regard to inequality because, in the change from A to Z, the number of unequal relations increases from 1 to 999. Likewise, according to Temkin's ICT, since the worst-off person has many more complaints in Z as compared to in A, 999 complaints versus 1.

Although AD and the Gini coefficient yield the right result in this case, a version of it will bring out a problem with these approaches. As we saw earlier, AD gives too much weight to equal relations. Actually, the same holds true for the Gini coefficient. Consider a sequence version of mere additions of better-off people, shown in Figure 6.5.

According to both AD and the Gini coefficient, B is better than A with respect to inequality since $AD(\text{A}) = 10$ and $GC(\text{A}) \approx 0.17$, whereas $AD(\text{B}) \approx 6.67$ and $GC(\text{B}) \approx 0.13$ (Z is better than both A and B with respect to inequality, see above). This might strike one as a bit odd. In A, there is one relation of inequality and no relations of equality, whereas, in B, there are two relations of inequality and one relation of equality. To judge B as better than A regarding egalitarian concerns is tantamount to judging that the positive value of one relation of equality outweighs the negative value of one relation of inequality. Moreover, this holds irrespective of how small the difference is between the best and worst off in A and B. This gives too much weight to relations of equality relative to relations of inequality, methinks. Rather, in the move from A to B, we may well judge that things have gotten worse with respect to egalitarian concerns since the doubling of the relations of inequality (making the aggregated complaints greater) outweighs the positive effect of creating just one relation of equality.

Hence, in regards to AD and the Gini coefficient on the one hand, and TD and Temkin's ICT on the other hand, we seem to be caught between Scylla and Charybdis: either we get the wrong result in regards to proportional variations (AD) and the mere additions of better-off people sequence (AD and Gini coefficient) or we get the wrong result in regards to the mere additions of better-off people (TD and Temkin's ICT) case. Can we do better?

Giving Positive Value to Relations of Equality

What the mere addition of better-off people cases brings out quite clearly, I think, is that, as egalitarians, we should care not only about relations of inequality but also about relations of equality. The idea is that the more people who are unequal, the worse in regards to egalitarian concerns, other things being equal; *and* the more people who are equal, the better in regards to egalitarian concerns, other things being equal. Hence, the egalitarian value of a population is a function both of pairwise relations of inequality (negative) and relations of equality (positive). Let's call this view "positive egalitarianism":

> *Positive Egalitarianism*: The egalitarian value of a population is a strictly decreasing function of pairwise relations of inequality and a strictly increasing function of pairwise relations of equality.[25]

This formulation leaves a lot of possibilities open as regards how to aggregate the value of equal and unequal relations. For example, the aggregation function for the negative value of unequal relations might be strictly linear, whereas the function for the positive value of equal relations might be a strictly increasing concave function with an upper limit. Nevertheless, with this approach, we can capture the intuitions regarding the cases just discussed.

Consider first Temkin's Sequence (Figure 6.2). What happens in this case, according to positive egalitarianism? Well, there are more relations of equality in "first" and "last" as compared to "middle" (498,501 as compared to 249,500). Moreover, there are fewer relations of inequality in "first" and "last" as compared to "middle." Thus, as we get closer to "middle," there is both an increase in unequal relations and a decrease in equal relations. Hence, like TD and ICT, positive egalitarianism implies that the sequence first gets worse, then better in regards to egalitarian concerns since the egalitarian value first decreases, reaches its lowest value at "middle," and then starts increasing again.

Consider now the case of proportional variations (Figure 6.3). Recall that, according to TD and ICT, proportional increases in population size always increase the badness of inequality, whereas, according to AD, proportional increases always decrease the badness of inequality. Although we agreed with TDA and ICT in connection with the particular case depicted in Figure 6.3, neither of these answers are satisfactory as general principles since whether proportional increases are good or bad from an egalitarian point of view should depend on the structure of the case. If there are few relations of inequality, then it should be possible that the badness of these relations is outweighed by the goodness of the increase in the number of equal relations. Moreover, if the inequalities are very small, then it should be possible that the badness of these is outweighed by a sufficiently great increase in the number of equal relations. In other cases, the badness of the increase in the unequal relations

[25] I think this principle is plausible at least as long as we are dealing with positive welfare levels. It might be that relations of equality involving negative welfare shouldn't be assigned a positive value. I'll say a bit more about this in the last section.

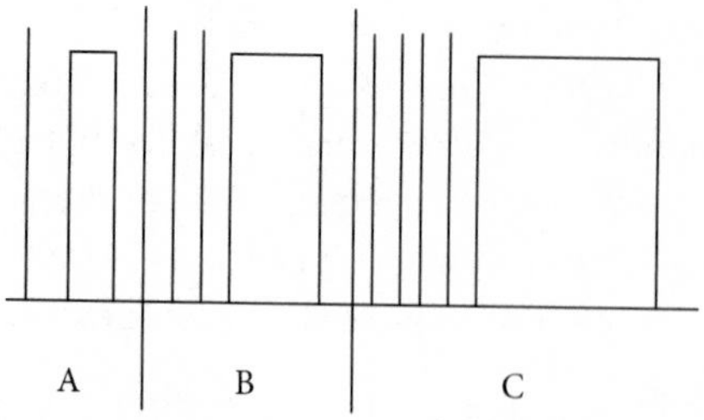

FIGURE 6.6 Proportional variations with few and small inequalities.

might outweigh the goodness of the increase in equal relations. Consider, for example, the version of proportional variations shown in Figure 6.6.

In this case, the inequality in welfare between the best and worst off is very small, and there is a small number of best-off people as compared to the number of worst-off. Hence, there is a greater increase in the number of equal relations as compared to the number of unequal relations when we move from A to B and from B to C. Still, TD and ICT imply that B and C are worse than A in regards to egalitarian concerns. Contrariwise, this is a case of proportional variations of which it is reasonable to claim that the goodness of the increase in equal relations outweighs the smaller increase in slightly unequal relations.

In difference from TD and ICT, positive egalitarianism can capture this structural dependence of the egalitarian value of proportional size increases since both the numbers of relations of inequality and equality increase with such increases. Depending on the weight we give to relations of inequality and equality, we can get the result that sometimes proportional increases makes the situation worse, sometimes better, and sometimes no different, in regards to egalitarian concerns.

Lastly, consider the mere additions of better-off people sequence (Figure 6.5). In this case, AD and the Gini coefficient implied that B and Z are better than A with respect to inequality. As we said, it is reasonable to judge that Z is better than A as regards egalitarian concerns since in A, there is one relation of inequality and no relations of equality, whereas, in Z, there are 999 relations of inequality but a whopping 498,501 relations of equality. Positive egalitarianism can, of course, capture this intuition since it also gives positive value to equal relations.

However, as we pointed out earlier, it doesn't seem reasonable that the doubling of relations of inequality in B relative to A is outweighed by the addition of one relation of equality. Hence, B is worse than A with regard to egalitarian concerns, and AD and the Gini coefficient get it wrong in this case. Positive egalitarianism, on the other hand, can accommodate this intuition. By assigning the right relative weights to the value of unequal and equal relations, positive egalitarianism will imply that the situation will first get worse and then better with regards to egalitarian concerns, as with the Temkin's sequence. For example, it is sufficient to give a slightly more negative value to one relation of inequality as compared to one relation of equality to reach this result in regards to A and B.

Another positive feature of positive egalitarianism is that it might help us handle a devastating objection that Temkin has directed against his own proposal:

> *The Repellant Conclusion*: For any world F, let F's population be as large (though finite) as one likes, and let the gaps between F's better- and worse-off be as extreme as one likes, there will be some unequal world, G, whose population is "sufficiently" large such that no matter how small G's gaps between the better- and worse-off might be G's inequality will be worse than F's (even if everyone in G is better off than everyone in F).[26]

The repellant conclusion follows from TD and ICT since the value of a sufficient number of small pairwise inequalities can add up to more than any number of great pairwise inequalities. However, it doesn't follow if we also give positive value to equal relations since population G will be very much bigger than F and thus there will be vastly greater number of equal relations in G as compared to F, and the positive value of these relations can overtake the negative value of the small inequalities.

Two Putative Objections

Let me end with two putative objections to positive egalitarianism. Consider the populations shown in Figure 6.7.

Positive egalitarianism implies that B is better than A with respect to egalitarian concerns since B has more equal relations, and there is otherwise no difference between these populations. One might find this bizarre since both A and B are perfectly equal populations. It might seem akin to claiming that, although both A and B are perfectly equal populations, B is more equal than A.

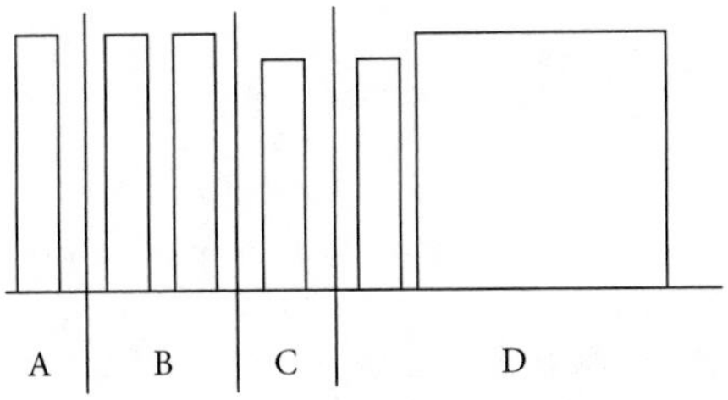

FIGURE 6.7 All populations are equal but some are more equal than others.

[26] Temkin (1993, p. 218).

There is, however, nothing like that going on here. Positive egalitarianism doesn't imply that B is more equal than A or that there is more or worse inequality in A as compared to B. Positive egalitarianism only implies that B is better than A in regards to what egalitarians should be concerned about. And, if I'm right in that egalitarians should care about the number of equal relations in a population, then there is nothing surprising with B being better than A in regards to egalitarian concerns. With this account of egalitarian concerns, there is no longer any perfect population from an egalitarian perspective since a population can always be made better in this respect by adding people and thereby creating more equal relations.

Positive egalitarianism might also imply that D is better than C with respect to egalitarian concerns since the positive value of the great increase in the number of equal relations might outweigh the negative value of the smaller increase in unequal relations. This might seem absurd since C is perfectly equal and D is unequal. How can an egalitarian prefer an unequal population over a perfectly equal one?

Again, however, positive egalitarianism doesn't imply that D is more equal than C or that there is more or worse inequality in C as compared to D but only that D is better in regards to egalitarian concerns. If we care about the number of equal relations, then the goodness of a big increase in the number of equal relations might sometimes outweigh a smaller increase in the number of unequal relations. Surprising as this first might seem, it follows that, even from an egalitarian perspective, we should sometimes prefer an unequal population over a perfectly equal one.

Another way to put this point is that this is a conflict between different conceptions of egalitarian concerns: patterned inequality, on one hand, and the number of unequal and equal relationship, on the other hand. As Temkin has long claimed, equality is an extraordinarily complex notion, and some notions point in different directions. This is another example of such a conflict between different accounts of what is of moral importance from an egalitarian perspective.

Conclusion and Discussion

It is commonly assumed among egalitarians that equality and inequality affect the goodness of outcomes only because inequalities give rise to complaints from the worse off and are thus unfair toward to those people. However, as we have seen in the context of population change, the positive value of equality also matters. Considering populations of different sizes gives us good reasons to reconsider what an egalitarian should be concerned about since the account of the value of inequality developed for same number cases have counterintuitive implications in several different number cases. I suggested a new way of conceptualizing egalitarian concerns that seems to capture our intuitions regarding the value of equality and the disvalue of inequality better, or so I argued. According to this view, which I called *positive egalitarianism*, the egalitarian value of a population is both a function of relations of inequality and relations of equality. More exactly, the egalitarian value of a population is a strictly decreasing function of pairwise relations of inequality and a strictly increasing function of pairwise relations of equality.

Positive egalitarianism can systematize our intuitions in a number of test cases and produce interesting and sometimes surprising implications. It should be pointed out, however, that we have merely provided a sketch of a theory, and there are lots of problems and questions that remain. For example, we have neither given a precise specification of the weight of the positive value of equal relations relative to the negative value of unequal relations, nor a function for aggregating these considerations to a measure of the egalitarian value of a population.

Another issue is that we have only discussed positive egalitarianism in connection with positive welfare levels. One might perhaps be less inclined to assign positive value to relations of equality that involve negative welfare levels. Moreover, if one does assign some small positive value to such relations of equality, then one would have to accept an implication akin to the leveling down objection:[27] Adding people with negative welfare to a population might make it in one respect better, although not all things considered better, since it might increase the value of equality in the population. More importantly, as this discussion indicates, how valuable equal relations are might arguably depend on the level of welfare involved.

Lastly, we also need to consider what we should do with small differences in welfare, small inequalities that can equally well be described as "rough equality." Is it only perfectly equal relations that have positive value, or is this also true of roughly equal relations? A promising approach that I think needs serious consideration is that inequality has a negative value when the inequality is sufficiently big but, when it gets smaller, we have rough equality that is of neutral value, and, when the welfare difference gets even smaller, it has positive value, which increases the closer we get to strict equality. So, for example, <5, 10> might have negative value from an egalitarian perspective; <8, 10> neutral value since we have reached rough equality; <9, 10> positive value since we are getting close to perfect equality; and lastly <10, 10> has maximal positive value regarding egalitarian concerns.

[27] According to the leveling down objection, one cannot make a situation better *in any respect* by only decreasing welfare of the better off (to the same level as the worse off). Many conceptions of the value of equality, like those discussed here, have this implication, but I don't find the objection very persuasive (it would be a different matter if a theory implied that it was all things considered better to level down).

As Temkin has shown, inequality is an extraordinarily complex notion. If I'm right in my suggestion that egalitarians should also value equal relations positively, then what an egalitarian should be concerned about is an even more complex notion than inequality since there is yet another aspect that we need to take into account.[28]

References

Arneson, R. (1989). Equality of opportunity for welfare. *Philosophical Studies, 56*, 77–93.

Arrhenius, G. (2000*a*). *Future generations: a challenge for moral theory.* Uppsala: University Printers. Available at http://people.su.se/~guarr/).

———. (2000*b*). An impossibility theorem for welfarist axiologies. *Economics and Philosophy, 16* 247–266.

———. (2003). The person affecting restriction, comparativism, and the moral status of potential people. *Ethical Perspectives*, 3–4, 185–195.

———. (2009*a*). Egalitarianism and population change. In A. Gosseries and L. Meyer (Eds.), *Intergenerational justice* (pp. 325–348). Oxford: Oxford University Press.

———. (2009*b*). Can the person affecting restriction solve the problems in population ethics?. In M. Roberts and D. Wasserman (Eds.), *Harming future persons: ethics, genetics and the nonidentity problem* (pp. 291–316). New York, Springer.

———. (2013, forthcoming). *Population ethics.* Oxford: Oxford University Press.

Barry, B. (1989). Utilitarianism and preference change. *Utilitas, 1*, 278–282.

Braybrooke, D. (1987). *Meeting needs.* Princeton, NJ: Princeton University Press.

Broome, J. (1999). *Ethics out of economics.* Cambridge: Cambridge University Press.

———. (2004). *Weighing lives.* Oxford: Oxford University Press.

Bykvist, K. (1998). *Changing preferences: a study in preferentialism.* Uppsala: University Printers.

Cohen, G. A. (1989). On the currency of egalitarian justice. *Ethics, 99*, 906–944.

———. (1993). Equality of what? On welfare, goods and capabilities. In M. Nussbaum and A. Sen (Eds.), *Equality of what? on welfare, goods, and capabilities the quality of life* (pp. 9–30). Oxford: Clarendon Press.

Dalton, H. (1920). The measurement of the inequality of incomes. *Economic Journal, 30*(119), 348–361.

Dworkin, R. (1981*a*). What is equality? Part 1: Equality of welfare. *Philosophy and Public Affairs, 10*(3), 185–246.

———. (1981*b*). What is equality? Part 2: Equality of resources. *Philosophy and Public Affairs, 10*(4), 283–345.

———. (2000). *Sovereign virtue: The theory and practice of equality.* Cambridge, MA: Harvard University Press.

---

[28] I would like to thank Krister Bykvist, Nir Eyal, Tom Hurka, Wlodek Rabinowicz, Larry Temkin, and the audience at the Brocher Summer Academy in Global Population-Level Bioethics, 12–16 July, 2010, for their very helpful comments. Thanks also to CERSES, CNRS, and IEA-Paris for being such generous hosts during some of the time when this chapter was written. Financial support from the Bank of Sweden Tercentenary Foundation and the Swedish Collegium for Advanced Study is gratefully acknowledged.

Feldman, F. (1997). *Utilitarianism, hedonism, and desert: Essays in moral philosophy.* Cambridge: Cambridge University Press.

———. (2004). *Pleasure and the good life: On the nature, varieties, and plausibility of hedonism.* Oxford: Oxford University Press.

Foster, J. E. (1985). Inequality measurement. In H. Peyton Young (Ed.), *Fair allocation. Proceedings of Symposia in Applied Mathematics* (vol. 33, pp. 31–69). Providence, RI: American Mathematical Society.

Griffin, J. (1990/1986). *Well-being: Its meaning, measurement, and moral importance.* Oxford: Clarendon Press.

Hare, R. M. (1981). *Moral thinking: Its levels, method, and point.* Oxford: Clarendon Press.

Hurka, T. (1993). *Perfectionism.* New York: Oxford University Press.

Kawchuk, R. (1996). *(In)Equality.* M.Phil. thesis. Department of Philosophy, University of Calgary.

Nielsen, K. (1996). Radical egalitarianism revisited: On going beyond the difference principle. *Windsor Yearbook of Access to Justice, 15,* 121–148.

Parfit, D. (1991/1984). *Reasons and persons.* Oxford: Clarendon Press.

Rabinowicz, W. (2003). The size of inequality and its badness—Some reflections around Temkin's inequality. *Theoria, 69,* 60–84.

Rawls, J. (1971). *A theory of justice.* Cambridge, MA: Harvard University Press.

Sen, A. (1980). Equality of what? In S. McMurrin (Ed.), *The Tanner Lecture on human values.* Cambridge: Cambridge University Press.

———. (1992). *Inequality reexamined.* Cambridge, MA: Cambridge University Press.

———. (1993). Capability and well-being. In M. Nussbaum and A. Sen (Eds.), *The quality of life.* Oxford: Clarendon Press.

Sumner, L. W. (1996). *Welfare, happiness, and ethics.* Oxford: Clarendon Press.

Tännsjö, T. (1998). *Hedonistic utilitarianism.* Edinburgh: Edinburgh University Press.

Temkin, L. S. (1993). *Inequality.* Oxford: Oxford University Press.

———. (2013). Inequality and health. In N. Eyal, S. A. Hurst, O. F. Norheim, and D. Wikler (Eds.), *Inequalities in health: Concepts, measures, and ethics* (Chapter 1). New York: Oxford University Press.

———. (2012). *Rethinking the good.* Oxford: Oxford University Press.

Wilkinson, R. G., and Pickett, K. (2009). *The spirit level: Why greater equality makes societies stronger.* New York: Bloomsbury Press.

PART } II

Health Inequality and Egalitarianism

7 }

Egalitarian Critiques of Health Inequalities

Daniel M. Hausman

My 2007 essay, "What's Wrong with Health Inequalities?" argued that information concerning the distribution of health among individuals without reference to how health covaries with other variables is usually of little interest from the perspective of justice. I maintained that health inequalities are not themselves *pro tanto* injustices. With the exception of incompensable health conditions, they do not imply the overall inequalities that raise questions of justice. I also argued that health inequalities among individuals are less suitable as indicators of overall inequalities than are inequalities in income or wealth. In this chapter, I first review the argument of my 2007 article and then criticize the contrary positions some egalitarians have taken. I focus on the views of two egalitarians: Norman Daniels, the most influential defender of egalitarian views of health and health care, and Shlomi Segall, whose recent book provides the first extended argument for egalitarianism with respect to health from a so-called luck-egalitarian perspective.

It might seem obvious that facts about health are of great importance to egalitarians concerned with social policy because health is both an important component and cause of well-being. If inequalities in well-being are relevant from the perspective of justice—as may seem evident—then it appears that health inequalities should be of interest to egalitarians. Furthermore, at the level of "rules of regulation,"[1] egalitarians want epidemiologists, doctors, nurses, and public health officials to take note of patterns of inequalities in individual health outcomes and to figure out how to mitigate them. But more needs to be said about what information about health inequalities grounds conclusions concerning justice and how.

I am indebted to the participants of the Brocher Summer Academy on Health Inequalities, including especially Shlomi Segall. I am also indebted to Paul Kelleher, anonymous referees, and to the editors of this volume for many detailed criticisms. They are of course not responsible for mistakes that remain.

[1] Cohen (2008, p. 3). See also Kasper Lippert-Rasmussen's contribution to this volume (Lippert-Rasmussen 2013, Chapter 4, this volume).

Until recently, egalitarians who were concerned with health focused on differences in health or in access to health care between different social classes, ethnic groupings, or geographical regions. Although it is possible to examine inequalities in specific health conditions such as heart attacks or cancer rates, much of this literature, like this chapter, is concerned with the distribution of "overall health" as measured by some indicator such as longevity, quality-adjusted life years (QALYs) or disability-adjusted life years (DALYs). In effect, those concerned with health inequalities have for the most part been concerned with correlations between health and other variables, such as class, income, education, housing, and so forth. Let us call the data comparing how health varies with other variables "health correlations."

Since different groups and variables are important in different societies, it is difficult to make international comparisons of health correlations. Comparisons among groups also ignore inequalities within groups (Illsley and Le Grand 1987; Murray et al. 1999; Asada 2013; Lippert-Rasmussen 2013). Furthermore, one can ask what principled reason there is to focus on health comparisons between some groups but not others. Accordingly, as part of their effort to compare health and health systems, staff members at the World Health Organization (WHO) sought to substitute measures of the extent of inequality in health across individuals in different countries and regions for the examination of health correlations (Murray et al. 1999, 2000; Gakidou et al. 2000). Their intention was to gather data concerning the extent of inequality in DALYs across individuals, just as economists study inequalities in income or wealth across individuals or families.[2] Let us call these data "individual health inequalities."

Despite the possibility of making international comparisons, I contend that individual health inequalities are generally of little relevance to questions of justice. In contrast to information concerning health correlations, which is often of great importance to the appraisal of social justice, data concerning individual health inequalities do not usually justify any conclusions concerning whether the society or its health policy is just. Health inequalities across individuals need not be *pro tanto* unjust.

Two remarks about this thesis: first, this chapter is concerned with health inequalities—inequalities in QALYs or DALYs—not with inequalities in health care or health-related resources. Second, this chapter (like my previous article) is concerned with what inferences concerning injustices can be drawn from data concerning health inequalities across individuals, not with whether those health inequalities are causes or effects of injustices. Some health inequalities involve grave injustice, and some do not. It is clearly unjust that African-American infants die at more than twice the rate of American infants of European ancestry. However, the fact that members of college athletic teams

---

[2] For further discussion of the contrasts between health correlations and individual health inequalities and a defense of studying individual health inequality, see Asada (2013, Chapter 3, this volume) and Lippert-Rasmussen (2013, Chapter 4, this volume).

are on average healthier than other college students implies no injustice. This chapter is concerned with the implications of particular *information about individual health inequalities*. What use can egalitarians make of information concerning inequalities in QALYs or DALYs across individuals?[3]

Which Inequalities Are Morally Significant?

In this chapter, I assume that there are two varieties of egalitarians, about which more will be said later. The first variety consists of *luck egalitarians*. Luck egalitarians are concerned about inequalities in outcomes (welfare) for which individuals cannot be held responsible. Those who criticize inequalities in resources, capabilities, or opportunities for welfare that are the result of "brute luck" are luck egalitarians. Victims of bad brute luck (such as those who come down with pancreatic cancer), unlike victims of bad "option luck" (such as unlucky investors), have not intentionally assumed the risks they face (Dworkin 1981, p. 293). The parties engaged in the "equality of what" debate of the 1980s and 1990s were luck egalitarians (Arneson 1989; Cohen 1989, 1993; Dworkin 1981; Le Grand 1991; Sen 1992). The other group of egalitarians are concerned about "standing"—that is, impartial treatment by the state, mutual respect, and nondomination. I call them "relational egalitarians" because their focus is on the relations among people. Elizabeth Anderson's well-known critique of luck egalitarianism (1999) defends a version of relational egalitarianism. Others whom I regard as relational egalitarians include Rawls (1971, 2001), Daniels (1985, 2008), and Scheffler (2003). Elsewhere, following Miller (1982) and Scanlon (2003), I have argued that there are several varieties of egalitarians, not just two, whose ultimate concerns differ (Hausman and Waldren 2011), but this dichotomous classification is a reasonable first approximation for the purposes of this chapter. See also O'Neill (2008).

The reason why information concerning individual health inequalities is not usually of use to an egalitarian is simple: the fact that Ann's health is worse than Albert's does not constitute information about either their comparative welfare or their comparative standing. A first approximation to the argument of my chapter can thus be stated as follows:

1. What matters to egalitarians are inequalities in welfare or standing.
2. Data concerning inequalities of health across individuals do not permit inferences concerning inequalities of welfare or standing.
3. Thus, data concerning inequality of health across individuals do not tell egalitarians about what matters to them.

---

[3] As noted in Asada, Hedeman, and Hausman (2002), it is only in virtue of possessing properties shared by others that one can assign a health expectation to an individual. So, data concerning inequalities in individual health expectations (and we do not have much) are in fact data concerning health inequalities among groups.

I take premise 1 for granted here. My case thus depends on premise 2, that data concerning individual health inequalities do not permit inferences concerning inequalities in welfare and standing.

Premise 2 requires an important qualification: when health inequalities are *incompensable*—that is, when the only way to repair the loss of standing or welfare due to people's ill health is to improve their health—then those who are in ill health are *ipso facto* worse off with respect to standing or welfare than those who are in good health. Data concerning incompensable health inequalities do permit inferences concerning inequalities in welfare or standing, and they thus provide relevant information for egalitarians. The reason why this is a qualification rather than a refutation of my position is that information concerning the distribution of QALYs or DALYs across individuals does not distinguish between compensable and incompensable health inequalities. Extremely large differences in QALYs or DALYs are typically incompensable, but moderate differences are often compensable.

In addition to distinguishing between compensable and incompensable health states, I also distinguished between *remediable*—that is, preventable or treatable health conditions—and irremediable health conditions. In my view, health inequalities that are neither remediable nor compensable—for example, inequalities due to conditions such as Tay Sachs disease—are tragic but neither just nor unjust.[4]

So, a more accurate statement of my argument is:

1. What matters to egalitarians are inequalities in welfare or standing.
2. Data concerning compensable inequalities of health across individuals do not permit inferences concerning inequalities of welfare or standing.
3. Thus, data concerning compensable inequalities of health across individuals do not tell egalitarians about what matters to them.

The rest of my 2007 article, which I do not summarize here, was devoted to arguing for premise 2, responding to objections, and criticizing the view that data concerning health inequalities, like data concerning income or wealth inequalities, are useful indicators of overall inequalities.

To forestall misunderstanding, let me emphasize that the pressing practical case for a redistribution of health-related resources toward the poor and oppressed does not depend on whether information concerning health

[4] Although the notions of compensation and remediation and the distinction between them are quite intuitive, exactly what counts as compensation or remediation is a tricky issue that I do not address here. Some of the complexities are discussed in Hausman (2007). I do not count leveling down of health differences as a form of remediation. Compensation usually falls short of remediation, and helping someone to adapt is as much compensation as remediation. If massive redistribution is required in order to accomplish compensation, I do not count the condition as compensable. A broken arm is both remediable and compensable. A diabetic coma is remediable but not compensable. Congenital blindness is compensable but not remediable.

inequalities permits inferences concerning injustice. Even if one had no concern for justice and were only interested in alleviating suffering, there would be an overwhelming case for redistribution. In some parts of the world, such as sub-Saharan Africa, few things, if any, have a higher moral priority than addressing health needs. Even though mitigating health inequalities and improving the life prospects of those whose lives are stunted go hand in hand in the world today, it is important to ask why the current distribution is objectionable.

Information about health correlations and social group health differences, in contrast to data concerning individual health inequalities, will often be relevant to conclusions about justice, not because group differences matter and individual differences do not matter, but because information about correlations between health and other factors often licenses conclusions about the inequalities in welfare or standing that egalitarians care about. Because in many societies there are large differences in other variables relevant to well-being, such as incomes, status, and opportunities across geographic regions and across ethnic and religious boundaries, knowing in addition the extent of the health differences can tell one a great deal about inequalities in overall welfare or standing across these groups. For example, the differences in quality-adjusted life expectancy between Americans of African and European ancestry show how large the welfare differences are between members of the two groups.

Data concerning the variance across individuals of health outcomes or expectations may give rise to inquiries whose findings could be of great importance to egalitarians. But simply knowing the distribution of health licenses few moral conclusions. From an egalitarian perspective, a state of affairs in which those who are otherwise worse off are healthier than those who are otherwise more fortunate is, other things being equal, more just rather than less just than a state of affairs that is exactly the same except that health is equally distributed.

Luck Egalitarianism

The case just summarized for the limited relevance of information concerning health inequalities has been implicitly rejected by those luck egalitarians and relational egalitarians who have argued that individual inequalities in health are unjust. In this section and the next, I examine Shlomi Segall's luck egalitarian condemnation of health inequalities, before turning in the next three sections to Norman Daniels's relational egalitarian case against health inequalities. In addition to defending my claims against their positions to the contrary, I shall make a number of criticisms of their specific proposals and arguments.

Luck egalitarianism stems from a powerful intuition, which many people (including me) share: it appears not only unfair but outrageous that, owing to brute luck, some people have stunted lives while others live well. It is unjust that some children are born with prospects for bleak, impoverished, and short lives that could be greatly improved while others can expect to live long, rich, happy, and secure lives. This intuition can be explained by the following candidate principle of justice:

> *Luck Egalitarianism*: Inequalities in welfare for which individuals cannot be held responsible are *pro tanto* unjust.

In G. A. Cohen's words, egalitarians aim "to eliminate…disadvantage for which the sufferer cannot be held responsible" (1989, p. 916). In his recent book, *Health, Luck and Justice*, Segall formulates luck egalitarianism as the view that "it is unfair for one person to be worse off than another due to reasons beyond her control" (2010, p. 10).

Luck egalitarians accordingly owe us an account of which actions individuals should be held responsible for. According to Cohen and Arneson, agents are responsible for actions if and only if the actions are freely chosen (Cohen 1989, 1993; Arneson 1989). According to Ronald Dworkin, in contrast, what distinguishes those actions for which individuals should be held responsible from those that one should regard as matters of luck is whether the actions stem from identity-defining features of agents (1981, p. 303). Segall argues instead that egalitarians should hold agents responsible for those actions that it would have been reasonable to expect them to avoid having chosen. The fact that outcomes depend both on things for which people are responsible and on things for which they are not responsible raises further difficulties. Should a luck egalitarian hold people responsible for outcomes that depend in any way on actions for which they are responsible? Doing so would eviscerate egalitarianism. If, on the other hand, the egalitarian judges that people are not responsible if the outcome was in any way influenced by factors for which individuals cannot be held responsible, then the concern with responsibility disappears. So, some way must be found to allocate shares of responsibility to the individual and to chance. "Only" one of seven smokers gets lung cancer. What does this imply about their responsibility? Julian Le Grand proposes that people be held responsible for the expected value of their choices rather than for the actual outcomes (1991). This distinguishes the effect of risk and uncertainty, but the expected value still depends on factors beyond an individual's control.

Although luck egalitarianism explains our moral outrage at the differences in people's life prospects, if it is not supplemented with other principles, it has (as argued by Anderson 1999) seriously counterintuitive implications. It apparently implies what she calls the "abandonment of the imprudent"—that those who fare badly as the result of choices for which they should be held responsible are not owed (as a matter of justice) any assistance. Like Segall, most egalitarians respond by invoking additional moral principles that justify such assistance, but the fact that luck egalitarianism by itself grounds no objection to this abandonment is still damaging. Implementing a luck egalitarian social policy also requires determining what individuals are responsible for, which in turn implies a disquieting intrusiveness into private lives. Some of our intuitions also appear to be directly in conflict with luck egalitarianism. Consider the case of someone who is taken ill because of his choice to take care of others, despite their highly contagious disease. His responsibility for his illness, unlike the responsibility of a reckless driver who injures herself, seems not to diminish his claims (as a matter of justice) to assistance.

To offer a satisfactory response to these objections, something should be done to put luck egalitarianism on a firmer foundation, because there are competing explanations for the intuition that there is something terribly wrong about the inequalities in life prospects that people face. That intuition might, for example, instead be explained by the wrongness of the avoidable suffering of those whose lives are stunted (Raz 1984; Frankfurt 1987). Both to justify luck egalitarianism and to explain how it should cope with the difficulties canvassed in the last two paragraphs, more needs to be said about the moral foundations of egalitarianism.

One way to defend luck egalitarianism, which differs from Segall's, can be found in Larry Temkin's contribution to this volume (2013, Chapter 1, this volume). Temkin argues that the basis of luck egalitarianism lies in "comparative fairness," which in turn derives from desert. In Temkin's view, "undeserved inequality is always objectionable; whether or not it is unavoidable, any one is responsible for it" (1993, p. 12). "In fact, I think that deserved inequalities... are not bad at all. The reason for this is simple. *Undeserved* inequality is unfair, but *deserved* inequality is not" (2003, p. 767). In this volume, he writes, "But among unequally deserving people it [inequality] isn't bad, because it isn't unfair, for someone less deserving to be worse off than someone more deserving, even if the former is worse off through no fault or choice of his own" (Temkin 2013, Chapter 1, this volume).[5] What makes desert theory to some extent egalitarian is the fact that much of what people deserve is equal and that equality is the default. The desert theorist can explain why misfortunes that are due to noble choices are still owed compensation because noble choices do not diminish what one deserves (Temkin 2013, Chapter 1, this volume). Similarly, even if those who drive recklessly or smoke may be responsible for their injuries or cancers, they may still be deserving of assistance.

---

[5] Shelley Kagan argues for the general thesis that desert preempts equality: once one recognizes the demands of desert, insisting on equality adds nothing (1999). Serena Olsaretti responds to Kagan by arguing that valuing equality makes a difference when one is considering starting points, where there is as yet no desert (2002). One can also respond, as Fleurbaey suggests, that, instead of determining a just distribution, desert depends on a prior theory of distributional justice (2008, chapter 10).

Most luck egalitarians are not desert theorists, and Segall explicitly distinguishes luck egalitarianism from any considerations of desert (2010, pp. 16–17). If not desert, what then justifies luck egalitarianism beyond our intuitive condemnation of actual inequalities, which can be explained by competing moral principles? In my view, not much.

Luck Egalitarianism and Health Inequalities

Let us turn to Segall's specific arguments for universal health care and egalitarian policies with respect to lifetime health expectations, which he claims to derive from luck egalitarian premises. To justify universal health care, he needs to show that it mitigates inequalities due to brute luck, and, to defend the provision of health care to those who are responsible for their illness, he must respond to the abandonment of the imprudent objection. To carry this out, Segall begins by assuming what I have disputed, that individual inequalities in health are themselves of concern to egalitarians, regardless of whether they coincide with inequalities in welfare. He then responds to the abandonment of the imprudent objection by arguing that luck egalitarians need not find anything unjust about *equalities* for which individuals are not responsible (2010, chapters 1, 2). Even though luck egalitarianism does not require treating smokers who have contracted lung cancer, it does not imply that treating them is unjust. What justifies universal health care is an additional principle that society, to the extent to which it is able, must meet everyone's basic needs. Since this principle is also egalitarian, and satisfying it does not conflict with the requirements of luck egalitarianism, Segall regards the combined theory as a version of luck egalitarianism. But what justifies universal health care is the principle that society should meet everyone's basic needs, not luck egalitarianism. The fact that luck egalitarianism is not doing any work is not, of course, an objection to the pluralist position Segall defends, but it does challenge the claim that luck egalitarianism supports universal health care.

When Segall turns from questions concerning the provision of health care to questions concerning the distribution of health itself, he abandons luck egalitarianism in favor of what he calls "luck prioritarianism"—the view that people's welfare claims are stronger if they are worse off and not responsible for being worse off.[6] What motivates the shift is a desire to avoid in any way favoring "leveling down," even *pro tanto*. (Leveling down in this context is diminishing the health of those who are healthy in order to lessen health inequalities.) Since, as Segall correctly points out, health is not mainly a positional good—that is, a good whose value to an individual depends on how

[6] The label, "prioritarian," and the classic statement of prioritarianism can be found in Parfit (1991).

much of it others have—leveling down is, as Segall maintains, particularly repugnant.

Segall's luck prioritarian view of health inequalities among individuals is problematic. First, enhancing the health *expectations* of those who have been unlucky fails to capture what the luck egalitarian or luck prioritarian cares about. Two individuals, one of whom dies of pancreatic cancer at age 30, while the other who is healthy until she dies of a sudden heart attack at age 87, may have had equal health expectations, but their brute luck has obviously been unequal. Second, apart from conforming to the intuition driving luck egalitarianism, nothing has been said to justify prioritarianism either in general or with respect to health. Consider Ann and Albert, who both have excellent lives. Albert is nevertheless better off than Ann, and Ann is currently healthier than Albert. Setting aside for the moment questions about responsibility, why should one give priority to either, and to whom should one give priority? Segall would give priority to Albert, if he is indeed less healthy than Ann, but Segall does not make clear whether the less healthy is the one whose current health state is worse, whose health so far over his or her whole live has been worse, or whose health expectations are worse.[7]

Segall's account reveals additional difficulties. In determining whether Ann or Albert should have priority, Segall takes two factors to be relevant. First, there is the question of who is less healthy. Second, there is the question of who is more responsible. How should luck prioritarians weigh these two factors in determining the priority that should be assigned to improving people's health? Call this the *double-priority problem*. Segall's solution is to give priority to prudence—that is, to the answer to the second question. If Ann has been more prudent—if she is less responsible for her ill health—then, other things being equal, she has a greater claim to nonmedical means of improving her health than does Albert, even though he is less healthy. On Segall's view, from the perspective of justice, the poor health of the less prudent generates claims for help only if resources are left over after doing everything possible for those who have taken good care of themselves. Since those who take care of themselves will, on average, be healthier than those who are less careful of their health, Segall's principle of "prioritizing the opportunity for health of the worse off" in fact prioritizes improving the health of the healthier.[8]

Moreover—and here I return to my own argument—why should priority determine claims for health enhancement rather than claims for welfare enhancement, and why should priority depend on prudence and health, rather than prudence and welfare? It is hard to see what good answers the luck

---

[7] I am indebted here to Dan Brock.

[8] This is true from the perspective of egalitarian or prioritarian justice. Benevolence, in the form either of a concern for the suffering of those who are very ill or from a quasi-utilitarian concern to improve population health, could justify a more reasonable policy.

egalitarian has to these questions, even if the luck egalitarian were able to provide a rationale for objecting to inequalities in welfare for which individuals are not responsible. Given the shaky philosophical foundations of luck egalitarianism and the many difficulties it faces, the luck egalitarian has little basis to condemn individual health inequalities.

Relational Egalitarianism

Relational egalitarians are not directly concerned with the distribution of goods, except for crucial positional goods, which affect an individual's standing. Whether Ann has a happy family while Albert is in the midst of a divorce or whether Ann is earning $150,000 per year while Albert is earning $100,000 is, according to the relational egalitarian, of little relevance to justice. If, on the other hand, Ann has the right to vote but Albert does not, or Ann has so much more wealth than Albert that she has appreciably more political influence, then there is a *pro tanto* injustice.

Like luck egalitarianism, relational egalitarianism derives from widely shared intuitions. It seems unjust if one individual subjugates another or if the government does not treat individuals impartially and with equal respect. Unless they have forfeited their status by immoral or criminal actions, each individual should have the same standing and should command equal respect. Social relations should be relations among equals. Inequalities in health are of concern to relational egalitarians if they limit the possibility of people interacting as equals or indicate unequal standing. Equality in health expectations across all salient social divides would seem to be sufficient (with respect to the distribution of health) to meet such a concern.

The best developed relational egalitarian discussion of health is Norman Daniels's recent book, *Just Health* (2008). Although it is concerned with the distribution of health (unlike his earlier book, *Just Health Care* [1985]), much of what Daniels has to say about the principles that should govern the distribution of health are developed in the course of his discussion of health care. Accordingly, it is tricky to draw out of *Just Health* precisely what Daniels believes justice requires with respect to the distribution of health, and I am not fully confident that the following discussion captures his view.

Daniels's egalitarianism derives from Rawls, whose two principles of justice I interpret to embody a relational egalitarianism:

> First, each person is to have an equal right to the most extensive basic liberty compatible with a similar liberty for others (1971, p. 60).
>
> Second, social and economic inequalities are to be arranged so that they are both (a) to the greatest benefit of the least advantaged and (b) attached to offices and positions open to all under conditions of fair equality of opportunity (1971, p. 83).

The first principle is prior to the second principle, and part (b) of the second principle "fair equality of opportunity" is prior to part (a), which Rawls calls "the difference principle." "Benefit" and "advantage" in the second principle are measured in terms of "social primary goods"—goods that are needed for the exercise of the fundamental moral capacities of formulating and executing a life plan and adhering to principles of justice. The first principle and part (b) of the second principle (fair equality of opportunity) express a relational egalitarian view that rules out domination and (along with the difference principle) grounds a firm sense of equal respect. Fair equality of opportunity requires that social contingencies such as parents' socioeconomic status have no effect on opportunity. Unlike luck egalitarianism, fair equality of opportunity permits talents and motivation to affect opportunity. It rules out only the influence of social contingencies. In insisting on equal liberties and fair equality of opportunity, Rawls is insisting on equality of standing. Hence my reading of his views as a form of relational egalitarianism.

When Rawls formulates his two principles of justice, he idealizes and supposes that everyone is in full health. Daniels relaxes this idealization. Rather than abstracting from questions concerning the justice of health inequalities, as Rawls does, Daniels points out that, just as poverty and poor education limit opportunity, so does bad health. Rather than thinking of opportunities narrowly in terms of access to offices and positions, Daniels is concerned with opportunities to form and carry out life plans; and instead of thinking of fair equality of opportunity exclusively as counteracting socioeconomic inequalities, Daniels thinks of fair equality of opportunity as securing equal life prospects to those whose talents and motivation are equal. More specifically, he formulates the notion of the "normal opportunity range" for a given society, which consists of those life plans that are feasible for any member of that society. Each individual has some share of the normal opportunity range—some set of life plans that are accessible given his or her talents, motivation, and circumstances. Fair equality of opportunity requires that individuals have "fair" shares of the normal opportunity range. Shares of the normal opportunity range are fair only if those whose talents and motivation are the same have the same shares.[9] Just as justice (as embodied in fair equality of opportunity) requires the elimination of social barriers that limit opportunities, so it requires protecting and restoring health, subject to feasibility constraints, resource limitations, and competing moral considerations. Daniels says little about the claims of those who cannot be restored to normal functioning and suggests that obligations to care for them are not matters of distributive justice (1985, p. 48).

---

[9] This is only a necessary condition on fair shares. A society that provided all those whose talents limit them to menial jobs with the same life prospects would satisfy this necessary condition, no matter how abysmal those prospects may be and how lavish the prospects of those with more specialized abilities.

Daniels maintains that, other things being equal, justice with respect to health requires that everyone possess their "fair share" of the normal opportunity range, and he employs this claim as the central premise in his argument for universal access to health care. The principle that all should possess their fair share of the normal opportunity range also governs the distribution of health itself. Daniels maintains that fair equality of opportunity requires (a) the prevention or cure of health deficiencies to protect or restore normal species functioning and (b) a fair distribution of the (nonmedical) socially controllable factors influencing the risks of disease. "Normal species functioning" is "full" health—the absence of any pathology that limits an individual's share of the normal opportunity range. The normal opportunity range is relative to the society, and an individual's fair share depends on his or her talent level.

Daniels speculates that the fair distribution of factors influencing the risks of disease matches the distribution implied by Rawls's two principles of justice (Daniels 2008, chapter 3). But there are reasons to doubt this speculation. The distribution required by Rawls's two principles of justice maximizes the level of primary goods of the least advantaged *representative* individual or social group. The distribution across individuals is a matter of pure procedural justice. What this means is that provided that the basic institutions satisfy Rawls's principles of justice, there are no further questions to be asked about the distribution of goods across individuals. Daniels, in contrast, seems to be concerned about the distribution of health across individuals. Although adhering to Rawls's principles of justice might suffice to eliminate the health gradient,[10] it would leave inequalities in health and, hence, inequalities in opportunities among those in the same social class. If fair equality is prior to the difference principle, it seems that Daniels should call for equalizing health, which would demand a more strongly egalitarian distribution than that required by Rawls's difference principle.

Health and Fair Equality of Opportunity

Suppose one grants Daniels's view that the relevance of health to an egalitarian lies mainly in its effects on opportunity. Do Daniels's conclusions concerning what justice demands with respect to the distribution of health and health care follow? Has he shown that I am mistaken to maintain that (with the exception of remediable but incompensable health states) justice does not require that health care be singled out for special treatment? What is his argument for equalizing access to health care and for the injustice of health inequalities?

---

[10] The *health gradient* refers to the significant correlation between socioeconomic status and overall health one finds in virtually all contemporary societies. See, for example, Marmot (2004).

Daniels begins with an account of health that he attributes to Christopher Boorse. Boorse argues that health is species-typical part functioning.[11] He conceives of organisms as physiologists do, as functionally organized systems whose parts and processes enable them to survive and reproduce. When some part or process is operating at a statistically abnormally low level of efficiency, then there is a pathology, and the organism is in diminished health. Many pathologies are trivial, whereas the effects of others may be mitigated by redundancies built into the organism. The malfunction of one kidney, for example, is a pathological condition, even though it may have no consequences for an individual's survival, reproduction, or day-to-day functioning.

What is at issue in Boorse's account of health is the normal function of parts or processes, *not* the normal functioning of the person as a whole. When Daniels speaks of "species typical functioning" or "normal species functioning," he could mean normal overall functioning or species-typical functioning of component parts and processes. These are not the same. If Daniels is following Boorse and Wakefield, he must mean the latter, but, as the kidney example illustrates, what matters to opportunity is in fact overall rather than part functioning.

In other regards, Daniels is more faithful to Boorse. In particular, as Boorse notes and Daniels recognizes, Boorse's account of pathology allows for the existence of pathological conditions that do not call for treatment or prevention and for conditions that are not pathological but that call for medical treatment or prevention. Daniels thus supports providing medical treatment for some nonpathological conditions, such as, notably, pregnancy and unwanted fertility. But, unlike Boorse, Daniels is concerned with medical treatment or social concern, not with a theoretical notion of health. The existence of nonpathological conditions that call for medical treatment suggests that what should matter morally to Daniels is not literally health, but how functioning affects opportunities.

Daniels maintains that fair equality of opportunity requires prevention and treatment of disease or disability, but that it does not require enhancement of nonpathological traits. This is problematic, because nonpathological traits may diminish opportunity in just the same way that pathological conditions do. For example, Daniels believes that fair equality of opportunity requires that someone whose opportunities are limited by short stature that is due to a (pathological) growth hormone deficiency be treated with growth hormone, but it does not require treating someone of equal stature who is

---

[11] See Boorse (1977, 1987, 1997). Jerome Wakefield (1992*a*, 1992*b*, 2007) defends a similar view. Although Boorse's view of health is, in my view, the best one thus far proposed, it has some serious problems (Schwartz 2007; Kingma 2010; Hausman 2011, 2012). Boorse's view of functions (2002) is also controversial.

equally sensitive to growth hormone but whose short stature was not caused by a pathology.[12]

Daniels's position on treatment versus enhancement is obviously inconsistent with luck egalitarianism. Whether one is short owing to a growth hormone deficiency or owing to the genes one inherits from one's parents is equally a matter of brute luck. Yet, in Daniels's view, egalitarians should be concerned only about inequalities due to the first cause. Why? Recall that his version of fair equality of opportunity requires mitigation of pathologies but tolerates inequalities due to differences in talents because talents define the fair share of the normal opportunity range whereas pathologies prevent individuals from enjoying their fair share. As Leslie Jacobs points out (1996, p. 337), this way of distinguishing the cases places a great deal of weight on the distinction between "low talent" and pathology (such as the difference between being a slow learner and possessing a learning disability). Yet, according to Boorse, this distinction is largely arbitrary.[13] Even if there were a principled way to draw the distinction, what reason could a relational egalitarian have to favor remediation or compensation for conditions depending on whether they are due to pathologies or to talent deficiencies? What is relevant appears to be how a condition affects people and the possibilities and costs of remedy or compensation, not whether this condition counts as a disease.

The fact that Daniels's version of fair equality of opportunity principle justifies the disparate treatment of conditions due to whether they result from pathology or merely reflect low "talent" casts doubt on the principle. In Rawls's hands, the principle had a clear rationale from a relational egalitarian perspective. Allowing social factors such as one's family's wealth and status to influence opportunities for careers and positions fails to show equal respect and facilitates domination of members of some groups by members of others, whereas allowing talents and motivation to influence opportunities for careers and positions arguably does not.[14] But, from a relational egalitarian perspective, there is no reason to be more concerned about inequalities due to poor health than there are to be concerned about inequalities due to differences in talents. Daniels's version of fair equality of opportunity apparently has no relational egalitarian rationale.

---

[12] This example is discussed at length by Buchanan, Brock, Daniels and Wikler (2000, pp. 115–126).

[13] According to Boorse, there is a pathology when the level of functioning or capacity to function is in the lower tail of the distribution of efficiency of part function. Exactly where to draw the line between low normal and pathological functioning is, in Boorse's view, arbitrary. There is nothing in theoretical medicine or biology that tells one whether the bottom 5 percent or 1 percent or 0.001 percent of liver function among some reference class divides the pathological from the nonpathological. For a critique of this view, see Schwarz (2007).

[14] One might question this on the grounds that different life prospects for those in different health states would undermine self-respect and mutual respect. If, however, the distribution also satisfies the difference principle (as Daniels would clearly support), then the difference in life prospects (or, in Rawls's framework, primary goods) for those in different health states, as for those with different talents, supports the good of the worst-off representative individual and, for that reason, should not undermine people's respect for one another.

What Does Fair Equality of Opportunity Imply?

From a relational egalitarian perspective, there is nothing special about health, yet Daniels claims to derive conclusions concerning the just distribution of health from his semi-Rawlsian starting point. Ignoring for the moment the absence of a relational egalitarian rationale for Daniels's version of fair equality of opportunity, let us examine how the derivation of conclusions concerning the just distribution of health care and health from fair equality of opportunity is supposed to go. In Daniels's view, Ann's share of the normal opportunity range depends on three classes of causal factors: (1) Ann's talents and motivation, (2) Ann's health, and (3) an array of social factors. Among individuals whose talents are the same, shares of the normal opportunity range depend on their health and on their social circumstances (and their health, in turn, depends in large part on their social circumstances). Daniels's version of fair equality of opportunity implies that these factors be distributed so that those with similar talents have similar opportunities. One way to bring about equal opportunity in Daniels's sense is to separately equalize both health and the social influences on opportunity. But this is not the only way. Inequalities in health and inequalities in the social causes of opportunity can cancel one another out. The healthy pauper and the sickly prince may have equal shares of the normal opportunity range. Curing the sickly prince would make opportunities less rather than more equal (Sreenivasan 2007, p. 22; Segall 2013, Chapter 10, this volume). If there are inequalities in nonhealth determinants of opportunity among those with similar talents, then fair equality of opportunity requires compensating *inequalities* in health, rather than protection and restoration of normal species functioning.[15]

Furthermore, once one recognizes that the effects of poor health on opportunity can be addressed in ways other than by restoring health, one can see a further reason why a relational egalitarian should not want to single out health. Preventing or treating pathological conditions is not the only way to address the consequences of poor health for an individual's shares of the normal opportunity range. Fair equality of opportunity, as understood by Daniels, can sometimes be achieved more efficiently by compensating for inequalities in health with inequalities in nonhealth determinants of opportunity. Indeed, in the case of irremediable health problems, the provision of additional non-health-related resources is the only way to address the limits on opportunity

[15] Daniels claims that fair equality of opportunity requires more than equalizing opportunity. He maintains that a hypothetical state of affairs in which everyone has a remediable health deficiency, such as anemia, which causes no inequalities among those with similar talents, violates fair equality of opportunity. Daniels explains his judgment by asserting, "But the opportunity account still helps us here, for it is not only a principle governing competitive advantage" (1985, p. 55; 2008, p. 146). This is puzzling because fair equality of opportunity appears precisely to be a principle governing comparative advantage.

caused by bad health. Except for the case of pathologies that are remediable but not compensable, there is no justification for attempting to separately determine a just provision of health care on the one hand and, on the other hand, a just distribution of non–health-related resources.

Conclusion

In my view, information concerning individual health inequalities does not typically permit one to draw any conclusions concerning whether individuals are being treated justly. Information concerning the correlation between health inequalities and inequalities in variables such as wealth, income, social status, geographical location, and so forth may also be uninformative, but, in many cases, such correlations reveal the extent of overall inequalities in standing or welfare, which are what matter to relational and luck egalitarians. In this chapter, I sketched my argument for this conclusion and then examined in detail two specific contrary views that maintain that individual health inequalities are *pro tanto* unjust. The failures of Segall's and Daniels's egalitarian arguments do not, of course, demonstrate the correctness of my position, but they illustrate how high are the hurdles confronting those who seek to argue that inequalities in health among individuals are *pro tanto* unjust.

Beneficence provides a simpler reason to be concerned about the grotesque health equalities that characterize our era than does egalitarianism: millions of people have unnecessarily stunted lives. What more reason do we need for action?

References

Anderson, E. (1999). What is the point of equality? *Ethics, 99*, 287–337.

Arneson, R. (1989). Equality and equal opportunity for welfare. *Philosophical Studies, 56*, 77–93.

Asada, Y. (2013). A summary measure of health inequalities: Incorporating group and individual inequalities. In N. Eyal, S. A. Hurst, O. F. Norheim, and D. Wikler (Eds.), *Inequalities in health: Concepts, measures, and ethics* (Chapter 3). New York: Oxford University Press.

Asada, Y., Hausman, D., and Hedemann, T. (2002). Health inequalities and why they matter. *Health Care Analysis, 10*, 177–191.

Boorse, C. (1977). Health as a theoretical concept. *Philosophy of Science, 44*, 542–573.

———. (1987). Concepts of health. In D. VanDeVeer and T. Regan (Eds.), *Health care ethics: An introduction* (pp. 359–393). Philadelphia: Temple University Press.

———. (1997). A rebuttal on health. In J. Humber and R. Almeder (Eds.), *What is disease?* (pp. 1–134). Totowa, NJ: Humana Press.

———. (2002). A rebuttal on functions. In A. Ariew, R. Cummins, and M. Perlman (Eds.), *Functions: New essays in the philosophy of psychology and biology* (pp. 63–112). Oxford: Oxford University Press.

Buchanan, A., Brock, D., Daniels, N., and Wikler, D. (2000). *From change to choice: Genetics and justice.* Cambridge: Cambridge University Press.

Cohen, G. A. (1989). On the currency of egalitarian justice. *Ethics, 99*, 906–944.

———. (1993). Equality of what? On welfare, goods, and capabilities. In M. Nussbaum and A. Sen (Eds.), *The quality of life* (pp. 9–29). Oxford: Clarendon Press.

———. (2008). *Rescuing justice and equality.* Cambridge, MA: Harvard University Press.

Daniels, N. (1985). *Just health care.* Cambridge: Cambridge University Press.

———. (2008). *Just health.* Cambridge: Cambridge University Press.

Dworkin, R. (1981). What is equality? Part 2: Equality of resources. *Philosophy and Public Affairs, 10*, 283–345.

Fleurbaey, M. (2008). *Fairness, responsibility and welfare.* Oxford: Oxford University Press.

Frankfurt, H. (1987). Equality as a moral ideal. *Ethics, 98*, 21–43.

Gakidou, E., Murray, C. and Frenk, J. (2000). Defining and measuring health inequality: An approach based on the distribution of health expectancy. *Bulletin of the World Health Organization, 78*(1), 42–54.

Hausman, D. (2007). What's wrong with health inequalities? *Journal of Political Philosophy, 15*, 46–66.

———. (2011). Is an overdose of paracetamol bad for one's health? *British Journal for Philosophy of Science, 62*, 57–68.

______. (2012) Health, naturalism and functional effficiency," *Philosophy of Science, 79*, 519–41.

Hausman, D., and Waldren, M. 2011. Egalitarianism reconsidered. *Journal of Moral Philosophy, 8*, 567–586.

Illsley, R., and Le Grand, J. (1987). The measurement of inequality. In Alan Williams (Ed.), *Health and economics.* London: Macmillan.

Jacobs, L. (1996). Can an egalitarian justify universal access to health care? *Social Theory and Practice, 22*: 315–348.

Kagan, S. (1999). Equality and desert. In L. Pojman and O. McLeod (Eds.), *What do we deserve: A reader on justice and desert* (pp. 298–314). Oxford: Oxford University Press.

Kingma, E. (2010). Paracetamol, poison, and polio: Why Boorse's account of function fails to distinguish health and disease. *British Journal for the Philosophy of Science, 61*, 241–264.

Le Grand, J. (1991). *Equity and choice: An essay in economics and applied philosophy.* London: Harper-Collins.

Lippert-Rasmussen, K. (2013). When group measures of health should matter. In N. Eyal, S. A. Hurst, O. F. Norheim, and D. Wikler (Eds.), *Inequalities in health: Concepts, measures, and ethics* (Chapter 4). New York: Oxford University Press.

Marmot, M. (2004). *Status syndrome: How your social standing directly affects your health and life expectancy.* London: Bloomsbury Publishing.

Miller, D. (1982). Arguments for equality. *Midwest Studies in Philosophy, 7*, 73–88.

Murray, C., Gakidou, E., and Frenk, J. (1999). Health inequalities and social group differences: What should we measure? *Bulletin of the World Health Organization, 77*(7), 537–543.

———. (2000). Response to P. Braveman, et al. *Bulletin of the World Health Organization, 78*(2), 234–235.

O'Neill, M. (2008). What should egalitarians believe? *Philosophy and Public Affairs, 36*, 119–156.

Olsaretti, S. (2002). Unmasking equality? Kagan on equality and desert. *Utilitas, 14*, 387–400.

Parfit, D. (1991). Equality or priority. Lindley Lecture. In M. Clayton and A. Williams (Eds.), *The ideal of equality*. New York: St. Martin's Press.

Rawls, J. (1971). *A theory of justice*. Cambridge, MA: Harvard University Press.

———. (2001). *Justice as fairness: A restatement*. Ed. E. Kelly. Cambridge, MA: Harvard University Press.

Raz, J. (1984). *The morality of freedom*. Oxford: Oxford University Press.

Scanlon, T. (2003). The diversity of objections to inequality. The Lindley Lecture 1997. In *The difficulty of tolerance: Essays in political philosophy*. Cambridge: Cambridge University Press.

Scheffler, S. (2003). What is egalitarianism? *Philosophy and Public Affairs, 31*, 5–39.

Schwartz, P. (2007). Defining dysfunction: Natural selection, design, and drawing a line. *Philosophy of Science, 74*, 364–385.

Segall, S. (2010). *Health, luck, and justice*. Princeton: Princeton University Press.

———. (2013). Equality of opportunity for health. In N. Eyal, S. A. Hurst, O. F. Norheim, and D. Wikler (Eds.), *Inequalities in health: Concepts, measures, and ethics* (Chapter 10). New York: Oxford University Press.

Sen, A. (1992). *Inequality reexamined*. Cambridge, MA: Harvard University Press.

Sreenivasan, G. (2007). Health care and equality of opportunity. *Hastings Center Report, 37*(2), 21–31.

Temkin, L. (1993). *Inequality*. Oxford: Oxford University Press.

———. (2003). Egalitarianism defended. *Ethics, 113*, 764–782.

———. (2013). Inequality and health. In N. Eyal, S. A. Hurst, O. F. Norheim, and D. Wikler (Eds.), *Inequalities in health: Concepts, measures, and ethics* (Chapter 1). New York: Oxford University Press.

Wakefield, J. (1992*a*). The concept of mental disorder: On the boundary between biological facts and social values. *American Psychologist, 47*, 373–388.

———. (1992*b*). Disorder as harmful dysfunction: A conceptual critique of DSM-III-R's definition of mental disorder. *Psychological Review, 99*, 232–247.

———. (2007). The concept of mental disorder: Diagnostic implications of the harmful dysfunction analysis. *World Psychiatry, 6*, 149–156.

8 }

Decide As You Would with Full Information!

AN ARGUMENT AGAINST *EX ANTE* PARETO

Marc Fleurbaey and Alex Voorhoeve

As policy makers and private individuals, we sometimes face choices of the following kind: either choose an alternative that has somewhat lower *expected* value for each person, but which will substantially improve the *outcomes* of the worst off, or choose an alternative that has somewhat higher expected value for each person, but which will leave those who end up worst off substantially less well off. By way of illustration, consider the following real-world mammogram case (U.S. Preventative Services Task Force 2009).

In 2009, the U.S. Preventive Services Task Force had to decide whether or not to recommend routine biannual breast cancer screening mammography for all women aged 40 to 49. For each woman in this age group, the potential costs of this method of screening include the small to moderate psychological and physical harms caused by initial testing and by follow-up testing.[1] Its potential benefits are improvements in length and quality of life due to the early diagnosis and more successful treatment of cancer.

The Task Force judged that, for each woman in this age group, the expected costs of screening outweighed the expected benefits by a modest margin.[2] The alternative that we call *routine screening* would therefore have a somewhat lower expected value for each woman in this group but considerably improve

Earlier versions of this chapter were presented at the Brocher Foundation, Carnegie Mellon University, Groningen University, the Hebrew University, Leeds University, the London School of Economics, the National Institutes of Health, Oxford University, University College London, and the University of Pennsylvania. We thank audience members for helpful discussions. We also thank Matthew Adler, John Broome, Boudewijn de Bruin, Nir Eyal, Johann Frick, Ipek Gençsü, Alex John London, Jerry Menikoff, Serena Olsaretti, Shepley Orr, Matthew Rendall, Jesse Saloom, Shlomi Segall, Peter Vallentyne, Andrew Williams, and two anonymous referees for comments. We are especially grateful to Michael Otsuka for lengthy discussion and detailed comments.

[1] For simplicity, we assume that the harms do not include an increased risk of breast cancer due to exposure to radiation in testing. This risk is thought to be very low (U.S. Preventative Services Task Force 2009, p. 271).

[2] This recommendation did not apply to women who are known to be at atypically high risk of developing breast cancer. For simplicity, our discussion excludes this subgroup.

the lot of those among them who, because of undiagnosed cancer, would otherwise be among the worst off. The alternative that we call *no routine screening* would have slightly higher expected value for each woman but would lead to more early deaths and greater inequality in health outcomes.

In this chapter, we analyze how one should decide such cases in which the alternative that has the highest expected value for each person also disadvantages those who end up worst off. One principle that is commonly invoked in such cases is *ex ante* Pareto. This principle holds that if an alternative has higher expected utility for every person than every other alternative, then this alternative should be chosen. Indeed, the Task Force was moved by this principle: it regarded the expected disvalue that routine screening would have for each woman as decisive and recommended against it. Notwithstanding the widespread support for *ex ante* Pareto, we argue that, in a certain type of case, it should be rejected because it conflicts with a requirement of rationality. This requirement is that, when one lacks information, but can infer that there is a particular alternative one *would* invariably regard as best if one had full information, then one should choose this alternative.

Our argument proceeds as follows. Real-world decision problems like the mammogram case typically involve a multitude of morally relevant factors. To focus our analysis on the key issue, we develop a stylized case in the first section of this chapter. In the next section, we introduce our rationality principle and show that it is inconsistent with *ex ante* Pareto in our stylized case. In the third section, we extend this rationality principle. In the fourth section, we show that it does not rule out other *ex ante* considerations, such as a concern for the fairness of equal-chance lotteries. In the last section, we discuss the relevance of our conclusions for real-world cases, including the mammogram case.

A Stylized Case

The mammogram case involves two morally relevant considerations that are extraneous to our core question. First, even if the Task Force had decided in favor of routine mammography, this would merely have involved advising women to have mammograms, coupled with steps to ensure that these mammograms were accessible to all. The choice of whether or not to have a mammogram would still have been up to each woman. Second, the officials on the Task Force or the doctors who would be acting on its advice may be regarded as agents of the women affected.[3]

---

[3] A further consideration is that testing women may lead to harm, whereas not testing them merely makes it less likely that one can do good for them. For simplicity, we set aside this aspect of the mammogram case. Note that our stylized cases do not involve the imposition of harm.

To focus on the conflict between *ex ante* Pareto and a concern for those who will end up worst off, we therefore devote much of this chapter to an analysis of the following stylized case in which there is no choice on the part of the affected individuals, and the benefactor is not an agent of the affected individuals but merely a morally motivated stranger.

Visual Impairment Case 1:

Imagine that two 10-year-old children, Adam and Bill, have excellent vision but will soon go totally blind due to natural causes unless a morally motivated stranger, Teresa, intervenes. Teresa can use a resource she rightfully controls to produce and administer only one of the following two medicines to both Adam and Bill.[4]

The egalitarian medicine (M_E) will ensure that Adam and Bill will both be equally, and considerably, visually impaired, although they will not become totally blind: they will be able to make out basic shapes at a moderate distance, but, even with glasses, they will be unable to recognize a friend on the other side of the street and will be able to read ordinary newsprint only with difficulty.[5]

The *ex ante* Pareto-optimal medicine (M_P) will either, with 50 percent probability, cause Adam to retain excellent vision and Bill to have a severe visual impairment (which differs from total blindness only in that one can make out basic shapes at a short distance), or, instead, cause Bill to retain excellent vision while leaving Adam with the severe visual impairment.

We will now make some assumptions about the utilities associated with these treatments. Throughout, we will assume a measure of utility that is derived from idealized preferences satisfying the Von Neumann-Morgenstern axioms. On this measure, an alternative has higher expected utility just in case it would be preferred for the individual's sake after calm deliberation using all pertinent information while attending to this individual's self-interest only.[6] Moreover, two alternatives have the same expected utility just in case such deliberation would yield indifference between them. If the individual is a normally capable adult with well-formed preferences, then the person expressing this preference can be taken to be an ideally rational version of this adult. If the individual is

[4] We assume those in need of aid are children in order to eliminate the consideration that a morally motivated stranger has reason to do what will maximize the expected utility of each out of respect for their autonomy. (One might argue that a respect for autonomy would require such expected utility maximization if one assumed a preference-based measure of utility of the kind elaborated later.) For further discussion, see Otsuka and Voorhoeve (2009, pp. 185–188).

[5] These descriptions of visual impairments and the associated levels of well-being are derived, with some modifications, from the well-known Health Utilities Index-3. See www.healthutilities.com.

[6] This is not a proposal regarding what utility *consists in*. Rather, it is a proposal about how to *measure* the magnitude of a person's utility. One can maintain that utility consists of something other than preference satisfaction while also maintaining that the specified idealized preferences faultlessly track the magnitude of this other thing.

TABLE 8.1 } **The distribution of utility in two cases**

Alternative	Person	State of the world (equiprobable). s_1	s_2
VISUAL IMPAIRMENT CASE 1			
M_E	Adam	0.8	0.8
	Bill	0.8	0.8
M_P	Adam	1	0.65
	Bill	0.65	1
VISUAL IMPAIRMENT CASE 2			
M_E	Adam	0.8	0.8
	Bill	0.8	0.8
M_U	Adam	1	1
	Bill	0.65	0.65

incapable of such deliberation (as we suppose Adam and Bill are), then the person expressing this preference can be taken to be an ideally rational guardian who has deliberated with exclusive focus on his charge's self-interest.

We will make one further assumption with regard to the interests that are taken into account in this measure of utility. We will assume that these reasons of self-interest do not include an interest in being fairly treated in the distributive process. Individual utilities therefore do not incorporate information on the degree to which the latter interest is satisfied.[7] This assumption makes it possible to represent fairness considerations separately from well-being considerations.

Suppose that 1 is the utility of being fully sighted, 0.8 the utility of the considerable visual impairment, and 0.65 the utility of the severe impairment. The utilities associated with treatments M_E and M_P in the two possible states of the world are shown in the top half of Table 8.1.

One of the aims of this chapter is to figure out how Teresa should decide Visual Impairment Case 1, under the assumption that she is an egalitarian who rightly cares both about reducing outcome inequality and about increasing individuals' well-being.[8] In cases of decision making under *certainty*, because of the moral importance of improving the lot of those who are less well off than others, she has decisive reason to (and therefore does) prefer a medicine that ensures that both Adam and Bill end up with the considerable impairment than to prefer a medicine that leads one of them to retain excellent vision and leaves the other with the severe impairment.[9] In other words, in a choice

[7] In this respect, we depart from the assumption made in Fleurbaey (2010, pp. 653–654).

[8] Note, however, that our argument against *ex ante* Pareto is equally effective if one instead gives priority to the worse off because one is a prioritarian who gives additional weight to utility gains when they occur at a lower absolute level of utility. (For a discussion of prioritarianism, see Parfit [2002].)

[9] We do *not* assume that she regards *any* improvement in the condition in the worst off, no matter how small, to be more important than *any* improvement in total utility, no matter how large.

between M_E and M_U in the lower half of Table 8.1, Teresa would rightly choose M_E even though it has lower total utility because, for the utility values in question, the improvement in the condition of the worst off is worth the sacrifice in total utility. We assume, therefore, that such cases of certainty should not be resolved by an appeal to what would be agreed to by Adam and Bill's representatives if they were placed behind a so-called "hypothetical veil of ignorance" that assigns an equal probability to each of ending up in any person's shoes (see Harsanyi 1953). (In this case, this would favor M_U, the alternative with the highest total utility.) As has been argued elsewhere, an appeal to such a device is an inappropriate way to make interpersonal tradeoffs because it violates the separateness of persons and leads to what are, intuitively, unacceptably inegalitarian decisions.[10] One of the central questions of this chapter is therefore this: given that Teresa ought to prefer M_E to M_U, how should Teresa decide between M_E and M_P?

Against *ex ante* Pareto

On the measure of utility here assumed, it is true by definition that a risky alternative like M_P has higher expected utility for each person than does a secure alternative like M_E just when, from the perspective of both Adam's and Bill's self-interest, the chance of the additional benefit offered by the risky alternative outweighs the risk of the foregone benefit associated with this alternative. If Teresa were to choose M_P over M_E, it may therefore seem that she could offer each of them the following justification for this choice:

> In making this choice, I had to balance a 50 percent chance of your having excellent vision rather than the considerable visual impairment against a 50 percent chance of your having the severe visual impairment rather than the considerable visual impairment. I balanced this potential additional gain and potential gain forgone from the perspective of your self-interest alone, in just the manner a guardian charged with looking after your interests who had the same information I had would have balanced them. On this way of balancing, the chance of the great benefit of unimpaired vision outweighed the associated risk of instead receiving the small benefit and thereby ending up with the severe impairment. In sum, by choosing M_P, I did the best I could for you, given the information I had at the time. I chose M_P for your sake.

However, this purported justification has a key difficulty.[11] It appeals to guardians who have the same information about their charges' possible fates

---

[10] See, for example, Nagel (1970, pp. 138–139).

[11] A similar objection to appealing to people's imperfectly informed preferences is offered in Fleurbaey (2010, p. 659).

as does Teresa. (We are here imagining that Adam and Bill each have a guardian entirely to themselves, so that there are two guardians.) Such guardians are imperfect insofar as their information is limited. Because of this limited information, things that *seem* to such a guardian to be the best that can be done for his charge may not, in fact, be in his charge's interests. A guardian who is less often in error about what is, in fact, in his charge's interests would be a better guardian for an individual to have. Indeed, an ideal guardian would know all relevant information about what would, in fact, best serve his charge's interest. From Teresa's perspective, an informed guardian would also be ideal. The role of the guardians in the preceding purported justification is to represent the interests of Adam and Bill; and, for each child, Teresa should want to know not merely which alternative seems to be in each child's interests, but also the extent to which each alternative will truly satisfy each child's interests.

The following considerations further underline that the justificatory force of the assent of uninformed guardians must be treated with suspicion. Suppose that Teresa must choose between M_E and M_U—she therefore knows the impact each treatment will have on each named individual. Suppose further that she is confronted with imperfectly informed guardians. Because of their lack of information, each guardian reasonably regards M_U as involving a 50–50 gamble between a full cure and the severe impairment for his charge (in just the manner in which M_P is regarded by the imperfectly informed guardians imagined in the purported justification for M_P). Each guardian therefore reasonably (given his beliefs) favors M_U for his charge. In these circumstances, Teresa obviously could not justify the choice of M_U to Bill on the grounds that his uninformed guardian regarded it as in his interest. After all, she knows that his guardian's preference for M_U over M_E is merely due to ignorance.

Now suppose that Teresa must choose between M_E and M_U but that, because of lack of information, she, Adam's guardian, and Bill's guardian all regard M_U as involving a 50–50 gamble between a full cure and severe impairment for each child. Suppose she can easily and costlessly acquire all relevant information about the impact of M_U. In these circumstances, Teresa obviously should acquire this information. Moreover, if she fails to do so, she cannot justify the choice of M_U to Bill on the grounds that she and his uninformed guardian regarded it as in his interest.

We conclude that, whenever possible, Teresa should base her decisions on what *fully informed* guardians who know their charges' true interests would tell her about the extent to which alternatives are in their charges' interests. Now, it may seem that this conclusion does not undermine the appeal to the assent of uninformed guardians in Visual Impairment Case 1. For, unlike in the two cases just mentioned, in this case, Teresa cannot know what Adam's (or Bill's) fully informed guardian would advise her. However, she *can* infer some of the things about the preferences of their fully informed guardians. For one, she can infer that there would be no unanimity among such fully informed guardians in favor of M_P. One of them would favor M_E on behalf of his charge; the other would favor M_P.

Teresa can also infer that if she consulted such fully informed guardians, insofar as she bases her decision on individuals' well-being, she would rightly no longer regard it as justifiable to each to provide both with M_P. For if these fully informed guardians knew that the state of the world would turn out to be s_1, and therefore told her that M_P was in Adam's interest but not in Bill's, then, insofar as she bases her decision on these interests, she would regard the choice of M_P as unjustifiable to Bill. She would not regard it as justifiable to Bill because, in line with the assumptions made in the first section of the chapter, it is unjustifiable to sacrifice the interests of someone who, as things turn out, will be no better off than the other person under either policy in order to make that other person better off still, at least for the size of the benefits under consideration. Moreover, if these fully informed guardians knew that the state of the world would turn out to be s_2 and therefore told Teresa that M_P was in Bill's interest but not in Adam's, then she would, for the same type of reason, regard the choice of M_P as unjustifiable to Adam.

Teresa also knows that, insofar as she bases her decision on how the available medicines will affect individuals' true well-being, she should favor M_E over M_P no matter what the fully informed guardians would tell her about their charges' interests. If these fully informed guardians knew that the state of the world would turn out to be s_1 and therefore told her that M_P was in Adam's interest but not in Bill's, then, in line with the extra weight she should assign to helping the worst off, she should resolve these conflicting interests in Bill's favor and choose M_E. And if these fully informed guardians knew that the state of the world would turn out to be s_2 and therefore told her that M_P was in Bill's interest but not in Adam's, then she should resolve these conflicting interests in Adam's favor and again choose M_E.

In sum, Teresa can infer that if she could consult both Adam's and Bill's fully informed guardians (a) M_P would not be justifiable to each, and (b) she should always favor M_E. As mentioned, both (a) and (b) hold insofar as she bases her assessment on the final distribution of well-being between Adam and Bill. Now, to consult such fully informed guardians is just to possess full relevant information. Because she cares about the real impact of alternatives on Adam and Bill's well-being, Teresa regards judgments made with full information about the well-being interests involved as superior to judgments made without full information. And, in this case, once she has gone through the foregoing reasoning, Teresa knows the alternative that she should strictly prefer if she had full information, no matter what that information turns out to be. It seems a basic principle of rationality that she should decide in line with this preference (Fleurbaey 2010; Adler 2011).

The principle of rationality here invoked can be put as follows:

> *Principle of Full Information (PFI), Part 1*: When one knows that, in every state of the world with positive probability, one would rightly rank two alternatives in a particular way, then one should so rank them.[12]

In sum, we have argued that in Visual Impairment Case 1, *ex ante* Pareto violates this principle of rationality and should therefore be rejected in this case.[13]

It is important to note that the scope of this argument is limited. This argument has no bite when one cannot infer *ex ante* that, with full information, one would always regard the same alternative as best. It therefore implies nothing about cases involving pure intrapersonal tradeoffs in which only one person's interests are at stake or in which everyone's well-being outcomes are perfectly correlated. By way of illustration, consider the following One-Person Case, which differs from our previous cases in that only Adam's interests are at stake. She must choose between the certain option

---

[12] This is weaker than the principle, common in decision theory, that if the set of feasible alternatives is unaffected by the acquisition of information, and one would not make any errors in deliberating on the basis of this information, it is always good or indifferent to acquire more information (Savage 1972). The former only pertains to cases in which one knows what one would decide with full information, whereas the latter would tell one to always decide as one would with *more* information than one has now.

Note also that, in applying the principle, one must take care when the outcome of a prospect depends on the absence of information at some earlier time. For example, suppose your alternatives are "go for a run" and "watch the Oxford-Cambridge boat race," that the possible states of the world are "Oxford wins" and "Cambridge wins," and that you do not know who will win. Suppose further that your ignorance of the outcome of the race does not affect the value of going for a run but is crucial to your enjoyment when watching the race. In applying the principle of full information, you must compare the outcome of each alternative in these two states of the world. Since your ignorance of who will win affects your experience of watching the race, this does *not* involve comparing the outcome of "go for a run" with the outcome of "watch the race knowing that Oxford will win" and "go for a run" with "watch the race knowing that Cambridge will win." Rather, it involves comparing the outcome "go for a run" with the outcome "watch the race in ignorance and Oxford wins," and so forth. The principle of full information then requires that if, in each state of the world, the outcome of watching in ignorance is better than the outcome of going for a run, then you should prefer watching the race.

[13] This argument directly questions the soundness of the *ex ante* Pareto principle. An indirect argument is also available by reference to Harsanyi's aggregation theorem (Harsanyi [1955]; for a nontechnical presentation and detailed discussion of its implications, see Broome [1991]). According to this theorem, the *ex ante* Pareto principle, combined with the assumption that social evaluation is made by a criterion that takes the form of the expected value of a social welfare function, implies that the social welfare function must be affine in individual utilities. Affine functions are such that the weight of a particular individual's utility is fixed and does not vary with how well off the individual is. If one assumes, as we have done here, that some priority must be given to the worse off, such affine functions are unacceptable. If, in addition, one assumes that social evaluation must be an expected value criterion, then Harsanyi's theorem implies that *ex ante* Pareto can no longer be satisfied.

Here, we did not make the expected value assumption about Teresa's evaluations, but only assumed that if Teresa would make the same decision in every state of the world, she should make it *ex ante*. This dominance principle is logically weaker than the expected utility hypothesis, but is enough to imply a rejection of *ex ante* Pareto. (A version of Harsanyi's theorem in which the expected social value hypothesis is replaced by the dominance principle is given in Fleurbaey [2009]).

M_E,[14] which will ensure Adam ends up 0.8, and M_P, which will give Adam a one in two chance of ending up at 1 if s_1 turns out to be the state of the world, and a one in two chance of ending up at 0.65, if s_2 turns out to be the state of the world. In this case, if Teresa knew that s_1 will turn out to be the case, then she would prefer M_P; if she knew that s_2 will turn out to be the case, then she would prefer M_E. In this case, therefore, Teresa cannot now ensure that her choice will be consistent with how she would choose with full information. The PFI therefore says nothing in this case, and our argument does not challenge the application of the *ex ante* Pareto principle to such cases.[15]

Extending the Principle of Full Information

In Visual Impairment Case 1, Teresa can infer that she would always strictly prefer the same alternative with full knowledge. It is natural to extend the PFI to cases in which Teresa is not certain which of two alternatives she would strictly prefer with full knowledge, but in which she correctly infers that, with full knowledge, she might disprefer one of the two alternatives but would never disprefer the other. In this case, it seems straightforward that she should avoid the risk of choosing an alternative she would disprefer with full knowledge and choose the alternative she knows she will never disprefer with full knowledge. She can thereby ensure her choice is consistent with her perfectly informed preference. This reasoning yields:

> *Principle of Full Information, Part 2*: When one knows that there is only one way of ranking two alternatives that will ensure one will never choose an alternative that one would rightly disprefer in full knowledge of the state of the world, then one should so rank them.

By way of illustration, consider the case described in Table 8.2 (in which M_M might, but need not, generate outcome inequality). Insofar as she is concerned with well-being, Teresa can infer that, if she were to learn that s_1 will be the case, then she would prefer M_E to M_M, whereas, if she were to learn that s_2 will be the case, then she would be indifferent between these two medicines. Once she has made this inference, she knows that she can certainly avoid choosing contrary to her fully informed preference by choosing M_E. It seems obvious that she should so choose.

---

[14] Note that, insofar as Adam's well-being is considered in isolation from how well or badly off others are, egalitarianism has nothing to say on the choice between M_E and M_P. In this sense, and unlike in our two-person cases, M_E is not the egalitarian option in this case.

[15] Indeed, elsewhere, we argue that, in such cases, insofar as she considers Adam's well-being in isolation, it is reasonable for Teresa to do what the *ex ante* Pareto principle recommends. See Voorhoeve and Fleurbaey (2012) and Otsuka and Voorhoeve (2009).

TABLE 8.2 } The distribution of utility in one case

Alternative	Person	State of the world (equiprobable)	
		s_1	s_2
VISUAL IMPAIRMENT CASE 3			
M_E	Adam	0.8	0.8
	Bill	0.8	0.8
M_M	Adam	1	0.8
	Bill	0.65	0.8

A final extension concerns cases in which Teresa can infer that, with full information, she would always be indifferent between two alternatives. In this case, it seems she should regard both as equally good. This yields:

> *Principle of Full Information, Part 3*: When one knows that, in every state of the world with positive probability, one is indifferent between two alternatives, then one should be indifferent between these alternatives.

By way of illustration, suppose that Teresa must choose between M_P and M_U alone, as in Table 8.3.[16]

Insofar as Teresa is concerned with final well-being alone, she is indifferent between the outcomes of these medicines in both s_1 and in s_2. If well-being outcomes are all that is relevant, then she should therefore be indifferent between these medicines.

So far, we have considered only one part of the evaluation of alternatives, namely, their impact on individuals' well-being interests. But other things besides well-being interests might matter. One might think, for instance, that M_P is less unfair than M_U, because M_P, but not M_U, offers Bill a chance of the benefit of unimpaired vision. We will now examine such fairness claims and show how an appeal to the PFI is consistent with giving them due weight.

TABLE 8.3 } The distribution of utility in one case

Alternative	Person	State of the world (equiprobable)	
		s_1	s_2
VISUAL IMPAIRMENT CASE 4			
M_P	Adam	1	0.65
	Bill	0.65	1
M_U	Adam	1	1
	Bill	0.65	0.65

[16] In this case, our mnemonic names for the medicines are less apt because both M_P and M_U are *ex ante* Pareto optimal, and both maximize expected utility. However, we continue to use them because the effects of these medicines are the same as in our central case.

Fairness and the Principle of Full Information

Broadly speaking, there are two leading explanations of the idea that an alternative such as M_P, which gives each person an equal chance at a great benefit that only one can receive, is fairer than an alternative such as M_U, in which it is known at the time of choice who will receive the great benefit. Following Wasserman (1996), we will refer to these as the "prophylactic view" and the "distributive view."

The prophylactic view holds that giving each an equal chance of this benefit is fairer when and because it ensures the absence of partiality or favoritism in the distribution of a good. We will assume that Teresa is publicly known to be fair in this sense. Teresa therefore has no prophylactic reasons for favoring alternatives that give each person an equal chance of ending up in the best position, nor does she have reasons to choose such an alternative to express or demonstrate her impartiality, unless, of course, impartial consideration of the interests of each already favors such an alternative.

On the distributive view, a given outcome inequality among people with equally strong claims to a benefit is less unfair when each person has a chance to end up better off than when the worse off have no such chance because, in receiving this chance, each person receives an equal share of something of expected value.[17] On this view, the more equally this expected value is distributed at a relevant point in time, the fairer the distribution. Of course, the *well-being value* of a chance for a person evanesces once it is clear that this chance is unrealized.[18] In this sense, having a chance at a benefit that does not materialize neither compensates a person for the well-being foregone nor offers any satisfaction of his well-being interests. However, a chance's contribution to fairness does *not* evanesce—it remains true of someone who received an equal chance at an indivisible benefit of a given size, but for whom the benefit did not materialize, that he had a fair chance of receiving it. For this reason, this equal chance contributes to the satisfaction of each individual's interest in being treated fairly in the distributive process, in which this fair treatment involves more than just having his interests given equal consideration.[19]

---

[17] This view's judgment that a given pattern of outcome inequality is less unfair when individuals have equal chances of ending up in any position is widely shared. See, for example, Diamond (1967), Broome (1990), and Otsuka (n.d.).

[18] In our cases, it is assumed that individuals' chances of receiving a good are nontransferable, so that they have no opportunity to exchange their as-yet-unrealized chance for some other good that will contribute to their well-being. We can also assume that the individuals concerned do not know their chances of receiving a benefit, so that they derive no benefit from the mere anticipation of the possible gain. The chance of receiving a benefit therefore makes no contribution to the quality of life of a person who does not end up receiving it.

[19] As mentioned in the first section, we assume that the satisfaction of this interest does not figure in our measure of utility.

Now, some, including Wasserman (1996), reject the distributive view and, with it, the idea that equal chances make a contribution to fairness beyond their contribution to ensuring and expressing impartiality. We will not here pronounce on whether the distributive view is correct. Instead, we explore how Teresa should choose if only the prophylactic view is correct and how she should choose if, instead, the distributive view is correct.

Let us start with Visual Impairment Case 4 (Table 8.3). If only the prophylactic view is correct, then all that matters is individuals' well-being, so that Teresa is rationally required to be indifferent between M_P and M_U. By contrast, if the distributive view is correct, then the well-being information listed in Table 8.3 is not all that is relevant to the evaluation of these alternatives. When considering the outcomes of these alternatives in each state of the world, we need to consider *both* each individual's well-being *and* the chance he had to achieve a different outcome (Broome 1991, pp. 111–115). The relevant outcomes for the choice between M_P and M_U are then those depicted in Table 8.4.

When the consequences are specified in this manner, the PFI requires that M_P be chosen in this case, as it is preferable to (because less unfair than) M_U in every state of the world.

Let us now return to Visual Impairment Case 1. If only the prophylactic view is correct, then the reasoning of the second section applies, and Teresa should choose the egalitarian option. If the distributive view is correct, then the relevant outcomes are depicted in Table 8.5.

If the distributive view is correct, then the PFI requires that Teresa's preference should entirely track her preference over the following outcomes: (a) Adam and Bill both have the considerable impairment and never had a chance of anything better; (b) one of them is fully sighted, and one of them has the severe impairment, with the unfairness of this outcome being mitigated by the fact that the severely impaired person had a one in two chance of instead ending up unimpaired, which is equal to the chance that the unimpaired person had of instead ending up with the severe impairment.

TABLE 8.4 } **The outcomes in one case if the distributive view is correct**

Alternative	**Person**	**State of the world (equiprobable)**	
		s_1	s_2
VISUAL IMPAIRMENT CASE 4			
M_P	Adam	1, and had a one in two chance to be severely impaired.	0.65, and had a one in two chance to be fully sighted.
	Bill	0.65, and had a one in two chance to be fully sighted.	1, and had a one in two chance to be severely impaired.
M_U	Adam	1, and had no chance of any other outcome.	1, and had no chance of any other outcome.
	Bill	0.65, and had no chance of any other outcome.	0.65, and had no chance of any other outcome.

TABLE 8.5 } **The relevant outcomes in one case if the distributive view is correct**

Alternative	Person	State of the world (equiprobable)	
		s_1	s_2
VISUAL IMPAIRMENT CASE 1			
M_E	Adam	0.8, and had no chance of any other outcome.	0.8, and had no chance of any other outcome.
	Bill	0.8, and had no chance of any other outcome.	0.8, and had no chance of any other outcome.
M_P	Adam	1, and had a one in two chance to be severely impaired.	0.65, and had a one in two chance to be fully sighted.
	Bill	0.65, and had a one in two chance to be fully sighted.	1, and had a one in two chance to be severely impaired.

Now, the choice between (a) and (b) depends on how much weight Teresa should give to improving the lot of those who end up worst off and how significant it is that the unfairness of receiving the lesser benefit is mitigated by the fact that one could have ended up with the greater benefit. If Teresa should give great weight to improving the lot of those who are less well off than others, and if equal chances do little to mitigate the unfairness of unequal outcomes, then she should prefer M_E over M_P. If, by contrast, Teresa should not sacrifice much total utility for the sake of the worst off, then the fact that the equal chances offered by M_P mitigate the associated outcome unfairness may tip the balance in its favor. Whatever the right way to balance these concerns, it is important to note that Teresa can ensure that the alternative she chooses is one she would regard as best with full knowledge of the relevant outcomes.[20]

We can conclude that, so long as Teresa knows which view of fairness is correct in Visual Impairment Case 1, she can make a decision that she can be sure will be in line with the preferences she would have with full information. If she knows that only the prophylactic view is correct, then she can infer that, with full information, she would always choose the egalitarian alternative. If, by contrast, she knows the distributive view is correct, then, in order to arrive at a decision she would approve of with full information, she should ask herself: "Is an outcome in which both people are considerably impaired at least as good as the outcome in which one person ends up fully sighted and the other severely impaired, and this severely impaired person had a fair, equal chance at a full cure?" and choose the egalitarian option just in case the answer is "yes."

[20] At least, so long as she also knows the nature of the chances involved (e.g. whether they are merely subjective, objective, or indeterministic). This caveat is required because one might argue that objective or indeterministic chances make a greater contribution to fairness than merely subjective chances (Otsuka, n.d.).

Return to Real-World Cases

Our discussion of our visual impairment cases has implications for closely analogous real-world cases. As relatively wealthy private individuals, most of us in the developed world may find ourselves in Teresa's position when we consider how to allocate resources that can do good for the children of strangers. If our argument is correct, then *ex ante* Pareto should play no role in our deliberations about such cases.

Our conclusions about real-world cases that are less like our stylized case must be more speculative. With this caveat in mind, what can we say about a case in which Adam and Bill are not children, but rational adults who have the same information that Teresa has? Adam and Bill will then prefer that Teresa administers the *ex ante* Pareto-optimal medicine. One may think that, because they are rational adults, Teresa has reason to defer to their judgment in order to promote their autonomy. We would question this defense of *ex ante* Pareto on two grounds. First, Adam and Bill's judgment is imperfectly informed. Even if deferring to their *fully* informed preferences promotes their autonomy, it is not clear that deferring to their *imperfectly* informed preferences promotes their autonomy (Harsanyi 1982).

Second, a plausible understanding of individual autonomy requires only that one defer to a person's wishes regarding choices he has a right to make. On this understanding, neither Adam's nor Bill's autonomy would be threatened if Teresa acted contrary to their wishes by giving them the egalitarian treatment. Since, by hypothesis, she rightfully controls the treatments, if she were to give them the egalitarian treatment, Teresa would not interfere with any choices they have a right to make.[21]

In sum, even if Adam and Bill are adults, it is doubtful that Teresa has an autonomy-based reason to do what they want. We tentatively conclude that even in cases in which adults' well-being is at stake, someone in Teresa's position should regard *ex ante* Pareto as having no force.

What if the decision maker is not a stranger, but is instead Adam and Bill's agent, charged by each of them with doing what is in his expected interest? In this case, such a decision maker may well have good reason to do what both prefer her to do. This is relevant for the mammogram case, insofar as the officials on the Task Force and the doctors who would be acting on its recommendations are such agents of the women affected. Insofar as they are agents of this kind, in this case, it would be inappropriate for them to advise women to do something that is not expectedly beneficial for these women.

Nonetheless, it seems to us that the members of the Task Force are not *merely* agents charged by these women with promoting their *ex ante* prudential

[21] See Otsuka and Voorhoeve (2009, p. 186).

interests. As public officials, they are also tasked with ensuring distributive justice in health-related quality of life. As such, we take it that, in cases of certainty, they should give special weight to improving the condition of those who end up worse off than others. Moreover, in cases of risk, they should be interested in what is truly in each woman's well-being interests and not merely in what, due to lack of information, seems to be in these women's interests. Members of the Task Force should therefore not regard the fact that an alternative is marginally expectedly beneficial for each as a sufficient justification for choosing this alternative.

By way of illustration, imagine that the feasible set of the Task Force is expanded to include an alternative that we will call *reallocation and routine screening*. This involves the use of medical resources to somewhat lower the expected costs of routine mammography to the point at which undergoing it is *not* a net expected burden to women. (This might be done, say, by investing in training or equipment that lowers the incidence of false-positive test results.) If this alternative were implemented, it would be unproblematic for doctors to advise their patients to undergo routine screening. Suppose that these resources would be reallocated from services that provided modest benefits to each woman and that, as a consequence, this alternative is *ex ante* Pareto-inferior to no routine screening, which involves no such reallocation. However, because it prevents many early deaths, from the perspective of the distribution of the satisfaction of women's genuine well-being interests, the outcome of reallocation and routine screening might be better than the outcome of no routine screening. If so, then the members of the Task Force would have reason to choose the former, contrary to *ex ante* Pareto.

Conclusion

We have reviewed cases in which an alternative that is in the expected interests of each will leave those who end up worst off substantially less well off. We have argued that, in such cases, we should not heed the call of that famous Italian siren, *ex ante* Pareto. We should not base our decisions on what, due to a lack of information about the impact of our choices on each individual, merely seems to be in every individual's interest. Instead, we should ask what we would decide with full knowledge about the state of the world and choose accordingly.

References

Adler, M. (2011). *Well-being and fair distribution: Beyond cost-benefit analysis*. Oxford: Oxford University Press.

Broome, J. (1990). Fairness. *Proceedings of the Aristotelian Society, New Series, 91*, 87–101.

———. (1991). *Weighing goods.* Oxford: Blackwell.

Diamond, P. (1976). Cardinal welfare, individualistic ethics, and interpersonal comparison of utility: Comment. *Journal of Political Economy, 75*, 765–766.

Fleurbaey, M. (2009). Two variants of Harsanyi's aggregation theorem. *Economics Letters, 105*, 300–302.

———. (2010). Assessing risky social situations. *Journal of Political Economy, 118*, 649–680.

Harsanyi, J. C. (1953). Cardinal utility in welfare economics and the theory of risk-taking. *Journal of Political Economy, 61*, 434–435.

———. (1955). Cardinal welfare, individualistic ethics, and interpersonal comparisons of utility. *Journal of Political Economy, 63*, 309–312.

———. (1982). Morality and the theory of rational behaviour. In A. Sen and B. Williams (Eds.), *Utilitarianism and beyond* (pp. 39–63). Cambridge: Cambridge University Press.

Nagel, T. (1970). *The possibility of altruism.* Princeton: Princeton University Press.

Otsuka, M. (n.d.) "The Fairness of Equal Chances," (unpublished ms.).

Otsuka, M. and Voorhoeve, A. (2009). Why it matters that some are worse off than others. *Philosophy and Public Affairs, 37*, 171–199.

Parfit, D. (2002). Equality or priority?. In M. Clayton and A. Williams (Eds.), *The ideal of equality* (pp. 81–125). Basingstoke: Palgrave.

Savage, L. (1972). *The foundations of statistics*, 2nd revised ed. New York: Dover Publications.

U.S. Preventive Services Task Force. (2009). Screening for breast cancer: U.S. preventive services task force recommendation statement. *Annals of Internal Medicine, 151*, 716–726.

Voorhoeve, A. and Fleurbaey, M. (2012). Egalitarianism and the separateness of persons. *Utilitas 24*, 381–398.

Wasserman, D. (1996). Let them eat chances: Probability and distributive justice. *Economics and Philosophy, 12*, 29–49.

9 }

Uncertainty and Justifiability to Each Person

RESPONSE TO FLEURBAEY AND VOORHOEVE

Johann Frick

It is a sad truism that tradeoffs between the well-being of different individuals are sometimes unavoidable in medicine and population-level health policy. We can distinguish two ways in which such tradeoffs may arise. On the one hand, there are situations where, in order to further the interests of some (by bestowing a benefit or averting a harm), we must impose some cost or disadvantage on other persons. The group of potential beneficiaries and the group of potential victims are known in advance and non-overlapping. (Such tradeoffs also come in probabilistic variants, in which to give some people a *chance* of benefiting we must impose on others a *risk* of harm.) By definition, actions or policies that fall into this first category are not in the *ex ante* interest of everyone affected. The tradeoffs involved are what we may call *competitive ex ante*.

On the other hand, there are tradeoffs that are merely *competitive ex post*. Suppose that a risky medical intervention is administered to multiple individuals. In such cases, especially in situations involving large numbers of patients, statistical knowledge often allows us to predict with a high degree of confidence the *overall pattern* of outcomes that the intervention will produce: we can foresee that X percent of patients will benefit to this-and-that extent, whereas Y percent will be harmed to such-and-such a degree. However, with regard to the outcome that our intervention will have for *particular* individuals, we find ourselves behind a "natural veil of ignorance." Although we know the approximate number of individuals whose well-being will be promoted or set back, we cannot know in advance *who* will be benefited and *who*

A version of this chapter was presented at the Foundation Brocher in July 2010. For helpful feedback and criticism, I thank Eric Beerbohm, Selim Berker, Dan Brock, Norman Daniels, Tom Dougherty, Nir Eyal, Marc Fleurbaey, Samia Hurst, Frances Kamm, Dave Langlois, Ekédi Mpondo-Dika, Tim Scanlon, Gerard Vong, Alex Voorhoeve, Dan Wikler, and two anonymous referees, as well as the participants in the graduate fellows' seminar at the Edmond J. Safra Center for Ethics at Harvard University.

will be disadvantaged. Tradeoffs of this type are not competitive *ex ante*; if the gamble offered by the risky intervention is sufficiently attractive, it may be in *every* patient's interest *ex ante* to receive the risky treatment—despite the fact that, *ex post*, there will be winners and losers.

In their paper, "Decide As You Would with Full Information! An Argument Against *ex ante* Pareto,"[1] Marc Fleurbaey and Alex Voorhoeve argue against a popular principle for deciding how to act in cases involving tradeoffs of this latter kind. According to

> *Ex Ante Pareto*: "If an alternative has higher expected utility for every person than every other alternative, then this alternative should be chosen." (Fleurbaey and Voorhoeve, Chapter 8, p. 114, this volume).

Despite its prima facie plausibility, Fleurbaey and Voorhoeve believe that *ex ante* Pareto violates a "basic principle of rationality," the Principle of Full Information (PFI). In this response, I critically examine the key claims of their chapter.

Three Cases

Fleurbaey and Voorhoeve's core argument is built around three stylized cases, summarized in Table 9.1. In each of these cases, Teresa, a medical decision maker, has to decide which of two medicines to produce and administer to one or more young children to prevent them from going completely blind (which would give them a utility-level of 0.6).

In the *Single-Person Case*, Teresa must choose whether to give Adam medicine M_E that will make him considerably visually impaired with certainty (utility = 0.8) or the risky medicine M_P, which gives him a 50 percent chance of retaining excellent vision (utility = 1) at the cost of a 50 percent chance of becoming severely visually impaired (utility = 0.65). Fleurbaey and Voorhoeve maintain that Teresa has good moral reason to take this gamble on Adam's behalf because M_P gives him greater expected utility than does M_E. In cases involving only a *single* individual, reasoning in accord with *ex ante* Pareto is morally unproblematic.

In *Visual Impairment Case* 2, Teresa must treat two children. Whereas M_E would give both Adam and Bill 0.8 for sure, M_U will allow Adam to achieve 1 while giving Bill 0.65 with certainty. The tradeoff here is competitive *ex ante* because only Adam will gain from Teresa's choosing M_U over M_P, whereas Bill is sure to be disadvantaged by this decision.

The key case for Fleurbaey and Voorhoeve, however, is *Visual Impairment Case 1*. Here, Teresa must choose between giving both patients M_E or the

[1] See 2013, Chapter 8, this volume.

TABLE 9.1 } **The distribution of utility in the three cases**

Action	Person	States of the world (equiprobable).	
		s_1	s_2
SINGLE-PERSON CASE			
M_E	Adam	0.8	0.8
M_P	Adam	1	0.65
VISUAL IMPAIRMENT CASE 1			
M_E	Adam	0.8	0.8
	Bill	0.8	0.8
M_P	Adam	1	0.65
	Bill	0.65	1
VISUAL IMPAIRMENT CASE 2			
M_E	Adam	0.8	0.8
	Bill	0.8	0.8
M_U	Adam	1	1
	Bill	0.65	0.65

risky medicine M_P, whose results for each patient are uncertain[2]: In state of world s_1, Adam will receive 1 whereas Bill gets 0.65; if the state of world is s_2, the results will be the reverse. S_1 and s_2 are equiprobable, but Teresa does not know which obtains. What she does know—since the individual outcomes under M_P are *perfectly inversely correlated*—is that the overall pattern of outcomes will be the same as would result from choosing M_U in Visual Impairment Case 2.[3]

Which medicine ought Teresa to choose in Visual Impairment Case 1? *Ex ante* Pareto gives a straightforward answer: just as in the Single-Person Case, Teresa ought to select the risky medicine M_P because, for both Adam and Bill, this option has higher expected utility than does M_E.

By contrast, Fleurbaey and Voorhoeve aim to show that "an egalitarian who...cares both about reducing outcome inequality and about increasing

[2] Economists and decision theorists sometimes draw the following distinction between "uncertainty" and "risk": situations involving risk have an unknown outcome, but we do know the underlying distribution of different possible outcomes and their respective probabilities. In cases of uncertainty, the outcome is also unknown, but we don't know what the underlying distribution looks like. In the following, I depart from this convention. To me, "risk" will signify the likelihood, probabilistically quantified, of some (bad) outcome occurring. "Uncertainty" is the epistemic predicament of not knowing which outcome will occur. However, as I understand the latter term, it does not imply ignorance about the probabilities of the various possible outcomes.

[3] Fleurbaey and Voorhoeve do not specify the causal mechanism by which the effects of medicine M_P come to be perfectly inversely correlated, rather than being (as would be more common in medicine) probabilistically independent. This stylized assumption need not detain us, however. The moral problem that Fleurbaey and Voorhoeve aim to investigate also arises under more realistic conditions. Even when the individual outcomes of a risky action are probabilistically independent, we can often

individuals' well-being" ought to reject the conclusion suggested by *ex ante* Pareto (Fleurbaey and Voorhoeve 2013, Chapter 8, this volume). In a footnote to this passage, they add: "our argument against *ex ante* Pareto is equally effective if one instead gives priority to the worse off because one is a prioritarian who gives additional weight to utility gains when they occur at a lower level of absolute utility."

On the strength of these passages alone, it may seem like Fleurbaey and Voorhoeve have set themselves an excessively simple task. Both outcome (or "telic") egalitarianism and prioritarianism are impersonal principles that rank outcomes based solely on their overall pattern of distribution. If we assume the truth of one of these positions, it is not hard to see that this will contradict the deliverances of *ex ante* Pareto. A plausible outcome-egalitarianism will clearly recommend that Teresa pick M_E in Visual Impairment Case 1 because this achieves an equal distribution at only a small loss in total well-being. Prioritarianism gives the same verdict because, under M_E, the worst off fare considerably better than under M_P.

If this were the extent of Fleurbaey and Voorhoeve's opposition to *ex ante* Pareto, it would be of limited dialectical power. It would "refute" *ex ante* Pareto by assuming the truth of an impersonal position that implies its falsity. Such a move would be only as strong as the outcome egalitarian or prioritarian intuitions that underlie it. It is safe to assume that it would fail to persuade a committed proponent of *ex ante* Pareto.[4]

In fact, however, Fleurbaey and Voorhoeve have a further, more interesting objection *to ex ante* Pareto. The intuitive attraction of *ex ante* Pareto is that it is an "individualistic" moral principle. Without requiring us to appeal to controversial interpersonal distributive principles, it seems that an action that satisfies *ex ante* Pareto can be justified to each affected individual in the following manner: "I am doing on your behalf what you *yourself* would have done, had you been solely concerned with maximizing your own expected utility."

It is precisely this individualistic appeal of *ex ante* Pareto that Fleurbaey and Voorhoeve set out to challenge. They aim to show that, in cases like Visual Impairment Case 1, the actions endorsed by *ex ante* Pareto are *not*, as a matter of fact, justifiable to each person. They therefore fail a broadly contractualist

---

predict, with a high degree of confidence, the overall pattern of individual outcomes that will arise—as long as the number of individuals affected is reasonably *large*. Hence, in population-level bioethics and other areas of public policy, the Law of Large Numbers often does the work that the assumption of perfectly inverse correlation does in Fleurbaey and Voorhoeve's example.

[4] As a matter of fact, Fleurbaey and Voorhoeve's dialectical position would be even more precarious than that because they are on record as *critics* of both telic egalitarianism and prioritarianism. For arguments against prioritarianism, see Michael Otsuka and Alex Voorhoeve (2009); for objections to telic egalitarianism, see Alex Voorhoeve and Marc Fleurbaey (in press).

standard of moral rightness according to which an action is right if and only if it is justifiable to each person.

T.M. Scanlon, the most prominent defender of moral contractualism, fleshes out this standard as follows: an action is justifiable to each person if and only if a principle licensing the performance of the action could not be reasonably rejected by any individual for personal reasons. Personal reasons, for Scanlon, are "reasons that are... tied to the well-being, claims, or status of individuals in [a] particular position" (Scanlon 1998, p. 219). They exclude appeals to how an action will affect *other* individuals, as well as to *impersonal* concerns, such as the goodness of the overall outcome that the action will produce. A principle licensing the performance of the action in question cannot be reasonably rejected if any alternative action would give another person yet stronger reasons for rejection.

In Visual Impairment Case 2, contractualist reasoning clearly favors the selection of medicine M_E over the alternative, M_U. Bill has stronger personal grounds for rejecting a principle licensing Teresa to pick M_U (it will make him *severely* visually impaired with certainty, when he could have been merely significantly visually impaired), than has Adam against M_E (he will be significantly visually impaired when he could have remained fully sighted) As Fleurbaey and Voorhoeve put it: "it is unjustifiable to sacrifice the interests of someone who... will be no better off than the other person under either policy in order to make that other person better off still, at least for the size of the benefits under consideration" (Fleurbaey and Voorhoeve 2013, Chapter 8, p. 113, this volume).

By contrast, it seems far from clear that, in a choice between M_E and M_P, it wouldn't be justifiable to each person to choose the risky medicine M_P. Defenders of *ex ante* Pareto could avail themselves of the following powerful argument:

> *The Argument from the Single-Person Case*: In terms of expected benefit, the gamble that M_P offers to Adam and Bill in Visual Impairment Case 1 is just the same as the one Adam was offered in the Single-Person Case. And, in that case, Fleurbaey and Voorhoeve agreed that it would be justifiable to Adam to choose M_P over M_E. By giving both patients M_P, Teresa therefore does for both Adam and Bill what a guardian concerned *solely* with promoting Adam's interests ought to do for him in a case in which he is her only concern. Given that M_P was deemed justifiable to Adam in the Single-Person Case, how could it not be justifiable to both Adam and Bill in Visual Impairment Case 1?

I confess to finding this argument extremely plausible. If the Argument from the Single-Person Case goes through, however, then—although there may be *impersonal* grounds for privileging medicine M_E in Visual Impairment

Case 1—from the point of view of justifiability to each person, there is no objection to Teresa's selecting M_p.

In the next section, I review Fleurbaey and Voorhoeve's objections to the argument from the Single-Person Case. I will attempt to show that their main argument, the *Argument from Omniscient Guardians*, is defective because it overlooks the normative significance of uncertainty.

Nothing I say in the following is meant to provide an *all-things-considered* account of what we ought to do in Visual Impairment Case 1. I agree with Fleurbaey and Voorhoeve that, in addition to making our action justifiable to every person, we may also have reason to attend to impersonal concerns, such as outcome equality or priority for the worst off. (I return to these points in the final section of this chapter.) My aim in this chapter is merely to show that, to the extent that these impersonal concerns are valid in Visual Impairment Case 1, they pull in the *opposite* direction as arguments from justifiability to each person.

The Argument from Omniscient Guardians

Fleurbaey and Voorhoeve consider the argument from the Single-Person Case, but attempt to rebut it with the following argument, which I summarize from their chapter:

> *The Argument from Omniscient Guardians:* Whenever possible, Teresa ought to base her decision on what *fully informed* guardians would ask her to do on their charges' behalf. Unlike Teresa, such omniscient guardians know which of s_1 and s_2 obtains and would thus be able to object to Teresa's choice of M_p if they foresaw that it was contrary to their charge's "true interest." If Teresa was able to consult such omniscient guardians and was informed by one of them that his charge would lose out under M_p, she would no longer regard it as justifiable to his charge to select M_p because this would mean knowingly sacrificing the interests of someone who, as things turn out, will be no better off than the other person under either policy in order to make that other person better off still.
>
> In reality, of course, Teresa does not know which state of the world obtains; however, she does know for sure that *one* of s_1 and s_2 obtains. Consequently, Teresa can infer that, if she were advised by fully informed guardians, she would necessarily regard the choice of M_p as unjustifiable to either Adam of Bill.
>
> Moreover, when she can, Teresa should therefore adopt the judgments about the justifiability to each that she can infer she would have under full information.

> Despite not knowing which state of the world obtains, Teresa ought, therefore, to conclude that giving M_P fails the test of justifiability to each person.

Fleurbaey and Voorhoeve claim that this conclusion is required by a "basic principle of rationality," which they dub the

> *Principle of Full Information, Part I*: "When one knows that, in every state of the world with positive probability, one would rightly rank two alternatives in a particular way, then one should so rank them." (Fleurbaey and Voorhoeve 2013, Chapter 8, p. 120, this volume).

What are we to make of this argument? It seems to me that talk of what Teresa would regard as unjustifiable to Adam or Bill upon consulting a "fully informed guardian" is just a picturesque way of saying that if Teresa *knew* for sure that s_1 (s_2) obtains, she would rightly regard it as unjustifiable to Bill (Adam) to choose M_P. The Argument from Omniscient Guardians can thus be restated as follows:

1. If Teresa knew that s_1 obtains, her choosing M_P would be unjustifiable to Bill.
2. If Teresa knew that s_2 obtains, her choosing M_P would be unjustifiable to Adam.
3. Teresa knows that either s_1 or s_2 obtains.
4. Therefore, Teresa can infer that, with full information, she would always regard her choosing M_P as unjustifiable to either Adam or Bill.
5. Judgments made with full information about a person's interests are superior to judgments made with lack of information.
6. When she can, Teresa should therefore adopt the judgments about the justifiability to each that she can infer she would have under full information.
7. Teresa can infer and adopt these fully informed judgments about justifiability. Therefore, Teresa should regard choosing M_P as unjustifiable to either Adam or to Bill.[5]

The critical step in this argument is the move from premise 5 to 6. To imagine a situation in which Teresa has full information about the effects of M_P on Adam and Bill is to make her choice equivalent to a case of decision making under certainty; namely whether to give either M_E or M_U in Visual Impairment Case 2. Now, it is undeniable that the assessments we can make under full information about what is in Adam and Bill's interests are "superior" in the sense of being more *accurate* than Teresa's judgments in Visual Impairment Case 1, where she cannot know in advance how M_P will affect each individual patient.

[5] This reconstruction of the argument was suggested to me by Alex Voorhoeve (in correspondence).

But does this also mean—as premise 6 asserts—that applying Teresa's *moral* judgments about Visual Impairment Case 2 to Visual Impairment Case 1 yields a morally "superior" or more plausible assessment than *ex ante* Pareto? That is, does it follow from the fact that Teresa would deem it unjustifiable to give M_P in a situation in which she knew for sure that this would amount to sacrificing Bill's interest in being merely significantly visually impaired in order to allow Adam to retain perfect eyesight, that she ought also to regard M_P as unjustifiable to some person even if she *doesn't* know whose interest will be set back by M_P and even though it gives *both* patients higher expected utility than M_E?

I believe that appealing to the Principle of Full Information to answer this question is a red herring. Let me explain why. As it is stated, the PFI is ambiguous between two possible interpretations. Fleurbaey and Voorhoeve might mean

> *Interpretation 1:* When one knows that in every state of the world with positive probability, and *given no uncertainty about which state of the world one is in*, one would rightly rank two alternatives in a particular way, then one should so rank them [no matter what state of the world one turns out to be in].[6]

On this interpretation of the PFI, we *could* directly infer what Teresa ought to do in Visual Impairment Case 1 from the fact that, in either variant of Visual Impairment Case 2 (a case where there is no uncertainty about which state of the world Teresa is in) she ought to choose M_E.

Unfortunately, on Interpretation 1, the PFI is unsound. To see why, consider the Boat Race Case from footnote 12 of Voorhoeve and Fleurbaey's chapter (the case is derived from a similar counterexample that I proposed in an earlier draft of this response): suppose that, given full information about the outcome of the Oxford-Cambridge boat race (i.e., given no uncertainty about which state of the world she is in), Teresa prefers to go for a run rather than watching the race, because watching the race would be boring. Interpretation 1 of the PFI then implies that, even if she *doesn't* know which side will win the race, Teresa ought to go for a run—since this is what she would do in every state of the world with positive probability, given no uncertainty about what state of the world she is in.

But this reasoning is obviously fallacious: the fact that Teresa doesn't know which state of the world she is in makes a potentially decisive difference to her reasons for watching the boat race—namely, that watching the race might be exciting. Interpretation 1 of the PFI is unsound because it overlooks that certain reasons that bear on how two alternatives ought to be ranked under conditions of uncertainty may depend on an agent's ignorance about the true

---

[6] I assume, as Fleurbaey and Voorhoeve seem to do, that the state of the world one is currently in includes timeless facts about how future gambles will turn out.

state of the world. Conversely, properties (like that of being boring) that may count against an alternative in each possible state of the world, *provided* the agent knows which state of the world she is in, do not obtain when all the agent knows is that the state she is in is a member of some exhaustive disjunction. This is because knowledge, and properties that depend on it, do not distribute over disjunction. That is

(A) Teresa knows that ($s_1 \vee s_2$)

does not entail

(B) Teresa knows that s_1 $\vee$ Teresa knows that s_2

Consequently, properties that obtain when (B) is the case need not obtain when only (A) is true.

Now, according to proponents of *ex ante* Pareto, "being justifiable to each person," just like "being exciting" or "being boring," *is* a property that may be highly sensitive to whether or not the agent knows what state of the world she is in. (The point is not, of course, that uncertainty about individual outcomes affects how Teresa should rank M_E and M_P in just the same way as it does in Boat Race. In latter case, as Fleurbaey and Voorheove note, uncertainty matters because it alters the *value* of one of the alternatives (watching the race); by contrast, proponents of *ex ante* Pareto merely claim that, in comparing Visual Impairment Cases 1 and 2, uncertainty may impact the correct ranking of alternatives by altering a *normative* fact; namely, whether not choosing M_E in favor of the other medicine is justifiable to each person.)

By contrast, Interpretation 1 of the PFI implicitly assumes that uncertainty about individual outcomes is morally irrelevant. Rather than making M_P justifiable to both Adam and Bill, uncertainty about individual outcomes merely masks the *identity* of the person to whom M_P is not justifiable. This assumption not only begs the question against defenders of *ex ante* Pareto; it is also embedded in a general principle that, as we have seen, is demonstrably unsound.

There is a second way of reading the PFI that avoids some of the pitfalls of Interpretation 1. Fleurbaey and Voorhoeve may instead intend:

> *Interpretation 2*: When one knows that in every state of the world with positive probability, and *given uncertainty about which state of the world one is in*, one would rightly rank two alternatives in a particular way, then one should so rank them [no matter what state of the world one turns out to be in].[7]

Interpretation 2 avoids the fallacious reasoning in Boat Race. If Teresa knows that, lacking information about the eventual outcome, she will prefer watching

---

[7] If this is the interpretation that Fleurbaey and Voorhoeve have in mind, then seems a misnomer. In simplified language, Interpretation 2 of the PFI amounts to little more than this: "if you don't know which state of the world you are in, rank the alternatives as you should, given that you *don't* know which state of the world you are in".

the boat race to going for a run—irrespective of who eventually wins—then she ought to watch the boat race. The problem for Fleurbaey and Voorhoeve is not that Interpretation 2 is unsound. It is rather that if *this* is how they intend the PFI to be understood, they cannot appeal to the PFI to solve the debate between proponents and opponents of *ex ante* Pareto: to *apply* the PFI on Interpretation 2, we already need to know which of these two views is the correct one.

To see this, suppose that the *ex ante* Pareto is correct and, given uncertainty about outcomes, it is justifiable to each person to select M_P because this gives both Adam and Bill greater expected utility than M_E. In that case, given uncertainty about the eventual outcome, Teresa ought to rank alternative M_P above M_E, no matter what state of the world she turns out to be in. In other words, if *ex ante* Pareto is sound, selecting M_P would be sanctioned by Interpretation 2 of the PFI.

To arrive at the opposite conclusion—that Teresa ought to choose M_E—Fleurbaey and Voorhoeve must assume that uncertainty about the eventual outcome does *not* make M_P justifiable to every person. I will review their arguments for this assumption in a moment. But the point to note here is that, *contra* Fleurbaey and Voorhoeve, we cannot appeal to the PFI to *show* that *ex ante* Pareto violates a basic requirement of rationality. Rather, to apply the PFI, we must first settle the independent normative question of whether *ex ante* Pareto is true. The PFI is of no help in this context.

What, then, are Fleurbaey and Voorhoeve's independent grounds for thinking that Teresa's judgments about the justifiability of M_P in Visual Impairment Case 1 should track her judgment that choosing M_U over M_E in Visual Impairment Case 2 would be unjustifiable to either Adam or Bill? Their chapter contains two arguments in support of this claim.

The first argument can be summarized as follows:

> *Argument 1:* If Teresa knew *more* than the guardians (i.e., if, from her perspective, the situation was akin to Visual Impairment Case 2, whereas for the guardians it was like Visual Impairment Case 1), then Teresa shouldn't listen to the guardians and give no weight to the fact that they would assent to M_P on their charge's behalf. Given what she knows, she should regard M_E as the only option that is justifiable to both Adam and Bill. This shows that it is the judgments about justifiability made with *full* information (i.e., the judgments of Visual Impairment Case 2) that should guide Teresa's actions in Visual Impairment Case 1.

I agree that what ultimately matters is what Teresa knows or can know, not what the guardians know—they are merely an illustrative device. The point, however, is that, unlike the case imagined in Argument 1, Visual Impairment Case 1 is such that Teresa *cannot* know who will win and who will lose, only that *one of* Adam and Bill will win and the other lose. It is not clear, therefore, that anything follows for Visual Impairment Case 1 from what Teresa ought to do if she herself knew how M_P would end up affecting Adam and Bill. To deny this, Fleurbaey and Voorhoeve would have to assume that the difference between the case imagined in Argument 1 and Visual Impairment Case 1—namely, Teresa's lack of information about individual outcomes in Visual Impairment Case 1—is normatively irrelevant. But to do so is simply to beg the question against proponents of *ex ante* Pareto.

Fleurbaey and Voorhoeve's second argument goes like this:

> *Argument 2:* It is obvious that if Teresa could easily and costlessly acquire more information—thus transforming Visual Impairment Case 1 into Visual Impairment Case 2—she ought to do so. But, if this is so, then, once again, it is the judgments about justifiability made with *full* information (i.e., the judgments of Visual Impairment Case 2) that should guide Teresa's actions in Visual Impairment Case 1.

Pace Fleurbaey and Voorhoeve, I do not regard the claim that Teresa ought to acquire more information if she could easily do so as *obvious* (although it may still be correct). After all, neither Adam nor Bill, if they are self-interested, would *want* Teresa to acquire more information. (I assume that once Teresa has the information, it will be unjustifiable for her not to choose M_E; but *ex ante*, the expected utility of Teresa's acquiring more information and then selecting M_E is lower, for both Adam and Bill, than her not acquiring the information and picking M_P).[8]

In any event, it is not clear what lessons we ought to draw from what Teresa should do in a case in which she could acquire more information for a case in which she *cannot* acquire more information. As in Argument 1 above, it would beg the question against defenders of the *ex ante* view to simply assume that this difference is normatively irrelevant.

I conclude that Fleurbaey and Voorhoeve lack convincing grounds for opposing *ex ante* Pareto and the Argument from the Single-Person Case. I do not disagree with their point that Teresa should want her action to be justifiable to Adam and Bill in terms of their *true* interests, rather than their merely apparent interests. But this doesn't rule out taking a gamble in Visual Impairment Case 1. Given her limited knowledge, M_P *is* the best way for Teresa to attempt to promote her patients' true interests: for each patient, the expected value of M_P—in terms of their true interests—is greater than that of M_E.

The Argument from Omniscient Guardians thus fails to show that selecting M_P in Visual Impairment Case 1 would be unjustifiable to either Adam or Bill.

---

[8] I owe this point to Dan Wikler (in conversation). Note also that Argument 2 has a curiously self-undermining quality. If Fleurbaey and Voorhoeve are right and what Teresa should do, lacking access to full information, is anyway the same as what she ought to do if she had full information, then why would Teresa "obviously" need to acquire more information if she could?

Before closing the book on this question, however, it will pay to take a brief detour via the arguments of another philosopher to see whether a better case can be made against using *ex ante* Pareto to resolve *ex post* tradeoffs like Visual Impairment Case 1.

The Argument from Certain Loss

In "Contractualism and Aggregation," Sophia Reibetanz proposes an account of contractualist justification under conditions of uncertainty that would provide a different basis for rejecting *ex ante* Pareto. She writes:

> As long as we know that acceptance of a principle will affect someone in a certain way, we should assign that person a complaint that is based upon the full magnitude of the harm or benefit, even if we cannot identify the person in advance. It is only if we do not know whether acceptance of a principle will affect anyone in a certain way that we should allocate each individual a complaint based upon his expected harms and benefits under that principle. (Reibetanz 1998, p. 304)

In Visual Impairment Case 1, of course, it is certain that *someone* will end up losing the gamble offered by M_P. If Reibetanz is right, therefore, whoever ends up losing should have as great a complaint against M_P as Bill would against M_U in Visual Impairment Case 2. We could then replace the Argument from Omniscient Guardians with the simpler

Argument from Certain Loss:

1. If Teresa knows that *someone* will lose if she selects M_P, then, if she chooses M_P and Adam loses, her action is unjustifiable to Adam.
2. If Teresa knows that *someone* will lose if she selects M_P, then, if she chooses M_P and Bill loses, her action is unjustifiable to Bill.
3. Teresa knows that someone will lose if she selects M_P.

Therefore, Teresa knows that her choice of M_P will be unjustifiable to either Adam or Bill.

However, I have misgivings about the Argument from Certain Loss and the view of justification that underlies it. Premises 1 and 2 imply that the reason why Teresa cannot justify her action to the person who ends up being disadvantaged is in virtue of information that she possesses about the *overall* pattern of outcomes that will result from her action. But why should Adam have a greater personal complaint against Teresa, just because, had things turned out differently, *Bill* might have lost (and vice versa)? This essentially amounts to allowing the *aggregation* of complaints across different individuals (and states of the world)—something that contractualism strictly rejects.[9]

Remember that, in terms of expected benefit, the gamble offered to Adam and Bill by M_p is the same we deemed justifiable to Adam in the Single-Person Case. The fact that, in Visual Impairment Case 1, there is bound to be a loser changes nothing about the attractiveness of the gamble for Adam and Bill *as individuals*. Contractualist justification is owed to persons, with determinate identities and interests, not placeholders in a pattern of outcomes.

Perhaps there are other ways in which Teresa's knowledge of the eventual pattern of outcomes might matter? For instance, it might be claimed that if Teresa knows for sure that someone will be disadvantaged from her choice of M_p, then selecting M_p nonetheless shows too little concern for the eventual loser.

This complaint also misses its mark. It might be argued, with some justification, that choosing M_p shows too little concern for avoiding that *there will be* a loser. This, however, expresses a preoccupation with the overall outcome, as it would arise from an impersonal moral principle such as telic egalitarianism or the priority view. By contrast, what cannot be said, either by Adam or by Bill, is that Teresa's choice shows too little concern for avoiding that *he will be* a loser. Again: Teresa takes no greater risk with the well-being of either patient than she did in the Single-Person Case, and there Fleurbaey and Voorhoeve agreed that taking the gamble on Adam's behalf did not show insufficient concern for his well-being. Unequal outcomes are not always evidence of unequal concern or treatment, especially when they are produced by a chancy causal mechanism.

In sum: it appears that, in Visual Impairment Case 1, despite her knowledge that her choice of M_p is sure to end up disadvantaging someone, Teresa treats both patients in just the way she ought to, were she acting on their behalf alone. She gives them the same attractive gamble as in the Single-Person Case, and she shows each the same concern that she had for Adam in that case. All told, it is hard to see how the fact that Teresa can predict the overall pattern could affect Adam's or Bill's grounds for reasonable rejection. The Argument from Certain Loss fails because it conflates the moral significance of "Teresa knows that *someone* will lose" with "there is someone who Teresa knows will lose."

Remarks on Fairness, Lotteries, and Risk Taking

So far, I have examined Fleurbaey and Voorhoeve's arguments presented in the first three sections of their chapter (2013, Chapter 8, this volume), in which

[9] See Scanlon (1998, chapter 5).

they sought to establish that, as far as justifiability to each person in terms of their true well-being interests is concerned, selecting the risky option M_P in Visual Impairment Case 1 is morally on a par with choosing M_U in Visual Impairment Case 2 (and inferior to picking M_E in either case).

However, in the fourth section of their chapter, Fleurbaey and Voorhoeve explore a way in which M_P and M_U may differ morally after all: unlike M_U, which is *certain* to benefit Adam at the cost of *certainly* setting back Bill's interests, M_P gives both patients an equal chance of receiving the benefit of being fully sighted. This may make M_P *fairer* than M_U.

The fact that M_P gives both patients an equal chance of benefiting would be especially significant, Fleurbaey and Voorhoeve maintain, if we subscribed to what David Wasserman (1996) calls a "distributive" view of equal chances. As Fleurbaey and Voorhoeve characterize this view, "a given outcome inequality among people with equally strong claims to a benefit is less unfair when each person has a chance to end up better off than when the worse off have no such chance because, in receiving this chance, each person receives an equal share of something of expected value" (Fleurbaey and Voorhoeve, p. 123). Let us call the kind of unfairness that is avoided by giving the patients equal chances of being fully sighted "*procedural* unfairness." If the distributive view is sound, this would make M_P morally preferable to M_U, at least in terms of procedural fairness.

I do not disagree with Fleurbaey and Voorhoeve that M_P may indeed be preferable to M_U on account of its greater procedural fairness (although I would not have treated this as a consideration that is *separate* from the question of justifiability to each person). However, Fleurbaey and Voorhoeve make two further claims that I believe deserve critical scrutiny. I will first spell out these claims and then address them in reverse order.

CLAIM 1: THE OUTCOME INEQUALITY PRODUCED BY M_P IS UNFAIR, TO SOME EXTENT

If the distributive view is correct, Fleurbaey and Voorhoeve maintain, this increases the moral distance between M_P and M_U. *How* different we deem M_P and M_U to be from one another depends on how much the unfairness of inequality produced by M_P "is *mitigated* by the fact that the severely impaired person had a one in two chance of instead ending up unimpaired, which is equal to the chance that the unimpaired person had of instead ending up with the severe impairment" (Fleurbaey and Voorhoeve 2013, Chapter 8, p. 124, this volume; emphasis mine).

The fact that Fleurbaey and Voorhoeve write that the unfairness of M_P is "mitigated" by of offering equal chances to Adam and Bill suggests that they think that M_P may still suffer from residual unfairness, according to the distributive view, on account of the unequal *outcome* it produces.[10] I will return to this point below.

CLAIM 2: IF THE DISTRIBUTIVE VIEW OF EQUAL CHANCES IS CORRECT, THEN IT MAY BE ALL-THINGS-CONSIDERED PERMISSIBLE TO SELECT M_P OVER M_E AFTER ALL

Fleurbaey and Voorhoeve think that if the distributive view of fairness is correct, this doesn't only affect how we ought to choose between M_P and M_U. It may also impact the choice between M_P and M_E in Visual Impairment Case 1:

> "If Teresa should give great weight to improving the lot of those who are less well off than others and if equal chances do little to mitigate the unfairness of unequal outcomes, then she should prefer M_E over M_P. If, by contrast, Teresa should not sacrifice much total utility for the sake of the worst off, then the fact that the equal chances offered by M_P mitigate the associated outcome-unfairness may tip the balance in its favor". (Fleurbaey and Voorhoeve 2013, Chapter 8, p. 125, this volume)

The problem with this second claim is not that I take it to be false, but that I do not see how Fleurbaey and Voorhoeve are entitled to it, given their preceding arguments.

Fleurbaey and Voorhoeve state explicitly that the Argument from Omniscient Guardians appeals only to Adam and Bill's welfare interests and that these do not include considerations of fairness: "We will assume that these reasons of self-interest do not include an interest in being fairly treated in the distributive process. This assumption makes it possible to represent fairness considerations separately from well-being considerations" (Fleurbaey and Voorhoeve 2013, Chapter 8, p. 116, this volume). Therefore, if Teresa's choosing M_P in Visual Impairment Case 1 is rejected by the Argument from Omniscient Guardians, this must be for reasons *other* than a concern with fairness.

But, in that case, even if the presence of equal chances mitigates any outcome unfairness arising in M_P, how could this help make M_P all-things-considered preferable to M_E? Because claims of unfairness play no role in the

[10] As Fleurbaey and Voorhoeve point out, David Wasserman himself actually rejects the distributive view. However, other philosophers, such as Gerald Lang (2005), do defend similar positions. Like Fleurbaey and Voorhoeve, Lang maintains that even perfect procedural fairness need not make an action entirely fair. Besides being unfair by giving people unequal chances of benefiting, Lang argues, an action can also be unfair in virtue of the unequal outcome it produces. He writes: "Outcomes, as well as chances, matter to fairness. To put it in another way, *expected* harm is not the only thing that matters, even when we are considering fairness, rather than goodness. *Actual* harm matters too. After all, a morally significant result of being awarded an equal chance of being saved is that *you might get to be saved.* So why should not the prevalence of actual harm be relevant to an assessment of fairness?" (Lang 2005, p. 336).

Argument from Omniscient Guardians, the claim that any outcome unfairness arising under M_P is mitigated by the existence of equal chances cannot reduce the force of the *original* objection to M_P. Moreover, note that by the standard of the distributive view of fairness, M_E does *at least* as well as M_P because it involves neither an inequality of outcomes nor of chances. If, as Fleurbaey and Voorhoeve believe, M_P fares worse than M_E in terms of the Argument from Omniscient Guardians and, at best, does no worse in terms of unfairness, then how, by their own lights, could M_P be all-things-considered more choice-worthy than M_E?

I now return to Claim 1. Like Fleurbaey and Voorhoeve, I believe that the fact that M_P gives both patients an equal chance of receiving the benefit of being fully sighted makes it considerably fairer than M_U, which creates a certain winner (Adam) and a certain loser (Bill), relative to the baseline of M_E. But, unlike Fleurbaey and Voorhoeve, I am unsure to what extent the outcome inequality arising from M_P in Visual Impairment Case 1 gives anyone a residual claim of unfairness—at least not the kind that could generate a legitimate moral complaint on the part of Adam or Bill.

The distributive account of fairness, with its distinction between procedural and outcome unfairness, was put forward by Wasserman and Lang as a possible explanation for the moral importance of lotteries in the allocation of *scarce, indivisible* goods. These are situations in which two or more claimants are entitled to some good in equal measure but where an "equal division of the good to which they have a claim is not possible or can only be achieved with a *significant* loss of value" (Wasserman 1996, p. 30).

In such contexts, it is not implausible that even a procedurally fair lottery, which assigns the scarce good to one claimant but not the other, cannot remove a residue of outcome unfairness. Using a lottery to give both individuals an equal chance of receiving the good only assigns them equal chances of being treated *unequally*, since only one of them will receive the good, whereas the other will not. Because the good in question cannot be divided without losing most of its value, there is no way in which *both* claimants could have satisfied their claims to a significant degree. It is unavoidable that, through no fault of their own, one of the individuals won't have his or her claim to the good satisfied.

The situation to which Fleurbaey and Voorhoeve attempt to apply the distributive view is arguably quite different. In Visual Impairment Case 1, in addition to M_P, we have the alternative of M_E, which, despite involving a small loss in total welfare, would give both Adam and Bill a significant benefit (significantly better than both a baseline of total blindness and one of severe visual impairment). Thus, there is a way in which Teresa could, to a significant extent, satisfy the claims of both Adam and Bill; namely, by choosing the riskless option.

However—and this is the crucial point—Adam and Bill, if they are self-interested, would not *want* Teresa to choose M_E. It is in both persons' *ex ante* interest that we take a gamble on their behalf by choosing M_P. The question is: to what extent could either Adam or Bill complain of "outcome unfairness" when any outcome inequality under M_P results from having forgone an option, in line with their own self-interest, that would have satisfied both of their claims to a significant extent and produced no inequality? We might think that, by receiving M_P, Adam and Bill "exchanged" their claim to the significant benefit that they could have gotten from M_E in return for the chance of getting an even greater good—a gamble that was in both persons' self-interest. It is not clear that, having made this exchange, either Adam or Bill is left with any valid complaint of unfairness if M_P does not turn out in his favor.

If this argument is sound, it would have the following interesting implication: an identical set of outcomes—those produced by the gamble M_P—may count as residually unfair or not depending on whether there existed an alternative like M_E that would have given each person a significant benefit without creating outcome inequality. This would be true, despite the fact that, had M_E been available, it would have been in neither person's self-interest that it be chosen.[11,12]

Conclusion

This concludes my response to Fleurbaey and Voorhoeve. If I am right, their Argument from Omniscient Guardians fails: the Principle of Full Information is either unsound or else cannot settle the debate between defenders and opponents of *ex ante* Pareto; and Fleurbaey and Voorhoeve's independent arguments to the effect that choosing M_P in Visual Impairment Case 1 is unjustifiable to either Adam or Bill are weak, because they risk begging the question against proponents of *ex ante* Pareto.

I then examined an alternative argument, the Argument from Certain Loss, adapted from the writings of Sophia Reibetanz, which suggests a different way

---

[11] Consider the following rough, nonprobabilistic analogy: suppose that, if offered a choice between two employment contracts, one paying $150,000 per annum for 80 hours of work per week, the other paying $50,000 per annum for 40 hours of work per week, I would regard it as in my self-interest to choose the former contract. I nevertheless believe that, had the former contract been the *only* contract I was offered, I would have standing to complain about long working hours in a way that I wouldn't if both contracts had been on the table.

[12] Note that this result does not challenge the axiom of "independence of irrelevant alternatives" (IIA) familiar from classical decision theory. IIA dictates that, if, for a given individual, X is the most preferred option from a choice set consisting of {X, Y, Z}, eliminating option Y from the choice set ought not to make Z preferable to X for that individual. What I am claiming is not that the presence or absence of M_E from the choice set {M_P, M_E, no intervention} affects the *preferability* of M_P—assuming that this is indeed Adam and Bill's most preferred option from the three-member set. I am merely claiming that the availability of M_E can alter a *normative property* of option M_P by making it the case that the outcome inequality created by M_P is not something against which either Adam or Bill have a legitimate complaint of unfairness.

in which a contractualist may object to *ex ante* Pareto. This argument, I tried to show, is also unsuccessful. It conflates the moral significance of "Teresa knows that someone will lose" with "there is someone who Teresa knows will lose."

Finally, I briefly considered Fleurbaey and Voorhoeve's remarks on fairness from the fourth section of their chapter. I agreed with them that the fact that M_P gives both patients an equal chance of retaining excellent vision, whereas M_U does not, increases the moral distance between these two options. But, *contra* Fleurbaey and Voorhoeve, I argued that—by the lights of their own earlier argument—this fact could not make it the case that, all things considered, we ought to prefer M_P to M_E in Visual Impairment Case 1.

The purpose of this response was not to defend *ex ante* Pareto as a correct *all-things-considered* principle for cases like Visual Impairment Case 1. Like Fleurbaey and Voorhoeve, I am sensitive to the force of impersonal moral principles, such as telic egalitarianism or the priority view, which may militate against selecting M_P. Indeed, I have argued elsewhere that a contractualist focus on justifiability to each person must be balanced against such impersonal considerations.[13] My aim in this response was the more limited one of showing that, although impersonal considerations may pull us in the opposite direction, there is no objection, as far as justifiability to each person is concerned, to choosing the risky option in Visual Impairment Case 1.

References

Fleurbaey, M. (2010). Assessing risky social situations. *Journal of Political Economy, 118*, 649–680.

Frick, J. Contractualism and social risk: How to count the numbers without aggregating claims. (unpublished ms.).

Lang, G. (2005). Fairness in life and death cases. *Erkenntnis, 62*, 321–351.

Otsuka, M., and Voorhoeve, A. (2009). Why it matters that some are worse off than others: An argument against the priority view. *Philosophy and Public Affairs, 37*, 171–199.

Reibetanz, S. (1998). Contractualism and aggregation. *Ethics, 108*, 296–311.

Scanlon, T. M. (1998). *What we owe to each other.* Cambridge, MA: Harvard University Press.

Voorhoeve, A., and Fleurbaey, M. (2012). Egalitarianism and the separateness of persons. *Utilitas, 24*, 381–398.

———. (2013). Decide as you would with full information! An argument against ex ante Pareto. In N. Eyal, S. A. Hurst, O. F. Norheim, and D. Wikler (Eds.), *Inequalities in health: Concepts, measures, and ethics* (Chapter 8). New York: Oxford University Press.

Wasserman, D. (1996). Let them eat chances: Probability and distributive justice. *Economics and Philosophy, 12*, 29–49.

[13] See my manuscript "Contractualism and social risk: How to count the numbers without aggregating claims" (available upon request).

10 }

Equality of Opportunity for Health

Shlomi Segall

Equality of opportunity has been central to thinking about justice in health care ever since Norman Daniels started publishing his seminal work on the topic. Daniels's is the dominant theory to date, and it famously grounds the provision of health care in John Rawls's "fair equality of opportunity principle" (FEOP) (Daniels 1985, 2008). There are potential weaknesses, however, to the way in which equality of opportunity figures in Daniels's account. I recount here some of these problems (this is the concern of the first section) and then propose an alternative account, namely "equality of opportunity for health." The second section of this chapter presents that account and discusses some initial objections to it. I then address two other potential objections to equality of opportunity for health. These objections concern (respectively) the claim that equality of opportunity can regulate only competitive goods and, as such, is not suitable for regulating health (third section), and the claim that equality of opportunity (EOp) is restricted to social rather than natural inequalities (in the fourth and fifth sections). I hope to disprove these two objections and, more generally, to present EOp for health as a plausible and attractive account of justice in health.

Let me quickly make one qualification. My proposed account of EOp for health is a narrower, as it were, account of justice in health care than Daniels. Thus, for reasons to be elaborated in the next section, it is more modest in its ambitions compared to Daniels. It is only fair to stress this now because, about some aspects of justice in health care on which Daniels's theory fails, my proposed account is simply silent.

I am grateful to Dan Hausman, Efrat Ram-Tiktin, and two anonymous referees for their written comments and suggestions. I have benefited also from the comments and suggestions made by the participants of the Brocher Summer Academy in Measurement and Ethical Evaluation of Health Inequalities and those made by the students at my "Justice After Rawls" graduate seminar. Financial support for this research has been provided by the Israel Science Fund (Grant no. 436/08).

Daniels's "Fair Equality of Opportunity"

I want to begin the inquiry by recalling the challenge that Daniels faced in offering his theory of justice in health care and the way in which he met this challenge. I then want to outline the shortcomings of his proposed solution. I then want to quickly present the idea of EOp for health and explain how it differs from Daniel's. I shall then briefly present two potential problems with EOp for health, two problems that I have addressed elsewhere (Segall 2010*a*). (I suspend addressing the two abovementioned objections until the next section.)

Central to Daniels's approach is the straightforward yet important observation that we need to be healthy to be able to pursue the life plans that we have each formed for ourselves. Health and, by derivation, health care is thus crucial for EOp to fulfill one's life plans. This insight lead Daniels to resist locating the distribution of health care under what would appear to be the obvious place, namely John Rawls's difference principle (DP) and rather to place it under the lexically prior fair EOp principle (FEOP). This has the happy result of justifying an egalitarian, rather than a prioritarian, distribution of health care. In this way, health care makes a modest but important contribution to equalizing individuals' opportunity to pursue their life plans. Daniels's approach, however, is vulnerable to at least three fundamental objections. The first objection shows that the theory has difficulty justifying *in kind* universal health care. Even worse, says the second objection, Daniels's principle fails to justify *universal* health care. And, worse still, according to the third objection, the principle does not justify public provision of health care *at all*. Let me recount these objections in turn.

Think of a patient who needs and is thus entitled to some expensive medical treatment, but who would much rather have the cash equivalent of that treatment. She might argue that she can use that same amount of money to boost her opportunity set in a far more effective way. A cancer patient with a 50 percent chance of survival may rather use the cash equivalent of her chemotherapy to sail around the world one last time (Jacobs 2004, pp. 196–200; Segall 2010*a*, pp. 83–86). Similarly, a paraplegic violinist might prefer a Stradivarius to an expensive wheelchair (Dworkin 2000, p. 61). A commitment to boosting one's opportunities to fulfill one's life plans appears not to justify *in-kind* medical treatment. This, it is plausible to think, is a major weakness in a theory of justice in health care. In reply, one thing that the proponent of Daniels's principle might say is that the principle does not speak of equal opportunity to fulfill each and every person's particular life plan, but rather speaks of a fixed range of plausible life plans (or life plans that it is reasonable for individuals in a particular society to entertain). Indeed, that latter interpretation does cohere with some other things that Daniels says, such as the relativity of that range of opportunities to one's particular talents (an issue which is not the focus of my criticism here; see Segall [2007]). Although this may get around the problem of patients whose particular life plan would benefit less from a certain medical care than from its cash equivalent, it is hard to see what would substantiate such a limitation. Recall that Daniels's account of justice justifies medical aid on the basis of its contribution to people's ability to pursue their life plans. Given that, it is not at all clear why a theory premised this way should limit itself to some average of life plans rather than to what individuals actually need to fulfill their particular life plans.

Here is the second problem. Daniels's justification for a universal system of health care, I said, is premised on its impact on EOp (to pursue one's life plan). But EOp to pursue life plans does not justify universal access to health care. Rather, it justifies providing superior treatment to those who otherwise suffer inferior opportunities, namely the poor.[1] Daniels's fair opportunity account would thus justify selective treatment that prioritizes the poor—or perhaps even one that turns the rich away from emergency rooms!—all in the name of EOp. Daniels is aware of this problem, but, as I have shown elsewhere, the argument he employs in reply, mainly resorting to depicting health care as a special and isolated sphere, is incompatible with other components of his theory (see Segall [2007; 2010*b*]).

Using the health care system to narrow the gap in opportunities in society (e.g., between the rich and the poor), as we can see, leads to consequences that are counterintuitive. But even if we did not think the latter to be counterintuitive, it is still doubtful that the health care system could be counted on to have such an impact on EOp. This is the third abovementioned objection. Daniels's fair opportunities account relies on the health care system to narrow inequalities in health. But this goal, it turns out, is beyond its capacity. In other words, the health care system is not an effective tool for narrowing inequalities in health. If we believe the epidemiological literature of the past 20 years or so, differences in access to health care could account for only about 20 percent of inequalities in health. The other 80 percent of health-determining inequalities are owed to "the social determinants of health." These include factors such as income, education, housing, and autonomy in the workplace (Marmot 2004; Marmot and Wilkinson 2006; Marmot 2013, Chapter 18, this volume). The ethical implications of these empirical findings cannot be exaggerated. Recall that the premise of Daniels's thesis is that justice requires narrowing health inequalities because of the way in which health impacts individuals' opportunities to fulfill their life plans. But to narrow down health inequalities most effectively we ought to divert resources away from hospitals and into the more significant determinants of health (equal distributions of income, education,

---

[1] For more on the dilemma between prioritizing the ill or prioritizing the poor, see Larry Temkin, "Inequality and Health," Chapter 1, this volume, and Daniel Hausman, "Egalitarian Critiques of Health Inequalities," Chapter 7, this volume.

housing, diet, jobs, and so forth). In fact, some critics of Daniels have gone so far as to suggest that a commitment to narrowing down health discrepancies would force us to shut down hospitals altogether (Sreenivasan 2007). We can see, therefore, that grounding the justification of public provision of health care in its impact on EOp to pursue one's life plans proves multiply problematic.

Equality of Opportunity for Health

The alternative to Daniels's account that I want to examine here says that individuals ought to have an equal opportunity to obtain the best health possible.[2] This view, in effect, turns Daniels's principle on its head. Instead of speaking of health (care) as a means to EOp, we speak, instead, of EOp *for* health.[3] The principle could be formulated as follows:

> *EOp for Health:* It is unfair for individuals to suffer worse health than others owing to factors that they do not control.

It is easy to see that this principle avoids the three problems that afflict Daniels's account. First, EOp for health focuses attention on, well, health. Whatever other opportunities the agent may want for herself in life, EOp for health requires that she has an equal opportunity to be as healthy as possible.[4] It therefore does not follow that she may convert her entitlement to good health into other opportunities (say, a trip around the world or a Stradivarius).[5] Second, stipulating that all individuals, irrespective, among other things, of social background, are entitled to the best health they can get avoids the second problem, that of discriminating against the rich. In other words, EOp for health justifies universal care. Finally, the principle also avoids the third problem observed, the one concerning the social determinants of health. "EOp for health" speaks

---

[2] The principle is rooted in a more general requirement of justice according to which individuals ought to have an equal opportunity for welfare. See Arneson (1989). More on this later.

[3] The term is not new, of course. See for example Roemer (1998, chapter 8). We may mention, in this context, another variant that turns Daniels's "health care as a means to EOp" on its head, namely "equality of opportunity for health *care*." This is a view held by John Harris (1999). For Harris, "equal opportunity for health care" means, rather controversially, that individuals' access to health care should not be determined either by their age or by their likelihood to benefit from the treatment. More on the former, in a moment.

[4] As mentioned, Daniels treats health care as an isolated sphere. My account takes health itself to be such an isolated sphere. In that respect, I follow John Roemer's "equality of opportunity for health" (see Roemer [1998, p. 52]).

[5] Another difference between my account and Daniels is that his account relies on the (quite plausible, I concede) assertion that health is a good that individuals want whatever else they might want in life. EOp for health does not even have to make that assumption. It guarantees to individuals the opportunity for health, *if they so choose*. In that sense, the principle proposed is more in line with liberal neutrality than is Daniels.

about individuals' health, without specifying whether it ought to be achieved by the means of clinical care (e.g., hospitals) or by other nonclinical means. Justice requires narrowing the gap in opportunities for health between individuals,[6] whichever resources it might take to do so.

This proposed approach, however, may generate its own set of problems. Let me briefly (briefly, because I have dealt with them elsewhere) mention two such potentially problematic implications. EOp for health speaks of guaranteeing to individuals the opportunity to be as healthy as they themselves choose to be. But what if individuals choose to waste, as it were, their opportunity for health? What does EOp for health say about society's obligations toward those who have damaged their own health through smoking, lack of exercise, unbalanced diet, not following their doctors' orders, and so forth? An opportunity-based principle would have to prioritize the treatment of the prudent over the imprudent, and that may strike many people as counterintuitive.[7] I shall not attempt to respond to this worry here (see Segall 2010*a*, chapter 4),[8] but simply offer the following thought. EOp for health will favor the nonsmoker over the smoker only when both individuals truly had an equal opportunity to quit smoking, as well as, obviously, an equal opportunity not to pick up the habit to begin with (Roemer 1993; 1998, chapter 8). Likewise, the principle of EOp for health would favor the compliant over the noncompliant patient only when both individuals truly did have an equal opportunity to exercise; namely, that they had equal access to safe parks in which to jog, equal availability of flexible working hours around which one might find time to exercise, and so forth (see also Le Grand 2013, Chapter 19, this volume). Since our nonideal world does not yet come close to leveling the playing field in that respect, it will very often be the case that "EOp for health" will not, in fact, abandon the (so-called) imprudent.

Here is the other potential problem with a principle that guarantees to all individuals EOp for health. We do not normally (cf. Harris 1999) think that a 30-year-old and a 70-year-old should be accorded an equal chance of receiving a (scarce) heart transplant (say, by tossing a coin to decide this). It may be problematic, then, to speak of EOp for health, pure and simple (see also Hausman 2013, Chapter 7, this volume). Obviously, that particular problem

---

[6] One way, of course, to narrow down inequalities in health is to level them down, something that does not seem very attractive. This, however, is a problem common to all egalitarian approaches to health, including Daniels (see Kamm 2001) and not just to the one proposed here. It is possible to avoid it, though, by reverting to prioritizing the opportunities for health of the worse off. I cannot, however, go into this issue here; see Segall [2010*a*, chapter 8]).

[7] On the tendency of opportunity-based theories of justice to abandon, as it were, the imprudent, see Fleurbaey (1995), Wolff (1998), Anderson (1999), and Hausman 2013, Chapter 7, this volume.

[8] Julian Le Grand was probably one of the first to defend a responsibility-sensitive account of justice in health and health care (Le Grand 1987). See also his contribution to this volume (Le Grand 2013, Chapter 19, this volume).

may be averted if we adopt what is often referred to as a "complete life view" of EOp. We may then say that, over the course of their lives, individuals should have an equal chance to lead a long and healthy life. But that would only seem to take care of differences of age. What about differences of sex? We know that, even in the best social circumstances, men and women do not have an equal opportunity to live a long and healthy life.[9] The ideal of EOp for health would commit us to narrowing the gap in life expectancy between men and women, something that would strike many readers as counterintuitive. Endorsing EOp for health thus entails defending it from this "inequality between the sexes" objection. I shall not address this objection here (see Segall 2010*a*, pp. 105–110), but will say that it might be the case that, on further reflection, the widespread intuition regarding the acceptability of health inequalities between the sexes may turn out to be not all that founded.[10]

If EOp for health could be successfully defended from the two abovementioned objections, then it may present an attractive alternative to Daniels's Rawlsian approach. In fact, the view that individuals should have an equal opportunity for health and that health ought not to depend on social *and* natural factors, I want to suggest now, could be traced back to Rawls. Of course, Rawls had very little to say about health, let alone specifying some ideal of EOp for health. But he did hold that "[t]here is no more reason to permit the distribution of income and wealth to be settled by the distribution of natural assets than by historical and social fortune" (Rawls 1971, p. 74).[11] With a change of one letter, as it were, we could read Rawls to be speaking here about how the distribution of health should be determined neither by social factors nor by natural ones. That, in a nutshell, is the very idea behind EOp for health. EOp for health strives to neutralize inequalities in health that are due to both social factors (over which the individual had no control) and ones that are due to differences in natural assets, such as one's genetic makeup.[12]

These are the merits and potential weaknesses of EOp for health as an alternative to Daniels's approach to justice in health. In the rest of this chapter, I discuss two other potential objections to EOp for health. The first of these objections says that EOp is a principle that is suitable only for the distribution of *competitive* goods. If true, this would prove problematic in the present context if we think (as I concede I do) that neither health nor health

---

[9] It may be of interest to note, though, that the more advanced a society is, the narrower the gap in life expectancy between men and women becomes (see Murray 1996, p. 18).

[10] See also the unusual and rather courageous position taken by Marmot on this point toward the end of his contribution to this volume (Chapter 18).

[11] Rawls reiterates a similar position in *Political Liberalism*: "What the theory of justice must regulate is the inequalities in the life prospects between citizens that arise from social starting positions, natural advantages, and historical contingencies" (Rawls 1996, p. 271).

[12] Since I focus on health (in contrast to how health figures more generally in EOp for welfare), I set aside the complication entailed in health conditions (whether owed to natural or social factors) that are neither remediable nor compensable. On the latter, see Hausman, Chapter 7, this volume.

care ought to be thought of as a competitive good, the way jobs or enrollment in a university potentially are. In other words, health, unlike jobs or medals, say, ought not to be a subject of a competition. That is the first challenge. The second objection to EOp for health is this. EOp for health purports to regulate inequalities in access to health. But "inequalities," some people say, can only refer to social inequalities. This is so because, the objection goes, there is no such thing as natural inequalities, only natural *differences*. If this is true, then the only obstacles that EOp for health would then be removing are social ones. And this, crucially, is a weakness in an account of justice in health. For, if EOp for health removes only social obstacles, then there is nothing in it to justify treatment for ill health that is due to natural causes, something that should be highly counterintuitive. I address this objection in the last two sections of this chapter.

Is Equality of Opportunity Necessarily Competitive?

The first claim we are investigating, then, says that EOp for health is false because the concept of EOp should only be used to regulate competitive goods (Cavanagh 2002, p. 124), and health, we all agree, ought not to be treated as a competitive good (Jacobs 2004, chapter 3).

Perhaps the first thing to notice about this objection is that it is not unique to the principle defended here. EOp for health is, in a sense, a special case of the more general principle, traced back to Richard Arneson, of EOp for welfare. Now, if there is one good that egalitarians agree ought *not* to be treated as a subject of competition it is surely the good of welfare. We might say, then, that if EOp for health is in trouble, then, at the very least, it is in good company.[13] Another point worth mentioning, one which is perhaps even more pertinent, is that the present "competitiveness objection" would spell trouble also for Daniels's account. Recall that Daniels justifies health care based on its contribution to EOp to pursue one's life plans. But are life plans a competitive good? This seems unlikely (Segall 2007, §3). If we may quote from Robert Nozick: "life is not a race in which we all compete for a prize which someone has established; there is no unified race, with some person judging swiftness" (Nozick 1974, p. 235). If the competitiveness thesis is correct, then it would follow that the core of Daniels's account, the pursuit of one's life plan, is also not a suitable subject of EOp.

[13] Admittedly, though, some of the things that John Roemer (who is often in accord with Arneson) says point to the fact that he actually has a competitive view of EOp in mind. "Thus there is, in the notion of equality of opportunity, a 'before' and an 'after': before the competition starts, opportunities must be equalized, by social intervention if need be, but after it begins, individuals are on their own" (Roemer 1998, p. 2).

None of the above, of course, serves as a rebuttal of the competitiveness objection to EOp for health, which is what I want to turn to now. In addressing this objection, I concede that the distribution of health should not be a subject of competition, but I dispute that EOp is necessarily competitive (or competitive in a way that makes it unsuitable for regulating the distribution of health). To see this, we need to delve a little into the nature of "opportunity." Often, when we speak of opportunities, we speak of them in terms of *chances* (Cavanagh 2002, p. 120). We may speak of the opportunity, as in the earlier example, to receive this or that organ for transplantation. On those occasions, we are speaking of opportunities as a matter of a zero-sum game, and these, of course, *are* competitive. But not all linguistic usages of "opportunity" comport to that. Think, for example, of one's opportunity to gaze at a sunset on the beach. "Opportunity" here signifies that one has the *choice* of whether or not to go to the beach and watch the sunset. Opportunities, then, could be understood either as chances, which are a matter of a zero-sum game, or, alternatively, as what has been termed "non-competitive opportunity" (Thomas 1977, p. 391). Here, "opportunity for X" signifies the fact that the agent may take advantage, or use, X, *if she so chooses*. Opportunity in that sense of the word, it is obvious, is not necessarily competitive. We may refer to these two common uses of opportunity, then, as (the by now familiar)[14] chance as opposed to choice.[15]

We have distinguished competitive opportunities, understood as chances, from noncompetitive ones, understood as choices. But the critic might persist that even opportunities of the latter sense are in a way competitive. Even a simple case such as one's opportunity to gaze on the sunset on the beach is in some sense competitive. To enable one's opportunity to get to the beach to watch the sunset, one requires various resources (means of transportation, time away from work, child care). All of these are scarce resources, and, as such, they are competitive. It therefore may seem as if one's seemingly noncompetitive opportunity to travel to the beach depends on a series of opportunities that *are* competitive.[16] It is perhaps this observation that may explain why some people conceive of opportunities as necessarily competitive. But a moment's reflection reveals that to speak of opportunities as competitive in this sense is trivial. This is so for the simple reason that any good that is the subject of distributive justice is for that matter scarce (at least insofar as we follow Hume's circumstances of justice). In as much as the claim regarding the competitiveness of EOp refers

[14] To recall the title of Allen Buchanan, Dan Brock, Norman Daniels, and Daniel Wikler's book on justice and genetics (*From Chance to Choice: Genetics and Justice*, Cambridge: Cambridge University Press 2000).

[15] For more on the distinction between opportunity as chance and opportunity as choice see Green 1989, p. 10.

[16] There is a good discussion of this in Green 1989, pp. 12–13.

to its ultimate reliance on the distribution of goods that are finite and scarce, then that claim is surely true but trivial. In that respect, Nozick's famous remark that to boost Smith's opportunity (in the name of EOp) without being willing to trample on (what Nozick believes to be) Jones' rights is to believe in EOp by means of "a magic wand" (Nozick 1974, p. 236). In one sense, he is certainly correct: EOp cannot be achieved without the redistribution of scarce, competitive goods. Health is no exception. Its redistribution relies on the distribution of medical care, income, education, jobs, and so forth. These are all, to a lesser or greater extent, scarce goods. (They may not necessarily be a matter of a zero-sum game, but they are nevertheless finite.) In that respect, EOp, including EOp for health, is indeed competitive. But if that is what is meant by "competitive" (as in relying on a distribution of scarce resources), then we might find that other ethical approaches to health are also guilty of relying on a competitive view of health. Think of the view that health equity requires setting some threshold of decent healthy living (Buchanan 1984) or the view (such as Daniels's) that resources should be spent so that individuals would get the best health care they require. All these patterns of distributing health rely on a redistribution of scarce, competitive resources. If EOp for health applies a competitive approach to a noncompetitive good (health), then so are its conceivable alternatives. In a sense, that is precisely Nozick's point. Nozick's objection to EOp is consistent with his objection to distributive justice more generally. Both involve the redistribution of scarce goods (goods that Nozick believes already belong to other people). And, accordingly, if one does not find the concept of distributive justice to be objectionable in itself, then neither should she find EOp for noncompetitive goods such as health to be objectionable (at least not for the reason invoked by the competitiveness objection).

EOp has traditionally been associated with meritocracy, as the idea of careers open to talent (Thomas 1977, p. 397; Green 1989, p. 5). That is probably why it was thought to be a procedure suitable for the regulation and distribution of competitive goods alone. But, fortunately, we no longer think of EOp as restricted to jobs and careers. More recent egalitarian thought, such as the abovementioned work by Richard Arneson, demonstrates this (Arneson 1989, also Roemer 1998). This scholarship, we shall see now, is relevant also in addressing the other objection to EOp for health; the one concerning natural inequalities.

Equality of Opportunity: Natural or Only Social?

EOp for health says that individuals ought to have an equal chance to be healthy, irrespective of social background or natural endowment. It is the latter requirement, the fact that EOp for health does not accept natural inequalities as given, that triggers the objection with which we are concerned here. Let me offer a formal presentation of the objection under consideration:

1. EOp for X regulates inequalities in obstacles to X.
2. To be attractive, EOp for health would have to regulate both social and natural obstacles to good health.
3. But there is no such thing as "natural inequalities."
4. EOp for health thus can only remove social inequalities in access to health.
5. EOp for health thus cannot (on its own) justify treatment for ill health that is owed to natural factors.
6. EOp for health is therefore unattractive.

In responding to this objection I shall concede premises 1 and 2, as well as the inference from 3 to 6, and restrict myself to contesting premise 3.

EOp for health aspires to remove social and natural impediments to good health, and I concede that it would not be an attractive guide to just health if it didn't. EOp for health is therefore forced to consider as unjust both inequalities in health that are owed to social factors (over which individuals have no control) and ones that are owed to natural factors. EOp for health is therefore committed to the view that differences in genetic propensity constitute unjust inequalities and, as such, warrant rectification. EOp for health thus depends on the view that there are natural inequalities. To bring out the force of the objection discussed here, let me explain why it is particular to EOp for health and does not afflict Daniels's account. As premise 1 shows, EOp for X is concerned with equalizing obstacles to X. EOp for health thus implies identifying, and leveling, inequalities in access to health. If social impediments are the only *inequalities* that affect the distribution of health, then EOp would level them and only them. This proves problematic in as much as there are natural factors that lie behind ill health (which there obviously are). Daniels's principle is not vulnerable to that problem. It says, recall, that justice requires bringing everyone's level of health up to normal species functioning. It is an attractive feature of Daniels's principle (or at least prima facie so) that it does not concern itself with distinguishing social from natural causes of ill health[17] but seeks to bring each individual up to the highest level of health. It does not hinge on the existence of "natural inequalities."

In difference to Daniels, EOp for health considers differences in genetic propensity to constitute unjust inequalities. Interestingly, until relatively recently, this last sentence would have been rather incomprehensible, let alone convincing. But, with the hindsight of Arneson's and Roemer's work on EOp, it no longer

[17] And whether or not there is, indeed, a sharp distinction between natural and social causes of ill health is yet another matter. One possible interpretation of the famous Whitehall study, for example, would suggest that there is a strong link between social determinants and basic human biology entailed in social hierarchies. (See Marmot, Chapter 18, this volume). I am grateful to an Oxford University Press referee for pointing out the relevance of this to my discussion.

strikes us as bizarre to think of EOp as entailing this rather radical implication. It is worth recalling, however, that before the late 1980s EOp was often objected to, by egalitarians, precisely on the grounds of its alleged complicity with these innate inequalities.[18] Pre-Arnesonian, as it were, EOp was considered a license for allowing inequalities in natural talent to legitimize the resulting inequalities in income and welfare. EOp, John Schaar wrote, "is really a demand for an equal right and opportunity to become unequal" (Schaar 1967, p. 238, cited in Jacobs 2004, p. 48). Rawls was equally critical: "Equality of opportunity means an equal chance to leave the less fortunate behind in the personal quest for influence and social position" (Rawls 1971, pp. 106–107). Luck egalitarians, such as Arneson, Cohen, and Roemer, have infused traditional understanding of EOp (in Cohen's case, "equality of access") with a new and radical content (Arneson 1989; Roemer 1998; Cohen 2009, p. 17).[19] Namely, their "equality of opportunity" requires leveling the playing field not just with regard to socioeconomic inequalities, but also with regard to natural ones (of talent, and indeed, health). Whatever one might think is wrong with the concept of EOp and with its application to health, it cannot be (or be thought to be) some alleged anti-egalitarian consequences (and we have Arneson's and Roemer's work to thank for that).

All this is worth bearing in mind when addressing the claim according to which the principle of EOp for health is counterintuitive because it presumes to regulate something that, in fact, does not exist, namely, natural inequalities. The objection is based on the following argument. When people speak of so-called natural inequalities, what they actually mean is natural *differences*; differences that are then transformed by social institutions into inequalities (i.e., disadvantages and advantages) (Jacobs 2004, chapter 3).[20] The deaf, to take a standard example, are at a disadvantage compared to the hearing not because they suffer from some natural inferiority. Rather, deafness, which is a natural trait, is transformed into a (social) disadvantage when the deaf individual finds herself in a society designed by and for those who hear ("normal" people) (Silvers 1998). In this way, natural traits are transformed into social disadvantages and thus give rise to inequality. There is therefore nothing natural, only social, about that inequality.[21] I object to nothing in the account describing how some natural traits are contingently translated into social disadvantages. What is true of

[18] Lesley Jacobs (2004, pp. 48-49) offers a nice summary of these views.

[19] For an application of luck egalitarianism to health see Larry Temkin (2013, Chapter 1, this volume).

[20] Notice that I treat inequalities and disadvantages as one and the same here. But it is worth pointing out that a critic of luck egalitarianism might not insist on the impossibility of natural inequalities (she might admit the natural inequality between two individuals who have different blood pressure, say), but rather on the impossibility of natural disadvantages. (I am grateful to Dan Hausman for pointing this out to me.) My discussion below covers both variants of the claim.

[21] And, consequently, any putative injustice here would be social, not natural. As Rawls writes: "The natural distribution [of talents] is neither just nor unjust; nor is it unjust that persons are born into society at some particular position. These are simply natural facts. What is just and unjust is the way that institutions deal with these facts" (Rawls 1971, p. 102).

deafness is true enough also of high cheekbones. It, also, is a natural trait that is translated into a social advantage because of a particular ideal of beauty prevalent in a given society at a given time. What I do object to is the claim that the abovementioned institutional and social aspect exhausts the way in which deafness, high cheekbones, or blindness gives rise to disadvantage.

To see this, consider a society consisting of blind and sighted individuals. Suppose (not implausibly) that some of the blind prefer to gain their sight back and none of the sighted wishes to become blind. (Of course, if any of the latter did wish to become blind that would be much cheaper and easier to bring about than would be the reverse, but leave that aside.) In as much as this is the case, we may say that the blind who wish to regain their sight are at a disadvantage compared to the sighted. Of course, it could be the case that the preferences (both of the blind to regain sight and of the sighted to remain so) are biased by the fact that their particular society is one tailored for the interests of the sighted (again, not an implausible assumption). Suppose, then, that everything conceivable (short of say, blocking the sun or banning fire and electricity) has been done to reform society such that it does not favor the sighted. And suppose further that, under those circumstances, some of the blind still prefer to regain their sight while none of the sighted prefers to lose theirs.[22] Under these circumstances, we may say, there is an inequality in terms of preference-satisfaction with regard to eyesight.[23] Is this inequality natural or social? By this stage of the discussion, this may not be a particularly interesting question (once the crucial fact of inequality has been observed), but, for what it's worth, it is difficult to see what is "social," as opposed to "natural," about this particular instance of inequality.[24]

From Equality of Opportunity to Affirmative Action in Health

The objection to speaking of "natural inequalities" (including speaking of them as the subjects of EOp) proves unsustainable. But there might be a

[22] Or suppose, to complete the picture, that the blind were given full mandate to use society's resources either to redesign social institutions so that they are more accommodating to the blind or use these resources to regain sight through some medical treatment, and that they have chosen the latter.

[23] This is, of course, precisely what Dworkin's "envy test" of inequality undertakes (see Dworkin 2000, pp. 67–68). Notice that another inequality not captured by the "social inequalities" account concerns pain. Consider Smith, who suffers from chronic migraines, and Jones, who does not. It is hard to deny that there is an inequality between them regarding pain. And yet it is difficult to see what is "social," as opposed to "natural," about this inequality. I am grateful to Tami Harel for pointing this out to me.

[24] The critic might still insist that the fact that discerning this particular inequality (in sight preferences) depends on a comparison (or envy) that makes it "social" (Jacobs 2004, p. 58.) But that comparison (of the blind to the sighted) does not make the inequality (in preference-satisfaction concerning sight) any more "social" than it is, well, "human." Inequality, in any normative sense, is based on comparisons between (human) individuals. (Something Jacobs is well aware of; see Jacobs 2004, p. 59, fn. 34.) There seems nothing social, as distinct from human, about the very act of comparison.

different, more tacit, basis for this objection. The objection might be motivated by the thought that speaking of inequalities as natural is in some sense "morally complacent." Some have used this phrase in their criticism of framing the debate on IQ differences between the races in the United States in terms of "natural inequalities."[25] Doing so is thought to be morally complacent because such statements seem to legitimize something that is essentially a social construct, and moreover, an outcome of unjust institutions.

Notice, though, that even if speaking of natural inequalities in IQ between the races is repugnant in some way, this is less obviously the case with regard to health. There seems nothing "complacent" about taking notice of the natural inequality in life expectancy between those suffering from a degenerative illness and those who don't. So, there is nothing problematic about targeting natural inequalities. Perhaps, then, there is something problematic about targeting natural inequalities when these overlap with some salient group membership (as opposed to an ad hoc one). A case in point would be gender. But we do not normally think there is something problematic about gynecology, say, as a branch of medicine. In other words, we do not think that targeting women for medical purposes is, as such, repugnant. To take an even more controversial example, there does not seem anything "morally complacent" about addressing the natural inequality in life expectancy between men and women (if anything, quite the contrary). So neither mere natural inequalities nor natural inequalities that overlap with some salient group membership are, as such, repugnant. Perhaps the problem lies elsewhere. It is generally (although not universally) thought that women and men form distinct biological categories. Targeting health inequalities between other social groups, whether on socioeconomic lines (the poor) or racial lines (blacks) is quite different in that respect. Such a practice may carry the suggestion that races and classes form distinct biological categories, which is, of course, not only controversial but also potentially repugnant.

We have a clearer view of the potential objection now. EOp for health can be problematic, then, in as much as it leads to targeting the health needs of groups that we otherwise resist seeing as forming a medical category. Think, for example, of the debate concerning the approval, in 2005, by the U.S. Food and Drug Administration (FDA) of the first ever drug specifically targeted at a racial group (African Americans). The decision was based on research (itself questionable, but set that aside for a moment) suggesting that heart patients who are black benefit significantly more from this particular drug (BiDil) than do white patients. The case is interesting

---

[25] Jacobs quotes Claude Fischer et al., who use this term to criticize the thesis of the famous *Bell Curve* (Hernstein and Murray 1994), regarding natural inequalities in IQ (see Jacobs 2004, p. 65).

for all sorts of reasons, but it is particularly interesting in the present context for the following reason. Given that, in the United States, blacks have a (significantly) lower life expectancy compared to whites, research into drugs specifically aimed at African Americans helps curb overall inequalities in health. The FDA's action, in other words, seems to follow directly from the ideal of EOp for health. (Daniels's approach, notice, would not prohibit such measures, but neither would it require taking them.)[26] Since the approval of BiDil has raised serious moral concerns, these, in turn, may reflect unfavorably on EOp for health. In particular, the FDA's decision has raised a series of concerns about turning what is essentially a social construct (race) into a medical category, adding further to the stigma suffered in the United States by people of color (Kahn 2004, cited in Hellman 2008, p. 184).[27] Does this case show that it is wrong to speak of natural inequalities in health? And, in turn, is EOp for health wrong for recommending such a policy? My answer is: not necessarily, and I want to try to explain this in the rest of this chapter.

I said that the data on which the FDA based its decision to approve BiDil were suspect. But suppose these was not. Suppose a significant correlation was indeed discovered between benefit from the use of BiDil and being African American. Even under those circumstances, notice, the approval of that drug might be thought of as problematic. For it could be the case that race is operating here as a proxy for something else, such as diet, income, and other such factors that would explain why black patients responded better than whites to the drug (Hellman 2008, p. 65). If that is the case, then perhaps the FDA was wrong to approve a drug designated for African Americans rather than insist on finding out what the fundamental correlation was. If it did the this, BiDil could have been marketed for what it truly was, namely, as a drug for "heart patients who have a high carbohydrate diet," or "patients who do not have time to exercise," or even "heart patients whose income falls below so and so." (Of course, these options may be stigmatizing in their own right and carry the risk of having the drug dubbed as one for "the poor, fat, and lazy.") And, if this is the case, then it also follows that the inequality that the drug was helping to correct was not a natural, but a social, one.

Suppose, however, that "black" is not a proxy here for something else. Suppose that BiDil is genuinely more effective for African Americans due to

---

[26] Daniels's approach, recall, calls for bringing everyone together up to perfect health (normal species functioning). Its focus, as far as I understand it, is on individuals rather than groups. EOp for health, in contrast, focuses on groups because it targets individuals who are *ex ante* worse off. Given that life expectancy is, for the most part, a group attribute, in practice, then, targeting ex ante worse-off individuals translates into identifying *groups* that suffer low life expectancy. Hence, the endorsement by EOp for health of such measures as BiDil.

[27] For more on the dilemmas that racial inequalities in health pose for bioethicists, see Norman Daniels (2013, Chapter 12, this volume).

some mysterious genetic factor.[28] Would then the FDA's decision to market it as such be the correct one? And, more to the point for us here, would such a decision reflect badly on EOp for health, given its insistence on curbing natural inequalities in health? With Deborah Hellman (who discusses this issue in the more general context of discrimination), I answer the first question in the affirmative. "If the social category 'African American' is helpful in predicting who will likely benefit from the drug and no other substitute can be found (such as diet or income), perhaps the use of this classification does not—after all—demean blacks" (Hellman 2008, p. 67). In other words, the use of racial categories would not only be medically warranted in this case, it would also not be morally suspect.[29] If certain ethnic or racial groups do have some unique biological attributes (which is, to be sure, a big "if"), then offering members of such groups, on occasion, separate medical treatment would not be troublesome.

But moreover, I want to say that developing drugs specifically targeted at such disadvantaged minority groups is a desirable policy precisely because it could be seen as a sort of "affirmative action in health." We may recall that, historically, racial categories in medical research have been used to demean and disadvantage blacks (e.g., the infamous Tuskegee syphilis experiment). At the very least, we may say, the medical establishment has been less than attentive to the medical (and other) needs of racial minorities. In the ideal scenario we have been sketching here, the approval of BiDil could be seen as a corrective step.[30] Rather than pointing out some weakness in the ideal of EOp for health, the case of "drugs for blacks," we can see now that it actually points out a potential advantage. Just as pursuing real (as opposed to merely formal) EOp in education has given us the ideal (and practice) of affirmative action, so the ideal of EOp for health allows us to start thinking in terms of affirmative action in health. It allows us to correct for persistent inequalities in health, whether owed to nature or to society.

Conclusion

EOp for health can be an attractive alternative to traditional thinking of justice in health. My aim in this chapter has been to sketch the way in which EOp for

[28] More recent research has hypothesized that BiDil's increased effectiveness for African Americans stems from the fact that people of that ethnic group are known to have lower levels of nitric oxide (NO) in their blood. Nitric oxide is a gas molecule in the air (and in the human blood) known to decrease the chances and severity of heart failure. Since the primary component of BiDil (isosorbide dinitrate) has the effect of increasing the levels of nitric oxide, and the secondary component (hydralazine HCl) increases its effectiveness, it was hypothesized that a combination of both will have a greater effect on African Americans (Taylor et al. 2004).

[29] More generally, on the permissibility of using racial categories in combating racism and other instances of inequalities, see Anderson (2010, chapter 8).

[30] Another such measure, perhaps, is the recent project of genetic research known as the African Diaspora Biobank conducted at Howard University. See http://connection.ebscohost.com/c/articles/10124904/howard-university-looks-create-dna-bank

health might improve on the currently dominant approach, namely Norman Daniels's "health care *as a means to* (fair) equality of opportunity" account. I have attempted to address here only two potential objections to EOP for health: the charge that EOp only regulates competitive goods, something that health is clearly not, and the claim that EOp for health cannot rectify ill health deriving from natural factors. Both objections, I hope to have shown, are unpersuasive. If so, EOp for health (as well as its derivative ideal of affirmative action in health) might be a useful way of thinking of justice in health.

References

Anderson, E. (1999). What is the point of equality? *Ethics, 109*, 287–337.

———. Anderson, E. (2010). *The imperative of integration.* Princeton, NJ, and Oxford: Princeton University Press.

Arneson, R. J. (1989). Equality and equality of opportunity for welfare. *Philosophical Studies, 56*, 77–93.

Buchanan, A. (1984). The right to a decent minimum of health care. *Philosophy and Public Affairs, 13*, 55–78.

Buchanan, A., Brock, D., Daniels, N., and Wikler, D. (2000). *From chance to choice: Genetics and justice.* Cambridge: Cambridge University Press.

Cavanagh, M. (2002). *Against equality of opportunity.* Oxford: Clarendon Press.

Cohen, G. A. (2009). *Why not socialism.* Princeton, NJ, and Oxford, England: Princeton University Press.

Daniels, N. (1985). *Just health care.* New York: Cambridge University Press.

———. (2008). *Just health: Meeting health needs fairly.* Cambridge: Cambridge University Press.

———. (2013). Reducing health disparities: No simple matter. In N. Eyal, S. A. Hurst, O. F. Norheim, and D. Wikler (Eds.), *Inequalities in health: Concepts, measures, and ethics* (Chapter 12). New York: Oxford University Press.

Dworkin, R. (2000). *Sovereign virtue: The theory and practice of egalitarian justice.* Cambridge, MA: Harvard University Press.

Fleurbaey, M. (1995). Equal opportunity or equal social outcome. *Economics and Philosophy, 11*, 25–55.

Green, S. J. D. (1989). Competitive equality of opportunity: A defense. *Ethics, 100*, 5–32.

Harris, J. (1999). Justice and equal opportunities in health care. *Bioethics, 13*, 392–404.

Hausman, D. (2013). Egalitarian critiques of health inequalities. In N. Eyal, S. A. Hurst, O. F. Norheim, and D. Wikler (Eds.), *Inequalities in health: Concepts, measures, and ethics* (Chapter 7). New York: Oxford University Press.

Hellman, D. 2008. *When is discrimination wrong?* Cambridge, MA and London: Harvard University Press.

Hernstein, R. J., and Murray, C. A. (1994). *The bell curve: Intelligence and culture structure in American life.* New York: The Free Press.

Jacobs, L. A. (2004). *Pursuing equal opportunities: The theory and practice of egalitarian justice.* Cambridge: Cambridge University Press.

Kahn, J. (2004). How a drug becomes "ethnic": Law, commerce, and the production of racial categories in medicine. *Yale Journal of Health Policy, Law, and Ethics, 4*, 1–46.

Kamm, F. (2001). Health and equality of opportunity. *American Journal of Bioethics, 1*, 17–19.

Le Grand, J. (1987). Equity, health, and health care. *Social Justice Research, 1*, 257–274.

———. (2013). Individual Responsibility, health, and health care. In N. Eyal, S. A. Hurst, O. F. Norheim, and D. Wikler (Eds.), *Inequalities in health: Concepts, measures, and ethics* (Chapter 19). New York: Oxford University Press.

Marmot, M. (2004). *The status syndrome: How social standing affects our health and longevity.* New York: Times Books.

———. (2013). Fair society healthy lives. In N. Eyal, S. A. Hurst, O. F. Norheim, and D. Wikler (Eds.), *Inequalities in health: Concepts, measures, and ethics* (Chapter 18). New York: Oxford University Press.

Marmot, M., and Wilkinson R. G. (2006). *Social determinants of health.* Oxford: Oxford University Press.

Murray, C. J. L. (1996). Rethinking DALYs. In Christopher J. L. Murray and Alan D. Lopez (Eds.), *The global burden of disease.* Cambridge, MA: Harvard School of Public Health, World Health Organization, World Bank.

Nozick, R. (1974). *Anarchy, state, and utopia.* Oxford: Blackwell.

Rawls, J. (1971). *A theory of justice.* Cambridge, MA: Harvard University Press.

———. (1996). *Political liberalism.* New York: Columbia University Press.

Roemer, J. E. (1993). A Pragmatic theory of responsibility for the egalitarian planner. *Philosophy and Public Affairs, 22*, 146–166.

———. (1998). *Equality of opportunity.* Cambridge, MA: Harvard University Press.

Schaar, J. (1967). Equality of opportunity and beyond. In J. Roland Pennock and J. W. Chapman (Eds.), *Nomos IX: Equality.* New York: Atherton Press.

Segall, S. (2007). Is health care (still) special? *Journal of Political Philosophy, 15*, 342–363.

———. (2010*a*). *Health, luck, and justice.* Princeton, NJ: Princeton University Press.

———. (2010*b*). Is health (really) special: Health policy between Rawlsian and luck egalitarian justice. *The Journal of Applied Philosophy, 27*, 344–358.

Silvers, A. (1998). Formal justice. In Anita Silvers, David Wasserman, and Mary B. Mahowald (Eds.), *Disability, difference, discrimination: Perspectives on justice in bioethics and public policy.* Lanham, MD: Rowman & Littlefield.

Sreenivasan, G. (2007). Health care and equality of opportunity. *Hastings Center Report, 37*, 21–31.

Taylor, A. L., Ziesche, S., Yancy, C., Carson, P., D'Agostino, R. Jr., Ferdinand, K., Taylor, M., Adams, K., Sabolinski, M., Worcel, M., and Cohn, J. N. (2004). Combination of isosorbide dinitrate and hydralazine in Blacks with heart failure. *New England Journal of Medicine, 351*, 2049–2057.

Temkin, L. Inequality and health. In N. Eyal, S. A. Hurst, O. F. Norheim, and D. Wikler (Eds.), *Inequalities in health: Concepts, measures, and ethics* (Chapter 1). New York: Oxford University Press.

Thomas, D. A. L. (1977). Competitive equality of opportunity. *Mind, 86*, 288–404.

Wolff, J. (1998). Fairness, respect, and the egalitarian ethos. *Philosophy and Public Affairs, 27*, 97–122.

11 }

When in Doubt, Equalize

PRESUMPTION OF EQUALITY JUSTIFIED

Wlodek Rabinowicz

This chapter examines *presumption of equality* (PE), which enjoins us to treat different individuals equally if we cannot discriminate between them on the basis of the available information. Obviously, a presumption of this kind is applicable in many different kinds of context. It is applicable in health contexts when it comes to the distribution of limited medical resources under circumstances in which our information about the recipients' medical needs is limited. Cases of this kind can arise, in particular, in situations of emergency, when it is impossible or too time-consuming to acquire more information about the individuals involved.[1]

I will view PE as a requirement of justice—more specifically, as a procedural principle whose goal is to promote *justice in outcome*, with the latter understood broadly as *suum cuique*—a state in which everyone receives his or her due.[2] The objective is to make PE so understood more precise and to clarify why and under what conditions it should be obeyed.

Why, then, should PE be obeyed? One natural answer is that, in the absence of relevant discriminating information, treating some individuals better than others is *arbitrary*, which is a bad thing. There's certainly some truth in this explanation. But, although arbitrariness considerations are important, they are not decisive. In some cases in which the discriminating information is missing, unequal treatment might still be right, despite its arbitrariness. To illustrate, suppose two individuals compete for two medications, *A* and *B*, of which the

[1] In some cases, relevant information that discriminates between individuals might be available, but, for some reason, it might be considered inadmissible. Cases of this kind are common in legal contexts, but they might conceivably arise even in the distribution of medical resources. I am indebted to Nir Eyal for this observation.

[2] What is due to a person might be partly dependent on noncomparative considerations (i.e., on that person's merits or deserts considered by themselves) and partly on comparative ones (i.e., on how a given person's merits compare with the merits of others). Here, both kinds of considerations are run together: We take it that both are taken into account.

former is more effective. Your task is to make the decision, but the medicine supply is limited: one dose of *A* and one dose of *B* is all you have. In this case, what is due to a person—what that person deserves—is explicated in terms of medical needs. You know that both persons are deserving (i.e., both need medication), but you have no clue which individual, if any, is in a greater need of a more effective medicine, and you have no opportunity to gather further information. Since the medications aren't equally effective, to give one to one individual and the other to the other is to treat them unequally, which is arbitrary and to that extent unsatisfactory. At the same time, you *could* treat them equally by withholding medicines from both. Such "leveling down," however, would be grossly unjust, given that both of them need to get a medication. Avoidance of arbitrariness is thus not all that matters. To justify equal treatment, when such treatment *can* be justified, we have to rely on other considerations.

At this point, I expect an objection: why not decide who gets what by a toss of a coin? This would give each individual a 50–50 chance of getting the more effective medication, but even the loser would not come away empty-handed: she would receive the less effective medication instead. Such a lottery, it seems, is itself a form of equal treatment because it gives each person equal chances. By tossing a coin, we avoid arbitrariness, but, at the same time, we see to it that both persons get medication, which they deserve.

It is true that, in the case at hand, drawing lots or tossing a coin is the obvious thing to do. Avoidance of arbitrariness *is* important. I would deny, however, that an equal lottery on unequal treatments is on a par with equal treatment. On an outcome-oriented approach to justice, which is adopted in this chapter, this is not so. Inequality in outcome may well matter from the point of view of justice. Although an equal lottery on unequal outcomes gives different individuals equal chances, the outcome of the lottery will still be unequal.[3]

Here is the suggestion I want to examine instead: principles of justice can be constraints on procedures or constraints on outcomes. Presumption norms constrain procedures, but procedural constraints can often be justified in terms of the expected outcomes of the procedures they regulate. This avenue is pursued in this chapter: the suggestion is that equal treatment should be chosen because, and to the extent that, it *minimizes the expected injustice* in outcome. When the available information does not discriminate between the individuals concerned, it will normally be the case that expected injustice will be at its lowest if individuals are treated equally. Normally, but not always. As will be seen, the medication example described above provides an exception to this rule. It violates the crucial condition on the measure of injustice that will be shown to be both necessary and sufficient for the validity of PE.

[3] This conclusion would follow, as a referee has pointed out, even on the conception of justice that gives *some* weight to the procedural aspects. As long as the final outcome also counts, equal lottery on unequal treatments is not on a par with equal treatment.

It has been suggested that the core reason behind presumption norms is to be found in the differential costs of potential errors.[4] For example, presumption of innocence in criminal law is often justified by the asymmetry in the moral costs of punishing an innocent as compared with letting a guilty person go free. Luis Katzner applied this idea to the choice between presumption of equality and its opposite, presumption of inequality:

> The only possible basis for opting for one of them rather than the other is which state of affairs one would rather see—that in which some of those who are similar are treated differently or that in which some of those who are different are treated similarly.[5]

My approach to PE is different. As will be seen, for this principle to hold, the moral cost of treating equals unequally need not be greater than that of the equal treatment of unequals.

Some presumptions might have, instead, more to do with the differential probability of errors. What is being presumed is deemed to be more probable.[6] But my argument does not assume that equality in deserts (i.e., in what is due to different persons) is probabilistically privileged in this way. Indeed, PE might well be justified even in those cases in which it is very *im*probable or even excluded that the individuals are equally deserving.

Although the justification I offer does not appeal to the differences in the costs of errors or in the probabilities of errors, it does appeal to the differences in the *expected* costs of errors. The suggestion is that, in the absence of discriminating information, we should treat individuals as if they were equal because this minimizes the expected moral cost of error: the expected injustice in treatment. To get an idea of why it is so, note that injustice might be seen as a kind of distance between how individuals are treated and how they deserve to be treated. A treatment's expected injustice can be seen as its expected distance from the just treatment. We can think of the set of possible treatments as a set of points forming a spatial area. One of these points is the just treatment but, in the absence of information, we don't know which point it is. Now, the conjecture is that equal treatment lies in the center of the area. In the absence of information that discriminates between individuals, no directions in the area

---

[4] See Ullmann-Margalit (1983, p. 159): "It is the justification of presumptions in normative terms which touches what I take to be the core of the concept of presumption.... [T]his normative type of consideration has to do with the acceptability of error." Making a presumption is grounded in "certain evaluative considerations which are primarily concerned with the differential acceptability of the relevant sorts of expected errors: the fact that one sort of error is judged to be, in the long run and all things considered, preferred on grounds of moral values or social goals to the alternative sort(s) constitutes an overriding reason for the decision underlying the presumption rule" (Ullman-Margalit 1983, p. 162).

[5] See Katzner (1973, p. 92, quoted in Ullmann-Margalit 1983).

[6] Cf. Ullmann-Margalit (1983, p. 157): "with presumption rules relating to presumptions that accord with the normal balance of probability the chance of an error . . . is reduced."

are more privileged than other directions. Therefore, by positioning ourselves in the center, we minimize our expected distance from the just treatment (i.e., keep the expected injustice at a minimum). Now, I want to examine under what conditions on the injustice measure equal treatment will have this feature of centrality. Unfortunately, as we shall see, this project is unfinished: there is still some work that remains to be done.

Individuals and Treatments

The model used here allows for different substantive interpretations. Its main components are a nonempty finite set $\mathbf{I} = \{i_1, \ldots, i_n\}$ of *individuals* and a non-empty set $\mathbf{T} = \{a, b, c, \ldots\}$ of possible *treatments* of individuals in **I**. Every treatment a in **T** is a vector $(a_1, \ldots, a_n)$, where a_k $(1 \leq k \leq n)$ is the way individual i_k is treated in a. We shall sometimes use the notation $a(i_k)$ for a_k. Treatment a is *equal* if, for all individuals, i_k and i_m, $a_k = a_m$. Other components of the model will be introduced later.

The three interpretations of the model that follow are all relatively abstract. Each may in turn be exemplified in many different ways.

INTERPRETATION 1: CAKE DIVISIONS

A "cake" is a homogeneous object or resource that is to be divided, without remainder, among the individuals in **I**. A treatment a is a vector of real numbers, $(a_1, \ldots, a_n)$, with each a_k being the share of the cake assigned by a to individual i_k. Each such share is non-negative, and together they sum up to one. **T** is the set of all possible vectors of this kind. The equal treatment, $(1/n, \ldots, 1/n)$, divides the cake equally among the members of **I**.

Representing cake divisions in this way means that we view them as *types* rather than tokens. Thus, to illustrate, if a cake is divided into pieces of equal size, it doesn't matter who gets which piece. There is therefore no reason to make this distinction in the model. This is a general feature of our approach. Treatments are interpreted as types that specify the relevant characteristics of their tokens. As a result, any two treatments in the model are supposed to be relevantly different from each other.

In health contexts, we might encounter cake-division problems when a limited supply of some medical drug is distributed among different individuals. The drug comes, say, in a liquid form, so that we can, for simplicity, treat every distribution $a = (a_1, \ldots, a_n)$ as possible. Justice considerations become relevant in a situation in which there are better or worse distributions in terms of the drug's effectiveness, but the value of the distribution depends on the medical status of the individuals involved.

INTERPRETATION 2: RANKINGS

On this interpretation, **T** is the set of all possible rankings of the individuals in **I**. That a treatment *a* ranks *i* above *j* means that *i* is treated better than *j* in *a*. A tie in *a* between *i* and *j* means that they are treated equally well. The ranking interpretation of treatments is appropriate when *ordinal* differences between the individuals are all that matters from the point of view of justice (i.e., when justice only requires that the more deserving individuals should be better treated and that the equally deserving individuals should be treated equally well).

Formally, a ranking may be represented as an assignment of ordinal numbers to individuals, with 1 being the highest level in the ranking, 2 the second highest level, and so on. The assignment of levels starts from the highest one and continues downward. Thus, equal treatment is the ranking in which every individual is assigned the highest level: (1, . . ., 1). (For another logically equivalent representation of rankings see the section on "Injustice Measure.")

In health contexts, this kind of interpretation might be applicable when we need to determine the order in which different sick or injured individuals are to be treated. Ideally, from the point of justice, this order should reflect the order of urgency that is determined by the medical status of the individuals in question.

INTERPRETATION 3: INDIVISIBLE GOODS

Suppose that *G* is a set of indivisible objects that are to be distributed, with or without remainder, among the individuals in **I**. *a*(*i*) is the subset of *G* that treatment *a* assigns to an individual *i*. For some *i*, *a*(*i*) may be empty, and, for distinct *i* and *j*, *a*(*i*) and *a*(*j*) have no elements in common. Some objects in *G* may be withheld from the distribution.

The medication case described at the beginning of the chapter provides an example drawn from a health context. In this example, *G* consists of two medications, *A* and *B*, and possible treatments amount to different partial or total distributions of *G* among the two individuals involved. The equal treatment is the distribution in which every individual is assigned the empty set.

I now move to general comments on the model. For simplicity, I exclude decision problems in which there is no equal treatment or in which there is a choice between several equal treatments (The former restriction would be violated, for example, in the interpretation in terms of rankings, if only linear rankings were available as treatments. The latter restriction would be violated in cake division if we allowed divisions in which part of the cake were withheld from distribution. The number of equal treatments would then increase from one to infinity.) I will also assume that **T** is closed under permutations on individuals. Thus, we impose two conditions on the set of treatments:

A1. For every permutation f on **I** and every a in **T**, **T** contains some b. such that, for every i in **I**, $b(f(i)) = a(i)$.

A2. There is a unique element of **T**, call it **e**, such that **e** is an equal treatment.

As we have seen, A2 is a substantial restriction. So is A1, which is a kind of completeness requirement on **T**. If **T** is the set of actually *available* treatments, this set sometimes might be too small for A1 to be satisfied. Here, however, I will ignore this difficulty and assume that **T** is sufficiently "roomy" for A1 to be satisfied.

Let me explain why I think A1 can be assumed. There are two ways of looking at **T**. If **T** is seen as the set of *conceivable* treatments, it is plausible to suppose that **T** is large enough to satisfy such conditions as A1. This way of looking at **T** is appropriate if we think of the elements of **T** as possible ways in which the individuals might *deserve* to be treated. But if **T** instead is interpreted as the set of ways in which we can treat the individuals (i.e., as the set of *available* treatments), A1 is not that plausible. Still, in the context of our discussion, the simplifying assumption that the set of available treatments is as large as the set of conceivable treatments is innocuous: remember that we want to know whether equal treatment minimizes expected injustice (and/or maximal possible injustice), as compared with available alternatives, in the absence of information that discriminates between the individuals. If this conjecture turns out to hold when the set of available treatments is large, it will obviously still hold if that set is diminished.

Given A1, every permutation f on **I** induces the corresponding permutation on **T** that to every treatment a assigns some treatment b in which it holds for every individual i, that b treats $f(i)$ in the same way as a treats i. I will refer to the union of f and the permutation f induces on **T** as an *automorphism* and use symbols p, p', and so forth to stand for different automorphisms. Intuitively, then, an automorphism is a simultaneous permutation of individuals into individuals and of treatments into treatments, in which the former permutation induces the latter:

DEFINITION An automorphism, p, is a simultaneous permutation of **I** and of **T** such that for all i in **I** and all a in **T**,

$$p(a)(p(i)) = a(i).$$

OBSERVATION Every permutation on **I** is included in exactly one automorphism.

This notion of an automorphism will come in handy later.

Here follow some examples of automorphisms. Suppose that **I** consists of three individuals, i_1, i_2, i_3, and let **T** be the set of cake divisions among the members of **I**. One automorphism would then permute i_1 into i_2, i_2 into i_3 and i_3 into i_1. This would effect the corresponding permutation on cake divisions. For example (0, 2/3, 1/3) would be permuted into (1/3, 0, 2/3). Analogously, if **T** is the set of rankings of i_1, i_2, and i_3, the automorphism that permutes i_1 into i_2, i_2 into i_3, and i_3 into i_1 involves the corresponding permutation on rankings. For example, it permutes the ranking with i_1 on top, followed by i_2 and i_3, in that order, into the ranking with i_2 on top, followed by i_3 and i_1.

It is easy to see that only equal treatment, **e**, stays invariant under all automorphisms: for all p, $p(\mathbf{e}) = \mathbf{e}$, and for all $a \in \mathbf{T}$, if $a \neq \mathbf{e}$, then for some p, $p(a) \neq a$.

We now define a relation between treatments that is going to be important in what follows:

> *Structural Identity:* A treatment a is *structurally identical* to a treatment b if and only if there exists some automorphism p such that $p(a) = b$.

Intuitively, this relation obtains between two treatments if we can get one from the other simply by reshuffling individuals while otherwise keeping the treatment unchanged. Structural identity is an equivalence relation: it is reflexive, symmetric, and transitive.[7] We can therefore partition **T** into *structures*, *S*, *S′*, and so forth, which are equivalence classes of treatments with respect to the relation of structural identity. For any treatment a in **T**, let S_a be the structure of a. As an example, suppose that **T** is the set of cake divisions among three individuals, i_1, i_2, and i_3. Consider a cake division a = (1, 0, 0). Its structure, S_a, consists of three treatments:

(1, 0, 0), (0, 1, 0), and (0, 0, 1).

To give another example, the structure of b = (1/2, 1/3, 1/6) consists of six treatments. In b, each individual gets a different share, and there are six ways in which we can assign these three different shares to three different individuals.

The number of treatments in a structure may vary but is always finite, given that **I** is finite: if **I** contains n individuals, the number of treatments in a structure is at most equal to $n!$, which is the number of possible permutations on **I**. Different automorphisms correspond to different permutations on **I**, and the number of treatments in a structure cannot exceed the number of automorphisms. But it can be smaller: for some a, several permutations on **I** induce automorphisms transforming a into the same treatment, which decreases the size of S_a. This will be the case whenever two or more individuals are treated equally in a. Thus, for example, there are two permutations on individuals

[7] This follows because it is true by definition that the set of automorphisms contains the identity automorphism and is closed under inverses and relative products.

that induce automorphisms transforming (1, 0, 0) into (0, 1, 0). Each of them assigns i_2 to i_1, but they differ in their assignments to i_2 and i_3: one assigns i_1 to i_3 and i_3 to i_2, whereas the other assigns i_1 to i_2 and i_3 to i_3. Since i_2 and i_3 are treated equally in (1, 0, 0), in both cases (1, 0, 0) is transformed into the same treatment, (0, 1, 0).

At one extreme, all the individuals are treated in the same way in **e**. Therefore, **e**'s structure contains only **e** itself. At the other extreme, if all the individuals are treated differently in *a*, any two distinct automorphisms will transform *a* into different treatments, which means that the number of treatments in *a*'s structure will equal the number of automorphisms.

Injustice Measure

Before I introduce the last component of the model, an injustice measure, let me make a further simplifying assumption: in the situations to be considered, the agent knows that *there is exactly one (perfectly) just treatment in* **T** (i.e., exactly one treatment in which everyone gets what he or she deserves). That there is at least one such treatment in **T** is plausible if we think of **T** as the set of possible ways in which the individuals might deserve to be treated. (See the earlier discussion in connection with A1.) But that the model does not contain several just treatments is a nontrivial constraint, which would sometimes need to be given up in more realistic settings. (Note that, if the model did contain several just treatments, they would need to be relevantly different from each other.)

The injustice measure **d** is based on this uniqueness assumption. **d** is a function from pairs of treatments to real numbers, with the following interpretation: **d**(*a*, *b*) specifies the degree of injustice of *a* on a hypothetical supposition that it is *b* that is the (perfectly) just treatment. This degree of injustice can be understood as *distance* from *a* to *b*: to the extent *a*'s injustice is greater, *a* is farther away from *b*. **d** can therefore be assumed to satisfy the standard conditions on a distance measure:

(D0) $\mathbf{d}(a, b) \geq 0$ (*Non-negativity*)
(D1) $\mathbf{d}(a, b) = 0$ if and only if $a = b$ (*Minimality*)
(D2) $\mathbf{d}(a, b) = \mathbf{d}(b, a)$ (*Symmetry*)
(D3) $\mathbf{d}(a, b) + \mathbf{d}(b, c) \geq \mathbf{d}(a, c)$ (*Triangle Inequality*)

Interpreting **d** as distance gives the model a geometric flavor. The pair (**T**, **d**) is then a *metric space*: a set of points with a distance measure defined on it. The set **I** of individuals may be seen as the set of *dimensions* of that space: a point $a = (a_1, \ldots, a_n)$ is defined by its coordinates on the different dimensions i_k in **I**.

As will be seen in the next section, interpreting injustice as distance goes well beyond what's needed for our purposes. In particular, it need not be assumed that the injustice measure is symmetric or that it satisfies triangle inequality. Nevertheless, this geometric interpretation is not implausible, and, in addition, it makes the model more intuitive and easier to grasp.

One further very natural condition on **d** is Impartiality, which requires **d** to be invariant under automorphisms:

IMPARTIALITY For all automorphisms p and all a, b in **T**, $\mathbf{d}(p(a), p(b)) = \mathbf{d}(a, b)$.

According to Impartiality, if one permutes the individuals in two treatments in the same way, the distance doesn't change. In other words, the injustice measure pays no attention to "who is who." Thus, for example, giving all of the cake to the individual who only deserves a small share is equally unjust independently of who it is who gets this unfair advantage.

How is **d** to be understood on the different interpretations of our model? Consider cake divisions first. It seems plausible that the distance between two cake divisions should be a strictly increasing function of the (absolute) differences, for each individual i, between the shares of the cake that go to i in these treatments. That is, the distance between treatments a and b should be a strictly increasing function of $|a_1-b_1|, \ldots, |a_n-b_n|$. The simplest function of this kind is the sum:

$$\mathbf{d}(a,b) = \sum_{i=1}^{n} |a_i - b_i|$$

This kind of measure is sometimes called the *city block* distance. If we instead go for the sum of the *squared* differences and take the square root of that sum, we get the Euclidean distance. The cityblock and the Euclidean measure are two instances of the class of *Minkowski distance* functions. **d** belongs to this class if and only if for some $k \geq 1$ and for all a, b in **T**,

$$\mathbf{d}(a, b) = \sqrt[k]{\sum_{i=1}^{n} |a_i - b_i|^k}$$

If $k = 1$, **d** is the city block distance; if $k = 2$, it is the Euclidean distance. The higher k is, the more disproportionate influence is given, by exponentiation, to the larger differences $|a_i-b_i|$, as compared with the smaller differences. Only if $k = 1$, are all the differences given influence proportionate to size.

How is the distance to be understood for rankings? Again, there are several possibilities, but the proposal by Kemeny and Snell is perhaps most well known. A ranking might be seen as a set of ordered pairs of individuals: a pair (i, j) belongs to a ranking a if and only if a ranks i at least as highly as it ranks j. The distance between two rankings, a and b, can then be measured by the number of pairs that belong to either a or b but not to both these rankings. It is easy to show that this definition satisfies our conditions D0 – D3.[8]

For the case of indivisible goods, we lack a plausible *general* definition of distance. Different situations that exemplify the general structure of indivisible goods require different specifications of the injustice measure. Let us therefore focus on the medication example we started the chapter with. The example involves two medications, one more effective, A, and the other, B, less so, and two individuals. Let us suppose that one of them is in a greater need of medical help.

There is no need to fully specify a suitable injustice measure **d**. I will only assume that the following holds: the distance between alternative treatments in which each individual gets a medication, that is, the distance between $a = (\{A\}, \{B\})$ and $b = (\{B\}, \{A\})$, is shorter than the distance to each of these treatments from the equal treatment $\mathbf{e} = (\varnothing, \varnothing)$, in which the medication is withheld from both individuals. To put it formally,

$$\mathbf{d}(\mathbf{e}, a) > \mathbf{d}(b, a) = \mathbf{d}(a, b) < \mathbf{d}(\mathbf{e}, b).$$

Intuitive motivation: if a is just or if b is just, both individuals deserve a medication. But then withholding the medication from both is even more unjust than giving the more effective medication to the less needy individual. Also, because **d** is symmetric, $\mathbf{d}(b, a) = \mathbf{d}(a, b)$.

Information Measure and Expected Injustice

Apart from fixed components **I**, **T**, **e**, and **d**, our model also contains one variable component: a probability distribution P on **T**, which reflects the agent's information about the case at hand. For every a in **T**, $P(a)$ stands for the agent's probability for a being the (perfectly) just treatment.[9]

---

[8] Cf. Kemeny and Snell (1962, pp. 9–23, in the chapter Preference Ranking: An Axiomatic Approach). They show that this measure is the only distance function on rankings that satisfies Impartiality (or Neutrality, as they call it), a couple of more or less technical axioms (Normalization and Reducibility), and the following important condition: *Betweenness*: If ranking b is "between" rankings a and c, in the sense that it is included in their union and includes their intersection, then $\mathbf{d}(a, b) + \mathbf{d}(b, c) = \mathbf{d}(a, c)$. The first formulation of this result was given in Kemeny (1959). For a recent account, which shows that one of the technical axioms (Reducibility) already follows from the other conditions, see Can and Storcken (2013). As for alternative proposals of distance measures on rankings, see, for example, Cook and Seiford (1978) and Duddy and Piggins (2012).

[9] Fixed components of the model are marked in bold, whereas the variable components are italicized. We take P to be variable because we want to examine whether equal treatment ought to be chosen for every P that does not discriminate between the individuals.

Since, as we have assumed, the agent knows that there is exactly one just treatment in **T**, we take it that the *P*-values for different treatments sum up to 1. There is a difficulty here, though. On some interpretations, such as cake divisions, the number of possible treatments in **T** is infinite. In such cases, the sum of *P*-values for different treatments might be lower than 1. It might even be zero if the probability is distributed uniformly over **T**. In such a uniform distribution, each treatment gets the probability zero (unless we allow infinitesimals as probability val ues), and the sum of zeros is zero. This difficulty can be dealt with by replacing summation with integration, but to keep things mathematically simple I will assume that there exists a *finite* subset of **T** such that the agent is certain that the just treatment belongs to that particular subset. Then the *P*-values of different treatments will sum up to 1, and, for any subset *Y* of **T**, we can define *P*(*Y*), the probability that *Y* contains the just treatment, as the sum of *P*-values assigned to the elements of *Y*:

$$P(Y) = \sum_{a \in Y} P(a).$$

To say that the available information does not discriminate between the individuals in **I** must mean that structurally identical treatments are assigned the same *P*-values. Thus, we are led to the following definition:

> *P does not discriminate between the individuals* if and only if, for all structurally identical *a* and *b* in **T**, $P(a) = P(b)$.[10]

Two treatments are structurally identical if there is an automorphism that transforms one into the other. Thus, *P* does not discriminate between the individuals if and only if it is *invariant under automorphisms*: for every *p* and *a*, $P(a) = P(p(a))$.

The *expected injustice* of a treatment *a* with respect to a given probability function *P* is the *P*-weighted sum of its distances to different possible treatments. Thus, in this sum, the distance from *a* to every treatment *b* is weighted with the probability of *b* being *the* just treatment.

$$\text{Expected injustice: } \mathrm{EI}_P(a) = \sum_{b \in \mathbf{T}} P(b)\, \mathbf{d}(a, b).$$

For the expected value to be a meaningful notion, it is enough if the underlying value function is unique up to positive affine transformations (i.e., up to the choice of unit and zero). Representing injustice as *distance* means that the only thing that is left for an arbitrary decision is the unit of measurement. The zero point for distance is not arbitrary: that each point's distance to itself, and only to itself, equals zero is a defining feature of a distance measure. But even apart from this nonarbitrary zero point, letting the injustice measure **d**

---

[10] Our finiteness constraint on *P* doesn't hinder *P* from being indiscriminative in this way. The reason is that every structure is finite if **I** is finite.

be a distance function is more than we need to give meaning to the notion of expected injustice. Neither symmetry nor triangle inequality are necessary for this purpose. Still, as suggested earlier, treating injustice as distance is not implausible and makes the model easier to grasp.

Expected Injustice and Equal Treatment

Consider the following hypothesis:

> *Minimization of Expected Injustice*: For every P that does not discriminate between the individuals and every treatment a in $\mathbf{T}$, $\mathrm{EI}_p(\mathbf{e}) \leq \mathrm{EI}_p(a)$.

In other words, on this hypothesis, equal treatment minimizes expected injustice in the absence of discriminating information. This is one way of accounting for the reasons behind PE. We want to know under what conditions this hypothesis is going to hold.

If Y is a finite set of treatments, let $\bar{\mathbf{d}}(a, Y)$ stand for a's *average distance* to the treatments in Y:

$$\bar{\mathbf{d}}(a, Y) = \textstyle\sum_{b \in Y} \mathbf{d}(a, b)/\mathrm{card}(Y).$$

The following condition on $\mathbf{d}$ can be shown to be both *necessary and sufficient* for the minimization of expected injustice:

> *Structure Condition:* For every structure $S \subseteq; \mathbf{T}$ and every $a \in \mathbf{T}$, $\bar{\mathbf{d}}(\mathbf{e}, S) \leq \bar{\mathbf{d}}(a, S)$.

The condition states that, for every structure, equal treatment has a minimal average distance to that structure, as compared with other treatments.

> *Sufficiency*: Structure Condition $\Rightarrow$ minimization of expected injustice.
>
> *Proof of Sufficiency:*
>
> *Claim:* If P does not discriminate between the individuals, then for every $a \in \mathbf{T}$, $\mathrm{EI}_p(a) = \sum_{S \subseteq \mathbf{T}} P(S)\, \bar{\mathbf{d}}\,(a, S)$.

That is, in the absence of discriminating information, a's expected injustice is a weighted sum of its average distances to different structures, with weights being the probabilities of these structures. Here's the proof of the claim:

> *Proof of the Claim:* $\mathrm{EI}_p(a) = \sum_{b \in \mathbf{T}} P(b)\, \mathbf{d}(a, b)$ [by the definition of EI] $= \sum_{S \subseteq \mathbf{T}} \sum_{b \in S} P(b)\, \mathbf{d}(a, b)$ [since $\mathbf{T}$ can be partitioned into structures] $= \sum_{S \subseteq \mathbf{T}} \sum_{b \in S} (P(S)/\mathrm{card}(S))\; \mathbf{d}(a, b)$ [since P is indiscriminative] $= \sum_{S \subseteq \mathbf{T}} P(S) (\sum_{b \in S} \mathbf{d}(a, b)/\mathrm{card}(S))$ [by algebra] $= \sum_{S \subseteq \mathbf{T}} P(S)\, \bar{\mathbf{d}}(a, S)$ [by the definition of $\bar{\mathbf{d}}$]

Given the Structure Condition, the average distance from $\mathbf{e}$ to a structure S never exceeds the corresponding distance from any a to S. Consequently, the Claim implies that $\mathrm{EI}_p(\mathbf{e}) \leq \mathrm{EI}_p(a)$. □

We now want to prove that the Structure Condition is *necessary* for minimization of expected injustice:

> *Necessity*: Structure Condition $\Leftarrow$ minimization of expected injustice.
>
> *Proof*: We need to show that if the Structure Condition is violated by our model, i.e., if for some structure S and treatment a, $\bar{\mathbf{d}}(a, S) < \bar{\mathbf{d}}(\mathbf{e}, S)$, then minimization of expected injustice is violated as well. The latter means, more precisely, that there exists a probability function P that does not discriminate between the individuals and is such that, with respect to P, the expected injustice of a is lower than the expected injustice of **e**. To construct a P like this, we simply let it be the uniform probability distribution on S. □

To forestall possible misunderstandings, it should be pointed out that for a *particular* P that does not discriminate between the individuals, **e** might minimize expected injustice with respect to that P even if the underlying injustice measure **d** happens to violate the Structure Condition. However, that condition is necessary if **e** is to minimize expected injustice for *all* possible Ps that do not discriminate between the individuals, as required by the hypothesis of minimization of expected injustice.

Is the Structure Condition satisfied by the different interpretations of our model? I think it is fair to say that this condition *usually* holds. It can be shown to hold for all Minkowski-distance measures on cake divisions.[11] It can also be shown to hold for the Kemeny-Snell distance between rankings.[12] But this condition is violated in the medication example presented at the beginning of the chapter. There, the distance between treatments $a = (\{A\}, \{B\})$ and $b = (\{B\}, \{A\})$ is shorter than the distance to each of them from the equal treatment $\mathbf{e} = (\varnothing, \varnothing)$. Since the set $\{a, b\}$ is a structure, it immediately follows that the average distance from a to this structure is shorter (in fact, more than twice as short) than the corresponding average distance from **e** to the structure in question:

$$\bar{\mathbf{d}}(a, \{a, b\}) = (\mathbf{d}(a, a) + \mathbf{d}(a, b))/2 = \mathbf{d}(a, b)/2 < (\mathbf{d}(\mathbf{e}, a) + \mathbf{d}(\mathbf{e}, b))/2 = \bar{\mathbf{d}}(\mathbf{e}, \{a, b\}).$$

Since the Structure Condition is violated in this case, it follows that there exists a probability function P that does not discriminate between the individuals and with respect to which **e**'s expected injustice exceeds the expected injustice of a: one such P is the uniform probability distribution on $\{a, b\}$. If we are certain that the just treatment is either a or b, with each of these treatments being an equally likely candidate to the title, treating the individuals equally by withholding the medications from both will not minimize expected injustice.

[11] For the proof, see Rabinowicz (2008, appendix A).

[12] For the proof, see Rabinowicz (2008, appendix B).

As we have seen, the Structure Condition is both sufficient and necessary if equal treatment is to minimize expected injustice. But this condition is neither especially transparent nor intuitive. It has a feel of a constraint that itself should be derivable from some more basic and simple conditions. What these conditions might be is not clear to me, however. One of them would probably be Impartiality, mentioned earlier, from which it follows that, for each structure, all its elements are equidistant from the equal treatment. But we obviously need other conditions as well.[13] These would have to guarantee, together with Impartiality, that equal treatment lies, so to speak, in the center of each structure[14] and thus give us the Structure Condition. Finding these underlying conditions is a major outstanding problem that is left for further inquiry.[15] Another outstanding problem, or a set of problems, is the investigation of PE in various possible extensions of the model: with more than one equal treatment, with indiscrimination between individuals that is limited to a proper subset of the set of all individuals, with more than one just treatment, and so on.

References

Cook, W. D., and Seiford, L. D. (1978). Priority ranking and consensus formation. *Management Science, 24*, 1721–1732.

Can, B., and Storcken, T. (2013). A re-characterization of the Kemeny distance. Working paper RM/13/009. Maastricht: Graduate School of Business and Economics.

Duddy, C., and Piggins, A. (2012). A measure of distance between judgment sets. *Social Choice and Welfare, 39*, 855–867.

Katzner, L. I. (1973). Presumptions of reason and presumptions of justice. *The Journal of Philosophy, 70*, 89–100.

Kemeny, J. (1959). Mathematics without numbers. *Daedalus, 88*, 577–591.

Kemeny, J. G., and Snell, J. L. (1962). *Mathematical models in the social sciences*. Cambridge, MA: MIT Press.

Rabinowicz, W. (2008). Presumption of equality. In Martin L. Jönsson (Ed.), Proceedings of the 2008 Lund-Rutgers conference, Lund Philosophy Reports (pp. 109–155). Lund: Department of Philosophy.

Rabinowicz, W. (2010). If in doubt, treat'em equally—A case study in the application of formal methods to ethics. In T. Czarnecki, K. Kijania-Placek, O. Poller, and J. Wolenski (Eds.), The analytical way. Proceedings of the 6th European congress of analytic philosophy (pp. 219–243). London: College.

Ullmann-Margalit, E. (1983). On presumption. *The Journal of Philosophy, 80*, 143–163.

---

[13] Impartiality is satisfied in the medication example despite the fact that this example violates the Structure Condition.

[14] I.e., in the center of a regular geometric figure whose vertices are the elements of a given structure.

[15] I am indebted to the participants and the organizers of the conference on measurement and ethical evaluation of health inequalities at Fondation Brocher in Geneva 2010 for helpful comments and encouragement. This paper is a significantly revised and radically shortened version of Rabinowicz (2010), which in its turn was a short and revised version of Rabinowicz (2008).

12 }

Reducing Health Disparities

NO SIMPLE MATTER

Norman Daniels

It is a commonplace in recent public health discussions to suggest that we should give some priority in our policies to reducing health inequities between social groups. This theme has emerged as important in the United States, where race "disparities" (a euphemism for "inequities") are significant and generally thought to be unjust (Institute of Medicine [IOM] 2002). It is a more developed feature of public policy in Europe, where a Health For All strategy has evolved (World Health Organization [WHO] Europe 1999). In the United Kingdom, health inequalities by class, and more recently by ethnicity, have been the subject of major reports leading to policy initiatives both within the health sector and across sectors aimed at "narrowing the health gap" (Secretary of State 1999, p. 5, cited in Graham 2004; Department of Health 1999, 2003; Graham and Kelly 2004). These initiatives address the social determinants of health and the ways inequalities in their distribution produce health inequalities across social groups. In Sweden, special attention has been paid to limiting social inequality as a way of reducing health inequalities (Ostlin and Diderichson 2001). In Europe, more generally, reducing health disparities has emerged as a major policy theme (WHO Europe 2002). Globally, the World Health Organization (WHO) and some of its regional organizations have made equity in health central to their agenda.[1]

I have argued elsewhere (Daniels et al. 1999, Daniels 2008) that a health inequality between social groups is unjust when it results from an unjust distribution of the socially controllable factors affecting population health. We can illustrate what counts as an unjust distribution of those factors, I claim, using Rawls's account of justice as fairness because his principles of justice capture key socially controllable determinants of health. This account of health inequities

[1] For example, the Pan American Health Organization (PAHO) highlights work on equity at http://www.paho.org/English/AD/GE/Ethnicity.htm. Accessed March 10, 2011. The WHO World Health Report 2006 emphasizes work in reducing health inequalities: See http://www.who.int/hrh/whr06_consultation/en/index9.html. Accessed March 10, 2011.

is intended to be quite general, capturing our concerns about race or gender inequalities in health, as well as about socioeconomic inequalities: when any of these inequalities is the result of socially controllable factors, they count as inequities. We might need to allow for some variation among these causes, which may differ in their tractability, and that may complicate the story; but for the sake of discussion, leave that issue aside. Arguably, if social policy has produced the health inequality, we may have additional reasons for wanting to reduce it. I say "additional reasons" because we, in any case, have reasons based on our social obligations to meet health needs, however they arise.

Life is not so simple, however, even when injustice is involved. I argue in what follows that unexpected complexity faces policy makers when they aim to reduce injustice in this way. Many policies that would reduce inequities between groups encounter the same issues of distributive justice that I have elsewhere called "unsolved rationing problems" (Daniels 1993): the priorities problem, the aggregation problem, and the best outcomes/fair chances problem.[2] These unsolved distributive problems, so common in medical resource allocation contexts, describe the baseline distributions of health neutrally. Although some people are clearly in worse health to start with than others in the priority problem, for example, no judgment is made about whether that inequality is itself unfair or unjust. The baseline is taken as a given, without prior moral judgment about how it arose.

This moral neutrality regarding the baseline may carry over from the neutrality that seems appropriate in medical contexts. In those contexts, we properly focus on the medical need and not on a moral account of how the need arose. Thus, emergency medical personnel treat beating or gunshot victims whether they initiated the attack or were innocently caught up in it. Doctors attend to the broken leg whether it comes from a fall while fleeing the police, from skiing, from a mugging, or from a slip on the ice. In these contexts, there is a deliberate detachment from moral evaluation of the baseline.[3] Similarly, the unsolved distribution problems focus on relevant health needs without the complication of a moral account of their origin.

The morally problematic features of the baseline are what make health inequalities into inequities. Inequalities in the prevalence of some diseases between blacks and whites are the result of the unjust distribution of many

[2] The priorities problem is posed by the question of how much priority should we give to those who are worst off. The aggregation problem asks when we should allow a modest benefit to a larger number of people outweigh a significant benefit to a smaller number. The best outcomes/fair chances problem asks when we should give people fair chances at a benefit rather than favor getting a best outcome. Reasonable people will disagree about the tradeoffs permissible in each problem.

[3] When the Chinese government decided to expand antiretroviral treatments for HIV/AIDS patients, it gave priority to people who were infected by contaminated blood. Since giving priority to these "innocents" wronged by the state can reinforce the stigma attaching to people infected by sex workers or intravenous drug use and make it harder to fight the epidemic, there are strong public health reasons for not deviating from some cases of moral neutrality in the name of rectifying injustice.

socially controllable factors, including income, job opportunity, education, housing quality and location, and racial discrimination itself. Other inequalities in the health outcomes for specific diseases, when many other factors are controlled for (education, insurance coverage, income), appear to be the result of racially distinct utilization decisions by clinicians—perhaps conscious or unconscious stereotyping. Similarly, the higher prevalence of HIV/AIDS among more young females than males in southern Africa is the result of an unjust distribution of property and marriage rights, with extreme poverty leading to transactional sex and the lack of empowerment of women to control their sexual and reproductive choices. Justice opposes the health inequality—the health inequity—in all these examples.

The unsolved rationing problems interact with efforts to reduce health inequities. Suppose we are able to improve the condition of worst-off groups, say those victimized by some form of racism, only by targeting interventions for them in ways that reduce significantly the benefits we can deliver to others. To give a high degree of priority to reducing an unjust racial inequality in health, we may have to forego using resources more effectively to improve the health of larger numbers of other people. What price in aggregate health should we pay to reduce unjust health disparities? Does the answer depend on the type or degree of injustice? Or, on the relative gains and losses to the different groups? In either case, reasonable people are likely to disagree about the fairest policy. I claim that we must appeal to fair process to legitimize decisions of this sort.

The tradeoff between reducing health inequalities and promoting population health arises as a result of well-intentioned policy. Frequently, measures intended to improve population health have a differential impact on subgroups in the population. A smoking cessation campaign may be more effective for better-off groups, say professionals and groups with higher income and higher educations levels, than for manual workers or lower socioeconomic status (SES) groups (Barbeau et al. 2004). Given that smoking levels are already higher for lower SES groups, the inequality in smoking rates may increase, along with attendant health effects. What should we do when efforts to improve population health increase health disparities? Does it matter if we think the initial disparity is itself unjust and we therefore make it worse while trying to improve health? Is it fair if better-off groups improve more and increase their relative advantage as long as worse-off groups improve somewhat? Our goal here is to examine this troubling conflict between reducing unjust health disparities and promoting population health fairly.

Race and Gender Inequities Illustrated

In what follows, it is important that we have clearly in mind some examples of health inequalities between groups that we agree are unjust. Consider the following examples of health inequalities that most people would consider unjust:

> *A. Race inequity in access.* Controlling for type of payer, treatment site, and clinical condition, physicians underutilize important treatments, such as cardiac catheterization (Schulman et al. 1999) and renal transplantation (Epstein et al. 2000) in blacks as compared to whites. The Schulman study used black and white, male and female actors in videotapes. They were dressed similarly and had matching educational and occupational profiles and were given identical clinical descriptions. Blacks were offered catheterization less often than were whites, and women less often than were men, with black women receiving the lowest referral rate. The Epstein study noted that there was overutilization among whites even while there was underutilization for blacks.

Whether we think there is overt racism among providers, or subconscious stereotyping that has no malicious intent, the effect is an inequality of access to crucial, even lifesaving, interventions. This inequality of access by race (as well as gender, in the Schulman study) makes this an example of a health inequity (even if we believe that some of the socially controllable factors are more tractable than others). A significant research effort is needed to uncover the exact features of provider beliefs about patients that contribute to these differences (van Ryn 2002), although we know that there is a negative perception of blacks and lower SES patients on such important issues as intelligence, affiliation with patients, and the likelihood of patient compliance (van Ryn and Burke 2000). Understanding the source of the discrimination will be important in devising interventions that remedy the problem.

> *B. Health inequity directly induced by the experience of racism.* There is substantial evidence for direct, negative health effects of the experience of racism. A comprehensive review of recent literature (Williams et al. 2003) showed a preponderance of studies evidencing a strong association between the experience of discrimination and (a) psychological distress, (b) major depression, and (c) physiological measures of stress, such as blood pressure (Harrell et al. 2003).

With regard to the latter, there is some evidence that people who "internalize" rather than "resist" discrimination have higher blood pressure, so coping strategies moderate the effects of discrimination for some people (Krieger and Sidney 1996; Noh and Kaspar 2003). Since the racism people experience is diverse in its source, remedying the health inequity that results from it is likely to be more difficult than altering the discriminatory behavior of providers, as in the catheterization and renal transplant example. Of course, it is an empirical question whether this claim about tractability is correct.

C. Health inequity resulting from cumulative exposures to health risks as a result of institutional racism. In 1990, black men at age 20 could expect to live 47 more years, 9 of which would be with some level of disability. White men at 20 could expect 54.6 more years, with at least a year less of disability (Haywood and Heron 1999). Compared to white males, black males aged 51–61 have higher prevalence of hypertension, stroke, diabetes, kidney and bladder problems, and stomach ulcers; whites have a higher prevalence of cardiac and chronic obstructive pulmonary disease, high cholesterol, and back and eye problems. In sum, blacks have a higher mortality rate and rate of disability in middle age.

Socioeconomic status explains most of the aggregate black-white differences in health, but we should not infer that it is only class and not race that is to blame. The broad legacy of racism, overt and institutional, in American society, disproportionately confines blacks in lower SES groups. As a result, merely pointing to the significance of SES in explaining race disparities in health understates the role of unfair social and economic disadvantage suffered by blacks. This point is true even if we cannot counter race inequalities without simultaneously addressing class inequalities (Kawachi, Daniels, Robinson 2005).

Despite the importance of SES, within each SES level, the health of blacks is worse than that of whites (House and Williams 2000). In addition, segregation—including hypersegregation and other severe forms of segregation—is associated with multiple risks factors for blacks as compared to whites (Acevedo-Garcia et al. 2003). These health risks accumulate over a lifetime, beginning in infancy and early childhood, so that much of the middle-age increase in black mortality rates as compared to whites must be understood as one of cumulative disadvantage and exposure to a wider range of health risks.

Although risky individual behaviors contribute to the health inequality, all the major health behaviors (smoking, immoderate drinking and eating, lack of exercise) explain only 10–20 percent of SES inequalities in health. If, however, all SES-associated risk factors are considered, including environmental exposures and stress factors from economic vulnerability and weaker social supports, lower levels of control over work and life, a much larger proportion (50–100 percent) of SES-associated health inequalities can be explained, thus suggesting a broad pattern of accumulated risk over childhood and adult life. Since the health inequalities produced by SES and race vastly exceed in scope those produced by inequalities in access to health care, broad intersectoral efforts will be needed to reduce these health inequalities.

D. Gender inequity in the HIV/AIDS epidemic. Girls and young women (aged 15–24) have a significantly higher incidence of HIV/AIDS than do comparable males in sub-Saharan Africa (UNFPA, UNAIDS, and UNIFEM 2004). The factors that contribute to this difference are quite diverse. Although

> there is some biological vulnerability of young girls to HIV, the key determinants of the health inequality are diverse, including extensive poverty, which induces transactional sex at an early age, including to pay for school fees; and gender inequalities in property rights and marriage and divorce rights, which give women little room to protect themselves from unsafe sex and early marriage to much older men who may well be HIV positive. To reduce the health inequality would require not only preventive efforts in the health sector, but educational and legal reforms that eliminate the inequality in power between genders and restore to women in this setting a constellation of human rights that would protect them in this epidemic.

These examples are all relatively uncontroversial instances of health inequities. In addition, each would count as a race or gender inequity in health because each involves an unjust distribution of the socially controllable factors affecting health. This claim is true if we are talking about access to needed medical services, as in premise A. It is true if we are talking about the immediate health consequences of discriminatory practices that violate protections of equality of opportunity, as in premises B or C. And it is true if we are talking about violations of both basic liberties and the protection of opportunity, as in D.

In each of these cases, we have clear reasons of justice to intervene to reduce the health inequality. In some cases, it may be clearer just what the point of intervention is: perhaps we can change provider utilization decisions in A, and thus access, more easily than we can reduce the exposure to racism and its bad direct effects on health in B or indirect effects in C. Whatever we do, reducing inequities requires an investment of resources. We turn to the distributive implications of such investments now.

Encounters with Unsolved Rationing Problems

Pursuit of the health-related Millennium Development Goals (MDG) provides an interesting example of how the unsolved distributive problems arise within efforts to reduce health inequalities. Unlike the examples of race and gender just discussed, and to which we return shortly, the MDG goals of inequality reduction are not premised on the explicit judgment that the inequality is unjust. Still, it moves us beyond the moral neutrality of the medical rationing cases because it assumes that the inequalities are unacceptable and should be reduced. Five of the eight internationally negotiated MDGs are directly inequality reducing within each country that pursues them because their targets aim at poverty reduction or providing primary education to those who lack it. The three health targets, however, are stated in terms of reducing health outcome measures that apply to the whole population, that is, as an aggregate, such as the under-5 child mortality rate.

David Gwatkin (2002) models two extreme approaches to these aggregate health goals. A maximizing approach seeks rapid achievement of the target by directing resources to those subgroups in the population who are already better off but easier to reach and improve. It will increase intracountry inequality yet is likely to be attractive to international donors aiming to show rapid progress. From their perspective, the maximizing strategy may also reduce embarrassing inequalities across countries more rapidly. In contrast, an egalitarian approach aims to help those who are worst off (within each country) first, then the next worst off, and so on. It sacrifices some aggregate health benefit to the goal of giving priority to those who are worse off and whose under-5 mortality rate may be harder to improve. But how much priority? How much sacrifice of aggregate under-5 mortality should we accept to give greater benefits to worst-off groups? The problem also can be posed as a conflict between best outcomes and fair chances. Best (aggregate) outcomes would result by getting the numbers up quickly. But should we not give worse-off groups some fair chance at significant benefits instead? If we pursue the maximizing strategy, worst-off groups have little chance at some benefit.

In the Gwatkin example, nothing explicit is said about the injustice of the baseline inequality, although the MDG goals imply that high levels of poverty and avoidable child mortality are unacceptable. Nevertheless, reasonable people may still disagree about the tradeoffs involved and give weight to different policy alternatives. If the worst-off group with regard to under-5 mortality happens to be an ethnic minority that has long suffered exclusion and discriminatory policies, then Gwatkin's example more closely resembles cases of inequity discussed in the previous section. Similarly, if the next worse-off group lives in a very poor agricultural region that has been underserved by public health and medical interventions, their disadvantage also counts as an inequity. Does making the injustice of the baseline more explicit affect our thinking about what tradeoffs between equity and maximization we would consider acceptable?

How Much Priority to Reducing Existing Health Inequities?

We can consider the problem by focusing on an actual, clear example of a health inequity. When we understand the determinants of the gender inequality in HIV/AIDS prevalence among people aged 15–24 in sub-Saharan African, there is no question that the inequality is an inequity that should be redressed. With an international effort to provide antiretroviral treatments under way, we might think one indicator of fair access to treatments would be to match prevalence to treatment rates. That is, in this age group, we should treat more women than men. Suppose this goal would be difficult to achieve because of the social stigma facing infected women? Accordingly, suppose efforts to enroll proportionally more women for treatment meant treating fewer people over all because it is easier and quicker to enroll men?

Of course, higher rates of treatment will not redress the inequality in prevalence itself. That would require non–health sector efforts, such as changing gender-biased divorce and marriage laws, eliminating gender inequalities in property rights, eliminating school fees so young girls would not have to resort to transactional sex to pay them, and so on. It would also involve public health measures that reduced sexually transmitted diseases and provided effective education about safe sexual practices.

An international agency understanding this situation might conclude that it could more efficiently use its resources for treating HIV/AIDS patients if it maximized the numbers treated and did not invest heavily in trying to break down the gender barriers to treatment. Maximizing the numbers treated, rather than seeking treatment proportional to prevalence, is a best outcomes strategy. It ignores giving priority to the worst-off groups. Others, perhaps advocating from a human rights perspective, would accept lower treatment rates in order to invest in a more equitable policy. Reasonable people would disagree about how to make the tradeoffs between health maximization and health equity. And this would be true even if all agree that the gender bias against women and its resulting health inequity demand redress on grounds of justice.

A similar problem can arise in the case of racial inequality in access to renal transplantation or cardiac catheterization. Suppose we think that unconscious stereotyping is the explanation for the different utilization decisions by race (and gender, in the case of catheterization). Some might then propose addressing the problem by intensive sensitivity training of all relevant personnel, hoping to reduce the grip of the stereotyping and its racist effects. Let us suppose this strategy would have its biggest impact through increasing access for blacks and women, especially black women. An alternative strategy might involve a much broader retraining effort aimed at giving all practitioners a better grasp of relevant practice guidelines. Arguably, the latter might have a better aggregate impact on population health—for example, addressing the overutilization among whites of some interventions—although it may have a less focused impact on stereotyping and would not get as directly at underutilization by blacks. Reasonable people may well disagree about how to make this tradeoff in effects, despite agreement on the racial injustice involved.

With these examples in mind, what can be said about the priority problem? There is considerable force to the claim that we should increase the priority we grant to those worse off with regard to health if they have been made worse off as the result of racist or sexist social policy or individual acts of racism or sexism. After all, we have social obligations to avoid the racist or sexist treatment of people, whatever its effects, and we also have a social obligation to try to preserve normal functioning in the whole population. The latter would apply even if the baseline were morally neutral, but we now owe remedy to the worse off for two weighty reasons of justice, not one. This fact of extra reasons might translate into giving them more priority than they would otherwise have had.

In addition, suppose the better-off groups were partly responsible for the discriminatory practices. Suppose, furthermore, that they also derived benefit from them. Arguably, this may be somewhat the case in the gender disparity in HIV/AIDS example. Some argue that whites benefit from racism in the United States, but, although whites are better off than blacks and often obtain privileges that blacks lack, there is strong reason to think that racism prevents blacks and whites from uniting to seek better conditions for all (Kawachi et al. 2005). We might, on these suppositions, have further reason for increasing the priority given those who are made worse off as a result of the discrimination imposed by those who benefit. We might think, for example, that they forfeit some of the strength of their claim to have their own health needs met because they compromised the health of others. In any case, we should not be complicit in sustaining the advantage they illegitimately acquired by refraining from giving more priority to those they have harmed.

But how much more priority? We should not give complete priority, in the sense that we must redress the effects on health of racism regardless of what other sacrifices are involved to the health levels for others. Even if average health status for blacks is worse than for other groups, as it clearly is in our illustrations, it seems wrong to give priority to meeting the health needs of blacks whose health status is not as bad as that of more seriously ill members of other groups. We should not completely override our concern to meet more serious health needs over less serious ones (which is part of our obligation of justice to promote normal functioning) simply because the additional, but less important, health needs were the results of racism.[4]

Similarly, if devoting all the resources necessary to eliminating the race gap in health status for a group that is only 10 percent of the population means that a much larger proportion of the population foregoes aggregate health benefits that vastly exceed the gains to the minority, we are most likely assigning too much priority to the worse-off group.[5] Our concern to rectify intergroup inequities, reflected in giving some additional priority to meeting their needs and closing the gap, should not lead us to ignore other considerations of equity across individuals and should not lead us to ignore completely the aggregate impact on population health. Even if we increase priority to the group that is worse off as a result of injustice, we may not ignore the individual or aggregate health needs of better-off groups.

---

[4] Temkin (1993) makes a similar point when he emphasizes the importance of focusing on individuals, not groups, in making comparisons from an egalitarian perspective.

[5] Kubzansky et al. (2001, in Evans et al. 2001) distinguish the population "impact" of a policy from what happens to worse-off groups and suggest policy should address both issues.

The burden of responsibility or complicitness in racist or sexist practices might give us additional reason to increase priority to addressing the health gap of those who are victimized. Nevertheless, even if some groups enjoy relative health advantage and are largely responsible for racist or sexist practices, it does not follow that we should ignore their health needs altogether. In general, we do not believe that the proper punishment for even criminal misdeeds is the denial of medical care. For example, if the doctors who are involved in reducing the access of blacks to renal transplantation and cardiac catheterization all belong to a professional group whose health status is superior, proper remedy of their misdeeds would not include denying them proper medical treatment.

Although we may give additional priority to meeting a group's health needs if inequalities are the result of unjust social practices, we cannot give complete priority to doing so. We are back to the main features of our unsolved rationing problems: extreme views, such as no priority to those worst off or complete priority to them, are implausible. Reasonable people will continue to disagree about how much additional priority to grant. Some of this disagreement may be the result of the original disagreement about how to make the tradeoffs in the morally neutral distributive problems. But some of it may be specifically a result of disagreements about how much weight to give to the underlying fact of injustice, be it race or gender based.

Should it, for example, matter whether the denial of treatments in the renal transplantation or cardiac catheterization examples is the result of conscious racist attitudes or simply the result of stereotypes that have a racist impact and are readily absorbed in our culture? If we suppose the effect of either mechanism is the same—we get the same health inequity—should it matter how culpable we might hold those responsible? We might think it matters because we want to single out explicit racism for special sanction. But giving more priority to blacks is not a sanction against the attitudes of the providers; rather, it is felt by other patients competing for needed services. Whether the advantage enjoyed by the white patients competing for these resources is the result of explicit racism or merely stereotyping that has racist effects seems not to matter. We want to reestablish fair access for all to needed services.

In sum, the following points have emerged from our discussion. Knowing that the health inequality between two groups is unjust may justify giving some extra weight to the priority we assign to the worst off, or it may add to our concern that the worse off be given fair chances at some benefit. There are, however, limits to the sacrifices in population health that would be acceptable in attempting to reduce the health inequity. Other people also have claims of justice on measures that protect their health. In addition, the fact that we find racism and gender-bias reprehensible forms of injustice does not mean that those who may be complicit in them, or derive some benefit from them, lose all claim on health protection themselves. In short, reasonable people will disagree about how to make the tradeoffs involved.

Improving Health at the Expense of Exacerbating Inequities

So far, we have been discussing contexts in which we face an existing health inequity, we have reasons of justice for reducing it, and yet we encounter other questions about distributive fairness in trying to do so. We encounter conflicting claims about fairness as well as conflicts between concerns about equity and concerns to promote aggregate population health. Similar issues arise in an even broader range of health policy contexts. Consider now cases in which we aim to improve population health, but our methods either create or exacerbate health inequalities, some of which may be admittedly unjust.

David Mechanic (2002) notes that some interventions that improve population health avoid generating inequalities, but others do not. The kind of intervention that improves population health while not increasing health inequalities is relatively unusual and has distinctive properties. Fluoridation of water, for example, improves the health of all who must use the water supply, independently of their demographic and behavioral features. Other interventions—smoking cessation, for example, as we noted earlier—improve population health while disproportionately helping groups who are better off in income and education.[6] In vaccination campaigns in developing countries, better-off groups seek out vaccination at higher rates than poorer, less well-educated, and geographically more remote groups do. Unfortunately, many measures have this property.

Mechanic (2002) notes that black infant morality (IMR) rates in the United States were 64 percent higher than whites in 1954 but were 130 percent higher in 1998, even though white rates dropped by 20.8 per 1,000 and black IMR dropped by 30.1 per 1,000. One issue is how we make the racial comparison: should we focus on the more rapid decrease in black IMR, which emphasizes improvement, or on ratios between black and white rates, which emphasizes the gap? This is not a real choice because both matter. Mechanic concludes, about this and other cases, that it is reasonable to accept *increasing* health inequalities (as measured by the ratios) that result from policies that improve population health as long as the health of all groups is being improved. Accordingly, there should be no real complaint about the ongoing (and increasing, from the perspective of ratios) inequality, given the fact of improving black rates.

Mechanic's conclusion requires more careful consideration. Suppose that we have two interventions (in any sector and involving any novel technology) that both raise the health of all groups. If intervention A does less for those who are worse off than B but does much more for those much better off, then both satisfy Mechanic's criterion. His criterion then fails to tell us how to

---

[6] There is some evidence that lower status groups actually try to stop smoking as frequently as better-off groups, but they succeed less often (Barbeau et al. 2004).

choose between these options. We may have strong views about whether to pursue A or B, depending on further facts about the magnitude of the effects or other facts about the sizes of the groups and thus the total impact of the programs. In addition, if the initial inequality is one that society is responsible for causing through unfair policies, there may be, as we noted, a special obligation to give more weight to equity than to maximization of aggregate population health. If those who are better off are in part responsible for the inequality, or even if they simply benefit from it, there may be even more reason to trade some benefits to them in favor of a policy that emphasized giving priority to those unjustly worse off. But just how much sacrifice of benefits to others we should make is something reasonable people will disagree about.

In addition to the problems of magnitude—how much inequality is generated by alternatives and how much improvement is sacrificed if greater equality is pursued—there are issues of speed. Historical injustices that underlie many health inequalities, as in our racism and gender bias examples, are longstanding. Surely, we owe some reasonable rate of progress toward eliminating them—let alone not increasing them (Held 1973). But how fast is fast enough? Here, too, people are likely to disagree, in part because they may disagree about how much current responsibility society has for the historical injustice, but also because policies involving different rates of progress will carry with them new versions of the same distributive problems we have been discussing.

Some of the difficulty we have in addressing these issues comes from the lack of precision we have in quantifying how the strategies or interventions we pursue will affect population health as a whole and subgroups within it. We cannot, for example, simply look at the infant mortality record and pick out which kinds of interventions have made the biggest contribution to aggregate or disaggregate changes. Some other measures might offer a better promise of doing that: perhaps cardiac mortality or morbidity rates offer a better prospect because we may be able to note points at which specific interventions, including smoking cessation, dietary changes, introduction of screening measures, introduction of aspirin, statins and other treatments, had an impact and try to quantify that impact. We might then have better illustrations of the magnitude of effects in the aggregate and across groups so we can better model our discussion of hypothetical differences with some actual evidence. This may help us think about them more clearly in light of what matters most. This intersection of a social science and ethical agenda is clearly suggested by our discussion.

Mechanic's criterion, in short, runs afoul of the same distributive problems we have been considering. Reasonable people will disagree about which policy, A or B, to pursue. The scope of the problem raised by these unsolved rationing problems is very great: they go well beyond medical resource allocation for individuals and pose dilemmas for population health. They pose these dilemmas regardless of whether the baseline distribution is described in morally neutral terms or is a clear case of injustice. They pose these dilemmas whether we are trying to reduce health inequities or whether we are trying to avoid making them greater.

The Complexity of Inequality Itself

There is a further source of complexity to the problem of reducing health disparities, one that derives from what Larry Temkin (1993) has identified as the "complexity of inequality." Temkin gives a schematic description of situations in which two or more groups of individuals differ in their levels of well-being. He then asks the question, which situation has the worse inequality? The question is normative, not descriptive, for he is not asking which has more inequality. Specifically, someone who is worse off has a complaint, he argues, about the unfairness of the inequality. The strength of that complaint, however, depends on whether we compare those who are worst off (a) with those who are best off, (b) with all those better off than they are, or (c) with the average to determine the magnitude of their complaint. To determine when one inequality is worse than another, we must not only assess the strength of each complaint, but we must aggregate those complaints within each situation. Here, too, there are approaches to aggregation: we can adopt a maximin egalitarian view of how to sum up complaints, an additive view, or a weighted additive view.[7] The nine combinations of these bases for judging inequalities better or worse yield somewhat divergent judgments about cases, including ones with multiple groups and ones involving welfare transfers among groups. Although all nine approaches, for example, might prefer to make the worst-off individual or group better before adding comparable benefits to any of the other individuals or (equal sized) groups, they will differ on judgments about many other cases.

Temkin argues that none of these nine combinations can be dismissed outright as inconsistent or otherwise completely implausible. If so, then reasonable people—even egalitarians—will often disagree about which situation is worse, with regard to inequality, than another. This source of disagreement is likely to be present in our thinking about alternative scenarios for reducing admittedly unjust inequalities in health as well. Some such inequalities will be judged worse than others, and yet reasonable disagreement about how to make that judgment will persist.

Disagreement in judgments about when one inequality is worse than another may be part of what underlies disagreements about how much priority to give worst-off individuals or groups. After all, how much priority we might want to give may vary with how strong we think the claims of the worse off are and that,

[7] The additive view simply sums up complaints; the weighted additive views weights complaints by seriousness before adding them; the maximin egalitarian view aggregates the complaints of those who are worst off; see Temkin (1993, chapter 2).

in turn, may depend on whether we compare them to the best off, to the average, or to all who are better off. It may be, however, that the disagreement about how much priority is independent of some of the disagreements about when an inequality is worse. That would be the case if it is not primarily an egalitarian concern that underlies the judgment about priorities but, say, some other consideration of justice.

Temkin and I agree that the kind of disagreement he analyzes does not imply that the concept of inequality is inconsistent, incoherent, or even ambiguous. Accordingly, I conclude that the reasoning behind the disagreements is something that needs to be addressed through a fair, deliberative process. Temkin believes that, although unfair inequalities always count for *something* in our making judgments about what is the best outcome and the best thing to do, all things considered, equality is only one value among a pluralism of considerations. Since other values come into consideration, different people, including different types of egalitarians, may give different weight to the purely egalitarian consideration, given their different views about other values. In short, reasonable people will disagree. Temkin's seminal work on inequality and egalitarianism thus opens the door to a reliance on fair deliberative process for resolving disagreements about how much to weigh equality against other values, at least in real time and under the pressure of pragmatic considerations.

Despite this potential point of convergence between Temkin's egalitarianism and the account I have developed, there is an important difference as well, for my version of health egalitarianism (Daniels 2008) is not the strict egalitarianism Temkin argues for. To see the point, consider an implication of the account of health as normal functioning that I have proposed. Health, understood as the absence of departures from normal functioning (i.e., understood as pathology), is a finite or *limit concept*, unlike income or wealth. This conception matches how health is viewed in the actual work of medicine and public health, where it is treated as a threshold (or better yet ceiling) that we strive to reach but not exceed. In this regard, it is unlike money: we can always have more, without limit.[8] It is a consequence of this fact about health that the ultimate goal of what I think of as health egalitarians and health maximizers is identical: make all people completely healthy. Nevertheless, health egalitarians—who pursue just health as I have described it—and health maximizers clearly differ in their strategies for achieving this ultimate goal. The former, but not the latter, pursue some forms of equity in the distribution of health, even at the expense of aggregate population health. At the same time, my health egalitarians are not strict egalitarians of the sort Temkin defends; nor are they strict prioritarians (Parfit 1995), at least

[8] Nevertheless, some enhancements might make us super-healthy, for example, because we have better resistance to disease; some subjective views of well-being, such as welfare-based ones, may involve some psychological limits, making it a limit concept as well. Still, if well-being is a composite of various objective and subjective components, and income or wealth is included, then it shares the fate of income and wealth.

not ones who give strict priority to those who are worse off. This middle ground needs some clarification.

My health egalitarians are not strict Temkin-style egalitarians because they would not consider it better in any way to "level down" the health of those in better health, such as those with sight, to create more equality with those who are in worse health, the blind. Specifically, they would not see that as in any way better because more people, rather than fewer, would now fall short of full health, the health egalitarian's ultimate goal. (In contrast, if we forego some health benefits to those with better health status in order to give some priority to those who have worse health status, as my health egalitarians would, the "leveling down" is offset by benefits to those with worse health.[9]) Of course, Temkin does not view such leveling down as better, all things considered, but only better with regard to equality, which for him is one (important) value among others. My health egalitarians are also not strict prioritarians—or maximiners of health—who insist on maximizing health for those in the worst health before any effort to improve the health of others is permitted. Indeed, it is because of the reasonable disagreements about *how much priority* to give to those who are worse off (among other disagreements) that we must rely on accountability for reasonableness to arrive at fair and legitimate decisions. Health egalitarians, as I am using the term to characterize those pursuing just health, fall between strict egalitarians a la Temkin and strict health prioritarians. Although I here retain the term "health egalitarian," even though my health egalitarians might well be considered a species of prioritarian, I do not want to quarrel about the term. My account is a claim about what justice requires—and, here, that falls between strict egalitarianism and strict prioritarianism.[10] We need a fair, deliberative process to find an acceptable middle ground.

---

[9] This is not a real leveling down since only a potential health gain is not delivered and there is no reduction in actual health for anyone.

[10] Justice, on my view, agrees more with some versions of egalitarianism that Temkin distinguishes (some approaches to judging inequality better or worse) than with others. Given the ultimate health egalitarian goal of making all people fully functional over a normal lifespan, it makes sense to judge the magnitude of the complaint those in ill health have by comparison to the standard of the best-off group. (This comparison with the best-off group is similar to the method used in one important summary measure of population health intended to measure the total burden of disease in a population. Disability-adjusted life years (DALYs) measure the loss of health compared to a standard of what the best-off group in the world actually enjoys, the Japanese.)Adopting this perspective makes just health agree more with one of the forms of egalitarianism Temkin distinguishes than with others.To see the point, consider a health version of what Temkin (1993, p. 27)calls "the Sequence" (I here substitute health status for welfare). The Sequence consists of a set of situations that differ from each other in the following way: in the first, 99 people are completely healthy and one is in poor health. In the next, two are in poor health and 98 are completely healthy. Each successive situation adds one more to the number of those in poor health and subtracts one from the group of the healthy. The last situation has all in poor health except one, who remains completely healthy. Temkin argues that, from the egalitarian perspective of judging how bad each situation is, three views remain plausible: it gets worse then better, it gets worse and worse, and it gets better and better. From the perspective of my view of justice and health, however, the situation gets worse and worse—in agreement with what some but not all types of egalitarians might believe.

Reasonable Disagreements and Accountability for Reasonableness

My central argument has been that reducing unjust inequalities faces a complexity one might not have expected in the pursuit of justice. Even where health inequalities between groups are avowedly unjust, and we have good reasons of justice for reducing them, we still encounter unsolved distributive problems. We identified three sources of reasonable disagreement: (1) preexisting disagreements about how to address the priorities, aggregation, and best outcomes/fair chances problems that arise in all resource allocations, including these decisions aimed at reducing health inequalities; (2) disagreement about how much to weigh the injustice of the baseline against other issues of fair distribution posed by these distributive problems; and (3) Temkin-type disagreements about when one inequality is worse than another, which may interact with this second disagreement about weighting injustice. These three sources of disagreement arise in the more common case in which we are not setting out to remove injustice but only to improve population health, and we discover that our interventions tend to sustain or increase health inequalities, many of which are unjust. In short, the problem is both complex and pervasive.

What should we do about making decisions in the face of these controversies? We need to make these resource allocation decisions in real time and in a way that is perceived to be fair by all affected by them, despite the underlying moral disagreements. As in the simpler case of the distributive problems taken alone, we must resort to a form of procedural justice. In the absence of prior agreement on principles that can resolve our disputes, we must make decisions in a process that is fair to all (assuming we can agree on what that means). The outcome of the fair process can then be accepted as fair.

One proposal for such a process is that institutions be established at different decision-making levels in health systems and that the procedures for decision making meet these conditions (Daniels and Sabin 2002, 2008):

1. Publicity: rationales for decisions are made public;
2. Relevance: decision makers, ideally including a broad range of relevant stakeholders, make decisions on the basis of reasons that all consider relevant;
3. Revisability: decisions are revised in the light of new evidence and arguments;
4. Enforcement: the above conditions are met.

Meeting these conditions makes decisions accountable for their reasonableness. But why think that adhering to this process yields greater fairness, even if we concede there is enhanced legitimacy?

Following Rawls's discussion, we can distinguish two main forms of procedural justice. In pure procedural justice, we lack prior agreement on a relevant principle for determining just outcomes, and we accept the outcome of a fair process as fair. Rawls offers gambling as an example: we accept the outcome of a fair spin of the roulette wheel as fair. In contrast, criminal trials constitute an example of impure procedural justice because we have prior agreement on a relevant principle: convict all and only the guilty. We determine who they are through trials that pit adversaries against each other but are judged by neutral parties. If we later find conclusive evidence that someone we found guilty in a trial is innocent (say, through DNA evidence), then we should overturn the trial result.

Since we lack prior agreement on distributive principles specific enough to yield outcomes to decisions about allocating health care resources, the proposed process has some resemblance to pure procedural justice. On this view, we have no basis for denying fairness to the outcome of a fair process. But the situation differs in two important ways from Rawls's example of gambling. Unlike gambling we should reject outcomes that violate requirements of justice, say, about nondiscrimination. Furthermore, again unlike the case of gambling, we can imagine arriving at a philosophically persuasive view about how to solve the priorities problem or any of the other unsolved rationing problems. Such a view might "defeat" decisions about fairness arrived at through the process. The "defeasible" fairness that results is the most we can claim for the outcome of our fair process.

I conclude by emphasizing the work that still must be done if that process is to be implemented. First, there must be a body of research on how those features can best be achieved at the different institutional levels at which decisions are made about improving population health and reducing health disparities. Second, we are woefully ignorant of the actual magnitudes of the tradeoffs that are involved in one type of intervention rather than another. Our deliberations about options should be informed by the best evidence and arguments, but that is hard to do if there is inadequate understanding of what actually moves and how far when one or another lever is pulled. I see integrating these two bodies of research with clear normative thinking as a major challenge facing the bioethics of population health.

References

Acevedo-Garcia, D., Lochner, K. A., Osypuk, T. L., and Subramanian, S. V. (2003). Future Directions in residential segregation and health research: A multilevel approach. *American Journal of Public Health, 93*(2), 215–221.

Barbeau, E. M., Krieger, N., and Mah-Jabeen, S. (2004). Working class matters: Socio-economic disadvantage, race/ethnicity, gender, and smoking in NHIS 2000. *American Journal of Public Health, 94*(2), 269–278.

Daniels, N. (1993). Rationing fairly: Programmatic considerations. *Bioethics, 7*(2/3), 224–233.

———. (2008). *Just health: Meeting health needs fairly.* Cambridge: Cambridge University Press.

Daniels, N., Kennedy, B., and Kawachi, I. (1999). Why justice is good for our health: The social determinants of health inequalities. *Daedalus, 128*(4), 215–251.

Daniels, N., and Sabin, J. E. (2002). *Setting limits fairly: Can we learn to share medical resources?* New York: Oxford University Press.

———. (2008). *Setting limits fairly: Learning to share resources for health.* New York: Oxford University Press.

Department of Health. (1999). *Reducing health inequalities: An action report.* London: Author.

———. (2003). *Tackling health inequalities: A programme for action.* London: Author.

Epstein, A. M., Ayanian, J. Z., Keogh, J. H., Nonan, S. J., Armistead, N., Cleary, P. D., Weissman, J. S., David-Kasdan., J. A., Carlson, D., Fuller, J., Marsh, D., and Conti, R. M. (2000). Racial disparities in access to renal transplantation—clinically appropriate or due to underuse or overuse? *New England Journal of Medicine, 343*(21), 1537–1544.

Evans, T., Whitehead, M., Diderichsen, F., Bhuyia, A., and Wirth, M. (Eds.). (2001). *Challenging inequalities in health: From ethics to action.* Oxford: Oxford University Press.

Graham, H. (2004). Tackling inequalities in health in England: Remedying health disadvantages, narrowing health gaps or reducing health gradients. *International Social Policy, 33*(1), 115–131.

Graham, H., and Kelly, M. P. (2004). *Health inequalities: Concepts, frameworks, and policy.* London: Health Development Agency, National Health Service.

Gwatkin, D. R. (2002). *Who would gain most from efforts to reach the millennium development goals for health? An inquiry into the possibility of progress that fails to reach the poor.* Health, nutrition and population discussion paper, The World Bank. Retrieved from http://www-wds.worldbank.org/external/default/WDSContentServer/WDSP/IB/2004/05/17/000265513_20040517171154/Rendered/PDF/288740Gwatkin1WhooWould01Whole.pdf.

Hayward, M. D., and Heron, M. (1999). Racial inequality in active life among adult Americans. *Demography, 36*(1), 77–91.

Held, V. (1973). Reasonable progress and self-respect. *The Monist, 57,* 12–27.

House, J. S., and Williams, D. R. (2000). Understanding and reducing socioeconomic and racial/ethnic disparities in health. In B. D. Smedly and S. L. Syme (Eds.), *Promoting health: Intervention strategies from social and behavioral research* (pp. 81–124). Washington, DC: National Academy of Sciences Press.

Institute of Medicine (IOM). (2002). *Unequal treatment: Confronting racial and ethnic disparities in health care.* Washington, DC: National Academies Press.

Kawachi, I., Daniels, N., and Robinson, D. (2005). Health disparities by race and class: Why both matter. *Health Affairs, 24*(2), 343–344.

Krieger, N., and Sidney, S. (1996). Racial discrimination and blood pressure: The CARDIA study of young black and white adults. *American Journal of Public Health, 86,* 1370–1378.

Kubzansky, L. D., Krieger, N., Kawachi, I., Rockhill, B., Steel, G. K., and Berkman, L. F. (2001). United States: Inequality and the burden of poor health. In Evans, et al., *Challenging Inequalities in Health: From Ethics to Action.* New York: Oxford University Press, pp. 104–121.

Mechanic, D. 2002. Disadvantage, inequality, and social policy. *Health Affairs, 21*(2), 48–59.

Noh, S., and Kaspar, G. (2003). Perceived discrimination and depression: Moderating effects of coping, acculturation and ethnic support. *American Journal of Public Health, 93*(2), 232–238.

Ostlin, P., and Diderichsen, F. 2001. *Equity oriented national health strategy for public health in Sweden.* Policy Learning curve Series No. 1. Brussels: European Center for Health Study.

Parfit, D. (1995). Equality or priority? *Lindley Lecture.* University of Kansas. Lawrence, KS. Nov. 21, 1991.

Schulman, K. A., Berlin, J. A., Harless, W., Kerner, J. F., Sistrunk, S., Gersh, B., Dube, R., Taleghani, C. K., Burke, J. E., Williams, S., and Eisenber, J. M. (1999). The effect of race and sex on physician's recommendations for cardiac catheterization. *New England Journal of Medicine, 340*(8), 618–626.

Secretary of State for Health. (1999). *Saving lives: Our healthier nation. Cm4386.* London: The Stationery Office.

Temkin, L. (1993). *Inequality.* Oxford: Oxford University Press.

UNFPA, UNAIDS, and UNIFEM. (2004). *Women and HIB/AIDS: Confronting the Crisis,* 1–10, 51–56. New York and Geneva: Authors. Retrieved from http://www.unfpa.org/about/report/2004/hiv.html.

Van Ryn, M. (2002). Research on the provider contribution to race/ethnicity disparities in medical care. *Medical Care, 40*(1), 140–151.

Van Ryn, M., and Burke, J. (2000). The effect of patient race and socio-economic status on physicians' perceptions of patients. *Social Science and Medicine, 50*, 813–828.

Williams, D. R., Neighbors, H. W., and Jackson, J. S. (2003). Racial/ethnic discrimination and health: Findings from community studies. *American Journal of Public Health, 93*, 200–208.

World Health Organization. (2006). *World Health report 2006. Working together for health.* Geneva: Author.

World Health Organization (WHO) Europe. (1999). *Health 21: The Health for All policy framework for the WHO European region.* Copenhagen: World Health Organization Regional Office for Europe.

———. (2002). *The European health report 2002.* Copenhagen: World Health Organization Regional Office for Europe.

13 }

Leveling Down Health

Nir Eyal

Telic Egalitarianism and Leveling Down

Today, only 1 in 3,800 women dies from pregnancy or child birth in countries belonging to the Organization for Economic Cooperation and Development (OECD), but 1 in 16 still does in sub-Saharan Africa. Vast health inequalities exist inside countries as well. In developing countries, medically assisted birth is the privilege of 85 percent among the richest quintile and only 36 percent among the poorest one (Crow and Lodha 2011, pp. 71, 75). Likewise, about 90 percent of the world's visually impaired people live in developing countries (Vision 2020 Staff 2013), and, inside the United States, low-income and racial and ethnic minority populations tend to be at greater risk for undiagnosed and uncorrected eye and vision disorders and diseases than the general population (American Public Health Association 2009).

Such vast health inequalities are of great concern. To me, they are concerning not only insofar as they testify that more could have been done for the health of the worse off and not only insofar as they correlate, predict, or cause poor individual outcomes among the worse off or everyone. They are concerning in their own right.

A natural basis for concern about health inequalities in their own right is the following approach to equality:

> *Canonical telic egalitarianism:* If some people are worse off than others (through no fault or choice of their own), this is always in itself bad because

For their helpful comments, I am grateful to Roger Crisp, Tom Douglas, Johann Frick, Douglas Hanto, Iwao Hirose, Ole Norheim, Thomas Søbirk Petersen, Leah Price, Emma Ryman, Andrew Schroeder, Shlomi Segall, Lucas Stanczyk, Larry Temkin, Frej Klem Thomsen, Alex Voorhoeve, Dan Wikler, and seminar participants at the Harvard University Program in Ethics and Health, the Harvard University Health Policy Program, the International Society for Utilitarian Studies (ISUS) XI meeting in Lucca, and the MANCEPT Workshops in Political Theory, as well as to anonymous referees.

> it is unfair. More inequality makes things worse (and more equality, better) not only insofar as the inequality is instrumentally or inherently bad for anyone. In at least one respect, inequality is bad in itself.

Following Gerald Cohen, Larry Temkin, and others, I, too, believe in canonical telic egalitarianism (Cohen 1989, pp. 97, 910–911; Temkin 1993*a*, p. 282; 2003*a*, p. 73; 2013, Chapter 1, this volume; Lippert-Rasmussen 2001; Norheim 2011, Chapter 14, this volume; Eyal 2007, pp. 1–2). The most influential challenge to this approach is Derek Parfit's *leveling down objection*:

> If inequality is bad, its disappearance must be in one way a change for the better, however this change occurs... Similarly, it would be in one way an improvement if we destroyed the eyes of the sighted, not to benefit the blind, but only to make the sighted blind. These implications can be more plausibly regarded as monstrous, or absurd (Parfit 1997, pp. 210–211; Parfit 2012, p. 399; compare Temkin 1993*a*, pp. 247–248).

As Parfit correctly points out, what we intuitively feel is that there is nothing to recommend blinding the sighted, even though their loss of eyesight would increase equality. This draws Parfit and many others to doubt that increased equality improves distributions in any respect and, hence, to doubt that equality has any intrinsic worth. Of course, telic egalitarianism can be coupled with external constraints or overpowering external aims that, all things considered, prohibit leveling down (Temkin 2003*b*; Eyal 2007, pp. 1–2; Segall 2010, pp. 64–66). But that would not save telic egalitarianism from saying, counterintuitively, that leveling down remains, at least in one way, an improvement.

A related objection to canonical telic egalitarianism is purer in that active harmdoing is not considered:

> The *raising up objection* claims that there is no respect in which a situation is normatively worsened merely by improving some people's lives. But, it is claimed,... since raising up may undeniably increase inequality, this shows that there *is nothing* valuable about equality itself... (Temkin 2003*b*, p. 776).

To illustrate the raising up objection, imagine that everyone is blind, that we are able to cure or treat only some, and that we do so. Is there anything worse about the new situation, compared to everyone's remaining equally blind? Had we known that not all could be assisted, would we have any reason to refuse to assist some? Intuitively, the answer is negative. More broadly, most medical and public health interventions do not help all patients, and that does not make them a mixed blessing, only a less-than-complete blessing.[1]

---

[1] So the especially low availability of dialysis and kidney transplantation in India's public sector constitutes, intuitively, no reason to deny these services in Britain (except insofar as the British budget could be used to alleviate India's shortages): compare Harris (2010, pp. 29–30).

Larry Temkin defends canonical telic egalitarianism from the leveling down and the raising up objections. The next section of this chapter explains what is compelling and what is still missing in Temkin's defense. The third section of the chapter indicates that, despite some shortcomings of Temkin's own defense, the intuitions underlying these two objections must be false, and Temkin's canonical telic egalitarianism is probably correct. The final section considers why these false intuitions arise.

The Continuing Challenge for Temkin

Temkin advances two central responses on behalf of canonical telic egalitarianism. First, he reiterates that egalitarians can be pluralists who endorse not only fairness (which they understand in part as equality) but also other values, which may override this component of fairness (Temkin 2003*a*, 2003*b*). However,

> Appealing to [the distinction between pure egalitarianism and pluralist egalitarianism] does not help telic egalitarianism give a convincing response to the Levelling Down Objection, for it is implausible to suppose that, other things being equal, a state of affairs is better in even one respect than a state of affairs in which some are in this condition and others are better off. (Mason 2001, p. 252; see also Brock 2002, p. 364).

In other words, Temkin's response fails to account for some of our intuitions about the blindness examples, namely, those according to which there is nothing to recommend blinding the sighted or failing to help a selection of the blind.

Temkin provides an additional, far better response. He argues that the intuition that such egalitarian policies would improve nothing probably stems from false views. Therefore, on reflection, any such intuition must be discounted. Originally, Temkin formed this point as a critique of what he calls:

> *The Slogan*: One situation cannot be worse than another in any respect, if there is no one for whom it is worse in any respect.

Temkin discusses both the Slogan and Parfit's "*wide* person-affecting principle that assesses the goodness of alternative outcomes... in terms of how people are affected, for better for worse, in each outcome" (Temkin 1993*b*, p. 248; 2003*b*, pp. 776–777). He gives one response to both:

> Most firmly judge that there is at least *one* respect in which vicious sinners faring better than saints is worse than the sinners and saints both getting what they deserve, even if the saints are just as well off in the two alternatives. But neither the Slogan nor the wide person-affecting principle can

> capture this judgment. Thus, like the Slogan, the wide person-affecting principle is unable to capture the noninstrumental value of proportional justice, a value to which many are committed. More generally, the wide person-affecting principle... allows *no* scope for *any im*personal noninstrumental ideals. (Temkin 2003*b*, p. 777).

As a response to the Slogan and to the wide person-affecting principle, Temkin's point is quite compelling.[2] But the point does not fully address the leveling down and the raising up objections as responses to telic egalitarianism. It only shows that some impersonal factors—in the Sinners and Saints' case, perhaps proportion to personal desert—make things inherently better or worse. That does not show that any other impersonal factor makes things better or worse, certainly not that a specific impersonal factor does so. What is at stake in the blindness examples is impersonal equality—a quite different impersonal factor—and in most people's intuitions about the latter examples, some ways to achieve equality improve nothing. What if the determinate concern that canonical telic egalitarians, and immediate competitors like prioritarians, purport to articulate—call it intrinsic concern for the worse off—can only be met by serving the personal good of the worse off? Put differently, we should focus not just on any moral concern, but on the concern that, as an historical matter, attracted egalitarians and immediate opponents' attentions? That concern probably formed the impetus for many of the economic left's battles for redistribution and poverty-reduction over the years. We should ask: is *that* concern really served by policies that aid no one?[3]

This is not just an academic worry. Parfit's prioritarianism, along with a host of noncanonical interpretations of egalitarianism, avoids describing the bulk of equal outcomes that rest on leveling down (or on refusal to selectively raise up) as superior from the viewpoint of that concern (Parfit 1997; Mason 2001, pp. 248–249; Wolff 2001; Hirose 2009; Otsuka and Voorhoeve 2009, pp. 183–184; Daniels 2013, Chapter 12, this volume). Parfit and these renegade egalitarians could argue that, properly articulated, the left-wing concern for the worse off is in no direct way served by harming the more fortunate; that concern makes sense only within the bounds of promotion and protection of individual welfare and health (properly weighted in favor of the worse off). What the concern for the worse off demands is, according to that existing interpretation, fundamental commitment to serving the personal good of

---

[2] Note, in particular, that this response is not focused on the narrow person-affecting principle. Therefore, it is not vulnerable to nonidentity problem-based objections to Temkin's other attempted responses to the Slogan (Holtug 1998).

[3] Some, such as Kagan (1999), have sought to ground telic egalitarianism in desertarianism. Such a position would have translated the desertarianism supported by the Sinners and Saints example into a case for egalitarianism. Importantly, that is not how Temkin uses the Sinners and Saints example. Nor is it, in my view, a successful grounding for telic egalitarianism of a luck-egalitarian stripe (Eyal 2007, p. 8).

the worse off. Leveling down fails to express proper concern for the worse off, precisely because it lacks basic commitment to anyone's personal good.

Therefore, Temkin still needs to address:

> The *Targeted Slogan*: One situation cannot be inherently worse (or better) than another in terms of how it addresses the concern for the worse off as such, if there is no one (not even the worse off) for whom it is worse in any respect.

By "worse for someone," I mean worse for either an identified individual's welfare, prospects, health, and the like, or, in a "wide" sense, worse for a "statistical" person (i.e., worse for the welfare, prospects, health, and the like of a yet-unidentified person). Thus, what the targeted slogan asserts is that, for a distribution to be worse in terms of the concern to which canonical telic egalitarianism and Parfitian prioritarianism purport to give voice, it must be worse in terms of the conditions specified in the slogan and in the wide person-affecting principle; namely, it must be worse for someone. I now offer reasons to reject the targeted slogan and with it some of the prioritarian and egalitarian alternatives to canonical telic egalitarianism.

Signs That Temkin Is Nevertheless Right

The following five examples indicate that, despite the targeted slogan, concern for the worse off as such can benefit from uncompensated setbacks to personal welfare (and prospects, health, etc.) and from other developments that do not improve welfare, either for the worse off or for anyone else.

THE ORGAN POOL

A *directed organ donation* is an organ freely given for transplantation but earmarked to a specific named person or group. The organ can come from a live or deceased donor. Public solicitation for organ donors, often via commercial websites, is currently undertaken by patients who need organs and hope to receive a directed donation. It is likely that "permitting directed, living kidney donation would result in a very small increase in the number of people willing to donate to a stranger." Why? Because "some donors have come forward and indicated they would not have thought to do so except for the personal stories reported by [organ solicitors]" (Hanto 2007). To keep things simple, I set aside a number of ways in which permitting directed kidney donation and its solicitation may simultaneously decrease the number of donated kidneys.[4]

---

[4] Permitting directed, solicited donations may undermine trust in the organ distribution system, thereby dissuading some nonrelated donors and discouraging patients from asking family members for organs (Hanto 2007).

Assume then that permitting these donations results in a net increase in the kidney pool. To permit these practices would thus greatly benefit the recipients, move up everyone behind them on the waiting list, and set back no one's prospects of finding a kidney. It would seem to help some and harm no one. Nonetheless, many observers support disallowing public organ solicitation (Kluge 1989; Adams et al. 2002; Ross 2002; Caplan 2004; Hanto 2007).

Some of the observers point out that in the United States, the United Kingdom, and elsewhere, so-called racist/discriminatory organ donations are already rejected (Adams et al. 2002; Hanto 2007), despite similar potential for Pareto improvement. *A racist/discriminatory directed donation* is a donation to a specific social group, such as a certain race or denomination, or one that excludes a specific group (Hanto 2007). In a famous case from Florida, the family of a murdered Ku Klux Klan sympathizer agreed to donate his organs on the condition that they be transplanted into white recipients. Accepting the donation would have immediately moved everyone on the organ waiting list—nonwhites included—one spot ahead, with the exception of nonwhite patients at the top of the various organ lists. These patients would be denied the racist donor's organs; still, their chances of obtaining an organ would not decrease. If the racist donation were rejected (as it eventually was), there would simply be one fewer donation. Setting aside speculation on the long-term causal effects (which may go either way), the racist donation would not take away organs or higher placement on waiting lists, either from these patients or from anyone else on the list—white or nonwhite. If so, accepting racist directed donations would Pareto improve access to organs for transplantation: benefit some and harm none (Veatch 1998). It would, moreover, benefit nearly all affected nonwhite patients by moving them one spot ahead on the waiting list. That we nevertheless reject racist directed donations suggests that Pareto improvements hardly defeat all other moral considerations.[5]

According to some of the observers, public solicitation for directed donations is also somewhat unfair, even absent specifications of race or religion (Kluge 1989; Adams et al. 2002; Ross 2002; Caplan 2004; Hanto 2007):

> Some candidates will have greater media appeal than others. A six-month-old child...tugs at our heartstrings, while a middle-aged alcoholic may not...unless the alcoholic is a national hero.... But organ allocation ought to be based on need, and not on media appeal. (Ross 2002)

[5] Although my main argument is different, I believe that part of the reason that accepting racist directed donations seems so problematic is canonical telic egalitarian: accepting them could remain unfair toward some nonwhites.

For some of these observers, this concern with unfairness sufficiently justifies procrustean limitations on public solicitation and directed donations. We may disagree with them on that and still accept the observers' concern about unfairness. Indeed, a kidney patient's inability to tell a moving story and look "attractive" to potential donors does not somehow undermine his or her claims. Even when solicited directed donations enlarge the organ pool and cost no one an organ, they continue to be less than perfectly fair toward some nonrecipients, in comparative terms. Whatever the right policy on soliciting directed donations may be, organ solicitation illustrates an important theoretical point: the gap itself is unfair—in this case, toward those nonwhite patients whose acute needs give them claims to the next available organs.

From a canonical telic egalitarian standpoint, the sense of unfairness is understandable. A patient's inability to produce a moving personal narrative hardly justifies the momentous comparative disadvantage: comparatively lesser access to a potentially lifesaving resource. Between the inarticulate patient and the successful organ solicitor, there exists what Jerry Cohen in a different context calls *unequal access to advantage* (Cohen 1989). It is true that allowing organ solicitation would benefit many other patients on the waiting list, including many who are also much sicker than average and perhaps likelier to be relatively worse off in further ways. It would thus not only maximize organ availability but typically make its distribution fairer overall. Yet accepting it would remain unfair toward any patient heading a waiting list when his or her need is greater. Herein, I propose, lies the root of our concern. We notice the unfairness toward that patient, which the added fairness toward others might outweigh only in part. That unfairness seems to boil down to the same gap in welfare or health that canonical telic egalitarians are concerned about.

Defenders of the targeted slogan may try to deny the existence of any bad unfairness toward any of the worse off as such, referring any moral repugnance to accepting solicited directed donations to other fundamental problems. I believe that such a response would fail. Note, in particular, that the repugnance to accepting solicited directed donations does not seem to stem from mere:

1. Desertarian disproportion, as distinct from egalitarianism: The recipients are not sinners, and the nonrecipients not saints.
2. Complicity in extreme wrongdoing. To donate an organ to a complete stranger partly because he or she has a touching story remains praiseworthy on balance: solicited directed donations are unlike racist directed donations. Although it might have been even nicer to donate it to the patient with the greatest need—even more altruistic—keeping such a donation legal is not wrongful complicity in truly nefarious acts.
3. Procedural injustice: Admittedly part of the problem with the "solicitation of organs from deceased donors [is that it] bypasses the patient who is first on the waiting list" and in that procedural sense, "it violates the principles... of justice on which allocation policies are based" (Hanto 2007; see

also Kluge 1989; Adams et al. 2002).[6] But that procedural concern captures only part of the problem. On the rare occasions that the solicitor is known to be neediest and to rank low only because the sharing network uses medically outdated exclusion criteria, solicitation of organs from deceased donors seems much fairer. Certainly, this procedural concern cannot exhaust the problem with solicitation for *live* organs, in which there is currently no waiting list and, yet, allocation to the best e-narrators continues to seem somewhat unfair.[7]

4. Social inequality, as distinct from inequality in canonical telic terms: Allowing solicited donations may be thought to question needier nonrecipients' equal worths. But it would seem to do so because of the prior unfairness toward these nonrecipients of the action being tolerated. Why otherwise would an action that increases the organ pool question equal worth?[8]
5. Discrimination against minorities: It is true that some publicly solicited directed donations track minority racial, religious, or socioeconomic affiliation, formally (as in racist donations) or informally (Ross 2002; Hanto 2007). However, solicited directed donations seem to remain somewhat unfair even when they do not. Even donations that track nothing but the recipient's personal ability to write moving narratives seem somewhat unfair (Kluge 1989; Ross 2002; Caplan 2004; Hanto 2007). The unfairness of these Pareto-improving donations challenges the targeted slogan. What remains unfair about them is often the unequal access of inarticulate individuals to these potentially-life saving organs.[9]

In sum, solicited directed donations illustrate that Pareto improvements do not rule out unfairness toward the worse off. This is not to say that we should clamp down on organ solicitation, which in my personal view remains justified and welcome on the whole. The point is simply to question the targeted slogan.

---

[6] Indeed, a person may rank highest on an organ waiting list not because she is the worst off (e.g., the one with the worst prognosis), but because she would benefit the most from being the next recipient. Bypassing such a patient is problematic, not for affecting the worst off, but simply for procedural reasons.

[7] In correspondence, Shlomi Segall responded that if someone idiosyncratically offered a kidney only to the second in line on the waiting list, whomever the second in line turns out to be, but not to the first in line, that would also subvert procedures, but accepting their kidney would remain fair. My intuition is that if the first in line is worse off and needs the kidney more than the second in line, accepting it remains somewhat unfair; if their needs are equal, then accepting it fair.

[8] For more on this, see the subsection "The Swimming Pool" later.

[9] Dien Ho suggested to me that, intuitively, the unfairness is reduced if solicited donations are allocated by lottery among patients on the list—although this process does not allocate the organs equally or purely on the basis of need, either. Whether or not this would reduce unfairness, some unfairness would clearly persist. To allocate a rare medical resource to the less needy patient is somewhat fairer when resulting from a fair lottery, but it is not optimally fair.

THEM THAT'S GOT SHALL GET (SO THAT THEM THAT'S NOT SHAN'T LOSE)

Sometimes, the most effective way to help the sick and the poor is to give even better infrastructure, governance, health services, or income to the rich and the healthy. Let me give some examples. Frequently, we cannot bypass benefiting the developing world's urban elites if we are to finally reach the rural poor (Bloom and Sachs 1998; Wagstaff 2001)—for instance, it is usually most effective to locate a new hospital in a well-served urban center with regular electric power and accessibility from all surrounding rural areas rather than to locate it in one underserved rural area. During pandemic, healthy doctors and nurses are unlikely to show up for work, unless we give them privileged access to treatment or vaccination (Persad, Wertheimer, and Emanuel 2009).[10] Privileged and healthy high economic performers may threaten to "secede," taking with them their skills and capital, unless we expand their privilege (Cohen 1992). Some hold that we cannot maintain the quality of health services and other public services over time without inviting, or forcing, the already privileged classes to utilize and then politically support these services (Wagstaff 2001; Segall 2004; Eyal 2010). Giving to the poor alone can stigmatize reliance on services, shame recipients, and diminish utilization (Van Parijs 2004).

On some such occasions, there is no alternative policy that would benefit the poor more. For example, as I mentioned, locating a hospital in an underserved village would often make it nonaccessible to many sick and impoverished populations. Then, two things should be said: first, we probably ought to benefit the already privileged a lot, partly so that we may help the sick and the poor populations somewhat; second, to do so would be a compromise. We should benefit the rich despite something. A dilemma or an internal struggle may precede our decision. We may recall the injustices, the nepotism, the inheritance, and the sheer luck that brought the "haves" their brighter prospects, and we may lament that giving them more would increase an already unfair gap.

This duality is lost on the targeted slogan. It must deny that inequality-augmenting yet strongly Pareto-improving policies could raise concerns about the less fortunate. Pluralists who endorse canonical telic egalitarianism can respect this duality. They acknowledge that, although these policies benefit everyone and may be justified, all things considered, they increase unfair inequality.

ENHANCEMENTS

Imagine that, for a while, it seems as though we could develop a beneficial enhancement that I shall call *luxury vision*, to serve only the already healthier segment of the population. Luxury vision allows the onlooker to see objects

---

[10] I am grateful to Candice Player for this example.

with prettier backgrounds than in reality; for example, with a tropical island or an ancient wall background. Many other attractive features are available that safely and substantially enhance users' happiness. Alas, luxury vision cannot help the blind and the depressed, or those who cannot afford it. It requires regular monitoring and so will remain very expensive, with no chance of attracting government subsidies. What it does is to help the relatively healthy rich use their privilege to gain more pleasure. And because the rich would not donate money not saved on luxury vision to the needy, in no way does it serve—or harm—the greater society.

Eventually, however, it turns out that, for technical reasons, we will not be able to develop luxury vision The already privileged will have to do without the added pleasures that this enhancement would have enabled. The level of welfare equality will have to be greater than was expected.

The unavailability of this exclusive enhancement to the already privileged arguably preserves fairness in the population, a bit more than its availability would.[11] When it comes to luxury vision, my intuitions differ considerably from my intuitions on failure to raise up the blind by providing them basic eyesight. There, I shared the feeling that selectively raising up is strictly an improvement. A plausible interpretation is that what we distribute makes a difference. In the distribution of exclusive enhancements and luxuries for the well off, inequality can give rise to concern for the worse off even when the source of that inequality is a Pareto improvement. Here, failure to raise up selectively remains clearly fairer to worse-off parties for curbing inequality somewhat, even without benefiting anyone. In the case of raising up some of the blind by curing blindness, any reason (or bias) I felt in support of inegalitarian Pareto improvements could have stemmed from what is special to that case: from our special sensitivity to insufficiency and to unmet basic needs. That sensitivity is independent from and teaches little about the truth of canonical telic egalitarianism.[12]

ALL FOR ONE

Sometimes we must choose whether only some will suffer or all will suffer. A cruel enemy besieges our town, threatening that, unless we send out one

---

[11] In conversation, Temkin compared this case to his case of the immortality berries, in which he points out that children who are afraid when told that one day they will die are often consoled by hearing that everybody will. Temkin speculates that death's universality makes it more acceptable by making it fairer. An immortality berry that enhanced only some would make others' mortality harder for them to accept, by introducing unfairness (Temkin 2003b, p. 781). In my view, death's universality makes it more acceptable to children by making death seem species-appropriate, natural, and part of a "normal" cycle. Enhancements would spoil that normality, not only the fairness, which I suspect concerns children less. My own enhancement example cannot be similarly debunked.

[12] Likewise, imagine that some people are millionaires and some are billionaires. For reasons lying outside anyone's control, all the billionaires become millionaires and incur no further disadvantage. There are no other effects. Intuitively, isn't there, at least in one respect, an improvement?

person to die, we shall all die. A trade union deliberates whether to protest the sacking of some members by resigning collectively. The master of the ceremony must decide whether diners who received their dishes can start eating before others receive theirs.

Different ethicists would react to such cases in different ways. Few would say that egalitarian leveling down—dying, resigning, or awaiting food *as one*—is an obligation. But many would insist that leveling down is praiseworthy, or at least permissible, and certainly intelligible. This seems to recognize some sound reason to suffer as one. Something of genuine (although perhaps only partly commensurate) value is lost when someone suffers alone. What exactly is lost? Arguably, fairness toward the sufferer: through no fault or choice of her own, she fares worse than her peers. Canonical telic egalitarianism can accommodate defeasible reasons to level down to the sufferer's level as a matter of fairness. The targeted slogan cannot.

THE SWIMMING POOL

Occasionally, equality-enhancing leveling down and failure to raise up selectively are probably justified, all things considered, and not only in one respect. On some such occasions, the reason that they are justified seems to include unfairness toward the worse off. The latter cases cast strong doubt on the targeted slogan.

Consider Jonathan Wolff's case of a modern-day racially segregated public swimming pool in a Southern U.S. town. As Wolff says, when desegregation is unfeasible politically, it is probably right for the town mayor to shut down the pool, preferring that no one have access to a swimming facility over whites only having access. Further details make it clear that shutting down the pool is a genuine leveling down and is not, for example, mere strategic posturing to force desegregation (Wolff 2001).

Let us agree with Wolff that this is a case of justified leveling down. This would place obvious pressure on the slogan, but does it also challenge the targeted slogan? Wolff may answer in the negative: he suggests that the justification for leveling down here is the value of "social equality"—of a society in which all are treated as equals—and not the value of distributive equality (or distributive prioritarianism), whose significance he seems to dismiss (Wolff 2001, 2010). For example, Wolff correctly points out that what matters here is the thick meaning of pool segregation in a country where, historically, segregation often expressed racism and unequal respect.

Wolff is right that something like social equality is the primary justification for leveling down here. Closing the segregated pool is important for reasons far beyond allocating correctly the relatively trivial benefit of access to swimming. The direct justification is that a pool for whites-only would be widely understood as dismissive of nonwhites' basic status. However, I believe that it would do so in part because it flaunts their relevant entitlements to use the pool. Clearly, black citizens did nothing to deserve the "punishment" of reduced entitlements. Thus, far from questioning the existence of unfairness toward the worse off, the social inequality of the segregated pool could rely on and indicate that unfairness, thus challenging the targeted slogan. Wolff's example supports distributive egalitarianism and not only what Wolff seems to consider an incompatible alternative: social equality.

A natural interpretation of all this is canonical telic egalitarian. All things considered, leveling down is usually wrong. But, sometimes, fairness matters a lot, say, because the degree of fairness happens to command high symbolic value (say, in terms of expressing equal respect), higher than the relevant aggregative value. On such occasions, leveling down can make outcomes better. Elsewhere, I intend to prove that, when the comparative value of fairness exceeds a certain threshold, egalitarians must hold that leveling down is an improvement *tout court*. As Wolff's example illustrates, this implication is not necessarily an unappealing one.

Of course, there are additional reasons why the white-only pool may undermine social equality. For example, it may suggest that nonwhites are impure and dangerous to swim around; it wastes an opportunity for citizens to meet and "rub shoulders" with one another as friends would; it borrows meanings from a history of racist segregation. As a general matter, distributive injustice is neither necessary nor sufficient for social injustice. However, sometimes it is a contributor, and, here, the perspicuous unfairness in (otherwise unimportant) access to swimming seems to be a significant contributor to the disrespectful message of racial segregation.[13]

An Error Theory

> And how was the play otherwise, Mrs. Lincoln?
>
> —A FAVORITE JOKE

---

[13] What if, thanks to rare circumstances, pool segregation would increase distributive equality? Imagine that the relatively harsh Southern sun made it slightly too risky for whites to swim at the local beach, but just safe enough for nonwhites to do so. Therefore, whites would lack access to swimming at the beach, whereas everyone else could and often would swim at the beach. Now assume that the aforementioned swimming pool were a covered one, and that, because even beach-goers loved variety, the pool would be regularly overbooked, preventing whites from swimming at all. In such rare circumstances, equality in the distribution of access to swimming could be improved by keeping the covered pool for whites only. Otherwise, many whites would regularly be unable to swim. Perhaps, in this case, a segregated pool could increase distributive justice in that sphere. Still, such segregation would be only somewhat more tolerable—arguably not tolerable enough—because formal segregation would do violence to social equality. My point is only that such farfetched circumstances would make segregation *somewhat* less bad, precisely because the distributive unfairness and, hence, the threat to social equality, would be lesser.

The cases I presented suggest that the targeted slogan is false, and canonical telic egalitarianism is true. Why, then, does the intuition persist that equalizing achieves nothing in the blindness cases? Put differently, if, as I argued, Temkin is right and both leveling down and failure to selectively raise up are always improvements in at least one respect, why do we sometimes feel as though they aren't? Recall our feeling in the blindness cases—that there is nothing to recommend leveling down or failure to raise up. Let me suggest a new response.[14] Equal outcomes always have (defeasible) inherent value. They maintain it even when based on leveling down or refusing to selectively raise up basic health. But it is usually morally wrong to acknowledge this value, and our intuitions on the blindness cases reflect this wrongness more than they capture the truth.

Consider an analogy. Virtues like tact and consideration sometimes call on us to deny, to others and even to ourselves, that there is anything good about someone's calamity, even when there is something good about it (Heyd 1995). It is best not to tell people, "Your mother died after long hospitalization, which is awful, all things considered, but at least society saved money by not having to keep a bed for her." Usually, it is best not even to secretly think, "There was certainly a silver lining to his mother's death—one extra bed available." Such words and thoughts are nonempathetic and, when made public, likely to hurt the bereaved.

In the blindness cases, it admittedly *feels* as though there is nothing to be said for equality. However, that feeling may merely reflect practical reasons to say and feel that nothing is gained, without it being the case that nothing is gained. Practical reasons to deny what is the truth can encompass more than tact and consideration: a variety of moral and prudential reasons may be implicated (Stich 1990, chapter 5; Nozick 1993, chapter 3; Crisp 2000; Stroud 2006).

When basic needs are at stake, there can be stronger, more enduring reasons to deny the potential gain from leveling down and from failing to selectively raise up. Here is one candidate reason. Human beings are often callous or even cruel toward nonfamily, especially distant others—with potentially disastrous results. Therefore, there is usually reason to cultivate an approach of complete intolerance toward severe human suffering. In this way, when a proposal comes along to ignore or to cause severe suffering, any excessive willingness to accept the proposal is tempered by knee-jerk hostility toward it. Such immediate hostility makes it more likely that we will do the right thing most of the time. Although, occasionally, we have sound reason to ignore or to cause suffering, having this hostility remains preferable to lacking it. It probably helps us act correctly on more occasions than it leads us astray (Hare 1981; Adams 1976).

---

[14] Temkin (1993*b*, pp. 316–317) gives another error theory.

Partly as a result, we have cultivated strong reluctance to acknowledge that there is anything to be gained from neglecting or causing severe suffering. When we are asked if a certain good thing—in this case, equality—warrants blinding the sighted, "moral alarm bells" go off. We deny that there is anything to recommend leveling down. We have a documented tendency to resist both committing direct violence—which blinding the sighted would involve (Greene 2008, p. 63)—and refusing to rescue—which refusing to raise up a real subset of the blind would involve (McKie and Richardson 2003, p. 2407). Indeed, when someone needs rescue, we regularly deny that there is any reason not to attempt rescue, even when reasons of opportunity cost and the preemption of moral hazard probably exist (McKie and Richardson 2003, p. 2407). Given how rarely the value of equality overrides basic needs, it is usually fruitful to deny that there would be any point in frustrating basic needs on egalitarian grounds. Such uniform denial blocks the appeal to egalitarian excuses and makes self-serving, cruel miscalculations more difficult.[15]

Helpful as this policy may be in general, it instills tendencies to dismiss the value of equality when it competes against basic needs. It does so even when equality matters. Thus, on leveling down and failure to selectively raise up basic goods, we tend to feel that equality would gain nothing—although Temkin is right that it would gain something.

Consider this. Although we so readily shared Parfit's intuition that having the sighted join the blind is not even "in one way a change for the better," it quite obviously *is* in one way in the hypothetical scenarios that most of us probably imagined! In real life, very often there *is* value in leveling down seeing capacity: less envy and tension, a better power balance, and a stronger sense of social solidarity, shared fate, classlessness, and community. Leveling down that capacity also carries symbolic value: everyone's sharing one fate with respect to eyesight may contribute to social equality. Additionally, eyesight is in some ways a "positional" good. The blind could benefit from other people's becoming or remaining blind. There would be improved job prospects and probably greater political willingness to provide good services to the blind, resulting in fungible gains—say, more Braille books in public libraries.[16] And since everything else is equal between the average blinded and the average sighted person,

---

[15] Tom Douglas has pointed out to me that we are also callous about the importance of equality with remote others. Why, then, isn't it equally fruitful, then, to inculcate a similar tendency to deny that anything good can come out of inequality? If we inculcated such a tendency, we would reject inegalitarian leveling up. In response to this challenge, because suffering is usually much worse than inequality, it is usually far more urgent to inculcate strong hostility to causing and tolerating suffering than to inculcate one to causing or tolerating inequality.

[16] Contrast with Segall (2010, 112–114). On positional goods and leveling down in general, see Brighouse and Swift (2006). On how, when all are blind, blindness is so much easier that being sighted is considered a problem, see the short story "The Country of the Blind" (Wells 1999).

including personal deserts, some versions of desertarianism would consider it intrinsically good if the two groups had equal average welfare.

Some of these alleged values are instrumental, and some are intrinsic and logically inseparable from inequality. Some are personal and some, impersonal. Reasonable people would disagree on which are real values and how to characterize which. The matter is highly complex. In so readily agreeing with Parfit, we neglected these multiple potential gains from blinding the sighted. We immediately denied that anything stands to be gained from blinding them without, for example, first imagining a full-blown concrete case and confirming that no one stands to gain from the sighted becoming blind. Admittedly, such a gain would thwart true leveling down, and Parfit asked us to imagine true leveling down. But my point is that we didn't take enough processing time to do so. That unthinking response should give us pause. Was there nothing dogmatic about our response? Might we have deliberately "forgotten" something? One account of what happened is as follows. Parfit's question set off moral alarm bells, making us protective and strongly reluctant to admit that anything could be said for blinding the sighted. In the moments that followed, we denied the value of the equality that would be gained from blinding them. The reason we did so was not that nothing could be gained from that equality. In fact, several good things obviously could. Rather, we did it for some other reason, perhaps for the reason I speculated about earlier—our hostility toward any attack on basic needs. That reluctance to admit that there is any point in leveling down or in refusing to raise up basic health may be morally motivated. We may have good practical reasons to preserve that reluctance. But in blinding us to the value of telic equality, it leads us epistemologically, and sometimes morally, astray. For one thing, it disguises one reason for concern about inequalities in health.

References

Adams, P. L., Cohen, D. J., Danovitch, G. M., et al. (2002). The nondirected live-kidney donor: Ethical considerations and practice guidelines: A National Conference report. *Transplantation, 74*, 582–589.

Adams, Robert Merrihew. (1976). Motive utilitarianism. *Journal of Philosophy, 73*(14), 467–481.

American Public Health Association. (2009). Improving access to vision care in community health centers (Policy 200910). Retrieved from http://www.apha.org/advocacy/policy/policysearch/default.htm?id=1383

Bloom, David E., and Sachs, Jeffrey D. (1998). Geography, demography and economic growth in Africa. *Brookings Papers on Economic Activity, 2*, 207–295.

Brighouse, Harry, and Swift, Adam. (2006). Equality, priority, and positional goods. *Ethics, 116*, 471–497.

Brock, Dan W. (2002). Priority to the worse off in health-care resource prioritization. In R. Rhodes, M. Battin, and A. Silvers (Eds.), *Medicine and social justice* (362–372). Oxford: Oxford University Press.

Caplan, Arthur. (2004). Organs.com: New commercially brokered organ transfers raise questions. *Hastings Center Report, 34*(6), 8.
Cohen, Gerald A. (1989). On the currency of egalitarian justice. *Ethics, 99*(4), 906–944.
———. (1992). Incentives, inequality, and community. In G. Peterson (Ed.), *The Tanner Lectures on Human Values*, Vol. *13* (262–329). Salt Lake City: Utah University Press.
Crisp, Roger. (2000). [Review of the book *Value... And What Follows*, by Joel Kupperman. *Philosophy, 75*, 458–462.
Crow, Ben, and Lodha, Suresh K. (2011). *The Atlas of Global Inequalities*. Berkeley: University of California Press.
Daniels, Norman. (2013). Reducing health disparities: No simple matter. In N. Eyal, S. A. Hurst, O. F. Norheim, and D. Wikler (Eds.), *Inequalities in health: Concepts, measures, and ethics* (Chapter 12). New York: Oxford University Press.
Eyal, Nir. (2007). Egalitarian justice and innocent choice. *Journal of Ethics & Social Philosophy, 2*(1), 1–18.
———. (2010). Near-universal basic income. *Basic Income Studies, 2*(1), 1–26.
Greene, Joshua. (2008). The secret joke of Kant's soul. In W. Sinnott-Armstrong (Ed.), *Moral psychology* (pp. 35–79). Cambridge, MA: The MIT Press.
Hanto, Douglas W. (2007). Ethical challenges posed by the solicitation of deceased and living organ donors. *New England Journal of Medicine, 356*(10), 1062–1066.
Hare, Richard M. (1981). *Moral thinking*. Oxford: Oxford University Press.
Harris, John. (2010). *Enhancing evolution: The ethical case for making better people*. Princeton, NJ: Princeton University Press.
Heyd, David. (1995). Tact: Sense, sensitivity, and virtue. *Inquiry, 38*(3), 217–231.
Hirose, Iwao. (2009). Reconsidering the value of equality. *Australian Journal of Philosophy, 87*(2), 301–312.
Holtug, Nils. (1998). Egalitarianism and the levelling down objection. *Analysis, 58*(2), 166–174.
Kagan, Shelly. (1999). Equality and desert. In Louis P. Pojman and Owen McLeod (Eds.), *What do we deserve?* (pp. 298–314). Oxford: Oxford University Press.
Kluge, Eike-Henner W. (1989). Designated organ donation: Private choice in social context. *Hastings Center Report, 19*, 10–16.
Lippert-Rasmussen, Kasper. (2001). Egalitarianism, option luck, and responsibility. *Ethics, 111*, 548–579.
Mason, Andrew. (2001). Egalitarianism and the levelling down objection. *Analysis, 61*(3), 246–254.
McKie, John, and Richardson, Jeff. (2003). The rule of rescue. *Social Science & Medicine, 56*(12), 2407–2419.
Norheim, Ole F. (2013). Atkinson's index applied to health: Can measures of economic inequality help us understand trade-offs in health care priority setting? In N. Eyal, S. A. Hurst, O. F. Norheim, and D. Wikler (Eds.), *Inequalities in health: Concepts, measures, and ethics* (Chapter 14). New York: Oxford University Press.
Nozick, Robert. (1993). *The nature of rationality*. Princeton, NJ: Princeton University Press.
Otsuka, Michael and Voorhoeve, Alex. (2009). Why it matters that some are worse off than others: An argument against the priority view. *Philosophy & Public Affairs, 37*, 171–199.
Parfit, Derek. (1997). "Equality and Priority." *Ratio, 10*, 202–221.
———. (2012). Another defence of the priority view. *Utilitas 24* (special issue 3), 399–440.

Persad, Govind, Wertheimer, Alan, and Emanuel, Ezekiel J. (2009). Principles for allocation of scarce medical interventions. *Lancet, 373*(9661), 423–431.

Ross, L. F. (2002). Media appeals for directed altruistic living liver donations: Lessons from Camilo Sandoval Ewen. *Perspectives in Biology and Medicine, 45*, 329–337.

Segall, Shlomi. (2004). Bringing the middle classes back in. An egalitarian case for (truly) universal public services. *Ethics & Economics, 2*(1), 1–7.

———. (2010). *Health, luck, and justice.* Princeton, NJ: Princeton University Press.

Stich, Stephen. (1990). *The fragmentation of reason.* Boston: MIT Press.

Stroud, Sarah. (2006). Epistemic partiality in friendship. *Ethics, 116*(3), 498–524.

Temkin, Larry S. (1993a). *Inequality.* Oxford: Oxford University Press.

———. (1993*b*). Harmful goods, harmless bads. In R. G. Frey and Christopher Morris (Eds.), *Value, welfare and morality* (pp. 290–324). Cambridge: Cambridge University Press.

———. (2003*a*). Equality, priority or what? *Economics and Philosophy, 19*, 61–87.

———. (2003*b*). Egalitarianism defended. *Ethics, 113*, 764–782.

———. (2013). Inequality and health. In N. Eyal, S. A. Hurst, O. F. Norheim, and D. Wikler (Eds.), *Inequalities in health: Concepts, measures, and ethics* (Chapter 1). New York: Oxford University Press.

Van Parijs, P. (2004). Basic income: A simple and powerful idea for the Twenty-First Century. *Politics & Society, 32*(7), 7–39.

Veatch, Robert M. (1998). Egalitarian and maximin theories of justice: Directed donation of organs for transplant. *Journal of Medicine and Philosophy, 23*(3), 456–476.

Vision 2020 staff. (2013). *Vision 2020:* Global facts. Retrieved from http://www.iapb.org/vision-2020/global-facts

Wagstaff, Adam. (2001). Economics, health and development: Some ethical dilemmas facing the World Bank and the international community. *Journal of Medical Ethics, 27*, 262–267.

Wells, H. G. (1999). The country of the blind. In John Hammond (Ed.), *The complete short stories of H. G. Wells* (pp. 629–648). London: Phoenix.

Wolff, Jonathan. (2001). Levelling down. In Keith Dowding, J. Hughes, and H. Margetts (Eds.), *Challenges to democracy: The Psa yearbook* 2000: Macmillan.

———. (2010). Fairness, respect and the egalitarian ethos revisited. *The Journal of Ethics, 14*(3–4), 335–350.

14 }

Atkinson's Index Applied to Health

CAN MEASURES OF ECONOMIC INEQUALITY HELP US UNDERSTAND TRADEOFFS IN HEALTH CARE PRIORITY SETTING?

Ole F. Norheim

This chapter discusses fair distribution of health in the context of health care priority setting. I have elsewhere argued that a framework for analyzing the distribution of health could start with only two principles: maximize health and equalize health (Norheim 2010*a*; Norheim 2010*b*). This is almost all we need. I take as a starting point that every citizen has reasons to want a long and healthy life, and, also, because health is a necessary if not sufficient condition for fair equality of opportunities, that every citizen has reasons to want health to be distributed equally—with some exceptions explored below (Daniels 2008).[1] Concerns about health maximization and health equalization are therefore both legitimate. I call this a pluralist notion of fair distribution of health (Norheim 2009).

In the literature, health is often measured in terms of mortality and morbidity, as quality-adjusted life years (QALYs) or disability-adjusted life years (DALYs). We could even imagine a measure called capability-adjusted life years (CALYs) (Hausman 2010). It is beyond the scope of this chapter to discuss the choice of metric. Here, I assume we have agreed on a metric and, for simplicity, I call it *healthy life years*. In some examples, I use QALYs if other authors have used that metric.

The question is whether a pluralist notion integrating maximization with equality captures the structure of our concerns for fair distribution of healthy

---

I am indebted to the participants of the Brocher Summer Academy on Health Inequalities, including especially Yukiko Asada, Tony Atkinson, Dan Brock, Angus Deaton, Nir Eyal, Johan Frick, Dan Hausman, Samia Hurst, Rafael Lozano, Erik Nord, Toby Ord, Trygve Ottersen, Larry Temkin, Alex Voorhoeve, and Dan Wikler. This chapter was also presented at the Institute of Health Metric and Evaluation, Seattle, University of Washington, where I received helpful comments from Emmanuella Gakidou, Chris Murray, and Andrew Schroeder. I am also indebted to discussions with Dan Chisholm, Kjell Arne Johansson, Mira Johri, and the anonymous referees for constructive criticism.

[1] This view assumes that health is instrumental for achieving other goods that we have reason to value, although health may also have intrinsic value.

life years. To explore this issue, I examine Atkinson's measure of economic inequality applied to health (Atkinson 1970). Would it make sense to substitute income with healthy life years in such measures, as Sudhir Anand and Chris Murray, independently, have argued (Anand, Diderichsen et al. 2001; Murray 2001; Anand 2002)? There are obvious pitfalls in making this move, and I shall examine possible objections in turn.[2] The aim of this chapter is to explore if Atkinson's index can help us understand tradeoffs in health care priority setting, and, if yes, how to respond to possible objections to this use.

The Gini and Atkinson's Measure of Inequality Applied to Health

The Gini index was originally developed to measure income inequality (Sen 1997). The use of the Gini applied to health was first suggested by Le Grand and later applied and discussed by several others (Le Grand and Rabin 1986; Le Grand 1989; Gakidou, Murray et al. 2000; Anand, Diderichsen et al. 2001; Wolfson and Rowe 2001; Shkolnikov, Andreev et al. 2003; Petrie and Tang 2008; Smits and Monden 2009). Wagstaff suggested that the Gini can be used as a rank-dependent measure of overall health inequality, where the rank is determined by the achieved health of different groups (Wagstaff 2002). The Gini index is based on the Lorenz curve, a cumulative frequency curve that compares the distribution of a given variable with the uniform distribution that represents equality.

One problem with the Gini is that the weighting scheme is based only on the rank order of the health of persons, not on the relative difference in health between them. In a population with three persons, if one dies at age 1, one at age 5, and one at age 8, their relative weight is exactly the same as in a population where one person dies at age 1, one at age 50, and the third at age 51.

Anand et al. surveyed a range of different inequality measures applicable to health inequalities and suggested that Atkinson's measure of inequality satisfied all the desired properties of such a measure (Anand, Diderichsen et al. 2001). Atkinson's measure of inequality is a measure of relative differences (Atkinson 1970) and is therefore a more appropriate choice than rank-ordered measures. As the extended Gini, it also explicitly incorporates a weighting scheme that attaches higher weights to the worst-off groups (Norheim 2010*a*). Atkinson's measure of inequality can be written as follows:

$$I_A = 1 - \left[\frac{1}{n} \sum_{i=1}^{n} \left(\frac{h_i}{\mu} \right)^{1-\varepsilon} \right]^{\frac{1}{1-\varepsilon}} \qquad \text{for } \varepsilon > 0, \text{ and } \varepsilon \neq 1$$

[2] For an excellent formal discussion of related issues, see Bleichrodt and van Doorslaer (2006).

TABLE 14.1 } **Life expectancy, based on World Health Organization life tables (2006), Atkinson's measure of inequality (ranging from 0 to 1), and Atkinson's achievement index for five countries (inequality aversion parameter is set to ε = 0.9).**

	Life expectancy at birth	Atkinson's measure of inequality	Atkinson's achievement index
Niger	42.2	0.49	21.6
South Africa	51.3	0.22	40.0
Botswana	51.7	0.31	35.5
Rwanda	51.7	0.36	32.9
Japan	82.6	0.03	79.3

where n is the number of people in the population, h_i is the health variable (age at death or number of healthy life years achieved), μ is average health in the population (healthy life expectancy at birth), and ε is an inequality aversion parameter. When ε is zero, this index attaches no weight to inequality. When ε is a positive number, aversion to inequality is incorporated, and the higher the ε, the higher weight to inequality.[3] If ε approaches infinity, this measure gives absolute weight to the worst off.

EXAMPLE: ATKINSON'S MEASURE OF INEQUALITY USED AT POPULATION LEVEL

Before we examine the issue of priority setting, I provide an example of how the baseline distribution can be evaluated. I calculate inequality in age at death for five different countries, based on the life table method (using World Health Organization [WHO] life tables for 2006 [World Health Organization 2008]), to show that Atkinson's measure of inequality provides additional and relevant information to what is given in the summary measure life expectancy at birth. The calculations are done in an Excel spreadsheet (available from the author on request). I have used a parameter representing moderate aversion to inequality, ε = 0.9.

As we see from Table 14.1, Niger has the lowest life expectancy, Japan the highest, Botswana and Rwanda the same, and South Africa slightly lower. If we add information about inequality, we see that Atkinson's measure of inequality reveals that even if South Africa has lower life expectancy, there is less inequality in the age of death compared to Botswana and Rwanda. We also see there is less inequality in Botswana compared to Rwanda. This population summary measure of inequality adds information to what we have when we only compare differences in life expectancy. There is little inequality in Japan, and this is due to low mortality rates in younger age groups. Inequality in the sub-Saharan countries is, however, quite high. This is clearly of particular relevance for how to prioritize health interventions.

[3] Strictly speaking, this measure should therefore be called a measure of inequity because it incorporates aversion to inequality.

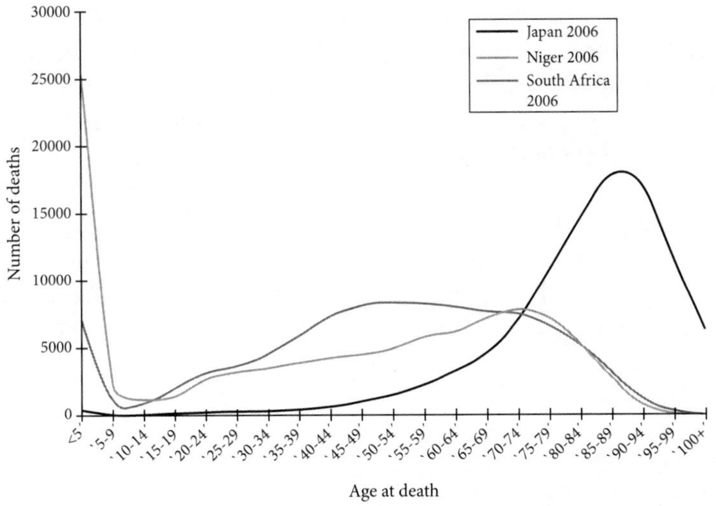

FIGURE 14.1 Distribution of age at death in three countries (*Source:* WHO life tables 2006).

The same information derived from the model life table is represented in Figure 14.1 for three of the countries, but the information in the summary measures is arguably easier to grasp than that presented in the figure or in the life tables themselves.

However, we are not only interested in comparing life expectancy alone or inequality alone. For example, how should we judge South Africa's achievement? South Africa has lower life expectancy than Rwanda, but less inequality. The combined achievement of both average health and the distribution of health is also of interest. In the income space, a widely discussed approach for evaluating complex distributions has been Atkinson's social welfare function that incorporates both an aversion for inequality and a concern for maximizing the average (Atkinson 1970). In his book *On Economic Inequality*, Sen showed that a general form this social welfare function can take is (Sen 1997):

$$W = \mu(1 - I),$$

where W is welfare (or more narrowly defined here as achievement), μ is average individual utility, and I is a measure of inequality. If we substitute income with health, we can write Atkinson's index (AI) as follows:

$$AI = \mu(1 - I_A),$$

where AI = Atkinson's index, μ = average health, and I_A = Atkinson's measure of inequality. Atkinson's index thus modified, integrates a concern for equality of health with a concern for improvements of the average health in a population. Welfare or achievement is here defined as equally distributed equivalent health (Anand 2002). I call this *Atkinson's achievement index for health.* It is interesting to note that the Inequality-adjusted Human Development Index (IHDI) published in 2010 is based on an approach that draws on the Atkinson

(1970) family of inequality measures. Life expectancy, one of three dimension of the HDI, is adjusted for distribution of age at death in exactly the same way as here (with data derived from model life tables, and the inequality aversion parameter set at 1.0). UNDP report similar results for a number of countries from all over the world (UNDP 2010).

We see from Table 14.1 that Japan has highest achievement and Niger lowest, whereas South Africa has higher achievement than Botswana and Rwanda, even if life expectancy is lower. If policy makers want to incorporate a concern for inequality into their evaluations, this index shows that South Africa's achievements are, all things considered, better than Rwanda and Botswana.

Possible Objections

This example shows that it is theoretically possible to measure inequality of health. The normative question is: are all inequalities in health inequitable? Does a measure of health inequality, or more broadly, a measure of health achievement, capture our concerns about unfair distributions? To explore this issue, here, I consider some possible objections to the use of Atkinson's index for health. I do so by moving to hypothetical cases much discussed in the priority-setting literature.

LEVELING DOWN

Before I consider other objections, I simply state, without much argument, that a pluralist framework that combines concerns for average health and equal health is not open to the leveling down objection. Compare two distributions (50, 50) and (50, 80). The first is more equal than the latter, but the first is not better and more fair—all things considered. Pluralist egalitarians are not committed to equality only. An index of health achievement that integrates both concerns will judge the latter as better and more fair than the former, as I have argued elsewhere (Norheim 2009).

DOES ATKINSON'S ACHIEVEMENT INDEX APPLIED TO HEALTH IGNORE SEVERITY OF DISEASE?

Empirical studies have shown that people seem to value health benefits for the very sick more than similar benefits to less ill patients (Nord 1993; Nord, Richardson et al. 1993; Nord 1995; Nord, Richardson et al. 1995; Nord 1999; Nord, Pinto et al. 1999). Erik Nord has pioneered the study of severity weights for health state evaluations. Through the person tradeoff technique, it is possible to elicit the value that respondents will assign to different health state improvements (Nord 1999). But as Fleurbaey and others have noted, this value combines both the valuation of the benefit and the distributive weight attached to it (Fleurbaey 2003). There might be good reasons to separate the two, and it may be argued that the QALY and DALY incorporate the "correct" individual priority weights to individual benefits—if such weights are assigned through proper methods (of which standard gamble is the "gold standard").

Distributive severity weights, conversely, can be justified by two different arguments. Daniels, for example, holds that securing fair equality of health-related opportunity is important for protecting the "capabilities of free and equal citizens" (Daniels 1985). The worst off have the largest deviation from equal health, and this justifies a special concern for the worst off (Scanlon 2002). This is an egalitarian argument. One may also provide a prioritarian argument. Derek Parfit calls his priority view nonrelational egalitarianism (Parfit 2002). On this view, health benefits to the worst off matter more. As Parfit notes, these benefits matter more *because* these people are worst off. This is a fact, not about the size of these benefits, but about their distribution. A valued health outcome (such as a QALY or a DALY) should therefore be given an additional distributive weight.

Leaving the proper justification aside, we may ask whether Atkinson's achievement index applied to health ignores severity of disease. Or, more correctly, does it ignore concerns for the worst off? I define the worst off as those with least lifetime health. Consider two terminal cancer patients: one is 60 years old, the other 30. Let us assume that we can extend the lives for both with five healthy life years. If we have to choose between treating A or B, we get the possible distributions illustrated in Table 14.2.

We see from Table 14.2 that distribution A is least unequal (0.07 vs. 0.14) and gives the highest Atkinson's achievement index (44.32 vs. 41.17). In this calculation, I have set the inequality aversion parameter (ε) to 2.0.

Is it possible within this framework to assign stronger weights to the worst-off person? I have defined the worst-off person (the most severely ill) as the one with least total number of lived healthy life years plus the number of extra healthy life years if an additional potential health gain is not provided. This is clearly patient 1 in our example. Changing the inequality aversion parameter ε will actually

TABLE 14.2 } **Distribution of healthy life years for two patients with different severity of disease and same gain from treatment (aversion to inequality, ε = 2.0).**

	Healthy years lived	Prognosis without treatment	Healthy life years gained from treatment	A	B
Patient 1	30	0.1	5	35.1	30.1
Patient 2	60	0.1	5	60.1	65.1
Average				47.6	47.6
Atkinson's measure of inequality				0.07	0.14
Atkinson's achievement index				44.32	41.17

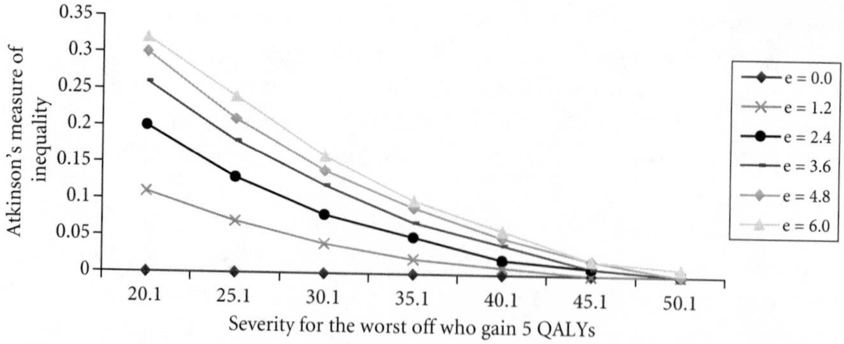

FIGURE 14.2 Atkinson's measure of inequality for distribution A with different degrees of severity and different values of ε.

assign higher weights to the difference between the two persons. To demonstrate this, I have calculated Atkinson's measure of inequality for distribution A with different degrees of severity and different values of ε (Figure 14.2).

Atkinson's measures make it possible to assign explicit weights to aversion to inequality and priority to the worst off. So it does not ignore concern for the worst off or the most severely ill. In this sense, Atkinson's measure is a prioritarian measure, not necessarily an egalitarian measure.[4] Whether this makes a normative difference is discussed elsewhere (Norheim 2009). It is also worth noticing that my proposed use of Atkinson's achievement index is very similar to the Williams "fair innings" argument (Williams 1997). It uses the same concept of health (healthy life years or QALYs), and combines the same two basic principles: health maximization and health equalization. The only difference lies in the specific functional form for equalizing health.

These frameworks do not, however, say anything about how strong the inequality parameter should be; that is a choice to be explored further by ethical analysis (different reasons may apply to different types of cases) or public deliberation.

AGE WEIGHTS

Some authors have suggested that the value of a healthy life year varies with age, and differentiated values can be captured by a marginal weighting function. A hump-shaped marginal weighting function of this kind was incorporated into the DALY measure of health through the use of age weights (Murray 1996). The DALY age-weighting function takes the form $\alpha x e^{-\beta x}$, where x denotes age and α and β are constants. Figure 14.3 provides a graphical illustration for

[4] I am indebted to Larry Temkin for discussions of this point.

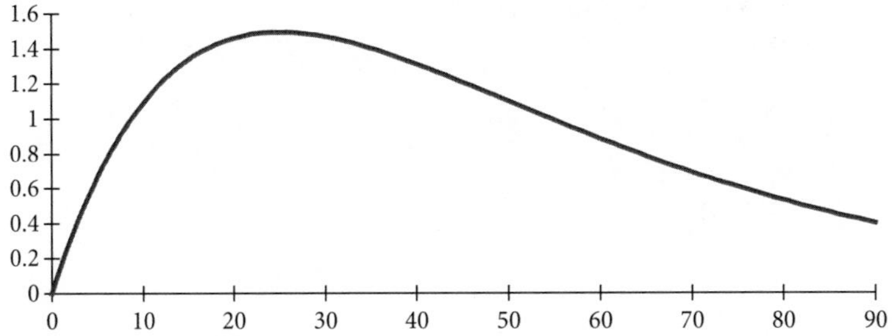

FIGURE 14.3 Disability-adjusted life year (DALY) age weights.

the case $\alpha = 0.16243$ and $\beta = 0.04$ (parameters used in the original global burden of disease study).

One interpretation of the DALY age weights is that the value of a marginal increase in the number of life years is higher at intermediary ages. Mestad and I have elsewhere defended the use of generalized age weights if they are used indiscriminately for all members of an age group (Mestad and Norheim 2012), although I acknowledge that there are competing views on this issue. The objection to an ideal of equal health goes like this: if a healthy life year gained for small children has lower value than for adults, is it then appropriate to incorporate "equity weights" based on a continuous declining weighting function? A continuously declining weighting function satisfies the principle of health transfers: a transfer of health from someone who is in better health to someone who is in worse health does not lead to a reduction in social welfare, provided the transfer does not change the ranking of the individuals in terms of health (Bleichrodt and van Doorslaer 2006). If people value life years approximately as shown in Figure 14.3, does this not show that the principle of health transfers (also called the *Dalton condition* applied to health) is inappropriate for a measure of inequity in health?

My response is both no and yes; it depends on the reasons we have for assigning lower values to the very young. I shall distinguish between age weights based on the *value of the individual health benefit* (that include the value of indirect health and nonhealth benefits to dependents and others) and distributive weights derived from *concerns about equal distribution*.

Low Age Weights to Children

Even if age weights are used, I am prepared to argue that they could be combined with distributive weights derived from concerns about each citizen's legitimate claim to equal health. Even if age weights are explicitly incorporated in Atkinson's measure of inequality, the combined weighing scheme will, in many cases, not change the main result. To see this, consider the following simple comparison concerning inequality in the age of death (Table 14.3).

TABLE 14.3 } **Distribution of age at death between two groups with $n = 10$ in each group, with and without age weights. Atkinson's measure of inequality incorporates distributive weights and is calculated for $\varepsilon = 0.9$.**

	Example			Example, age-weighted		
	N	A	B	N	A	B
Group 1	10	1	16	10	0.2	14.4
Group 2	10	45	30	10	55.1	35.0
Atkinson inequality		0.65	0.04		0.81	0.01

In this example, the difference between group 1 and 2 in age at death is 15 years. In distribution A, 10 people die at age 1 in group 1 and 10 die at age 45. In distribution B, 10 people die at age 16 in group 1, and 10 people die at age 30 in group 2. Atkinson's measure of inequality is calculated for $\varepsilon = 0.9$, and we see that distribution A is more unequal than distribution B (AI = 0.65 vs. 0.04). When DALY age weights are incorporated with Atkinson's measure of inequality, the same ranking according to inequality holds (AI = 0.81 vs. 0.01).[5] Distribution A is more unequal on both accounts. In conclusion, even if the age weight objection seems a possible objection to the use of any inequality measure (including Atkinson's) that satisfies the Dalton condition of transfers, it does not hold if we make clear the distinction between age weights and distributive weights.

The Incomplete Lives Argument

The incomplete lives argument is a greater challenge. Life extension for newborns who will not live to adulthood may lead to incomplete lives, as Persad and others have argued (Persad, Wertheimer et al. 2009). Life years gained early in life may therefore have lower marginal value than years gained as adults. Dworkin argues that a premature death for an adolescent girl is a greater tragedy than the death of an infant girl because that death "frustrates the investments she and others have already made in her life" (Dworkin 1993). Death before a person has developed relationships, ambitions, and expectations may be less important. Support for this argument can also be found in the fact that extra life years always come together with some kind of physical and mental change. In early stages of life, this development may enable gradually greater enjoyment of life, for instance through higher levels of awareness and physical capabilities.

The incomplete lives argument does not directly undermine measurement of inequality of age at death (or healthy life years more generally). It may do so if one wants to compare two distributions in which there is a change so that

[5] I am indebted to Kjell Arne Johansson for his suggestion of combining weights and to Ottar Mestad for discussions of this point.

the youngest only live a few years more. This rare complication may occur if some intervention, say, a health intervention for HIV-positive newborns, only increases life expectancy with some years (say, 10–15 years).

Although a change making the youngest live only a few years more would be measured as a reduction in inequality (as shown in Table 14.3), it may not be a positive change seen from a normative perspective. The wish to avoid incomplete lives is a separate concern that goes beyond concerns for maximization and equality. If this argument is accepted, it is clearly a limitation to the use of most measures of inequality applied to changes early in life.

When Is the Incomplete Lives Argument Not Valid?

Even if we accept the incomplete lives argument, it may not be valid when we consider the distribution of, say, DALYs, instead of life years. A DALY incorporates both risky prospects and quality of life. If we compare 15 additional DALYs to a newborn and to a person aged 30, the facts behind the figures may be that 15 DALYs to the newborn (who would otherwise die) is that he or she may be given a treatment that has a probability p of 0.19 to achieve 80 healthy life years (15 DALYs = 0.1875 × 80 × 1). The argument about incomplete lives is not valid here. The argument is neither appropriate if the newborn can gain for certain 80 extra life years with a quality of life of 0.19 (15 DALYs = 1 × 80 × 0.1875). The incomplete lives argument cannot be generalized to gains in healthy life years.

The Fair Innings Argument

What about lower age weight to the elderly? Alan Williams proposed that everyone is entitled to some "normal" span of health termed a "fair innings," estimated at roughly 70 years in the contemporary United Kingdom (Williams 1997; Williams 2001). His original article focused on differences in health outcomes by social class, but the argument has been widely discussed also as a claim about the value of health gains as such, regardless of class. QALYs gained above the age of a normal lifespan should have lower weights than QALYs gained before. Others have suggested that we can generalize this argument so that it justifies a continuous declining age weighting function (declining from young adulthood to the very old) (Nord 2005). Empirical studies of people's preferences have also supported such a marginal weighing function, although some studies suggest it may be hump-shaped.

In my view, the discussion about age weights fails to distinguish between the value of individual health gains and views about the distribution of health gains. Even if we accept the use of generalized age weights if they are used indiscriminately for all members of an age group, we may also accept additional *distributive weights* that are continuously declining from young adulthood to the very old.

Age may be a good proxy for when to assign values to individual health gains, but age is an imprecise proxy for those who have had much or little health. A more plausible formulation of a general criterion, such as "priority to the young," derived from the principle of equal lifetime health is "priority to those with least lifetime health." These are sometimes the young, but not always (Norheim 2010*b*).

THE DISABILITY PARADOX

How should we set priorities between interventions for persons with disability and healthy people who fall ill? Our concerns for the disabled are strong, but so are our concerns for those we can help more. This may create hard choices for decision makers who face resource scarcity (see also Kamm 2013, Chapter 16, this volume and Beckstead and Ord 2013, Chapter 15, this volume).

Consider the following hypothetical example. You, as a decision maker, have to choose between treating two 25-year-old persons: A or B. Person A was born severely disabled, has quadriplegia, and needs help with all daily activities. Person B has been healthy all her life up to now. Now both become severely ill and face immediate death without intervention. You can save only one of them. If you save A, she will live but with the same reduced quality of life as before. If you save B, she will live a normal life.

The health maximizing response to this dilemma is to bite the bullet and recommend saving B. Person B will gain more health-related utility (because she has a higher quality of life) than person A, and saving B therefore maximizes health. This priority strategy has been generalized for groups of patients and grounds the justification for cost utility analysis: choose the health program that maximizes health (measured as QALYs or DALYs) given the resource constraint (Drummond, Stoddart et al. 1987/97; Hutubessy, Chisholm et al. 2003).

Erik Nord's work on priority to the worst off is the most widely cited approach that has suggested a way out of the disability dilemma for cost-effectiveness analysis (Nord 1999). Nord has proposed an approach he calls "cost-value analysis." It is based on a multiplicative model of societal value that aims to incorporate concerns for severity of illness and a reluctance to discriminate against patients who happen to have lesser potentials for health than others. These concerns are incorporated in cost utility analysis by the use of equity weights. He also, importantly, suggests that, for chronically ill or disabled people, a life year gained should count as 1 and no less than 1 as long as the person concerned considers the year preferable to being dead. In a paper co-authored by Nord and several others, they clarify the proposed modification of QALY maximization: "A preference for non-discrimination in matters of life-saving may be encapsulated in QALY calculations simply by saying that for states

TABLE 14.4 } **A counterexample to nondiscrimination.**

	Age	Initial quality of life	Lifetime QALYs without treatment	Quality of life with treatment	Life years gained with treatment	QALYs gained with treatment	Priority to A Lifetime health (QALYs)	Priority to B Lifetime health (QALYs)
A (disabled)	70	0.5	35	0.5	10	5	40	35
B (previously healthy)	25	1	25	1	10	10	25	35

QALYs, quality-adjusted life years.

of chronic illness or disability that are preferred to death, all saved life years count as one.... [Values of health states other than 1] will only be relevant in estimating the value of health improvements for people with non-fatal conditions—relative to each other and to the prevention of premature death" (Nord, Pinto et al. 1999).

However, this nondiscriminatory approach of restricting priority setting to only involve people with nonfatal conditions is not an acceptable option. There must be other ways out from the health maximization straightjacket. Consider the following counter-example to the principle of nondiscrimination (Table 14.4). You have to choose between saving the life of A or B.

Person A was born disabled with a quality of life of 0.5. He is 70 years old. Person B is 25 years old and has been healthy up to now. Both become ill and face immediate death without intervention. If you save A, he will live for 10 years more, with the same quality of life as before (0.5). His potential gain is 5 QALYs. If you save B, he will live for 10 years more, with the same quality of life as before (1.0). His potential gain is 10 QALYs.

Nord and his colleagues will not discriminate between them—or save A. If we only look at future health benefits, there is no basis to discriminate between A and B. In lifesaving dilemmas, the value of each health year gained should be assigned the value 1.0. If we also look at initial quality of life (severity of disease as Nord defines it), person A (the disabled) has the worst initial health, and this tips the balance in his favor.[6]

Atkinson's framework applied to health is based on other principles. One objective is to equalize lifetime health; another is to improve average health for both. If we compare health outcomes with and without the intervention, nondiscrimination appears unreasonable as seen from the perspective of person B. Although not disabled, lifetime QALYs without treatment for B is 25 QALYs; for A it is 35 QALYs. Person B is worst off in terms of lifetime health in the absence of any intervention. With the intervention, the outcome for B is larger (10 QALYs) compared with the outcome for A (5 QALYs). So, both a concern

[6] An alternative interpretation for Nord et al. is that we should disregard previous health streams, including initial disability, and judge both A and B as having the same initial health and death without treatment. On this interpretation, A and B have equal claims on life saving.

for the worst off derived from equality and concern for maximizing the average points in the direction of giving some priority to B. Nondiscrimination derives its only justification from the existence of disability in one of the persons and disregards all other information. In this particular example, a pluralist egalitarian will not only give some priority to B, but will choose B because lifetime health will be equalized (35 QALYs to both), and average health is higher (32.5 under option A; 35.0 under option B).

END-OF-LIFE PALLIATIVE CARE

There seems to be arguments against both concerns for maximizing healthy life years and equalizing healthy life years for one particular type of care: end-of life palliative care.

In a study of the importance of age in allocating health care resources, Mira Johri et al. found that intervention type seems to matter for people's preferences (Johri, Damschroderd et al. 2005). Of particular relevance here is that distributive preferences for end-of life palliative care were less influenced by patient age than for other types of interventions. A possible normative argument underlying this view may be that end-of life palliative care is something everyone has reason to want (once in their life) regardless of its "effect" or "value" (incompletely captured by QALYs) and regardless of total lifetime health (the equity concern). The claim to palliative care derives it strength from its universal character. If an argument of this kind is accepted, it points to one important exception in which the principles of maximization and equality need to be supplemented by additional considerations.

THE FALSE PRECISION PROBLEM

Can equity or fairness in health distribution be measured? I have argued that tradeoffs between equality (with proper priority weights) and average health can be explored by the use of Atkinson's achievement index. A range of other issues also play a role in judgments of the overall fairness of health distributions. Without due consideration of these other issues, measures of inequality and health achievement is at risk of conveying false precision. Measures of health inequality may replace judgments of complex distributions and reduce them to simple numerical values. As argued by Asada, users rarely pay attention to the information selected, suppressed, or omitted (Asada 2007). It is therefore important to be clear about what other concerns are left out from the framework and measures discussed earlier.

Fleurbay and Schokkaert have postulated that the level of health and health inequality are determined by a number of factors: medical consumption (use of health care), consumption goods (including lifestyle goods), job characteristics, social background (including socioeconomic status), the genetically determined health endowment, and chance (Fleurbaey and Schokkaert 2009).

The Atkinson framework, as applied here, does not take into account consumption goods, including lifestyle goods such as smoking, drinking, and physical activities. How to factor in normative judgments about personal responsibility for health, if at all acceptable, is still an open question (Norheim and Asada 2009). Perhaps these are separate fairness judgments that have to be made in a context-specific political process?

Moreover, the discussion so far has only focused on overall health inequality without decomposing it into inequality associated with other determinants of health, such as job characteristics, social background, or socioeconomic status. Attempts to measure overall inequality in distribution may lead to ignorance of these other important concerns. A more comprehensive measure of inequity should ideally include other aspects of human well-being, including the social determinants of health. *Bivariate* measures are able to capture health inequity associated with socioeconomic status (Wolfson and Rowe 2001). Others have proposed multivariate measures that include health and many other elements of well-being, but it goes beyond the scope of this chapter to examine these alternatives (for more formal discussions of this issue, see (Fleurbaey 2005; Bleichrodt and van Doorslaer 2006; Fleurbaey and Schokkaert 2009; and Asada 2013, Chapter 3, this volume). This is probably the most important limitation to univariate measures (such as those described in this chapter) and bivariate measures (such as the concentration index): they do not take into account the combined effect of pure health inequalities and the distribution of nonhealth goods. It is therefore worth noticing that another specific functional form for combining health maximization and health equalization was proposed by Wagstaff in 1991: the constant elasticity of substitution social welfare function (Wagstaff 1991). This functional form is more flexible than the Atkinson index because it allows one to incorporate parameters indicating priority for particular subgroups as well as a parameter for general inequality aversion.

I am, however, prepared to argue that two other determinants of health, the genetically determined health endowment and chance, are taken into account in this framework. They will influence overall distribution of health, but because they can be seen as circumstances that go beyond individual choice, inequalities arising from these factors should count as inequitable. It is therefore appropriate that they are, or can be, captured in Atkinson's measure of health inequality (Norheim and Asada 2009).

OTHER ISSUES NOT EXPLORED

Finally, I mention two issues not explored sufficiently in this chapter: the choice between absolute versus relative measures of inequality and comparisons between two-peaked distributions.

First, both the Gini and Atkinson's index of inequality are relative measures of inequality. Atkinson, in this volume (2013, Chapter 2), argues that health is different from income and that there may be reasons to seek other measures such as absolute measures, or combinations of absolute and relative measures. For example, unlike income, age at death has an upper boundary of about 100 to 120 years. A relative measure would be invariant with respect to equal proportionate changes, so that a 20–40 age-at-death difference would be judged as the same as a 50–100 difference. With an absolute measure, the latter would be seen as a larger inequality than the former. The choice between absolute or relative measures of inequality in health is not straightforward and needs to be further explored (Asada 2007; Harper, King et al. 2010). It should be noted, however, that an absolute measure of inequality in the age at death would intuitively be easier to interpret than the Gini or Atkinson's index. Using data from Smits and Monden, who found the global life expectancy for women to be 68 years (Smits and Monden 2009), Atkinson estimates that, for global inequality, the expected absolute difference between the achieved age at death would be 24 years (Atkinson 2013, Chapter 2, this volume). This means that in a *random sample* of two women (sampled from anywhere in the world), we would expect that difference in age at death.

Second, comparisons between two-peaked distributions (as seen in Figure 14.1) might be problematic. Smits and Monden argues that this is problematic because similar changes in inequality may be caused by changes in the first (young age), the second (higher ages), or both peaks (Smits and Monden 2009).[7] This is clearly a problem for pure inequality measures (lower mortality in young age might be offset by higher mortality at higher ages), but more work is needed to explore whether this is also problematic for measures that combine concerns about inequality and the average.

Conclusion

Measures of economic inequality can help us understand tradeoffs between maximization and equality in health care priority setting. I have argued that Atkinson's index of inequality and the Atkinson's achievement index are able to (a) capture distributive concerns in cases involving inequality in the age of death at population level, (b) capture distributive concerns for the worst off,

[7] A critical point also raised by Angus Deaton after the Brocher presentation in Geneva.

(c) incorporate distributive weights in addition to age weight, and (d) provides an alternative perspective on the disability paradox encountered by cost utility analysis.

Limitations include distributions involving small health benefits at the beginning of life (the incomplete lives argument) and at the end of life (a special concern for palliative care for terminally ill patients regardless of how much health they have achieved previously). The univariate measures discussed in this chapter are only concerned about the distribution of health itself. If these measures are used, it should be made clear that they ignore other issues relevant for judging distributions, such as those captured in bivariate and multivariate measures. An avenue for further research would be to explore reasons for using relative versus absolute measures of inequality in health. If an absolute measure is more appropriate, Atkinson's index should be modified or replaced.

References

Anand, S. (2002). The concern for equity in health. *Journal of Epidemiology and Community Health, 56*, 485–487.

Anand, S., Diderichsen, F., Evans, T., Shkolnikov, V. M., and Wirth, M. (2001). Measuring disparities in health: Methods and indicators. In T. Evans, M. Whitehead, F. Diderichsen, A. Bhuiya and M. Wirth (Eds.), *Challenging inequities in health: From ethics to action* (pp. 49–67). Oxford: Oxford University Press.

Asada, Y. (2007). *Health inequality: Morality and measurement.* Toronto: University of Toronto Press.

———. (2013). A summary measure of health inequalities incorporating group and individual inequalities. In N. Eyal, S. A. Hurst, O. F. Norheim, and D. Wikler (Eds.), *Inequalities in health: Concepts, measures, and ethics* (Chapter 3). New York: Oxford University Press.

Atkinson, A. B. (1970). On the measurement of inequality. *Journal of Economic Theory II*, 2, 244–263.

Atkinson, A. B. Health inequality, health inequity, and health spending. In N. Eyal, S. A. Hurst, O. F. Norheim, and D. Wikler (Eds.), *Inequalities in health: Concepts, measures, and ethics* (Chapter 2). New York: Oxford University Press.

Bleichrodt, H., and van Doorslaer, E. (2006). A welfare economics foundation for health inequality measurement. *Journal of Health Economics, 25*, 945–957.

Daniels, N. (1985). *Just health care.* New York: Cambridge University Press.

———. (2008). *Just health.* New York: Cambridge University Press.

Drummond, M., Stoddart, G., and Torrance, G. W. (1997). *Methods for the economic evaluation of health care programmes.* Oxford: Oxford University Press.

Dworkin, R. (1993). *Life's dominion. An argument about abortion, euthanasia, and individual freedom.* New York: Knopf.

Fleurbaey, M. (2003). On the measurement of health and health inequalities. In D. Wikler (Ed.), *Goodness and fairness.* Geneva: WHO.

———. (2005). Health, wealth and fairness. *Journal of Public Economic Theory, 7*, 253–284.

Fleurbaey, M., and Schokkaert, E. (2009). Unfair inequalities in health and health care. *Journal of Health Economics, 28*, 73–90.

Gakidou, E. E., Murray, C. J., Frenk J. (2000). Defining and measuring health inequality: An approach based on the distribution of health expectancy. *Bulletin of the World Health Organization*, 2000; *78*(1), 42–54.

Harper, S., King, N. B., Meersman, S. C., Reichman, M. E., Breen, N., and Lynch, J. (2010). Implicit value judgments in the measurement of health inequalities. *The Milbank Quarterly, 88*(1): 4–29.

Hausman, D. M. (2010). "Valuing health: a new proposal." *Health Economics, 19*(3), 280.

Hutubessy, R., Chisholm, D., and Tan-Torres Edejer, T. on behalf of WHO-CHOICE. (2003). Generalized cost-effectiveness analysis for national-level priority-setting in the health sector. *Cost Effectiveness and Resource Allocation, 1*(8), 1–29.

Johri, M., Damschroderd, L. J., Zikmund-Fisherd, B. J., and Ubel, P. A. (2005). The importance of age in allocating health care resources: Does intervention-type matter? *Health Economics, 14*, 669.

Kamm, F. (2013). Rationing and the disabled: Several proposals. In N. Eyal, S. A. Hurst, O. F. Norheim, and D. Wikler (Eds.), *Inequalities in health: Concepts, measures, and ethics* (Chapter 16). New York: Oxford University Press.

Le Grand, J. (1989). An international comparison of distributions of ages-at-death. In J. Fox (Ed.), *Health inequalities in European countries* (pp. 75–90). Aldershot: Gower.

Le Grand, J., and Rabin, M. (1986). Trends in British health inequality 1931–1983. In A. J. Culyer and B. Jonsson (Eds.), *Public and private health services* (pp. 182–191). Oxford: Blackwell.

Mestad/Norheim (2012): A universal preference for equality in health? Reasons to reconsider properties of applied social welfare functions. Social Science & Medicine, 75(10):1836–43

Murray, C. (1996). Rethinking DALYs. In C. Murray and A. Lopez (Eds.), *The global burden of disease* (vol. 1, pp. 1–98). Cambridge, MA: Harvard School of Public Health, WHO, World Bank.

Murray, C. J., and Acharya, A. K. (1997). Understanding DALYs (disability-adjusted life years). *Journal of Health Economics, 16*(6), 703–730.

Murray, C. J. L. (2001). World health report 2000: Commentary: Comprehensive approaches are needed for full understanding. *British Medical Journal, 323*(7314), 680–681.

Nord, E. (1993). The relevance of health state after treatment in prioritising between different patients. *Journal of Medical Ethics, 19*, 37–42.

———. (1995). The person-trade-off approach to valuing health care programs [see comments]. *Medical Decision Making, 15*(3), 201–208.

———. (1999). *Cost-value analysis in health care*. Cambridge: Cambridge University Press.

———. (2005). Concerns for the worse off: Fair innings versus severity. *Social Science and Medicine, 60*(2), 257–263.

Nord, E., Pinto, J. L., et al. (1999). Incorporating societal concerns for fairness in numerical valuations of health programmes. *Health Economics, 8*(1), 25–39.

Nord, E., Richardson, J., et al. (1993). Social evaluation of health care versus personal evaluation of health states. Evidence on the validity of four health-state scaling instruments using Norwegian and Australian surveys. *International Journal of Technology Assessment in Health Care, 9*, 463–478.

Nord, E., Richardson, J., et al. (1995). Maximizing health benefits vs egalitarianism: An Australian survey of health issues. *Social Science and Medicine, 41*(10), 1429–1437.

Norheim, O. F. (2009). A note on Brock: Prioritarianism, egalitarianism and the distribution of life years. *Journal of Medical Ethics, 35*(9), 565–569.

———. (2010*a*). Gini impact analysis: Measuring pure health inequity before and after interventions. *Public Health Ethics,*

———. (2010*b*). Priority to the young or to those with least lifetime health? *American Journal of Bioethics, 10*(4), 60–61.

Norheim, O. F., and Asada, Y. (2009). The ideal of equal health revisited: Definitions and measures of inequity in health should be better integrated with theories of distributive justice. *International Journal for Equity in Health, 8*, 40 pages.

Ord, T., and Beckstead, N. Rationing and rationality: The cost of avoiding discrimination. In N. Eyal, S. A. Hurst, O. F. Norheim, and D. Wikler (Eds.), *Inequalities in health: Concepts, measures, and ethics* (Chapter 15) (pp. 232–239). New York: Oxford University Press.

Parfit, D. (2002). Equality or priority? In M. Clayton and A. Williams (Eds.), *The ideal of equality* (pp. 81–125). New York: Palgrave, Macmillan.

Persad, G., Wertheimer, A., et al. (2009). Principles for allocation of scarce medical interventions. *Lancet, 373*(9661), 423–431.

Petrie, D., and Tang, K. K. (2008). *A rethink on measuring health inequalities using the gini coefficient.* Discussion paper No. 381. The University of Queensland, School of Economics.

Scanlon, T. (2002). The diversity of objections to inequality. In M. Clayton and A. Williams (Eds.), *The ideal of equality* (pp. 41–59). New York: Palgrave, Macmillan.

Sen, A. (1997). *On economic inequality.* Expanded edition with a substantial annexe by James E. Foster. Oxford: Clarendon Press.

Shkolnikov, V. M., Andreev, E. E., et al. (2003). Gini coefficient as a life table function: Computation from discrete data, decomposition of differences and empirical examples. *Demographic Research, 8*(11), 305–358.

Smits, J., and Monden, C. (2009). Length of life inequality around the globe. *Social Science and Medicine, 68*, 1114–1123.

UNDP (2010). *The real wealth of nations: Pathways to human development.* Human Development Report 2010. New York: Author.

Wagstaff, A. (1991). QALYs and the equity-efficiency trade-off. *Journal of Health Economics, 10*, 21–41.

———. (2002). Inequality aversion, health inequalities and health achievement. *Journal of Health Economics, 21*(4), 627–641.

World Health Organization (WHO). (2008). WHO life tables for member states. Retrieved from http://who.int/en

Williams, A. (1997). Intergenerational equity: An exploration of the 'fair innings' argument. *Health Economics, 6*(2), 117–132.

Williams, A. (2001). The "fair innings argument" deserves a fairer hearing! [Comments on Nord and Johannesson.] *Health Economics, 10*(7), 583–585.

Wolfson, M., and Rowe, G. (2001). On measuring inequalities in health. *Bulletin of the World Health Organization, 79*, 553–560.

15 }

Rationing and Rationality

THE COST OF AVOIDING DISCRIMINATION

Nick Beckstead and Toby Ord

Since we cannot fund all of the health interventions that we would like to, we must use some method to decide which interventions to fund and which not to fund. Over the past 40 years, it has become standard to rank publicly funded health interventions in terms of how many quality-adjusted life years (QALYs) they produce for a fixed amount of money. A QALY is a unit that takes account of both the amount of life that a health intervention adds, as well as the intervention's effect on health-related quality of life. Length is measured in years, and quality is measured on scale of 0–1, with 1 being perfect health and 0 being equivalent to death. One determines total QALYs by multiplying years of life by their quality weight. Thus, 10 years of good health is equivalent to 20 years at a quality rating of 0.5 (a weight commonly assigned to blindness).

The QALY value of a health intervention is the difference between the total number of QALYs with the health intervention and the total number of QALYs without the health intervention. Some proponents of this metric favor ranking health interventions in terms of how many QALYs they produce for a fixed sum of money, then funding the most cost-effective interventions first. The rationale for this approach is clear: it produces the greatest amount of health for a fixed sum of money, provided the quality weights are assigned appropriately.[1] This approach has the potential to produce great gains in terms of efficiency of health interventions funded and transparency of decision making.

Despite its benefits, the QALY-maximizing approach has been attacked by disability rights advocates, policy makers, and ethicists on the grounds that

---

The main ideas of this paper were developed during the 2010 Brocher Summer Academy. We would like to thank the participants at Brocher Summer Academy for many helpful discussions on these issues and the Brocher Foundation for making the event possible. We are especially grateful to Erik Nord and Will Crouch for their insightful comments on late drafts of this paper.

[1] Of course, it only maximizes health gains if different health states are given appropriate weightings. We will assume that we are dealing with weightings that have been chosen appropriately because problems of choosing an appropriate weighting are orthogonal to our concerns here.

it unjustly discriminates against the disabled. The main complaint is that the QALY-maximizing approach implies a seemingly unsatisfactory conclusion: other things being equal, we should direct lifesaving treatment to the healthy rather than the disabled. This objection has been forcibly made by John Harris (who described it as "double jeopardy" for the disabled),[2] and it rose to national prominence in the United States after attempts to use the QALY approach in the state of Oregon were overturned on antidiscrimination grounds (Hadorn 1999).This argument pays insufficient attention to the downsides of the potential alternatives. We show that this sort of discrimination is one of four unpalatable consequences that *any* approach to priority setting in health care must face. Given the alternatives, it is far from clear that we should revise the QALY-maximizing approach in response to this objection.

Bubbles Under the Wallpaper

Attempts to avoid unequal treatment for the disabled have not met with great success. A solution favored by Erik Nord and others involves ignoring quality weights when deciding to whom we should give a lifesaving treatment, provided the people to be saved regard their lives as worth living (Nord et al. 1999). As Magnus Johannesson has pointed out, Nord's proposal would sometimes conflict with individual preferences: it would sometimes rank one treatment higher than another, although this would be worse for someone and better for no one (Johannesson 2001). Johannesson offers his own proposal, which also faces devastating objections (Nord et al. 2003). In looking at such proposals, one gets the feeling that the task may be like trying to get a bubble out from behind the wallpaper; pushing down in one place simply moves the bubble elsewhere.

Now for our main point: discriminating against the disabled is one of four highly counterintuitive consequences that any system of priority setting must face. To see why, consider the following case:[3]

---

[2] Harris (1987). See Singer et al. (1995) for a response to Harris.

[3] Note that, in this case, there is no preexisting disability. The case therefore differs from standard examples of "double jeopardy." This makes the case stronger, not weaker. In a case of preexisting disability, prioritarians and egalitarians can claim that it makes sense to choose *X* over *Y* on the grounds that *X* has had less health in life and therefore should be given priority. However, in our case, Alice and Beth had equal health prior to the disease. Therefore, prioritarian and egalitarian adjustments to the QALY framework cannot justify choosing *X* over *Y*.

Prioritarians and egalitarians might argue that, in this kind of case, there is nothing wrong with favoring the healthy over the blind, although priority/equality considerations tell against it in cases of double jeopardy. We could address this point by changing the case so that Alice became blind a couple of years ago. In this context, equality and priority would have insignificant weight, so this defense would not apply. Yet it would still seem objectionable to choose *Z* over *X* on the grounds that Alice is disabled. The analysis of the revised case would proceed, more or less, as it does here.

TABLE 15.1 } **The Alice-Beth dilemma**

	Option X	Option Y	Option Z
Alice	45 years (blind)	–	–
Beth	–	60 years (blind)	35 years (full health)

The Alice-Beth Dilemma: Alice and Beth were both perfectly healthy 20-year-olds, but have recently contracted an unusual disease. This disease will kill them very soon unless treated, and even then they will suffer from serious complications, such as blindness and/or a reduced lifespan. To make matters worse, there are not enough resources to treat them both. There are, however three possible treatment options. outlined in Table 15.1.

In *X*, Alice is treated and will live for 45 years, but will lose her sight. Because Beth was infected by a slightly weaker strain, there are two treatment options available to her: in *Y*, she will live for 60 years but will lose her sight, in *Z* she will live for only 35 years, but will retain her sight. After a due course of reflection, Beth finds that she strongly prefers 35 years of life with full health over 60 years of life with blindness, and Alice would, given the hypothetical choice between *X* and *Z*, have the same preference (a result in line with most people's preferences and with the commonly used QALY ratings).

However we decide to choose among these treatments, we will face severe difficulties.[4] To see this, compare *X* and *Y*, then *Y* and *Z*, and then *X* and *Z*. There are three problems we'll want to avoid here.

1. *Preference for Early Death: X* gives fewer years of life for Alice than *Y* does for Beth. This is the only difference between them. Since there is no reason to favor Alice over Beth, choosing *X* over *Y* would reveal a perverse preference for saving the person who would live for a shorter period of time.
2. *Pointless Violation of Autonomy: Y* is worse than *Z* for Beth, Beth has requested this treatment after a due course of reflection, and *Z* is not better for Alice. Choosing *Y* over *Z* thus violates Beth's autonomy and benefits no one.

[4] As a reviewer reminded us, the QALY approach is not typically used for bedside rationing, but for deciding which treatments should be available for the population as a whole. The case we have described is therefore not the typical setting for applying the framework.

Our example could easily be modified so that it fits a more typical application of the QALY-maximizing approach. One need only replace Alice and Beth with two groups of people with two diseases, *A* and *B*, that correspond to Alice and Beth's conditions in terms of prognosis and treatment options. We can suppose that the government only has enough funds to authorize one of three treatments, *X*, *Y*, or *Z*, as here, and our argument could be repeated, in analogous form, in that context. However, the example we have given is a bit simpler and makes all the same theoretical points, so we have decided to leave it as it is.

3. *Disability Discrimination:* *Z* provides fewer years of life for Beth than *X* provides for Alice. The only reason to choose *Z* over *X* could be that *X* would leave Alice disabled. Thus, choosing *Z* over *X* involves the very kind of discrimination derided by those who try to revise the QALY approach to priority setting. (This problem is also discussed by Ole Norheim [2013, Chapter 14, this volume].)

To avoid these problems, we must choose *Z* over *Y*, *Y* over *X*, and *X* over *Z*. This leads us directly to the classical problem of *cyclic preferences*.[5] Cyclic preferences violate the conditions of rational choice theory and open one up to being "money pumped." If it is important to choose *Z* over *Y*, then one should pay a penny to switch from *Z* to *Y*. For the same reason, one should pay a penny to switch from *Y* to *X*, and another penny to switch from *X* to *Z*, leaving one back where one started, but with less money. Worse, there seems to be nothing keeping one from going around in a circle until one runs out of money.[6] So, the fourth problem then, is this:

4. *Cyclic Preferences:* Choosing *Y* over *X*, *Z* over *Y*, and *X* over *Z*, involves cyclic preferences, which violate the conditions of rational choice theory and leave one open to irrational behavior, such as money pumping.

Since any way of setting priorities in health care will face one of these problems, we are forced to choose the least among these four evils. It is far from clear that the best way of resolving this problem will involve rejecting disability discrimination. Indeed, we find it doubtful that anyone will seriously contemplate *Preference for Early Death* or *pointless violation of autonomy*. For these reasons, we will consider other ways out in the next sections.

A Rights-Based Approach?

There is no way of choosing between these three options does not involve one of the four unappealing consequences just described. Some people respond by endorsing a certain rights-based approach that involves cyclic preferences, but avoids the other problems. On this approach, when we have equally expensive treatments but can save only one person's life, the person who stands to gain the most life years (ignoring any quality adjustments) is awarded the right to treatment. The person may then select the treatment that she most

---

[5] Note that we are using the term "cyclic preferences" in a broad sense, referring both to cycles of preferences within a given set of option and cycles of preferences across sets of options (such as the present case).

[6] The status of money pump arguments is somewhat controversial. This much, however, is not: if policy makers want to set health care priorities using a ranking system that they can follow in general, the ranking system will be susceptible to a money pump if the ranking is cyclic.

prefers to receive, under the advisement of her doctor. (This is the simplest modification of Nord's proposal that avoids *Pointless Violation of Autonomy*.) Although it sounds very sensible, we will now argue that this approach has serious problems.

Before discussing these problems, let's take a minute to understand how this approach works. When the options are *X* and *Y*, Beth gets the right to treatment and will choose *Y*; so this approach avoids preference for early death. If the options are *Y* and *Z*, Beth is again awarded the right to treatment. Since she prefers *Z* to *Y*, she will choose *Z*; this approach thus avoids pointless violation of autonomy. If the options are *X* and *Z*, Alice will be awarded the right to treatment because she stands to gain more years of life; thus, this approach avoids *Disability Discrimination*. Of course, this puts us back at cyclic preferences, violating rational choice theory and opening us to money pumps.

Although some people will regard *Cyclic Preferences* as enough to reject this kind of view outright, others may find this less objectionable, especially since it arises naturally out of the informed choices of individual people. Because we are unlikely to actually get money-pumped in practice, they may find that accepting cyclic preferences is preferable to the other alternatives.

The point of the money pump argument is not so much that we are afraid of bankrupting the public health budget if the situation ever arises, but that the possibility of being money pumped reveals a certain unreasonableness inherent in the policy. So, ultimately, this complaint that money pumping situations will not arise in practice is unpersuasive. Still, we think it is worthwhile to illustrate some additional problems faced by the rights-based approach.

Notice that the rights-based approach will deliver different results when seemingly irrelevant options appear or disappear. If the choices are *X*, *Y*, and *Z*, then treatment *Z* will be chosen. If the choices are *X* and *Z*, then *X* will be chosen. Since *Y* will not be chosen either way, it seems strange that adding this irrelevant option should change anything about which options are worth choosing. This strangeness can manifest itself in disturbing ways.

Consider, for instance, the following embellished version of the Alice and Beth case depicted in Table 15.1. Suppose that for each treatment (*X*, *Y*, or *Z*) that could be delivered, there is a corresponding vial of medicine that must be administered. After this, the patient must receive a very uncommon medicine, of which the clinic has only a single dose. Following the rights-based approach, the doctor decides on option *Z*, so he walks over to the table and selects vial *Z*, then fills a syringe with it. Just as he is about to inject Beth with this medicine, he hears a small crash: vial *Y* has just fallen off the table and shattered, making treatment *Y* unavailable. The doctor then realizes that it would now be wrong to give treatment *Z*, as it has become a choice between only *X* and *Z*, so he goes back to the table and fills a syringe from vial *X* to give to Alice instead.

This kind of behavior seems bizarre. The problem could arise in more ordinary contexts as well. A doctor might know that *X* and *Z* are available but not know whether *Y* is available. If *Y* is available, choosing *Z* would involve a pointless violation of autonomy and should be avoided. If *Y* is not available, choosing *Z* would involve discriminating against the disabled. Not knowing what to do until he knows whether *Y* is available, the doctor might be required to search the clinic or telephone suppliers, even though he knows he won't use the drug he's looking for. One could imagine more extreme versions of the case in which the doctor runs expensive tests to determine whether it is possible to use treatment *Y*. In still more disturbing versions of this example, the doctor would decide who to treat on the basis of how *Y* and *T* compare, where *T* is some other treatment that no one wants anyway (perhaps *T* and *Y* involve saving the most life years, but offer very low quality of life, so patients aren't interested in them anyway).

These objections suggest that, ultimately, the rights-based approach is untenable. Since problems of this kind arise as a result of *Cyclic Preferences,* they illustrate the unreasonableness of resolving the problem by embracing cyclic preferences.

A Lottery Solution?

In the section in which we presented the original problem, we assumed that the only options were *X*, *Y*, and *Z*. Someone might point out that, in practice, we would have many more options, corresponding to all of the lotteries over *X*, *Y*, and *Z*. Since many philosophers believe that fairness sometimes requires the use of lotteries when indivisible goods must be distributed, it is natural to wonder whether a lottery-based solution might avoid all of the problems we've been worried about.[7] In this section, we argue that any lottery solution—any method of allocating health-care resources on the basis of chance—will face problems analogous to those presented above.

At first glance, this solution is unresponsive to the philosophical problem. If the only options were *X*, *Y*, and *Z* (perhaps because there is no time to roll dice, or we are working in a community that forbids leaving important decisions up to chance), we would still like to know what to do. If an approach gives unsatisfactory results even in imaginary cases, that counts against using that kind of approach.

A second problem is that even if lotteries seem sensible in particular clinical cases, they will seem less reasonable in other contexts. The QALY approach can, in principle, to be used to rank many health options, including research

[7] See, for instance (Broome 1984).

options. To suggest that the public health organizations should sometimes roll dice to determine which research to fund seems rather implausible, although analogues of our problems would arise in this context. Therefore, it is doubtful that a lottery solution could have fully general scope.

But the most serious objection to a lottery solution is that it falls prey to a more general version of the problem that we've been worrying about. To see this problem, think about what probabilities we would assign to the different alternatives when the choices were *X* and *Y*, *Y* and *Z*, and *X* and *Z*. There are three problems we'll want to avoid:

1*. *Preference for Early Death**: When the potential treatments are *X* and *Y*, the lottery allows Alice at least as great a chance as Beth even though Alice and Beth are equally healthy and Beth would live for an additional 15 years.[8]

2*. *Pointless Violation of Autonomy**: When the potential treatments include *Y* and *Z*, we force Beth to gamble over *Y* and *Z*, rather than just letting her choose *Z*, even though she prefers *Z* and giving it to her would be worse for no one.

3*. *Disability Discrimination**: When the potential treatments are *X* and *Z*, the policy demands a lottery over *X* and *Z* that gives Beth at least as great a chance as Alice, even though (a) Beth stands to gain fewer years of life, and (b) we would favor Alice if she were not disabled.

If we avoid these problems, we introduce a fourth. Since *Z* merits more probability than *Y*, *Y* merits more probability than *X*, and *X* merits more probability than *Z*, we are back to another kind of cyclic ranking. Intuitively, one alternative should only get more probability than another if choosing that alternative would be preferable to choosing the other (if chosen deterministically). This would imply that the relation "is preferable to" is cyclic. If "is preferable to" is cyclic, that brings back all of the problems of *Cyclic Preferences*, which we were trying to avoid.

Conclusion

We have shown that it is impossible for a policy to provide guidance in interpersonal tradeoffs between length of life and quality of life without facing one of four very challenging conclusions. Of these, we think that those most likely

[8] Some people may be tempted to think that it isn't so bad to embrace *Preference for Smaller Benefits** on the grounds that a fair coin toss is the appropriate response to this case. A difference of 15 years should be enough to make this implausible. We could adjust the case by choosing a more debilitating condition and allowing an even larger gap in years. For this solution to work in general, one must be willing to do fair coin tosses even when the difference in benefits could be very great. This idea is absurd; it is anathema to the very idea of priority setting in health care.

to be accepted are *Disability Discrimination* and *Cyclic Preferences*. We argued that approaches involving *Cyclic Preferences* face severe problems and should be rejected.

Although we have not directly argued in favor of the QALY approach's treatment of the disabled, we have shown it to be substantially more plausible in light of the challenges faced by all of its competitors. This makes it a lot less clear that we should change the QALY system and thereby throw away the great health gains it has achieved.

References

Broome, J. (1984). Selecting people randomly. *Ethics, 95*, 38–55.

Hadorn, D. (1999). The Oregon priority-setting exercise: Quality of life and public policy. *The Hastings Center Report, 21*(3), 11–16.

Harris, J. (1987). QALYfying the value of life. *Journal of Medical Ethics, 13*, 117–123.

Johannesson, M. (2001). Should we aggregate relative or absolute changes in QALYs? *Health Economics, 10*, 573–577.

Nord, E., Pinto J. L., Richardson, J., Menzel, P., and Ubel, P. (1999). Incorporating societal concerns for fairness in numerical valuations of health programs. *Health Economics, 8*, 25–39.

Nord, E., Menzel, P., and Richardson, J. (2003). The value of life: Individual preferences and social choice: A comment to Magnus Johannesson. *Health Economics,12*, 873–877.

Norheim, O. (2011). Atkinson's measure of inequality: Can measures of economic inequality help us understand tradeoffs in healthcare priority setting? In N. Eyal, S. A. Hurst, O. F. Norheim, and D. Wikler (Eds.), *Inequalities in health: Concepts, measures, and ethics* (Chapter 14). New York: Oxford University Press.

Singer, P., McKie, J., Kuhse, H., and Richardson, J. (1995). Double jeopardy and the use of QALYs in health care allocation. *Journal of Medical Ethics, 21*, 144–150.

16 }

Rationing and the Disabled

SEVERAL PROPOSALS

F. M. Kamm

In this chapter, I first critically examine some recently published views of Peter Singer about rationing scarce health care resources, in particular to the disabled. For purposes of comparison, I will then briefly summarize some alternative proposals about rationing and the disabled that I have made in greater detail in earlier work. This will lead me to also compare my proposals to some of those more recently made by Dan Brock. Hopefully, distilling the essence of my proposals will make them more accessible, and comparing them with other proposals will show the need for distinctions they draw. Finally, I shall point to some concerns raised by my proposals.[1] Throughout, the discussion focuses on resources that are not under personal control and that it is impermissible to distribute according to purely personal preferences. I am particularly concerned with whether favoring the nondisabled over the disabled in distributing scarce resources involves invidious discrimination, mistakenly focuses on maximizing health benefits, or exhibits no moral fault at all.

Singer

Singer is concerned with maximizing health benefits per dollar spent using a quality-adjusted life year (QALY) measure.[2] For example, he thinks a teenager

---

[1] My remarks on Singer are in response to his "Why we must ration health care" (*N.Y. Times Magazine*, July 19, 2009). All references to Singer are to that article, which he wrote while the Obama administration's health care proposals were being discussed. A short extract of my discussion of Singer was published as a Letter to the Editor of the *N.Y. Times Magazine* August 13, 2009. My remarks on Brock are in response to his "Cost-effectiveness and disability discrimination," *Economics and Philosophy* 25 (2009): 27–47. All references to Brock are to this article. I am grateful for comments to the editors of this volume, and to audiences at the Conference on Rationing, Erasmus University, Rotterdam, December 2010; at the Bioethics Colloquium, New York University, April 2011; and at the Department of Clinical Bioethics, National Institutes of Health, June 2011.

[2] The QALY, which multiplies years of life times quality, was invented by Richard Zeckhauser; who also thinks we should allocate health resources to maximize QALYs per dollar. It is not clear why Singer favors maximizing health benefits rather than all benefits. Prima facie, the latter standard could imply that we ought to save the rich, beautiful, and productive rather than those who lack such traits.

should be saved rather than an 85-year-old person because we can expect much more future life from the teenager than from the old person. In response, it should be pointed out that this is also true if we compare a teenager with a 50-year-old. If we think the 50-year-old should not be disfavored relative to the teenager, it may be because sometimes persons have a right to certain types of health care independent of whether this maximizes health benefits per dollar.

On the other hand, suppose that the teenager could be saved for fewer good years than could the 85-year-old. It might be argued that we should still save the teenager because she would die having had much less life overall than the older person if she is not helped. Helping the person who will have had much less life overall if not aided so that she improves to some significant degree might also be relevant to how to allocate resources, not just maximizing expected health benefits per dollar. This is related to giving priority to the worst off.

Singer also considers how to compare the health benefit achieved in saving one person's life with another benefit achieved in curing a serious condition in another person that does not threaten that person's life (e.g., quadriplegia). He argues that the way to think about this question is to consider the tradeoff each person would reasonably make in his own life between 7 years lived and quality of life. For example, if every person (already disabled or not) would be indifferent between living 10 years as a quadriplegic and living 5 years nondisabled, this would indicate that people take living as a quadriplegic to be half as good as living nondisabled. Singer thinks that such data would show that using our resources to cure two quadriplegics is just as good as saving someone else's life, provided the life expectancy of all three people, if helped, would be the same (e.g., 10 years).[3] His reasoning (which he does not spell out but which I shall now try to supply) seems to be that if someone would give up 5 out of 10 years of his own life rather than be quadriplegic, that would justify curing one person's quadriplegia rather than saving someone else's life for 5 years. If there are two people whose quadriplegia we can cure, the combined benefit of curing both, he thinks, is equal to saving the life of another person who would live for 10 years.

There are several problems with this conclusion and the reasoning that leads to it, I think. First, in the tradeoff between quality and quantity that a person might make in his own life, it is that person who benefits from the

---

[3] He says: "How can we compare saving a person's life with, say, making it possible for someone who was confined to bed to return to an active life. . . . One common method is to describe medical conditions to people—let's say being a quadriplegic—and tell them that they can choose between 10 years in that condition or a smaller number of years without it. . . . If most . . . have difficulty deciding between 5 years of nondisabled life or 10 years with quadriplegia, then they are, in effect, assessing life with quadriplegia as half as good as nondisabled life. . . . (These are hypothetical figures. . . .) If that judgment represents a rough average across the population, we might conclude that restoring to nondisabled life two people who would otherwise be quadriplegics is equivalent in value to saving the life of one person, provided the life expectancies of all involved are similar."

tradeoff. When we make tradeoffs between different people, the people who get the improved quality of life are not the same people who suffer the loss of more life years. Rather, we are doing what results in the loss of life for one person who does not benefit for the sake of benefiting others. This raises different moral issues than the tradeoff within one life, I think.[4]

Second, the conclusion that curing two quadriplegics who would live for 10 years anyway is equal to saving someone else who would otherwise die so that he can live for 10 additional years depends on aggregating (adding up) the benefit to *two* people to weigh against the loss of the benefit to the third person of having his life saved for 10 years. However, calculating total health benefits produced by aggregating smaller benefits to a greater number of people can be problematic. For example, suppose the tradeoff test within one person's life showed that a small disability (e.g., a damaged ankle) made life only 95 percent as good as a nondisabled life. Then a person would rather have 9.5 years without the small disability than 10 years with it. On Singer's view, this implies both that we should cure one person's small disability rather than save someone who would otherwise die so he can live for an additional half year,[5] and that we should cure small disabilities in 21 people rather than save someone who would otherwise die so that he then lives for 10 years. This is the sort of reasoning that led to the discredited rationing plan in Oregon many years ago in which resources were to be allocated to cap many people's teeth rather than save a few people's lives. It can lead us to deny significant help to people who will be the worst off (and badly off in absolute terms) because they will die if they are not helped in order to help many who are disabled only in a small way and thus not very badly off.[6]

To see a third problem, notice that Singer's way of reasoning is independent of the particular values found through intrapersonal tradeoffs of quality and quantity of life. Suppose people who are severely paralyzed would trade off only a few days of life in order to live without their disability. This result in a tradeoff between quality and quantity of life would imply that their disability has only a slightly lower value than nondisability. Taking this data, Singer's

---

[4] On why this might be so, see my "Should you save this child? Gibbard on intuitions, contractualism, and strains of commitment," a comment on Allan Gibbard's Tanner Lectures, published in Gibbard's *Reconciling Our Aims* (Oxford University Press 2008).

[5] Such a rescue is different from deciding when someone is, for example, 20 whether to allocate resources in such a way that he lives to 60.5 rather than 60. I discuss this distinction briefly in "Aggregation, allocating scarce resources, and the disabled," in *Social Philosophy and Policy*, 26 (Winter 2009).

[6] In general, Singer believes that it could be morally correct to aggregate small benefits to many people, each of whom is not badly off, and produce a large overall benefit, rather than provide a significant benefit to prevent someone else from being much worse off. So, although he is known for his views on the duty to save people from famine, his theoretical position actually implies that it could be morally preferable to save many from headaches rather than save a few from death. For this and other criticisms of Singer's views, see my "Faminine Ethics," in *Singer and His Critics* Ed. D. Jamieson (Blackwells 1999), which, somewhat revised, is also chapter 13 in my *Intricate Ethics* (Oxford University Press 2007).

method of reasoning implies that we simply need a much larger number of people who could be cured of severe paralysis in order to compensate for not saving the life of someone who would go on to live for 10 years. A particular problem to which this case gives rise is that the conclusion to which Singer's method leads may now seem reasonable. That is, it may be said that curing thousands of severely paralyzed people *is* indeed to be preferred to saving one person so that he can go on to live for an additional 10 years. Aggregating benefits across people seems to give the right answer here. However, if we agree with this conclusion, it is probably because we are assuming that severe paralysis makes for a type of life that is very bad for each person in contrast with nondisability and, hence, that someone would trade much more than a few days of life in order to be unparalyzed. But Singer's reasoning implies that such a low value need not be attached to the paralysis in order for curing the many paralyzed people to outweigh saving the life. And this is why his reasoning is problematic.

Finally, Singer argues that if we accept that disability can make a person's life less good healthwise, other things equal, and we want to maximize the health benefits we get with our resources, we should save the life of a nondisabled person rather than someone whose disability cannot be cured, other things equal. The only alternative to this, he says, is to deny that disability per se makes someone's life not as good healthwise, and to say *that* would have the unpalatable implication that there is no reason to allocate resources to cure or prevent disabilities.[7] (Notice, in Singer's defense, that saying that "a life is not as good with a disability" in the sense that the quality of life for the person goes down does not itself imply that the person him- or herself is not as good as or not worth as much as a nondisabled person.)

---

[7] It is sometimes argued that people who are not disabled mistakenly believe that becoming severely disabled is very bad. This is because, it is said, they are poor predictors of how unhappy they would be if they were disabled, as shown by the fact that the disabled are as happy as the nondisabled due to adaptation and various protective psychological mechanisms (even including self-deception). These points are made by Timothy Wilson in his *Strangers to Ourselves* (Harvard University Press 2004). However, there are disturbing implications to basing rationing decisions on these findings, in addition to not allocating funds to cure disabilities. Suppose many people come to an emergency room with severe headaches that will last several hours. At the same time, someone else comes in with a spinal injury that will paralyze his legs if surgery is not done right away. Should we treat all the headaches or do the surgery if we cannot do both? Suppose that we can predict that someone will quickly adapt to paralysis but the people with severe headaches cannot adapt to them. If experienced well-being were all that mattered, we should cure the headaches. This is the wrong conclusion, I believe. This is an indication that experienced well-being and accurate predictions about it are not all that matter in rationing decisions. The fact that people can adapt to, and deceive themselves about, a bad condition does not mean that we should not prevent the bad condition. (In this connection, it is interesting to note that Daniel Kahneman, who reports that disfigured people's "daily mood" is the same as nondisfigured people's, also reports that the disfigured people themselves want to have the disfigurement removed (mentioned in his "Evolving notions of well-being," a lecture in the Mind, Brain, and Behavior Distinguished Lecture Series, Harvard University, April 17, 2008).

I have argued that there is another alternative that does not deny that disability makes life significantly worse for a person, other things equal, and yet does not lead to Singer's conclusions about allocation: we should recognize that a consideration can give us a reason to do something in one context but not another. For example, having a paralyzed finger can make life not as good in a small way, holding other factors constant. This can give us some reason to try to cure this condition while also recognizing that, when it comes to deciding whose life to save, it is an irrelevant consideration that one person has a paralyzed finger and another person does not. The additional admitted good of a nonparalyzed finger in the life of one person is what I called an "irrelevant good" when deciding whose life to save, and so equal chances should be given to each. It is not necessarily irrelevant when deciding whether to spend dollars on a curative treatment for finger paralysis.[8]

This explanation suggests that it is not the judgment that disability can make an outcome worse that has to go; it is the judgment that we should always maximize health outcomes with our resources that has to go.

It may be clear that small differences in victims, like a paralyzed finger, should not affect who is chosen for a lifesaving resource. But what is the explanation of this irrelevance? Here is a possible explanation: in this two-person contest for a scarce lifesaving resource, either person would get the greater part of the best possible outcome that can be gotten by someone (i.e., a worthwhile life whether with or without a paralyzed finger). It is also the case that the alternative for each to being saved would be very bad (death), and each wants to be the one to survive. It is crucial to this explanation that we are dealing with separate persons and that we think that, from a moral point of view, their different perspectives on an outcome (viz. each cares who survives) should influence what we should do. Otherwise, it would be clear that we should maximize QALYs. This is what we would do if we had a choice with respect to one person of merely saving his life or saving his life and also unparalyzing his finger, holding costs constant.

But what of larger disabilities that bring down quality of life as far as 0.5 or somewhat below, so that it is not true that either person would get the greater part of the best possible outcome that can be gotten by someone? I have

---

[8] This explanation and others I am about to describe are presented in greater detail in "Deciding whom to help, the principle of irrelevant goods and health-adjusted life years" (1999), unpublished but circulated as a working paper of the Center for Population Studies, Harvard University; "Deciding whom to help, health-adjusted life years, and disabilities," a revision of the working paper, published in *Public Health, Ethics, and Equity*, eds. S. Anand, F. Peter, and A. Sen (New York: Oxford University Press 2004); "Aggregation, allocating scarce resources, and the disabled," in *Social Philosophy and Policy* 26 (Winter 2009); and a slightly different, longer version, "Disability, discrimination, and irrelevant goods," in *Disability and Disadvantage*, eds. Brownlee and Cureton (New York: Oxford University Press 2009). I shall refer to these papers in the text by their dates or as "unpublished" only when some point is present in one version but not in another. I earlier discussed the Principle of Irrelevant Goods in my *Morality, Mortality*, vol. 1 (Oxford University Press 1993).

suggested at least two grounds for why we should still give equal chances for a lifesaving procedure to the disabled and nondisabled. Importantly, neither ground depends on the view that a disabled life is as good for someone as a nondisabled one, other things equal. First, each person can get what it is most important that people have, namely, a worthwhile life, and each wants to be the one to survive (call this the *Moral Importance Ground*). Second, when one's only option is to have a life at 0.5, it may be reasonable to care about keeping it as much as it would be reasonable to care about keeping a life rated at 1. (Call this the *Only Option Ground.*) Note that this is consistent with its being reasonable to care to have the life rated at 1 rather 0.5 and even its being reasonable to risk death to get it, were this possible. This implies that it could be reasonable to risk death to get a life at 1 about which it will not be reasonable to care once more one has it, than one should care about the life one has now (at 0.5) were it one's only option. All this may seem puzzling, yet I think it is true. Neither of these grounds applies when the quality of life rating falls very low (e.g., coma) and I will not consider such cases here.

But now imagine two nondisabled patients. One could live for 20 years if he had a scarce lifesaving surgery, and the other could live for 5 years. The *Moral Importance* and *Only Option Grounds* also seem to imply that it would be wrong to favor the person who would live much longer. If we disagree, we will need an argument that distinguishes allowing significant differences in length of life to count in rationing decisions whereas significant differences in quality do not. One suggestion I have made is that we distinguish between the "type" of person someone is, constituted by the qualitative features of his life, and how long any type of life goes on. Respect for persons might often require ignoring types when rationing but not big differences in how long any given type will persist. (Call this the *Respect Ground.*)

In sum, using quality of life considerations and comparing and aggregating benefits across different people, at least in the manner Singer recommends, to determine how good a health outcome is, often seems to be the wrong way to ration scarce resources. It is important to realize that we might be able to think seriously about how to allocate scarce resources among different people—and even be willing to endorse rationing sometimes—without necessarily reaching all of Singer's conclusions.

It is also worth pointing out (2009)[9] that in *cases* not involving life-and-death decisions (such as treating gastritis with a scarce resource), arguably it need not matter whether we treat the disabled or nondisabled even if we, like Singer, were only concerned with how much good health there will be in an outcome overall. This is because if a scarce treatment for gastritis is equally effective in a disabled or a nondisabled person, both people will continue to exist, and the same improvement in the gastritis will occur whomever we treat.

---

[9] See my "Aggregation, allocating scarce resources, and the disabled," p. 160, 169–170.

Using abbreviations makes this clear, where "cure gastritis" is C, P is "paralyzed person," and U "unparalyzed person." If we treat P so that we have P(C), U is still alive (unlike in a case in which we do not treat his life-threatening illness in order to save P), albeit with gastritis, and prima facie P(C) + U(– C) contains as much good as P(– C) + U(C), only distributed differently. It is true that there is no "perfect specimen" in the outcome if the nondisabled person is not treated—no U(C)—but medicine is not concerned with producing perfect specimens. (Of course, it might be a good reason to give the cure for gastritis to someone who will already have the problem of paralysis to deal with, rather than treat someone who has no such additional problem. This concern for the person who would be worse off is, arguably, independent of concern for the amount of good in the outcome overall, unless we think there is diminishing marginal utility of a gastritis cure to the nondisabled, which seems unlikely. It may simply be that there is greater moral value in giving the same amount of physical good to someone who otherwise has less physical good.)

Proposals for Counting Disability

Although I have provided some possible reasons for ignoring many quality-of-life differences in rationing, in earlier work, I have also suggested additional reasons why taking account of such differences sometimes does not involve the particular problem of invidious discrimination. This is so even if taking account of the differences raises the different problem of giving too much weight to what should be irrelevant goods and even if favoring the nondisabled over the disabled for scarce lifesaving resources sometimes does involve invidious discrimination. Consider some of the arguments for the view that there need not be invidious discrimination when deciding whether to treat someone just recently seriously paralyzed or, instead, some unparalyzed person.[10] One argument focuses on cases in which there are multiple causes of a condition such as paralysis. This condition gives us a reason to treat a specific illness with a scarce resource. For example, suppose we are equally able to treat two patients for a specific illness that causes both paralysis and pain, but we are most concerned with the illness because it causes paralysis. However, there is another cause of paralysis in one of the patients that we cannot treat. We can refer to such cases as "condition similarity cases."[11] I argued that there would be good reason not to treat the patient who will still be paralyzed due to the other cause even though our treatment against the specific illness is equally effective

[10] I deal with the recently paralyzed to factor out the relevance for rationing decisions of one candidate having had a worse life in the past than another candidate. See my *Morality, Mortality* vol. 1 for a theory of rationing that takes into account different pasts in candidates for a scarce resource.

[11] See my "Aggregation, allocating scarce resources, and the disabled," p. 172. There I called it "treatment similarity."

in both patients. It seems that it is better to get rid of both pain and paralysis than to just get rid of the lesser problem of pain. Hence, it may be permissible to leave the unavoidably paralyzed person with pain and treat pain and paralysis in the other person.

I also argued that we should distinguish treating a person differently on the basis of (a) disability as a component of someone's life, making him a certain type of person, versus (b) disability as a cause of other bad effects in the person's life. So when the presence of a disability has the causal effect of interfering with treatment of another condition (e.g., we cannot perform heart surgery as well because of paralysis), there might be no objectionable discrimination in providing treatment to a nondisabled person instead (2009). (This is consistent with there possibly being objectionable failure to prioritize the worse off.) Also, counting differences in life expectancy caused by the disability in deciding whom to help need not involve invidious discrimination if it is permissible to count an otherwise-caused difference in life expectancy.[12] Similarly, it can be permissible and nondiscriminatory to take into account obstacles to treatment that arise from *not* having a disability (e.g., we cannot perform heart surgery as well because someone has two legs rather than one). Or if nondisability reduced life expectancy, this may be taken into account consistent with nondiscrimination. Hence, someone's undeserved disability can sometimes determine that he suffers a further loss (his life), without this involving objectionable discrimination. This is what I called "linkage."[13]

I further distinguished between (1) producing a better outcome in one patient than in another by (what I call) "piggybacking" on the good property a patient already has or *will have* but that we do not, per se, produce, and (2) producing a better outcome in one patient than in another by causally producing the additional good property. For example, I discussed what I called "switch cases" (1999, 2004) (See Figure 16.1, where ⇒ signifies causing paralysis or nonparalysis and → signifies absence of such a causal role, all in cases in which we would cause the saving of life of any person we treat.) In all three cases, two people compete for a scarce lifesaving treatment. The difference is only in the impact on paraplegia.

In Case 1, two paraplegic people are up for a scarce lifesaving treatment. But, in the first person, the treatment, as a side effect, will undo the paralysis (i.e., P ⇒ U). In Case 2, two unparalyzed people are up for a scarce lifesaving treatment. But, in the first person, the treatment, as a side effect, will cause paraplegia (i.e., U ⇒ P). (Case 3 will be discussed later.) In Case 1, if we choose to save the paralyzed person whom we cause to become unparalyzed, we do

---

[12] See my "Deciding whom to help, health-adjusted life years, and disabilities," p. 240.

[13] Brock refers to "Kamm's nonlinkage principle" (p. 35) to describe the view that linkage might be morally objectionable in general, but he does not note that I specifically rejected this view. See "Deciding whom to help, health-adjusted life years, and disabilities," p. 240. I discuss this further in "Aggregation, allocating scarce resources, and the disabled," pp. 171–172.

	Case 1	Case 2	Case 3
Person one	P==>U	U==>P	P→U
Person two	P →P	U→U	U→P

FIGURE 16.1 Switch Cases.

not merely get a better outcome by saving an already unparalyzed person or one who will become unparalyzed independently of our treatment curing paralysis. Rather, we get a better outcome by saving a person *and* unparalyzing him. I argued that this different causal route to the same better outcome might make a moral difference to whether it is permissible to decide not to save a person who will remain paralyzed. That is, it might be permissible not to give a person who will remain paralyzed an equal chance to be saved relative to another person whom we can save *and* unparalyze. This is so even if it is impermissible not to give a person who will remain paralyzed an equal chance relative to another person whom we can save but whose being unparalyzed, per se, is not due to our efforts. This moral difference is not taken into account by those who, like Singer, claim that all that matters is how good the outcome is (i.e., that the person we save be unparalyzed). Nor is it taken into account by those who claim that deciding whom to save on the basis of whether they will be disabled always involves objectionable discrimination. (This is so even if we assume, for the sake of argument, that favoring U → U over P → P involves invidious discrimination and not just giving too much importance to maximizing QALYs.) To capture these results, I described the following principle:

> *The Causative Principle*: It may be morally permissible to take account of large differences in QALYs if and only if we cause them (1999, 2004).[14]

But how can we justify there being a difference between a better outcome achieved by piggybacking and one achieved by causing? Perhaps we have greater entitlement to decide on the grounds that a better outcome will come about (i.e., there will be a nonparalyzed person in existence rather than a different paralyzed person) if we cause the nonparalysis rather than piggyback on this property by saving a person already unparalyzed. This entitlement could weigh against other factors pulling in another direction. (Similarly, we might be entitled to avoid causing something bad like paralysis in U ⇒ P rather than piggybacking on it as in P → P, in Case 2.)

I argued that the causative principle could not simply be subsumed under what I called the *treatment aim principle* (2009).[15] The latter is the view that if our treatment for a particular problem would be equally effective in a narrow sense (e.g., cure heart failure) in either a disabled or nondisabled patient, each

[14] I first discussed Switch Cases and the causative principle in "Deciding whom to help, the principle of irrelevant goods and Health-adjusted life years, and again in disabilities" (2004); p. 238.

[15] In "Aggregation, allocating scarce resources, and the disabled," p. 178.

should have an equal chance for the treatment. This is a common justification for giving equal chances for a scarce lifesaving drug to a disabled and nondisabled person. However, the treatment aim principle also implies that if treatment outcome, in a narrow sense, would be different, we might permissibly decide to treat the patient who will get the better outcome. One reason I gave for not subsuming the causative principle under the treatment aim principle is that if a treatment aimed at curing heart failure unexpectedly cures or causes paralysis, as in the switch cases, this would ordinarily be considered a side effect of treatment, not part of the narrow sense of effectiveness of the heart treatment. By contrast, the switch cases and the causative principle are intended to suggest that the good or bad side effect we cause might also be relevant to deciding how to allocate the scarce lifesaving resource. I did note (2009)[16] that we might modify the treatment aim principle, so that it would take account of side effects in determining the effectiveness of treatments. (However, this would be a wide rather than narrow sense of equally effective treatment.) I also noted that if a drug's good side effect were consistently present in many patients, one might come to consider the drug as a treatment for two different problems, either together or alone (even though it was not developed with this in mind). If the drug were considered a treatment for two problems *at once*, its effectiveness might be judged, even in a narrow sense, by whether it cured both problems rather than just one.

The important point, I argued, is that sometimes having a causal role in making someone disabled or nondisabled might be a ground for deciding whether to treat someone with a scarce resource for a completely different problem, such as heart disease, without this involving objectionable discrimination. This could be true regardless of whether having this causal role means that our treatment is more effective for the different problem per se.

In sum, I argued that even those who disagree with Singer and think that picking U → U instead of P → P is objectionably discriminatory could agree with the following: there is no objectionable discrimination in taking disability into account when (1) our treatment causes or cures it; (2) the disability affects treatment; (3) the disability causes further bad effects, such as reduced lifespan; and (4) the disability is similar to the effects of an illness we are specifically trying to treat.

However, even if these four reasons for distinguishing people do not involve objectionable discrimination, attending to them may involve giving too much weight from a moral point of view to differences in outcome. That is, some differences in outcome may still be "morally irrelevant goods" in certain contexts. For example, given that life itself is at stake for either candidate for the scarce resource and that each wants to be the one to live, the fact that taking account of a minor difference in outcome that we cause did not involve objectionable

[16] In "Aggregation, allocating scarce resources, and the disabled," p. 179.

discrimination per se need not show that taking account of it is morally permissible. Hence, I suggested, objections to not treating the disabled in many contexts may have to rest on violating a principle of irrelevant goods rather than a claim of improper discrimination.[17]

Brock on Equally Effective Treatment

The distinction I drew between the causative principle and the treatment aim principle are relevant to evaluating some recent views of Dan Brock's on rationing and the disabled. By contrast to Singer, Brock suggests that we accept a narrow notion of equally effective treatment. It is a "treatment specific" understanding of effectiveness (p. 41). He considers the case of heart surgery. Brock says that surgery that fixes heart valves can be equally successful in each of two people even though we can predict that one person will live for 10 years and another will live for 1 year, because the second will be executed within the year (p. 41). The measure of the surgery's success on this account is how well the valves are fixed, independent of how long the person goes on to live. Similarly, he says, "specific medical treatments are developed for specific medical conditions and their effectiveness is determined by how well they correct that condition" (p. 41). This implies that if a treatment designed to remove an impairment does so entirely in one person (even for a limited time, before she is executed) but only partially in someone else, the treatment is more effective in the first person.

Given this narrow notion of treatment effectiveness, it is theoretically possible for a paralyzed person to have just as successful a heart surgery as a nonparalyzed person. Hence, contrary to what Singer suggests, Brock thinks that if surgery must be rationed, there is no reason to favor the nondisabled person. Indeed, it could be objectionably discriminatory not to give equal chances for surgery to each.

My concern is whether Brock's narrow notion of treatment effectiveness is consistent with some other claims that he goes on to make. This is where the discussion of my earlier work is relevant. First, in discussing a case of hip replacement, he says "a pre-existing disability in effect often acts as a co-morbidity that makes treatment less effective in improving a patient's health-related quality of life. Patients with COPD [chronic obstructive pulmonary disease], for example, have substantial limitations in mobility and ability to carry out a variety of activities requiring physical exertion; this would reduce the benefit they would otherwise receive from an intervention like a hip replacement, which is also intended to restore mobility and ability to carry out physical activities" (p. 30). If we were to decide not to

[17] In "Deciding whom to help, health-adjusted life years, and disabilities," p. 242.

treat the COPD patient for these reasons, Brock says it would be a "form of discrimination [that] seems less morally problematic because it is based on an arguably relevant and defensible difference in treatment effectiveness, although that difference in effectiveness is caused by a pre-existing disability" (p. 41–42).

What Brock means here is *not* that the hip cannot be replaced as successfully because the COPD makes surgery more difficult. Rather Brock is here considering that the disabled person *will get less out of what the new hip is meant to help provide* (e.g., mobility). But this does not seem to involve use of a narrow notion of treatment effectiveness because it considers what further benefits someone gets from a treatment in judging how effective the treatment is. This is a wider notion of treatment effectiveness. If we used this wider notion, then, if one person got more out of heart valve surgery because he got more of what it is was supposed to provide than someone else (e.g., longer life), then the first person's heart treatment would be judged more effective. This seems contrary to what Brock originally claimed to be the correct understanding of surgery that would fix each person's heart to the same degree. (Brock's case is also like the "condition similarity" case that I discussed earlier: We can treat one cause of absence of mobility equally well but only get mobility in one patient due to another cause of immobility in the other patient).

Second, Brock considers a hypothetical case considered by a government agency using the Americans with Disabilities Act (ADA). In that case, two people are imagined to have sustained life-threatening injuries in a car accident that also left them unable to walk (p. 29). We can save each person's life, but a cure for the disability only works in one of the people. The agency argued that automatically saving the person who could also be made non-disabled would be objectionable discrimination according to the ADA. One reason given for this conclusion was that judging an unparalyzed life to be better than a paralyzed life, other things equal, was itself discriminatory. This reason seems wrong for, as Singer noted, it is because we think an unparalyzed life is better for someone than a paralyzed life, other things equal, that we try to cure and prevent paralysis in cases where there is no conflict for a scarce resource. Doing so is not thought to involve an objectionable discriminatory judgment.[18] The agency also suggested that choosing to save the unparalyzed life implies that one thought the life of a paralyzed person was not worth as much. Brock thinks this complaint fails to distinguish between the equal worth of a person and the unequal worth of the contents of that person's life.

[18] It is possible that there is a different reason, in general, for trying to cure and prevent paralysis; namely, a life with the disability is harder even if not less good. It could be supererogatory to require for people to lead the harder life even if it were no less good. But it is also not objectionably discriminatory to judge that the paralyzed life is harder. For the "supererogation argument" see my "Disability, discrimination, and irrelevant goods."

Apparently, he thinks the latter can be relevant to allocation decisions consistent with respect for the equal worth of persons.

Brock's positive view about the hypothetical case considered by the government agency is that our treatment will be more effective if it both saves a life *and* cures a disability incurred in the accident. Therefore, it is not objectionable discrimination to save the person who will not be disabled.[19] Notice that we are probably considering this to be a case in which we are *aiming* to reverse all the damage—life-threatening as well as disability-causing—that has occurred in the accident. Hence, we are probably not conceiving of this as a case in which a treatment that is aimed only at saving someone's life also has *a foreseen but unusual side effect* of curing his disability, as in my switch cases.[20] Indeed, in the government's case, there may be two treatments; one is lifesaving and will work on each person equally well in the narrow sense. Another is a disability-curing treatment that will work on only one person. Suppose we are concerned not with whom we can treat most effectively (as Brock puts it), but with in whom *a treatment* will be most effective. Then the question becomes whether we should choose one of the patients to get a lifesaving treatment that works equally well in either patient simply because another treatment we have is effective in curing disability only in him. But loss of life is the most pressing concern (and length of the expected survival is not said to be different). So it seems that the narrow standard of treatment effectiveness implies, as it would imply in my switch cases, that we should ignore whether we can cure a disability in deciding whom to save.

Third, Brock says that if a treatment for an unrelated condition (such as heart disease) causes a disability (such as paralysis) in one person but not another, as it did in my switch case 2, the treatment is less effective in the first person, other things equal.[21] However, the idea of unequal effectiveness that Brock employs here seems inconsistent with his original, narrower notion of treatment effectiveness. Because if a treatment's causing disability counted against its narrow effectiveness, so should its causing reduced lifespan in one

---

[19] He says, "The fifth form of discrimination is where a particular treatment is less effective in some kinds of patients than in another kind, leaving the first kind disabled, but not due to any background conditions of pre-existing disability. This case seems simply to be a difference in treatment effectiveness, with disability entering the picture for some patients but not others only as a result of the treatment" (p. 41). This quote probably applies to both cases in which treatment does not cure disability acquired in an accident (as in the text) and where it actually causes a disability (as in my second switch case).

[20] In my switch case that involves life saving and a cure of disability in one patient but not another, the disability was recently acquired in both patients, but independently of the life-threatening illness. When I first wrote about the switch case in "Deciding whom to help, the principle of irrelevant goods and health-adjusted life years," I did not know about the hypothetical case considered by the government agency and its analysis of the case. Indeed, Brock informed me of it as a way of criticizing my conclusion that curing disability could matter morally in the switch cases. He seems to have changed his position on this.

[21] Although Brock cites "Deciding whom to help, health-adjusted life years, and disabilities" in his article, he does not mention the discussion in that article of the switch cases.

patient but not another. This limits the scope of Brock's view that we should not consider how long a patient survives after a lifesaving treatment in deciding on treatment effectiveness. (p. 41). Further, if a drug for heart disease caused paralysis, on the narrow view of treatment effectiveness, we would presumably consider it a bad side effect of the drug, just as if it caused dandruff; causing a bad side effect is not an indication of a less effective treatment for heart disease. We might seek another drug that treated the heart disease as effectively but without the bad side effect, but we would not describe this as seeking a more effective treatment, in a narrow sense, for heart disease.

It is only if we adopt a wide notion of treatment effectiveness that good or bad side effects will speak against treatment being equally effective in different people. Hence, it does not seem that the narrow standard implies that we should prefer to save the person in whom the treatment does not produce or does cure a disability. (This issue arises, in part, because Brock introduces the narrow notion of treatment effectiveness in conjunction with the idea that "specific medical treatments are *developed* for specific medical conditions." So it seems that it is only the condition for which the treatments are developed that matters for deciding whether effective treatment is present. Focusing on development for specific medical conditions, if this means specific illnesses, will also raise problems if we consider cases in which "condition similarity" due to different illnesses (as described earlier) exists, or in which a patient will be treated successfully for heart disease but soon die of liver failure anyway.

Brock himself specifically qualifies his conclusions based on the narrow notion of treatment effectiveness, saying that they hold "unless attending to treatment effectiveness is ruled out on other moral grounds" (p. 42). Still, I think that Brock does not correctly draw out the implications of the narrow conception of treatment effectiveness that he favors. Furthermore, the correct implications of the conception are often inconsistent with what seem to be the correct views about possible nondiscriminatory handling of cases. Hence, we have reason not to always rely on such a narrow notion in deciding whether allocating scarce resources is or is not invidiously discriminatory.

Problems with the Causative Principle and Ideas of Discrimination

Having distinguished the causative principle from a narrow treatment effectiveness view, I want to discuss some problems I have elsewhere raised for the causative principle. The problems show that the principle fails, despite avoiding some of the problems raised by the narrow treatment effectiveness view. Moreover, some of its failings involve (other) forms of invidious discrimination.

1. Recall that the causative principle states that it may be morally permissible to take account of large differences in QALYs if and only if we cause them

(rather than piggyback on them). Consider a case in which we must choose whether to give a lifesaving scarce drug to an unparalyzed person who will remain unparalyzed because we do not affect this property of his in any way (U → U) or, instead, to a recently paralyzed person in whom the lifesaving drug has the side effect of unparalyzing him (P ⇒ U), where ⇒ indicates our causal role in treating paralysis. (This case involves the second person in Case 2 and the first person in Case 1, Figure 16.1.) In this case, our causal role is greater in the originally paralyzed person than in the originally unparalyzed person. Yet I believe it would be morally wrong and even invidiously discriminatory to make this factor relevant in deciding whom to help. This is because both people will be unparalyzed in the outcome, and there is no difference in their past lives that would imply that one person will have lived a much worse life overall if he is not helped to live on. That is, suppose we endorse some morally acceptable role for the causative principle (on the basis of cases where the choice is between giving a scarce lifesaving drug to P who will remain P and P whom our treatment can make U, as in Case 1). Then we may make the wrong decision and, it seems, even an invidiously discriminating one, in some cases. This is so if we choose to aid the person on whom we have a much greater positive causal effect, in cases where the candidates' outcomes are the same. (Brock does not consider such cases and the problems they raise in his discussion of our greater impact on one patient than another. I shall comment on this further later.)[22]

In response to such same-outcome cases, I suggested that a mark of invidious discrimination may be that we hold it for or against someone in a contest for a scarce resource that he is disabled or nondisabled when we did not cause those states in him. In cases in which the outcomes for both patients would be U, if we count it in favor of one person that we would cause his being U, we will really be holding it against the other person that he would be U rather than P independently of anything we do.[23] This is because it is his being and remaining U that makes it true that we cannot have a causative role in producing U in him. Hence, sometimes, if we want not to be engaged in invidious discrimination against either the disabled or the nondisabled, we should *not* attend to the causative role of our treatment. (The same may hold when we must decide between saving U ⇒ P and P → P. The fact that our causative effect is negative in one person but not the other can be irrelevant if the outcome is the same. This is so even though we would be harming one of the people, especially since depriving him of a chance for the procedure that paralyzes him would result in a worse effect for him, namely, death.) This is why I suggested that we should move beyond the simple causative principle (and also beyond seeing

[22] I raised this issue in "Deciding whom to help, health-adjusted life years, and disabilities," pp. 239–240.

[23] A full discussion of this point would have to consider as an exception the idea of giving priority to a worse-off paralyzed person because her past and the past of the unparalyzed persons are very different. I owe this point to Carlos Soto.

where our treatment narrowly construed is most causally effective). Hence, in deciding how to allocate a scarce resource, insofar as we are concerned with quality in outcome and assume that invidious discrimination can occur when we piggyback, we should focus on whether *we would cause a significantly better or worse* outcome in one patient than in another.[24]

This solution to the problem raised by the simple causative principle for same outcome cases helps refine the idea of invidious discrimination.[25] As suggested by what I have said above, I do not think that judging paralysis to be worse than nonparalysis, other things equal, is itself an instance of an invidiously discriminatory value judgment. Now suppose it is sometimes not invidiously discriminatory to differentiate candidates for a scarce resource on the basis of the expected presence or absence of disabilities when our treatment for some other condition would cause or cure the disabilities. Then we also cannot conceive of invidious discrimination as taking account of someone's disability when this will lead to a worse outcome for him (e.g., he loses his chance for a scarce resource for another medical problem). But one sense of invidious discrimination seems to involve doing what holds someone's disabled or nondisabled state against or in favor of him just because our treatment does not cause the state *when outcomes are the same*. Finally, we have been supposing that someone believes that invidious discrimination occurs in attending to differences in outcome when they come about through piggybacking, yet he also thinks this is not true when the same difference is caused by us (as in the switch cases). Putting all this together, we get a conception of discrimination that seems to involve holding someone's abled or disabled state against or in favor of him in a contest for a lifesaving resource when our treatment does not cause the difference (i.e., whether outcomes are different or the same). (One exception is when the disabled state is similar to the condition that gives us reason to try to treat an illness with our scarce resource.)

---

[24] For a more detailed discussion of this, see "Aggregation, allocating scarce resources, and the disabled." In moving beyond the simple causative principle, I introduced another principle, the *principle of irrelevant (type) identity*. I omit discussion of it here to avoid unnecessarily complicating matters. Elizabeth Pike has suggested that in same outcome cases not involving life and death, we *should* attend to our causative role. For example, suppose that we could treat either P or U for gastritis. U would remain U if he is treated, but the drug for gastritis would also have the side effect of making P unparalyzed. Surely, she says, we should give the drug to P, for then the person who remains U will still be alive and U, albeit with gastritis, and we will both cure gastritis in someone and produce another unparalyzed person. I agree that, in this case, we should give the treatment to P. However, this case shows that it is not enough to focus on just the outcomes for the competitors for a scarce resource in order to know whether we will have produced the same outcome whomever we treat. Because if we treat U instead of P, we will have a world in which there is still a paralyzed person (P), whereas, if we treat P, we will reduce the number of paralyzed people and cure the same amount of gastritis. Hence our overall outcome will be different depending on whom we treat.

[25] I discuss this in "Deciding whom to help, health-adjusted life years, and disabilities," pp. 238–239.

2. Another problem with emphasizing whether our treatment causes or cures disability is the threat of *intransitivities*[26]: suppose we may sometimes take account of how we causally affect disabilities when deciding how to allocate scarce resources. Then it may be morally permissible to treat $P \Rightarrow U$ and $U \rightarrow U$ differently when they are each in contests for resources with someone who is $P \rightarrow P$. That is, $P \Rightarrow U$ may be preferred to $P \rightarrow P$ without invidious discrimination, but, if we assume the view that taking account of piggybacked disability is wrongly discriminatory, $U \rightarrow U$ may not be preferred to $P \rightarrow P$. Yet, it was argued earlier that $P \Rightarrow U$ and $U \rightarrow U$ should be treated as equals in a contest between them alone for a scarce resource. So individuals who are equals in a pairwise comparison behave differently when they are compared pairwise with a third party ($P \rightarrow P$). This gives rise to the (apparent) threat of intransitivity and the problem of whom we should select when all three of these individuals are present at once. (It also implies that it is being held against someone that he was U without our assistance since he fares worse relative to P than someone who began as P and whom we would *make* U. To avoid this problem, we could simply settle for avoiding invidious discrimination, as I described it earlier, in pairwise comparisons only.)

More specifically, the problem of (apparent) intransitivity can be put as follows, where > is "preferred without invidious discrimination": (1) $P \Rightarrow U > P \rightarrow P$; (2) $P \rightarrow P = U \rightarrow U$; and yet (3) $-(P \Rightarrow U > U \rightarrow U)$.[27] Brock does not speak to this issue because, as I noted earlier, he does not deal with cases in which our causative role in helping (or harming) one person would lead to the same outcome for both patients. That is, Brock's discussion considers the comparisons in (1) and (2), but not the comparison involved in (3). This may be why he does not notice that (1) and (2) imply what seems to be untrue, namely that $P \Rightarrow U > U \rightarrow U$.[28]

What should we do when all three individuals (i.e., $P \rightarrow P$, $U \rightarrow U$, and $P \Rightarrow U$) are in competition for the same lifesaving scarce resource? When all three are present, I suggested (2009) that it would not involve invidious discrimination to select one of the people who would have the best outcome. We could reason in the following way: $P \rightarrow P$ could be eliminated from the contest by $P \Rightarrow U$, and so not have to be directly compared with $U \rightarrow U$. Then we

[26] This was discussed in "Deciding whom to help, health-adjusted life years, and disabilities," p. 242, n. 13. Further discussion of this is in "Aggregation, allocating scarce resources, and the disabled."

[27] Also, $P \Rightarrow U = U \rightarrow U$, and $U \rightarrow U = P \rightarrow P$, yet $-(P \Rightarrow U = P \rightarrow P)$.

[28] Perhaps there is another reason for his not seeing this problem. It is possible that a treatment that did more for one patient than another should (as in [3]) still be considered equally effective in a wide sense in both, and so not be grounds for permissibly preferring one patient. This is because the treatment equally deals with all the problems each patient had, even if the nondisabled patient has fewer problems. It would be just as *effective* in a wide sense although it did not literally *affect* as much.

can give equal chances to P $\Rightarrow$ U and U $\rightarrow$ U. (There will be no cycling.) The underlying view is that we are morally permitted to seek a significantly better outcome, and to follow a path in decision making that leads us there, so long as our path to this end is not invidiously discriminatory and no other relevant moral principle is violated.[29]

3. Let me present a third problem I have discussed. I think it is a problem for those opposed to taking account of disability and nondisability in allocating lifesaving scarce resources when P $\rightarrow$ P and U $\rightarrow$ U, but who nevertheless think that significant differences in life expectancy—whether they come about through our causation or piggybacking—should sometimes matter in allocation decisions. Suppose candidate A for a lifesaving treatment will live for 1 year and B for 6 years, and this is a reason to select B. Suppose A is nondisabled and B was recently severely paralyzed. Other things equal, if we do not give the treatment to B, we would be holding his disability against him. Suppose B receives the treatment and subsequently wishes to take advantage of a new surgery that will unparalyze him although it reduces his life expectancy to slightly over 1ne year. (I called this a *switch-and-reduce case*.) He wants to do this because, let us suppose, it is a reasonable *intra*personal tradeoff to exchange 6 years of severely paralyzed life for slightly more than 1 year of nondisabled life. In fact, it makes him better off. With the switch-and-reduce surgery, B would be almost identical to the way A was; the difference in length of life expected (a month) would presumably be morally irrelevant in an interpersonal choice of whose life to save. Had B's prospects earlier been nearly identical to A's, the objection we raised to the simple causative principle implies that we should have given them equal chances for the lifesaving resource. Even if at the time of allocating the scarce treatment we only knew that B would have the switch-and-reduce surgery were his life to be saved, it seems we should have given A and B equal chances.

Might it be that if we select B over A because he will live for 6 years, we should elicit a promise that he will not have the later surgery so that the 5 additional years of life that gave us a reason to deprive A of his chance will come about? Limiting B's options subsequent to his selection would imply that there are moral reasons for his having to make decisions only about his own life from the same perspective that led to him rather than someone else being alive. (This would be even clearer if A would have been preferred over B [with a life expectancy of slightly over 1 year] because A had a significantly longer life expectancy than 1 year [e.g., 3 years]).

Further, suppose that, at the time of the choice with A, we could have saved B in two different ways: (1) so that he will live for 6 years paralyzed or (2) so

---

29 A round-robin procedure would lead to the same result, according to Peter Graham.

that we switch him to being unparalyzed with a lifespan of slightly more than 1 year. Then if B chose the switch-and-reduce option (2), it seems that equal chances should have been given to A and B. Hence, if, at the time of selecting a candidate, B chose the lifesaving procedure (2) that was better for him intrapersonally, he would eliminate the superior chances to live relative to A that he would have had if he chosen to be P for 6 years.[30]

The problem in these cases arises because we are refusing to allow the same tradeoff between quality and quantity of life interpersonally that (we are assuming) is reasonable intrapersonally. Such a tradeoff interpersonally (we are assuming) would make 6 years P in B equal to 1 year U in A. One ground for not allowing quality/quantity tradeoffs interpersonally was suggested earlier: when all one can have is a life with severe P, it may be reasonable to care about 1 year with such a life as much as someone else cares about 1 year with U (2004, 2009). However, we are also allowing the reasonableness of bringing about the intrapersonal tradeoff between a long life with severe P and a shorter one with U when this can be done. That is, someone who reasonably cares maximally for a year with severe P when it is all he can have, can consistently care to be U for even much less time, when that is an option. As a result of these two moves, B's P life lasting for 6 years is judged better *interpersonally* than A's U life lasting for 1, and yet B's U life for slightly more than 1 year, which would *intrapersonally* be better than the better *interpersonal* option, is not judged better *interpersonally* than A's year.

These cases may remind us of what Thomas Scanlon famously emphasized, that intrapersonal tradeoffs that are adequately reasonable for an individual to make can lack moral relevance from an interpersonal point of view. He described someone (call him Joe) who had a claim on us for food to meet his nutritional needs but for whom it was more important to build a monument to his god than to eat. Scanlon claimed that Joe would have no claim on us to provide him with funds to build the monument instead of spending the same amount for his food. Now suppose that our money is scarce, and both Joe and Alice have an equal claim on us for food. The amount we can purchase is the minimum necessary for survival, and so there is no point dividing it between them. Then, if other things are equal between them, we should give each a maximal equal chance for food. However, if Joe will sell the food we give him to get supplies to build the monument to his god, then, presumably, he should lose his equal chance for the food. His not unreasonable intrapersonal tradeoff

---

[30] A similar issue arises if B, who would be P for 6 years, confronts C, who would be P for 6 years, when only B has the option of another lifesaving treatment that would result in his being U for 1 1/8 years. Suppose the latter is his intrapersonally preferable option. Should B be deprived of his equal chance simply because he selects a better intrapersonal option that we would cause? It atleast seems so, because giving him an equal chance with A would involve counting the length of someone's life differently depending on whether he was U or P.

would not have a legitimate interpersonal role in his retaining an equal chance with Alice for food. This would be true even if Alice had the same preference ranking that Joe had but would not be able to act on it if she gets the food supply.[31]

[31] For Scanlon's case, see his "Preference and urgency," *The Journal of Philosophy*, 72(19), 655–669. Thomas Nagel reminded me of the relevance of Scanlon's case for my discussion of the switch-and-reduce cases. Suppose, however, that Joe used money of his own on monument building where he could have used it for food, and this forseeably left him without money for his food, Scanlon would think that Joe now had no claim on us to provide him with food. (Would he think that Joe had atleast a weaker claim on food than someone else whose hunger was not the result of having spent his money on this other project.) This case raises many interesting issues about the specificity of the use of our aid (after all, Joe will eat the food we give him) and also about responsibility for one's condition.

PART } III

Health Inequality and Public Policy

17 }

What Does the Empirical Evidence Tell Us About the Injustice of Health Inequalities?

Angus Deaton

How we should think about inequalities in health depends, in part, on the facts about health inequalities and on how we understand them. Causal interpretations are required to design policy. Hausman (2009, p. 237) notes that "understanding the health gradient helps to guide benevolent interventions" and emphasizes the need to clarify causal paths. Facts and correlations, without an understanding of causation, are neither sufficient to guide policy nor to make ethical judgments. Without getting causation right, there is no guarantee that interventions will not be harmful. It is also possible that an inequality that might seem to be *prima facie* unjust might actually be the consequence of a deeper mechanism that is in part benevolent or that is unjust in a different way.

I provide examples of good inequalities, of bad inequalities, and of inequalities that are neither. In each case, I reflect on judgments and policies. I discuss health inequalities within countries, in which differences in health are associated with differences in education, income, and status. I shall have something to say about the enormous differences in health between rich and poor countries, and I shall briefly consider the relationship between income inequality and health. Following Hausman (2007), I treat health inequalities as important to the extent that they involve inequalities in overall well-being, and I treat them as unjust when they are not compensated for by other components of well-being, when they do not play an essential part in some other good outcome, or when they cannot plausibly be attributed to freely undertaken personal choices. Health inequalities are unjust when they are part of an overall distribution of well-being that is different from what it ought to be. Finally, I offer some brief conclusions.

I am grateful to Anne Case, Marc Fleurbaey, Jeff Hammer, and Dan Hausman for comments on previous versions of this chapter, as well as to participants at the Brocher Summer Academy, July 2010, for discussion and suggestions. I gratefully acknowledge financial support from the National Institute on Aging, National Institutes of Health, Grants P30 AG024361 to Princeton and R01 AG049629 to the National Bureau of Economic Research.

The Birth of the Gradient

It is sometimes supposed that the gradient has always been with us, that rich people have always lived healthier and longer lives than poor people. That this supposition is generally false is vividly shown by Harris (2004, figure 2), who compares the life expectancies at birth of the general population in England with that of ducal families. From the middle of the sixteenth to the middle of the nineteenth century, there was little obvious trend in life expectancy among the general population. For the ducal families up to 1750, life expectancy was no higher than, and sometimes lower than, the life expectancy of the general population. This changed in the century after 1750, when the life prospects of the aristocrats pulled away from those of the general population, and, by 1850–74, they had an advantage of about 20 years. After 1850, the modern increase in life expectancy became established in the general population. Johansson (2010) tells a similar story for the British royals compared to the general population, although the royals began with an even lower life expectancy at birth.

Kings, queens, and dukes were always richer and more powerful than the population at large and would surely have liked to use their money and power to lengthen their lives, but, before 1750, they had no effective way of doing so. Why did that change? Although we have no way of being sure, the best guess is that, perhaps starting as early as the sixteenth century, but accumulating over time, there was a series of practical improvements and innovations in health, including inoculation against smallpox (not vaccination, which still lay many years in the future; Razzell [1977]), professional (male) midwives, cinchona bark against malaria, "Holy wood" against syphilis, oranges against scurvy, and ipecacuanha against diarrhea (Johansson 2010). Many of these innovations were expensive; indeed, in sharp contrast to what would happen later, the "miracle" drugs and methods were imports from afar, from Brazil, Peru, China, and Turkey. The children of the royal family were the first to be inoculated against smallpox (after a pilot experiment on condemned prisoners), and Johansson notes that "medical expertise was highly priced, and many of the procedures prescribed were unaffordable even to the town-dwelling middle-income families in environments that exposed them to endemic and epidemic disease." So the new knowledge and practices were adopted first by the better off—just as today, where it was the better off and better educated who were the first to give up smoking and to adopt breast cancer screening. Later, these first innovations became cheaper, and, together with other gifts of the Enlightenment—the beginnings of city planning and improvement, the beginnings of public health campaigns (e.g., against gin), and the first public hospitals and dispensaries (Porter 2000)—they contributed to the more general increase in life chances that began to be visible from the middle of the nineteenth century.

Why is this important? Absent some extraordinary constellation of offsetting factors, the absence of a gradient before 1750 shows that there is no general health benefit from status *in and of itself* and that power and money are useless against the force of mortality without weapons to fight it. The possession of power and money may have protected health in some ways and hurt it in others, but the overall point is the same: that without some understanding of causes and cures for ill health, high status affords no protection. Link and Phelan's (1995) "fundamental causes" hypothesis, that power and money seek out health improvements but that these take different forms in different eras, is an important insight and frequently useful for thinking about changing patterns of disease. It also implies that, in periods when there is nothing that power and money can do, there will be no gradient. Beyond that, when health improvements come through innovation and new knowledge, the first beneficiaries are likely to be those with the understanding and wherewithal to adopt them, which will usually be the better educated and better off. It would certainly be better still if all beneficent changes came to everyone at the same time, although this may not always be possible if, for example, the innovations are initially expensive. Moreover, if the initial health inequalities indicate that there are general health benefits to come, and if they provide incentives for the spread of innovation, we may be more tolerant of an initial temporary inequality. Clearly, the way to eliminate the inequality is to encourage the rapid diffusion of successful innovations, not to prevent the royal family from inoculating its children nor to suppress the knowledge that cigarette smoking causes cancer.

I am not arguing that innovations are the only cause of health inequalities; for example, we know that health inequalities differ between places and countries with the same health knowledge and technology and, as we shall see, there are many other causes of health differences between groups. Nor am I arguing that public policy should not target the health inequalities caused by new knowledge and treatments; indeed, such inequalities are likely to be a good target, if only because we know something about how to address them. The argument here is that these types of inequalities indicate the workings of a benevolent process, and policies to address inequalities should be designed so as not to hinder the diffusion of better health.

Men and Women

Men die at higher rates than women at all ages after conception. Although women around the world report higher morbidity than men, their mortality rates are usually around half those of men. The evidence, at least from the United States, suggests that women experience similar suffering from similar conditions but have higher prevalence of conditions with higher morbidity and lower prevalence of conditions with higher mortality so that, put crudely, women get sick and men get dead (Case and Paxson 2005). Perhaps the first reaction is that these inequalities are biologically determined and are not amenable to human action, so that they are neither just nor unjust. But biology cannot be the whole explanation. The female advantage in life expectancy in the United States is now smaller than for many years, 5.3 years in 2008 compared with 7.8 years in 1979, and it has been argued that there was little or no differential in the preindustrial world (Vallin 1991). The contemporary decline in female advantage is largely driven by cigarette smoking (Pampel 2002); women were slower to start smoking than men and have been slower to quit, so that the decline in associated mortality started much earlier for men. In some parts of Europe, female mortality rates from lung cancer are still rising. It might be argued that these gendered choices have no implications for overall well-being and are no more an injustice than it is unjust for women to choose Jane Austen over Dan Brown while men choose the opposite. Yet these choices are not made in a social vacuum nor without the constraints of economic or other circumstance, and injustice may (or may not) lie in these background arrangements. For much of the twentieth century, women were unjustly prohibited from smoking, and current outcomes are in part a reflection of that history. Yet that historical injustice of opportunity seems less important than other injustices, such as those of poverty and inequality, so that gender differences in smoking-related mortality are surely of less ethical concern than differences in smoking-related mortality between poor and rich.

It is hard to see health inequalities between men and women as a justification for differential treatment at the point of care, which would create a procedural injustice. Yet, at a systemic or research level, policy makers and administrators constantly prioritize one set of conditions over another so that, among other considerations, one might argue that the injustice of men's shorter lives calls for greater attention to diseases that are more likely to kill men. Alternatively, one might also argue that the male disadvantages in life expectancy reflect informed male choices of lifestyle and are fully compensated by the offsetting benefits of those choices. We should take the broader view that the inequalities that should concern us are those in overall well-being not in its components. If men are favored in most domains of well-being, such as power, earnings opportunity, or morbidity, the superior mortality experience of women might actually reduce overall inequalities. On this argument, we would be much more concerned if women had *higher* mortality than men, just as we are particularly concerned about the higher mortality of blacks, given that they suffer from a wide range of other disadvantages.

Children, Race, and Health Care

Children have worse health outcomes when their parents have less income or less education. The differences are relatively small at birth, but widen throughout childhood; Case, Lubotsky, and Paxson (2002) show that the income (but not the education) gradient of child health in the United States steadily steepens with age. Similar results have been found for Canada and for the United Kingdom (Currie and Stabile 2003; Case, Lee, and Paxson 2008).

What seems to happen is that the disadvantages at birth from a wide range of conditions (income, housing, nutrition, health care) widen with age because of the cumulative effects of bad conditions or because poorer parents are less able to deal with new health conditions as they occur, in part through the costs of doing so and in part through the difficulty of finding time to take children for treatment while holding down (often multiple) low-paying jobs. In consequence, conditions that could be fully treated are sometimes allowed to get worse or to have long-lasting consequences. In many places, the poor also face lower quality, less well-funded health services. As the children of poor people move into the labor force, their relatively worse health persists into adulthood, leading to poorer job opportunities and greater loss of earnings through a higher likelihood of episodes of ill health. People who are inadequately nourished as children are shorter in adulthood and earn less; in both Britain and the United States, an additional inch of height comes with 1.5–2 percent higher earnings (Case and Paxson 2008). As a result, the relationship between health and income steepens throughout the working life. After retirement, once the link from health to earnings from work is broken and selective mortality becomes important, health gradients flatten out again, although they never entirely disappear. Parental education also affects child education, and children who are in worse health are more likely to miss school or to learn less in school, so that there is also a mechanism running from health in childhood to lower earnings in adulthood, even conditional on good adult health. The evidence for the multiple pathways is reviewed by Currie (2009); Heckman (2007) develops a model of cognitive and noncognitive skill formation that integrates health and human capital formation.

These childhood gradients, with their long reach into adulthood, are unjust inequalities that ought to be addressed. Sen (2002) writes "What is particularly serious as an injustice is the lack of opportunity that some may have to achieve good health because of inadequate social arrangements." Heckman's work, with its emphasis on dynamic complementarities, through which investments in health and education have higher returns for better educated and healthier people, suggests high rates of return to interventions in early life (see Conti, Heckman, and Urzua 2010), so this is a case in which justice and economic expediency are well-aligned.

Racial inequalities in the United States are my second example of an unjust inequality although, once again, there is controversy about the cause of the inequalities and the nature of the injustice. In 2006, life expectancy at birth was 4.1 years less for African Americans than for white Americans. There are also pronounced racial differences in treatment patterns, for example, for cardiovascular disease (Smedley, Stith, Nelson 2002), or knee arthroplasty (Skinner et al. 2003). The conventional explanation for these inequalities, endorsed by a 2002 report of the National Academies of Sciences (Smedley et al. 2002), is that the encounter between health care providers and patients leads to poorer treatment of African Americans by largely white providers. More generally, the daily stress of living in a racist society is itself thought to be a cause of poor health outcomes.

There is no doubt something to these accounts, but there is another, perhaps more obvious explanation, which is that African Americans receive worse health care because the hospitals and clinics that serve them are of lower quality than the hospitals and clinics attended by other Americans. Hospitals in the United States are run on something close to an apartheid basis, with few white patients in the hospitals that treat mostly African Americans, and vice versa (Skinner, Chandra, Staiger, Lee, and McClellan 2005); doctors and nurses are much less segregated, with many white doctors in "black" hospitals and African-American doctors in "white" hospitals. The "black" hospitals have worse outcomes, are less well-provisioned, their pharmacies have fewer drugs, and their providers are less well-qualified (Bach et al. 2004). In consequence, people who live in cities with large African-American populations—both African Americans and whites who live in those areas—have poorer health care and higher mortality rates than those who live in cities with small African-American populations (Deaton and Lubotsky 2003).

Another disadvantage for African Americans is that they are more likely to live close to environmental hazards. Currie (2011) has recently documented the claims of the environmental justice movement using data on 11.4 million births in five large American states. According to her calculations, 61 percent of black mothers (67 percent of those without high school education), but only 41 percent of white mothers give birth within 2,000 meters of a site included in the U.S. Environmental Protection Agency's "Toxic Release Inventory." There is good evidence that pollution from such sites can compromise health at birth. It is possible that African Americans accept these conditions in return for other goods, such as cheaper housing near polluters. Even so, one might wonder whether they fully understand the tradeoffs that they are making and, even if they do, the injustice is shifted back to the distribution of income, not removed.

These explanations for racial inequalities, like the explanation for early life inequalities, although recognizing multiple determinants, put more emphasis on health care (and on environmental pollution) than is usually the case in the health inequalities literature, which tends to focus on more general economic and social forces, either of material circumstances (the effects of poverty on health) or of psychosocial stress (the effects of low status on health) (Marmot 2004). According to these explanations, the remedy for the injustice is redistribution of income and wealth, both to address material deprivation and to reduce the force of the status differentials that are associated with income and wealth; for example, by giving people more control in the workplace. The health care and environmental explanations, by contrast, are more narrowly focused on the provision of public goods, even though income is likely to be one of the upstream causes of environmental injustice, just as racism is certainly implicated in the general underprovision of public goods for African Americans or indeed of welfare benefits more generally in the United States relative to Europe (Alesina and Glaeser 2004). But the understanding of mechanisms is important, and it will often be easier and more effective to address the immediate causes rather than wait for more general social change.

One reason for pinpointing the effects of health care is the clear importance of health-related innovations for the decline in mortality in the developed world over the past half century. Life expectancy at birth in the United States rose by 7 years from 1960 to 2000, 70 percent of which was due to reduction in mortality from cardiovascular disease, approximately two-thirds of which is medical advance, with the rest attributable to the decline in smoking (Cutler, Deaton, and Lleras-Muney 2006). There has also been a substantial decline in infant mortality, much of it from the introduction of high-tech neonatal intensive care units (NICUs). There has been relatively little reduction in mortality from cancer, although even here, recent data suggest that innovations in treatment are reducing mortality from breast and prostate cancer. Although there are substantial international differences in smoking rates and in mortality from lung cancer, the patterns of decline in cardiovascular mortality are similar in different countries, much more similar than would be expected from different national patterns in economic and social environments, but exactly as would be expected from the spread of knowledge, drugs, and technology from one country to another, especially among rich countries where there are few barriers to adoption and implementation. Given the importance of these advances for mortality decline, and given that not everyone gets access at the same time—better hospitals adopt new advances more rapidly, and the use of drugs such as antihypertensives or preventive screening are more rapidly adopted by the more educated—it would indeed be surprising if the new innovations did not widen the gradients within countries, as was the case for the first gradients in Britain in the eighteenth century. And the same argument applies now as then: that although we should like to reduce the inequalities, we must be careful that our policies speed up the widespread adoption of beneficial treatments and do not discourage their introduction or the discovery of new treatments and thus kill the innovative goose that is laying the golden eggs. Wealth has a formidable record of generating new ways of improving health—wealthy nations have both the means and the desire to extend their lives—and we need to harness its power, not muzzle it on the grounds that it generates temporary inequalities in health.

Socioeconomic Status, Education, Income, and Health

Much of the epidemiological and sociological literature describes and analyzes health inequalities in terms of differences in socioeconomic status, which is taken to be some amalgam of income, education, rank, social class, and occupation, among other things; indeed, health inequalities are often described as "social" inequalities in health. The concept of socioeconomic status, although useful as a descriptive, portmanteau term, is unhelpful when we come to think about causation and, beyond causation, about policy. For example, there is much evidence, reviewed for example in Cutler, Lleras-Muney, and Vogl (2011), that education directly promotes health, not just that those who are educated are also likely to be healthy because of some third factor, but because the knowledge and life lessons that are learned in school and college enable people to take better care of themselves and to take good advantage of the health care system when they need it. We also know that being sick adversely affects the ability to earn and accumulate wealth—that is what the word "disabled" means. One of the many harms of ill health is that it limits the way a person can achieve his or her goals, such as developing a successful, well-paid career and accumulating wealth. Failing at those things is also a likely cause of ill health, but any credible investigation of that link must adequately deal with the obvious deleterious effects of ill health on income, position, and wealth. Wrapping education, position, income, and wealth into an ill-defined object labeled "socioeconomic status," taken to be the primary (and often only) cause, muddies the water and muddles the argument.

Almost certainly, the most famous and influential work on socioeconomic status and health comes from studies of Whitehall civil servants led over many years by Michael Marmot (see, e.g., Marmot et al. [1991], Marmot [1994], Marmot [2004]). This work shows a consistent link between civil service rank—in practice, measured by income—and a wide range of health outcomes, a link that is interpreted as the effect of high rank on promoting health and of low rank as a risk to health. These effects, attributed to psychosocial stress, appear to operate independently of standard risk factors, such as smoking and obesity.

It is easy to believe in the operation of these factors, but there are other mechanisms at work. In particular, even on their first day as civil servants, the future mandarins of Whitehall are not the same as the future clerks; they are better educated, their fathers come from higher social classes, they are taller, and they had better health as children. The later links between health and position within Whitehall are, to some extent, the working-out of these long-determined factors, "the long reach of childhood health." Not surprisingly, civil servants do not look like the general population—they are much better educated and more likely to be drawn from higher social classes—which means that analyses *within* Whitehall cannot correctly disentangle the competing effects on health of early events and of civil service rank. In an important recent paper made possible by the much-welcomed (but very recent) release of Whitehall data, Case and Paxson (2011) show that an uncorrected analysis of Whitehall data leads to an *understatement* of the effects of early life conditions and an *overstatement* of the effects of rank. The mechanism is straightforward. If a lower status youth is to make it through the Whitehall selection process, he or she must have some compensating ability or special talent, and those unobserved factors are almost certainly positively correlated with health. In consequence, the relationship between early life circumstances and health is attenuated within those who actually make it into Whitehall because those from poorer backgrounds are much better on other things that we cannot measure, and part of what should be attributed to early life finishes up being attributed to rank. Case and Paxson carefully document the reality of these biases by comparing the Whitehall civil servants with matched samples from two British cohort studies.

Much of the link between rank and health in Whitehall can also be explained by standard health behaviors. A paper by members of the Whitehall team, Stringhini et al. (2010), but writing without Marmot, shows that "the association between socioeconomic position and mortality...was substantially accounted for by adjustment for health behaviors, particularly when the behaviors were assessed repeatedly" (p. 1159). Earlier studies had measured behaviors at baseline only.

These two new studies, although only two among many, undermine one of the main conclusions of the Whitehall studies to date—that rank, in and of itself, is protective against mortality. When we also note that much of this literature makes no allowance for the "obvious" causality acting in the opposite direction—even in Whitehall, early-onset Alzheimer's disease or chronic emphysema must negatively affect promotion and income prospects—it is unclear how much evidence is left for the operation of psychosocial stress working through rank. Of course, none of this is to deny the importance of social forces on health and, in particular, why health behaviors are so socially graded, a topic that I turn to in the next section.

My own reading of the most important links is shown in the (over)simple account in Figure 17.1. This focuses on health and education in childhood, with

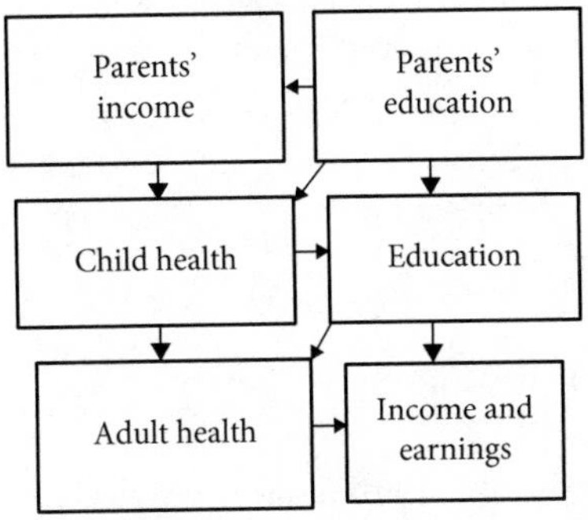

FIGURE 17.1 The main links between health, income, and education.

child health affecting both education and adult health, with education a major determinant of adult earnings, which may also be limited by ill health. Sick people earn less, they spend less time in the labor force, and they retire earlier. In this framework, little but confusion is generated by amalgamating a cause (education) and a consequence (income) into a single category labeled socioeconomic status, which in turn is supposed to cause health (both a cause and a consequence.) None of this is to argue against a role for income in adulthood in promoting health, but that the situation is more complicated is a further reason for conceptual clarity, not the opposite. Even more important are the implications for policy; correcting health inequalities through education is very different from correcting health inequalities through taxation, income, or benefit policies.

What do these conclusions imply for policies to correct injustice? Once again, there is a clear rationale for focusing on early childhood health, nutrition, and disease prevention and for trying to moderate the effects of parental deprivation on child outcomes. Here, the policies are identical to those that would be advocated by those who see causality as flowing from socioeconomic status to health. Among adults, however, there is some divergence of views. If adult earnings is seen as the primary cause of good health, health inequalities need to be addressed through income redistribution—more progressive taxes—or through policies that moderate the benefits of status—although it is not clear what these policies might be. If, by contrast, the mechanism runs from ill health to low incomes, we need to design policies that prevent the injustice of those who are sick having the added disadvantage of suffering material deprivation at the worst possible time. What is required is the construction of health insurance and disability schemes that insure, not health, but one's pocketbook against the depredations of a medical system or the inability to work. In my view, it is such policies, which are only poorly developed in the United States relative to Europe, that are required to address the major injustices of health inequalities among adults. Redistributing income is not only politically much more difficult, but it is likely to be ineffective because it is based on a largely mistaken diagnosis of the problem.

Even so, and as I shall note in my final section, income inequality may, in some circumstances, pose a threat to society's ability to offer equal opportunity to its children, and education and public health programs may not be able to do the job on their own. To this degree, income redistribution may be important for children, if less so for adults.

Unhealthy Behavior by the Poor

One of the major causes of health inequalities is differences in behavior across income and educational groups; in rich countries, poorer people are more likely to smoke, are more likely to be obese (at least among women), are less likely to exercise regularly, are more likely to work in jobs that pose a risk of injury or disability (physical labor in a modern economy is more likely to be bad than good for health—think of a delivery driver carrying heavy packages), are more likely to live in a polluted atmosphere, and are more likely to drink alcohol immoderately. Although there is an element of choice in occupation, location, and lifestyle, poor people lead heavily constrained lives, in terms of money, time, and choices, and some of these choices, even with their poor health consequences, may not be easily avoided under adverse circumstances. For example, without human capital from education or financial capital from inheritances, people must often rely on their physical capacities and energies and adopt occupations, as well as consumption styles, that involve heavy wear and tear on their bodies and on their health (Muurinen and Le Grand 1985; Case and Deaton 2005). If we believed that these lifestyle choices were freely enough made so that people can be held responsible for them, it might be argued that the health inequalities that they cause are not unjust. This may be true in part, but the social patterning of these behaviors should make us cautious about any such supposition.

The health inequalities that come about through these lifestyle and occupational "choices" are once again addressable, if only in part, by addressing early life inequalities in health and education, the same prescription that runs throughout this chapter.

International Health Inequalities

The differences in life expectancy between countries dwarf those between different groups within countries. (This is true for income inequalities too.) There is an 8-year difference in life expectancy between Japanese women (86.1 years) and Japanese men (78.0 years), but both Japanese men and women can expect to live almost twice as long as a newborn in the lowest life expectancy countries in sub-Saharan Africa (Zambia, Angola, and Swaziland). Infant mortality rates—which are the main drivers of differences in life expectancy between rich and poor countries—vary from 3 per 1,000 in Iceland and Singapore (who says the tropics must be unhealthy?) to more than 150 per 1,000 in Sierra Leone, Afghanistan, and Angola. According to the World Bank's World Development Indicators, in 1990, more than a quarter of children in Mali did not live to see their fifth birthdays, a marked *improvement* over 1960 when around half died in childhood—or put even more starkly, when median life expectancy at birth was only 5 years.

The children who die in poor countries would not have died had they been born in rich countries. The same is true of adults with AIDS, whose life expectancy is greatly prolonged in rich countries by the routine use of antiretroviral drugs that are far from universally available elsewhere. At a medical level, we know how to prevent the death of children in poor countries. They are not dying of exotic, tropical diseases for which there are no medicines, but from respiratory infections, diarrhea, diseases associated with malnutrition, lack of neonatal care, or from diseases like polio or measles, for all of which there are known, cheap cures or preventions. Children in rich countries do not die of these causes, although they once did, and, as with health inequalities within countries, these international inequalities are a consequence of the unequal adoption of once new methods and knowledge. If we think that where people are born has no moral relevance for assessing their outcomes, these deaths are surely the greatest of the health-related injustices. Yet matters are even worse because these health injustices are compounded by income injustices. As with health, between-country inequalities in income are much larger than within-country inequalities in income, and the countries that are at the bottom of the health heap are generally also the countries that are at the bottom of the income heap. A newborn child in Angola or in the Democratic Republic of Congo (DRC) not only has a life expectancy that is about half that of a newborn child in Japan but, while alive, can expect to "enjoy" an income level that is only 6.4 percent (Angola), or less than 1 percent (DRC) of Japan's.

For cosmopolitan philosophers who believe that national borders are morally irrelevant, international health and income inequalities are injustices that ought to be corrected by the international community, and in the absence of a world government, this is a task for individual donors working through international nongovernmental organizations (NGOs) and their own governments, as well as for the World Bank, the United Nations or its relevant arms, such as the World Health Organization (WHO) or the United Nations Children's Fund (UNICEF) (see, e.g., Pogge [2002], Singer [2002, 2009], or Sen [2008]). Other philosophers, such as Rawls (1999) and Nagel (2005), argue that the concept of justice does not apply in this international context and that these inequalities, however extreme, are neither just nor unjust. Justice, according to this argument, is part of the social contract within a state; it is what is owed by the state to its citizens: "A political community that exercises dominion over its citizens, and demands from them allegiance and obedience to its laws, must take up an impartial, objective attitude toward them all," Dworkin (2000, quoted by Nagel). No such obligation exists between different peoples. Indeed, Rawls argues that "decent" peoples have a moral standing of their own *as peoples*, so that interference from outside to enforce a global interpretation of justice would be no more justified than the interference by one family in the affairs of another on the grounds that it was insufficiently egalitarian. Similarly, a world government, whose putative powers of remediation might render international inequalities unjust, would bring injustice of another kind (Wenar 2006). That poor health in poor countries is internally unjust seems clear, especially in those cases where first-world medical care and outcomes are found side by side with some of the world's worst health conditions. But the remedy for this injustice falls not on the international community but on domestic governments, which sometimes seem to have little interest in or ability to address it.

An important counterargument is that the world is not a set of islands on which the different peoples live, but a deeply interconnected global community, within which at least some international organizations—think the International Monetary Fund or the World Trade Organization—have substantial powers over the global distribution of income, powers that arguably carry an obligation to international justice (Van Parijs 2007). Even Rawls and Nagel argue for an obligation to assist those peoples who do not have the resources to be "decent," at least to the extent that it is feasible for the international community to do so (about which Rawls himself expressed considerable skepticism, especially through financial transfers). Given the depths of poverty and ill health in much of the world, the obligation to assist and the obligation to justice may not look very different in practice. Yet there are clear areas where cosmopolitanism does indeed seem to risk injustice in its health practices. One example comes from important recent initiatives by the UN and the WHO to target noncommunicable diseases, especially heart disease and cancer, on the grounds that most deaths in poor countries—outside of Africa—are now from these causes. These initiatives may be helpful in finding new ways to treat these conditions in resource-poor contexts. Yet these international priorities may not be those that individual countries would adopt on their own; for example, India might very reasonably choose to give child malnutrition (largely among the poor) higher priority than treatment for (say) diabetes (largely suffered by the better off), even though there is more diabetes in India than anywhere else in the world. Yet international priorities often have a large effect on national policies.

Whether or not we adopt a cosmopolitan position, it is clear that neither the international organizations, private NGOs, nor the governments of rich countries have more than a very limited ability to correct international health inequalities, so that the practicalities are against the cosmopolitans. This is not a matter of the citizens of the rich world being unwilling to pay the (relatively low) financial costs of the required vaccines, medicines, and health clinics. International health inequalities cannot be eliminated without the construction of well-functioning domestic health care systems that provide to the citizens of poor countries the preventative, pre- and post-natal and maternal care that is routine in rich countries. These systems cannot be constructed from the outside, but require domestic state capacity, institutions, and responsibility to citizens that is often missing in poor countries, the very essence of domestic justice. The development of these institutions may actually be undermined by large financial flows from outside (Moss, Pettersson, and van de Walle 2008; Epstein 2007). If this undermining is important, as I believe it is, there is a risk that a well-meaning cosmopolitan attempt to address international health inequalities might actually make them worse and cause even greater suffering and (cosmopolitan) injustice.

None of this is to deny that much has already been done to improve health in poor countries by the application of first-world knowledge (the germ theory of disease) and techniques (vaccination, smallpox eradication). Nor that rich countries cannot do more through basic research (e.g., that AIDS is a sexually transmitted disease or the development of antiretroviral drugs) or international legal arrangements (e.g., trade rules governing the international prices for vaccines and medicines.) Yet the leading sources of mortality in poor countries, especially among children—respiratory infections, diarrheal disease, lack of vaccinations among hard to reach populations—are not addressable by "vertical" health campaigns run by or with the assistance of international organizations.

Income Inequality as a Risk Factor for Health

The health inequalities literature frequently argues that differences in incomes cause health differences, a position that I have argued is largely mistaken. A related but different view is that differences in income are themselves a risk factor for the *level* of health (as well as for the levels of other good social outcomes), so that the rich as well as the poor are hurt by large income differences (Wilkinson 1986; Wilkinson and Pickett 2010). In effect, income inequality is a form of social pollution which, like actual particulate or chemical pollution, risks the health of everyone, rich and poor alike. That income inequality should be a risk factor is sometimes referred to as the "relative income hypothesis," but this is a misnomer because it is possible for health to depend on income relative to others, on rank or on status, without income inequality having any effect on health (Deaton 2003). The evidence for the income inequality hypothesis, which has taken different forms over time, typically rests on correlations, across countries or across American states, of various health measures with various measures of income inequalities. I have argued elsewhere that these contentions are incorrect (Deaton 2003), and similar conclusions have been reached in the epidemiological literature (Lynch, Davey Smith, Harper, Hillemeier, et al. 2004; Lynch, Davey Smith, Harper, and Hillemeier 2004); nothing in the more recent literature invalidates these conclusions. Yet there are other arguments about inequality, injustice, and health that are quite different from those advanced by Wilkinson and that are at risk of being undermined or ignored because of the weakness of Wilkinson's evidence and the controversy that surrounds it.

Inequality has had important historical effects on health, but the mechanisms were not through pollution-type effects of *income* inequality, but through *political* inequality. Szreter (1988) has argued that the cleaning up of cities in Britain in the middle of the nineteenth century had to await the elimination of a political injustice, that working people—who suffered from the dreadful sanitary conditions produced by the industrial revolution—were not permitted to vote. After the Reform Acts and the extension of the franchise, new political coalitions were formed that led, in turn, to an emphasis on urban health. Another example comes from the effects of the Civil Rights Act in the United States on the desegregation of clinics in the American South (Almond, Chay, and Greenstone 2007). Again, when voting machines with candidates' photographs were introduced in Brazil between 1994 and 2002, illiterate or poorly educated voters were better enfranchised, and the spatial pattern of the introduction of the machines matched the spatial pattern of subsequent improvements in spending on public health, in prenatal care, and in the fractions of low birth-weight babies (Fujiwara 2012).

In the United States today, and to a lesser but parallel extent in the other rich English-speaking countries (Atkinson 2003), there has been an almost unprecedented expansion in the fraction of national incomes going to those at the very top of the income distribution. Writers from Plutarch to Hume have emphasized the risks that extreme wealth concentration pose for good government, and there is good evidence that American government today is much more sensitive to preferences of the rich than to the preferences of the poor or even the middle classes (Gilens 2005; Bartels 2008). Indeed, it is likely that at least some of the increase in the pre-tax incomes of top corporate executives and of financial managers have come about through the dismantling of regulations for which those interests have lobbied fiercely (Hacker and Pierson 2010). The very rich have no need of national health insurance, of disability or income support schemes, of public education, or of public policy that will limit the inheritance of deprivation from parents to children. They do not wish to pay taxes to support such schemes, and their immense wealth and political influence provides them with a potent weapon to prevent them having to do so. There is much to fear from the expansion of this kind of income inequality where injustices in one aspect of well-being can breed injustices in others.

Conclusion

Health inequalities are a matter of great moral concern. But whether we see them as an injustice, and whether and how we design policy to correct them, depends on how they come about. In this chapter, I have argued that childhood inequalities are the key to understanding much of the evidence and that public interventions would do well to focus on breaking or weakening the injustice of parental circumstances determining child outcomes. Among adults, the main priority should be the design of schemes that prevent the impoverishment that can come from ill health, through loss of the ability to work or through the costs of treatment. It is also important not to use health inequalities as an argument for limiting health innovations that will benefit all, although there will often be a role for public policy in ensuring that beneficial innovations spread rapidly through the population. As to the largest health inequalities of all, which come from poor health in poor countries, I do not believe that labeling them as an international injustice is either correct or helpful. To the extent that it is possible, individuals, individual nations, and the international community have an obligation to assist those who are suffering the worst of health and material deprivation, but the argument should be on the grounds of common humanity and not international justice. Whatever the motivation, feasibility is a serious concern. Assistance from outside, although sometimes possible and effective, may also undermine the institutions that are needed to support domestic health. Finally, I believe that the recent concentration of wealth at the very top of the income distribution in the United States (and other English-speaking countries) is a serious threat to well-being through its possible long-term effects on health, education, and democracy.

References

Alesina, A., and Glaeser, E. (2004). *Fighting poverty in the US and Europe: World of difference.* Oxford: Oxford University Press.

Almond, D. V., Chay, K. Y., and Greenstone, M. (2007). *Civil rights, the war on poverty, and black-white convergence in infant mortality in the rural south and in Mississippi.* Working Paper No. 07-04, Department of Economics, MIT.

Atkinson, A. B. (2003). Income inequality in OECD countries: Data and explanations. *CESifo Economic Studies, 49*(4), 479–513.

Bach, Peter B., Pham, H. H., Schrag, D., Tate, R. C., and Hargraves, J. L. (2004). Primary care physicians who treat blacks and whites. *New England Journal of Medicine, 351*(6), 575–584.

Bartels, L. (2008). *Unequal democracy: The political economy of the new gilded age.* New York: Russell Sage.

Case, A., and Deaton, A. (2005). Broken down by work and sex: How our health declines. In D. A. Wise (Ed.), Analyses in the economics of aging (pp. 185–205). Chicago: Chicago University Press.

Case, A., Lee, D., and Paxson, C. (2008). The income gradient in children's health: A comment on Currie, Shields, and Wheatley Price. *Journal of Health Economics, 27*(3), 801–807.

Case, A., Lubotsky, D., and Paxson, C. (2002). Economic status and health in childhood: The origins of the gradient. *American Economic Review, 92*(5), 1308–1334.

Case, A., and Paxson, C. (2005). Sex differences in morbidity and mortality. *Demography, 42*(2), 189–205.

———. (2008). Stature and status: Height, ability, and labor market outcomes. *Journal of Political Economy, 116*(3), 499–532.

———. (2011). The long reach of childhood health and circumstance: Evidence from the Whitehall II study. *Economic Journal, 121*, F183–F204.

Conti, G., Heckman, J., and Urzua, S. (2010). The education-health gradient. *American Economic Review, 100*(2), 234–238.

Currie, J. (2009). Healthy, wealthy, and wise: Socioeconomic status, poor health in childhood, and human capital development. *Journal of Economic Literature, 47*(1), 87–122.

———. (2011). Inequality at birth: Some causes and consequences. *American Economic Review, 101*(3), 1–22.

Currie, J., and Stabile, M. (2003). Socioeconomic status and child health: Why is the relationship stronger for older children. *American Economic Review, 93*(5), 1813–1823.

Cutler, D., Deaton, A., and Lleras-Muney, A. (2006). The determinants of mortality. *Journal of Economic Perspectives, 20*(3), 97–120.

Cutler, D., Lleras-Muney, A., and Vogl, T. (2011). Socioeconomic status and health: Dimensions and mechanisms. In S. Glied and P.C. Smith (Eds.), Oxford Handbook of Health Economics. Oxford and New York: Oxford University Press.

Deaton, A. (2003). Health, inequality, and economic development. *Journal of Economic Literature, 41*(1), 113–158.

Deaton, A., and Lubotsky, D. (2003). Mortality, income, inequality, and race in American cities and states. *Social Science and Medicine, 56*(6), 1139–1153.

Dworkin, R. (2000). *Sovereign virtue* Cambridge, MA: Harvard University Press.

Epstein, H. (2007). *The invisible cure: Africa, the West, and the fight against AIDS*, New York: Farrar, Strauss, and Giroux.

Fujiwara, T. (2012). *Voting technology, political responsiveness, and infant health: Evidence from Brazil.* Department of Economics, Princeton University, retrieved from http://www.princeton.edu/~fujiwara/papers/elecvote_site.pdf

Gilens, M. (2005). Inequality and democratic responsiveness. *Public Opinion Quarterly, 69*(5), 778–796.

Hacker, J. S., and Pierson, P. (2010). *Winner-take-all politics: How Washington made the rich richer and turned its back on the middle class.* New York: Simon and Schuster.

Harris, B. (2004). Public health, nutrition, and the decline in mortality: The McKeown thesis revisited. *Social History of Medicine, 17*(3), 379–407.

Hausman, D. M. (2009). Benevolence, justice, well-being and the health gradient. *Public Health Ethics, 2*(3), 235–243.

Hausman, D. M. (2007). What's wrong with health inequalities? *The Journal of Political Philosophy, 15*(1), 46–66.

———. (2009). Benevolence, justice, well-being and the health gradient. *Public Health Ethics, 2*(3), 235–243.

Heckman, J. J. (2007). The economics, technology, and neuroscience of human capability formation. *Proceedings of the National Academy of Sciences, 104*(33), 13250–13255.

Johansson, S. R. (2010). *Medics, monarchs, and mortality, 1600–1800: Origins of the knowledge driven health transition in Europe.* Retrieved from http://ssrn.com/absttract=1661453

Link, B., and Phelan, J. (1995). Social conditions as fundamental causes of disease. *Journal of Health and Social Behavior, 35*(extra issue), 80–94.

Lynch, J., Davey Smith, G., Harper, S., and Hillemeier, M. (2004). Is income inequality a determinant of population health? Part 2. US national and regional trends in income inequality and age- and cause-specific mortality. *The Milbank Quarterly, 82*(2), 355–400.

Lynch, J., Davey Smith, G., Harper, S., Hillemeier, M., Ross, N., Kaplan, G. A., and Wolfson, M. (2004). Is income inequality a determinant of population health? Part 1. A systematic review. *The Milbank Quarterly, 82*(1), 5–99.

Marmot, M.l G. (1994). Social differences in health within and between populations. *Daedalus, 123*(4), 197–216.

———. (2004). *The status syndrome: How social standing affects our health and longevity.* New York: Holt.

Marmot, M. G., Smith, G. D., Stansfeld, S., Patel, C., North, F. Head, J., White, I., Brunner, E., and Feeney, A. (1991). Health inequalities among British civil servants: The Whitehall II study. *Lancet, 337,* 1387–1393.

Moss, T., Pettersson, G., and van de Walle, N. (2008). An aid-institutions paradox? A review essay on aid dependency and state building in sub-Saharan Africa. In William Easterly (Ed.), Reinventing foreign aid (pp. 255–281), Washington, DC: Brookings.

Muurinen, J.-M., and Le Grand, J. (1985). The economic analysis of inequalities in health. *Social Science and Medicine, 20*(10), 1029–1035.

Nagel, T. (2005). The problem of global justice. *Philosophy and Public Affairs, 33*(2), 113–147.

Pampel, F. (2002). Cigarette use and the narrowing sex differential in mortality. *Population and Development Review, 28*(1), 77–104.

Pogge, T. (2002). *World poverty and human rights.* Malden, MA: Polity Press.

Porter, R. (2000). *The creation of the modern world: The untold story of the British Enlightenment.* New York: Norton.

Rawls, J. (1999). *The law of peoples.* Cambridge, MA: Harvard.

Razzell, P. E. (1977). *The conquest of smallpox: The impact of inoculation on smallpox mortality in eighteenth century Britain.* Firle: Caliban Books.

Sen, A. K. (2002). Why health equity? *Health Economics, 11,* 659–666.

———. (2008). The idea of justice. *Journal of Human Development, 9*(3), 331–342.

Singer, P. (2002). *One world: The ethics of globalization.* New Haven: Yale.

———. (2009). *The life you can save: Acting now to end world poverty.* New York: Random House.

Skinner, J., Weinstein, J. N., Sporer, S. M., and Wennberg, J. E. (2003). Racial, ethnic, and geographical disparities in rates of knee arthroplasty among Medicare patients. *New England Journal of Medicine, 349*(14), 1350–1359.

Skinner, J., Chandra, A., Staiger, D., Lee, J., and McClellan, M. (2005). Mortality after acute myocardial infarction in hospitals that disproportionately treat black patients. *Circulation, 112,* 2634–2641.

Smedley, B. D., Stith, A. Y., and Nelson, A. R. (Eds.). (2002). *Unequal treatment: Confronting racial and ethnic differences in health care.* Washington, DC: Institute of Medicine.

Stringhini, S., Sabia, S., Shipley, M., Brunner, E., Nabi, H., Kivimaki, M., and Singh-Manoux, A. (2010). Association of socioeconomic position with health behaviors and mortality. *Journal of the American Medical Association, 303*(12), 1159–1166.

Szreter, S. (1988). The importance of social intervention in Britain's mortality decline c. 1850–1914: A reinterpretation of the role of public health. *Social History of Medicine, 1,* 1–37.

Vallin, J. (1991). Mortality in Europe from 1720 to 1914: Long-term trends in patterns by age and sex. In R. Schofield, D. Reher, and A. Bideau (Eds.), The decline of mortality in Europe. Oxford: Oxford University Press.

Van Parijs, P. (2007). International distributive justice. In R. E. Goodin, P. Pettit, and T. Pogge (Eds.), A companion to contemporary political philosophy (2nd ed.). Oxford: Blackwell.
Wenar, L. (2006). Why Rawls is not a cosmopolitan egalitarian. In R. Martin and D. Reidy (Eds.), Rawls' law of peoples: A realistic utopia (pp. 95–113). Malden, MA: Blackwell.
Wilkinson, R. G. (1996). *Unhealthy societies: The affliction of inequality*. London: Routledge.
Wilkinson, R. G., and Pickett, K. (2009). *The spirit level: Why more equal societies almost always do better*. London: Allen Lane.

18 }

Fair Society Healthy Lives

Michael Marmot

I was invited by the British government to conduct a strategic review of health inequalities in England and to make recommendations for actions to reduce health inequalities. I had chaired the World Health Organization (WHO) Commission on Social Determinants of Health (CSDH 2008). The question for the British government, as for other governments, was how the CSDH recommendations could be applied in one country. We published the English Review in 2010, with the title, *Fair Society Healthy Lives* (Marmot Review 2010) The title was chosen for a positive and a negative reason. The negative was that I wanted to put "social justice" in the title, but was not sure exactly what I understood by the term. Although comfortable with having the debate—hence my pleasure as a non-philosopher in being part of the debate that is represented in this volume—I judged that a report to a government, recommending action, was not the appropriate venue for a philosophical discussion.

The positive reason for the title *Fair Society Healthy Lives* was a judgment, expressed in the report, that if fairness were put at the heart of all societal decision making, the health of the population would improve and health inequalities would diminish. Although that sounds close to a credo, an item of belief, it was in fact a judgment reached over several decades of research on health inequalities and a gathering of the evidence, globally in the CSDH and nationally in the Marmot Review.

Implicit in both the CSDH and the English Review were several conclusions that are the subject of philosophical discussion in the chapters of this volume. I reached these conclusions not by philosophical inquiry but as a doctor-epidemiologist conducting research on health inequalities and now trying to use those and other research findings to influence policy and practice. I will touch on them in this chapter:

- Health is of value in and of itself, not simply as an instrument to some other good.
- Taking action to reduce health inequalities should be taken for moral not economic reasons.

- In high-income countries, especially, the issue is not just the poor health of those in absolute poverty, but the social gradient in health: progressively worse health as the social hierarchy is descended. The implications of the gradient are that action needs to be taken across the whole of society, not only in reducing the health consequences of poverty.
- By common usage in Britain, when we use the term "health inequalities," we mean differences among social groups; in economics, the term inequality is commonly used to apply to differences among individuals—this is interesting but not what I mean by health inequalities.
- Related to the focus on social inequalities in health, evidence shows that actions aimed at encouraging individuals to make healthy choices will not be effective in reducing health inequalities—such action may make inequalities worse as those with more education, for example, take heed of health messages to a greater extent than do those of lesser education.
- Although personal responsibility is key, social action is required to create the conditions that allow people to take control of their own lives.
- The starting position of many economists is that none of the above makes any sense because we have the model wrong: social conditions do not cause health; health causes social position. Therefore, do not address social conditions to reduce health inequalities: instead, spend on better access to medical care, and that will lead to better education, higher incomes, and economic growth. Although the causal arrow may point in both directions, the evidence contradicts the assumption that it goes only from health to wealth. What purports to be an empirically based judgment is, in fact, an ideological position. There is good evidence to view health inequalities as the consequence of our set of social and economic arrangements. A concern with health implies that we need to focus not only on fair processes but also on fair outcomes.
- We should have two societal goals: improving health for everybody and reducing health inequalities. Others may see them as being in conflict, but they are two separable goals. Both are worthy and should be pursued. I have never argued that an overall improvement in health should be sacrificed in the pursuit of narrower health inequalities. Given my general thesis that, to oversimplify, good health results from a good set of social arrangements, I would look to sacrifice other social goals (a self-serving movement toward making the tax system less progressive, for example) before accepting that there had to be a tradeoff between these two health goals.

There was another reason for putting fairness in the title of the inequalities review. A predecessor of the Marmot Review was the Black Report. In 1978, Sir Douglas Black was invited by the British Labour government to conduct a review of health inequalities and make recommendations. By the time the Black Report (Black 1980) was published (Black 1980), Mrs. Thatcher's Conservative government had been elected. The Black Report was rejected by the government. Thirty years later, I had been commissioned by a Labour government, but the predictions were that, soon after I reported, the government would change (no causal link). Although social justice might sound like something rather nasty to some strands of political opinion, it seemed unlikely that any government would say that it was against "fairness." I assumed that Rawls's "justice as fairness," and the fact that fairness should really attract the same debate as justice, might not feature highly.

So it proved. Although the Conservative Secretary of State for Health in Britain (the most senior health minister) welcomed my report and made his response to it in the form of a commitment to taking action on the social determinants of health to reduce health inequalities a central feature of the government's public health white paper, the word "fairness" has been freely used. The government uses "fair" to describe all its policies, regardless of whether their impact may be regressive. My position in the public debate is that, as a doctor, I regard as unfair health inequalities that could be avoidable by reasonable means. Therefore I regard as unfair policies that exacerbate avoidable health inequalities. Of course, we can debate the nature of "reasonable means," but, as a starting position, it is a way of distinguishing, among all the policies that the government describes as fair, where I would concur.

Writing as a non-philosopher, one who has been involved in academic and now policy debates and has thought about these issues, but not in the way a philosopher would, I am very happy to, as it were, test the ideas out against more philosophical modes of thought.

Social Differences in Health

HEALTH IS VALUED

This is a value judgment, but one that has empirical support. Health is highly valued by individuals. Whereas some view health as an instrument to something else of higher value—income, happiness, a good tennis game—I do not. Or at least, it may have instrumental value, but that is not the primary reason for a concern with health.

It has been put to me that people are not concerned by health inequalities. The general population, says this view, is concerned that extremes of income inequality are unfair, but they do not regard some people living longer as unfair. My response is twofold. First, we conducted some informal polling on this issue. A general response was to regard as unfair the fact that some sections of society have worse health. Second, there is indeed empirical evidence, from Britain at least, that the public does regard the level of income inequality to be excessive and unfair. Given my approach—regarding arrangements that lead to avoidable health inequalities as unfair—it means that to the insult of unfair distributions of income has to be added the injury of avoidable health inequalities.

One, but not the only, way to interpret the term "value" is to put a monetary value on it. Murphy, a University of Chicago economist, agrees that people value health highly for its own sake, not simply as an instrument to something else. Murphy assesses the degree of value using a willingness to pay methodology (Murphy 2006). He says that if you want to know how much a person values his or her life, see how much he or she is willing to pay for another year of life. Murphy states that a year of life has greater value if people are willing to pay more (i.e., have higher income), are closer to the age of onset of illness (i.e., older), and are well (rather than sick). At a seminar at Rand, to discuss this approach, I began by saying that I had had lunch with an Indian historian recently and told him that the news from Chicago was that he didn't value his life. The reaction from the Chicago economists was that, indeed, Indians don't value their lives—they are not willing to pay much for another year of it. My retort was that we may behave as if Indian lives are not valuable but that does not mean we *should* regard them as such. My Indian colleague regards his life, and that of his countrymen, as more valuable than do these Chicago economists.

I tried what I assumed would be safer ground. I presented data from the Whitehall Study of British civil servants showing that the lower the grade of employment, the higher the mortality rate. I said that I understood that if a lower grade man dies, his widow is compensated at a lower level (by the pension arrangements) than if a higher grade man dies; but if a lower grade and a higher grade man get chronic renal failure, they have an equal right to be treated in a dialysis program. The Chicago reaction was violent disagreement: the high-grade man's life is worth more, treating him should have priority. It was put to me that if the lower grade man was offered some money rather than treatment, and he chose the money, surely I would be happy with that.

These economic calculations have an elegant simplicity and consistency. Value life in dollars, and society gains more by adding years to a rich person's than to that of a poor person. But that elegance in no way compensates for the ugliness of the assumptions that underlie it. My reaction to the question of whether I would be happy to compensate the low status man with money was along the following lines. "Let me see if I understand what you have just suggested. You would have me, as a physician, say to this low-status man that, because of his humble station in life, his life is relatively worthless. Therefore we are going to withhold treatment and condemn him to a slow, lingering, uncomfortable death. We know how to treat him but are not going to do it. Instead, we will offer him some money. Not a great deal of money. If we had a great deal, we would give him the treatment."

Yes, that is what they would have me say. My response is that I would not vote for a government that organized its affairs that way.

This is not to say that I think that the main determinants of inequalities in health lie within the health care system. They do not. Social determinants of health are far more important. In Britain, for example, the National Health Service comes close to guaranteeing equal access to health care, free at the point of use and regardless of ability to pay, but we still have steep health inequalities. It is not primarily a health care issue. Nevertheless, this exchange illustrates my view that we should treat loss of healthy life years as equally important, regardless of the social status of the individual concerned. Health inequalities are not less important (than average health) because, by definition, they affect people more the lower they are in the social hierarchy.

POVERTY AND INEQUALITY

The insight from the Whitehall studies is that ill health is not confined to poor health for the poor but follows the social gradient: the lower the social position, the worse the health (Marmot 2004). An insight that began, for me, with British Civil Servants has proved to be remarkably general. We updated it for the Marmot Review, from which Figure 18.1 is taken.

The graded nature of the link between neighborhood income deprivation and both life expectancy and disability-free life expectancy is quite remarkable.

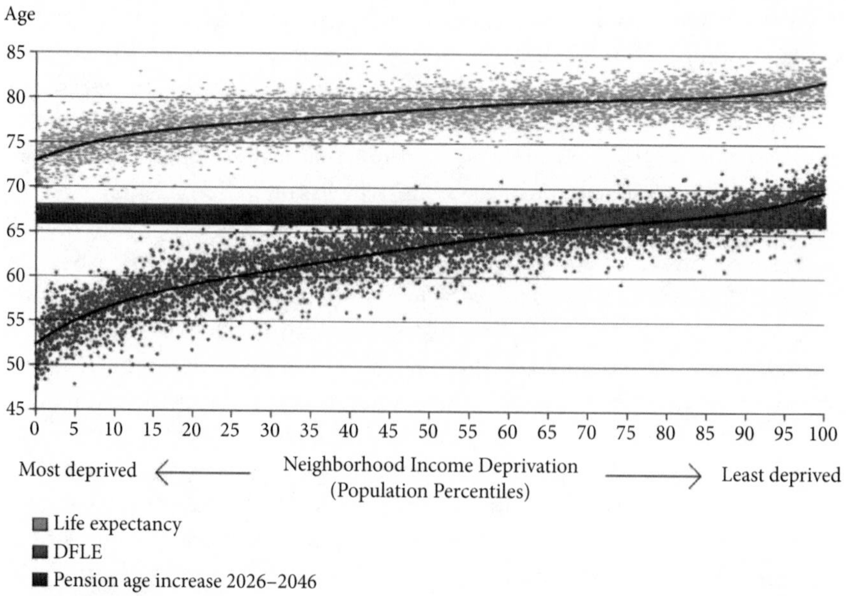

FIGURE 18.1 Life expectancy and disability-free life expectancy at birth by neighborhood income deprivation, 1999–2003.

The implication we drew from the gradient is that action to reduce inequalities in health has to be across the whole of society, not simply to reduce poverty—universalist solutions are needed, not targeted ones. To recognize that those most socially excluded may need more attention, we coined the awkward neologism *proportionate universalism*: universalist solutions with effort proportionate to the degree of disadvantage.

The gradient certainly implies that more than poverty is at play here. Does that mean that relative inequalities are more important than absolute? One way out of this dilemma is to follow Amartya Sen's formulation: relative deprivation with respect to income can translate into absolute deprivation in capabilities (Sen 1992). My view of capabilities is that it is important for people to have control over their lives and to participate fully in society.

INDIVIDUAL DIFFERENCES OR SOCIAL INEQUALITIES?

Many years ago, I realized that some of the confusion between disciplines related more to the dictionary than to the philosophy books—although ideology still plays a part (see the next section). In economics, for example, it is common to use the term "inequality" to mean the total variance (i.e., the sum of individual differences). In the United Kingdom, by tradition, when we in the health sector refer to "health inequalities," we mean the difference between socioeconomic groups. More recently, "equality" has taken on another meaning in the United Kingdom, one to do with equal and fair treatment for groups defined on the basis of race and ethnicity, gender, disability, age, and sexual orientation, as well as socioeconomic position.

It was put to me that socioeconomic position explains only a small portion of the variance in the occurrence of disease (i.e., of the totality of individual differences). True. But then so does smoking. I calculated in the Whitehall Study that smoking, age, and grade of employment "explain" only 7 percent of the variance in death from lung cancer. I conclude from this not that smoking is an unimportant cause of lung cancer, but that percent of variance explained is not a good measure (Marmot 2000). In defense of this position, I point to the fact that 95 percent of lung cancer deaths occur in smokers. Given that there are good reasons to believe that this link is causal, it means that we could abolish 95 percent of lung cancer deaths by abolishing smoking, even though it explains less than 7 percent of the variance.

The causes of individual differences and the causes of group differences, then, may not be the same. In the thought experiment of equalizing all relevant environmental conditions, there would still be individual differences in health. These may claim attention, both from geneticists and from those who sought to avert genetic destiny by improving the lives of people despite their inheritance, but for clarity I would not use the term "inequality" to describe these genetic differences among individuals. I would not think of the genetic lottery as unfair or unjust. Injustice may apply to lack of attention to make the lives of people as fulfilling as possible. For example, even if one were convinced that no injustice pertained to the causes of being confined to a wheelchair, it would still be unjust for buildings not to provide access to those disabled or for local authorities not to provide help to those who have visual impairment.

It is social inequalities in health that exercise me and, if avoidable, that I label as unfair. What if the gradient were the other way round, and the rich had worse health? They don't, but see section on "Improving Health for Everyone or Reducing the Social Gradient?"

INDIVIDUAL BEHAVIORS OR SOCIAL DETERMINANTS

Over the course of the Whitehall studies, we have asked how much of the social gradient could be explained by individual behaviors or risk factors. In the end, socioeconomic position has to "get under the skin" (Adler and Ostrove 1999). In the first Whitehall study, we showed that the usual cardiovascular risk factors accounted, statistically, for about a third of the social gradient in mortality (Marmot, Shipley, and Rose 1984). In the Whitehall II study, we first reproduced that figure and then showed we could explain about 60 percent of the gradient by adding in to the model indicators of the metabolic syndrome and height as a measure of early life nutrition (Marmot et al. 2008). A subsequent analysis from Whitehall II says that more of the social gradient could be explained by the conventional risky behaviors for heart disease (Stringhini et al. 2010). A further paper, however, using the same risk behaviors, shows that they explain only about 20 percent of the social gradient in a French cohort (Stringhini et al. 2011).

Whether these individual behaviors explain 20 percent of the gradient or 80 percent, the same question applies: why is there a social gradient in these risky behaviors? Parenthetically, if they explain only 20 percent, our interest in biological stress pathways is more important than if smoking, diet, and physical activity explain 80 percent. That said, the social gradient in exposures and risky behaviors is what should claim our attention.

Among some observers, the problem is irresponsibility on the part of individuals: the evidence is clear that smoking is causing ill health, as is obesity; for individuals not to act on the evidence is sheer irresponsibility.

I do not find that a helpful way to proceed. First, look at time trends. In Britain, as in many countries, smoking prevalence has declined, and obesity prevalence has increased. If increasing fecklessness accounts for the obesity epidemic, what accounts for our apparent outbreak of responsible behavior in relation to smoking? The decline in smoking has occurred because of concerted social action: price, bans on advertising, labeling of tobacco products, bans in public places, availability of nicotine replacement therapy—not simply because of the sudden onset of individual responsibility. The increase in obesity can be tracked to a complex web of causation relating to the food supply and lack of physical activity at work and at leisure, not simply an outbreak of laziness or indulgence.

Second, an assertion of irresponsibility has to account for the social gradient in smoking and, particularly in women, obesity. Is it accidental that these causes of disease should follow the social gradient? The whole approach we have taken with reports on social determinants of health is to examine the "causes of the causes"—a dubious concept philosophically, I am aware. Simply to ignore the social patterning of behavior and somehow assume that health is a matter of personal responsibility flies in the face of the evidence, whatever one's prior position.

Do We Have the Model Right?

I was due to give a lecture in Stockholm on ageing. Although there was snow in Stockholm and London, it was the closure of Heathrow airport in London that prevented me from traveling. I e-mailed my presentation and gave the lecture down a telephone line. I could not see the audience. At the end of my lecture, the Chair invited questions. The first question was: "Have you thought of the possibility that health leads to wealth rather than, as you suggest, wealth leads to health?"

My response: "That gentleman must be an economist." The chair acknowledged that he was indeed an economist, and how did I know? I have never given a lecture to a group containing economists and not been asked that question and have never been asked that question by someone from another discipline. I would quite like to get to the bottom of why this should be the case, but so far have not. Why is it that the starting position of public health scientists is that the conditions associated with people's social position cause their ill health, and the starting position of many economists seems to be that health "causes" socioeconomic position? Are we public health people sloppy scientists who are blinded by our penchant for do-goodism—to put right social injustice? And are the economists more careful scientists employing more rigor? Perhaps, but that cannot be all there is to it. When I have shared my findings with health economists seeking to investigate these matters, they start by putting to me the proposition that the relation between health and social position is endogenous. My response has been that evidence from birth cohorts show that social position precedes health. Economists have now reanalyzed the same birth cohort data and show the opposite: health leads to social position. Same data, opposite conclusions. Needless to say, analysts who find that social position leads to health do not accept that the economists have it right, and they have it wrong—they then continue the debate (Case, Paxton, and Vogl 2007).

As I said at the beginning of this chapter, the causal arrow goes in both directions, but evidence abounds for these differences in starting positions. The journal *Social Science and Medicine* commissioned eight groups of authors to write commentaries on the Marmot Review, *Fair Society Healthy Lives*. My colleagues and I were invited to respond to these eight commentaries. What follows, in this section, is taken from our *Social Science and Medicine* response (Marmot, Allen, and Goldblatt 2010).

Do We Know Enough to Take Action on Social Inequalities in Health?

Six of the commentaries are in little doubt that we do; although all, like us, want a stronger evidence base. What of the other two commentators (Canning and Bowser 2010; Chandra and Vogl 2010)? Their starting position, like that of many economists involved in the social determinants debate, is that peoples' health determines what happens to them. The Review's starting position was that what happens to people has a cumulative effect throughout their life course, progressively affecting their health.

As I have remarked (Marmot 2009):

> This is not just a polite, or even testy, academic debate. The policy implication of these two positions is quite different. If the main causal direction is from health to wealth, the appropriate intervention is to control illness in order to improve an individual's social and economic fortunes or, indeed, eradicate illness to improve the economy of a whole country. If, as I conclude, the main causes of health inequalities reside in the circumstances in which people are born, grow, live, work and age—the social determinants of health—then action to reduce health inequalities must be in those circumstances and the fundamental drivers of those circumstances: economics, social policies and governance.

Of course, not all economists share Chandra et al.'s approach to the evidence. Amartya Sen was a member of the Commission on Social Determinants of Health, and Sir Tony Atkinson was a Commissioner of the Marmot Review. Each signed up to the conclusions in the respective reports. Jim Smith, whose work showing how health affects income has been influential, also showed elegantly the powerful influence of education on health, such that income drops out of the model (Smith 2007).

The Role of Selection

Chandra et al. appear to believe that it is only through the logic of economic reasoning that causation can be understood. If we in public health were as rigorous about evidence as they, we would be more cautious. In the case in hand, social inequalities in health, everything is determined by "selection." They concatenate two forms of selection, widely discussed in the epidemiological literature: (1) health leads to social conditions, and (2) the health of any group (e.g., low-grade civil servants) is determined by its composition, not by the social conditions experienced by the group.

It is a fundamental tenet of science, with which we fully agree, that in making inferences about causation, associations should always be rigorously tested for the possibility of reverse causation—health leads to socioeconomic position—and confounding—an extraneous factor affects both health and the social condition with which it correlates. But it is mystifying to us why one should start from the position that health determines people's social circumstances rather than the other way round.

The issue and the debate have been around for a long time, both in science and the arts. Take a page from Dickens's *Hard Times* on housing for example: "In the hardest working part of Coketown, ... where Nature was as strongly bricked out as killing airs and gases were bricked in ... where the chimneys, for want of air to make a draft, were built in an immense variety of stunted and crooked shapes" (pp. 65–66) or a description of working conditions in a northern mill town: "all the melancholy-mad elephants, polished and oiled up for the day's monotony, were at their heavy exercise again.... Every man was in the forest of looms where Stephen worked to the crashing, smashing, tearing piece of mechanism at which he laboured."

Should we really assume that these dark satanic mills and airless places, rather than causing terrible illness and shortened lives, selectively employed sick people and those whose backgrounds accounted for all their subsequent illness? That subsequent improvement in living and working conditions, thus abating Victorian squalor, and associated improvements in health were correlation not causation? That although medical care improved health, housing also got better, and the public health profession mistook the improvement in housing and working conditions for causes of improved health?

If proponents of this set of assumptions dropped their guard for a moment and accepted the evidence that air pollution, crowded living conditions, and ghastly working conditions were causes of ill health in Victorian times why, a priori, do they start from the position that living and working conditions are not a cause of ill health in the twenty-first century? Why do they reject the evidence on selection from the 1970s and 1980s, that workers are selected into employment for good health and not illness (Goldsmith 1975; Fox and Collier 1976); that such effects are of limited duration (Fox and Goldblatt 1982; Marmot 2009); and are overtaken by cumulative exposure to work conditions; and that, rather than being sustained by selective mobility between jobs, social gradients in the workforce are dampened by selective movement out of the labor force (Fox and Goldblatt 1982; Goldblatt 1988; Goldblatt 1989)? Why do they appear to assume that Figure 18.1 in the Review, reproduced here, linking neighborhood deprivation to disability-free life expectancy could all be due to a remarkable ability of people to choose places to live depending on their level of health—ill health leads to neighborhood income, in other words? Which of their many coefficients proves that? At a regional level, it is equally difficult to see how selection explains why the social gradient is widest in the North East and narrowest in the South West, as both regions have a history of out-migration by those needing to find employment.

This disagreement between commentators is not just about evidence. It is also about ideology. We think that the health gradient in Figure 18.1 is a powerful demonstration of the graded relation between social and economic conditions and health. We are chastised, by Canning and Bowser (2010), for wanting a fairer society to put it right. Instead, they offer the following: "The health gradient should be seen as a flashing alarm that our health systems are failing to deliver cost effective health care and a call to allocate health sector resources more effectively."

Why should it? Where is the evidence for their counter-assertion? They are not being more rigorous about causation than we are, as they claim. They simply have a different starting position. This is ideology dressed up, condescendingly, as methodological rigor. We would go further. Given the vast research resources that have gone into evaluating medical interventions, the lack of clear evidence that the main cause of the social gradient in health is differential access to health care may mean that, indeed, it is not lack of health care that is the cause of the problem.

Angus Deaton (2013, Chapter 17, this volume) puts forward the view that childhood illness is a key determinant of adult socioeconomic position, the other major determinant being access to medical care. He assigns little role to the conditions in which adults live and work as being causative of health inequalities in adulthood, other than through effects on their children's health.

I have brought together a body of evidence that leads my colleagues and me to a sharply different view. In the Marmot Review, we made recommendations, based on evidence, in six domains:

- Give every child the best start in life.
- Provide education and life-long learning.
- Improve employment and working conditions.
- Ensure that everyone has the minimum income necessary for healthy living.
- Create sustainable housing and communities.
- Undertake a social determinants approach to prevention.

If one's view of the scientific evidence is that it does not support interventions on the middle four of these, we have scientific differences of the highest importance for policy. There needs to be continued scientific debate.

In my view, there is another meta-level issue, the one with which I began this section: why do scientists from different disciplines take such radically different views of what the evidence shows? Psychologists find evidence for individual differences; sociologists of a Durkheimian bent find evidence for social causation; economists find evidence for health selection. It seems clear that these debates are not simply about "evidence" but about a whole approach to the scientific endeavor. To assert that one discipline has the monopoly on scientific rigor is to focus on trees and miss the wood.

Consequences

I started a review of Norman Daniels's excellent book, *Just Health*, with the following:

> In Puccini's opera, candidates for Turandot's hand are given a fair choice: correctly answer three riddles and gain marriage to the princess; fail and be executed. No male, however ardent or focussed on the main chance, is forced into it—he can choose. One could, therefore, argue that the process is fair. The outcome, as distinct from the process, is anything but: a trail of dead suitors and one chaste princess (until, of course, the tenor arrives which usually spells the end of the soprano's chastity). On this evidence—fair process versus fair outcome—would we deem the society in which Turandot was a princess to be a just society? Clearly not, as we rig things in more subtle ways today. (Marmot 2008)

I then went on:

> For Daniels, we care about health because improving health enhances opportunities. Improving health, therefore, contributes to Rawlsian justice. I am sure it does, but is that why we care?
>
> In my role as chair of the Commission on Social Determinants of Health I have been pushing two arguments. First, everyone values health for its own sake; not simply for the opportunities it brings. I have been arguing that people would like to avoid heart attacks or malaria not because they might then get a better job or live in a better neighbourhood but because they value getting up in the morning free of major illness. Most certainly, health may lead to opportunities but that is not the only reason it is important. If it were would we say that premature death was only important because it restricted opportunities?
>
> Second, I have, in a sense, been arguing that opportunities lead to health i.e. arguing the other way round from "health leads to opportunity." Better jobs, more just distribution of power, the social bases of self-respect will lead to better health. So much so, that health and the distribution of health can be used to tell us how well a society is functioning and distributing its benefits. In this view, health, important for its own sake, is also important because it reflects, indeed in large measure is determined by, the meaningful opportunities that society affords its members. This is a view well articulated

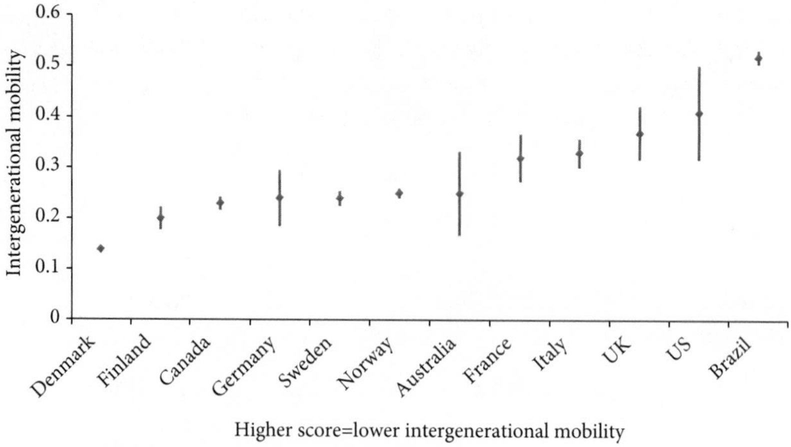

Source: NEP 2010[26]

FIGURE 18. 2 International comparisons of income mobility.
Source: National Equity Panel 2010.

> by Amartya Sen and is consistent with his general view of Development as Freedom (Sen 1999). Were I a signed-up Rawlsian, I might argue that Rawlsian justice would lead to better health rather than better health will lead to more Rawlsian justice.

I note that "opportunities lead to health" is the position taken by Segall (2013, Chapter 10, this volume). My view of opportunities is similar to his. Opportunities are not randomly distributed in society. Children born into poverty do not have the same opportunities as children born into affluence. Opportunities cumulate throughout the life course. As one illustration of the way opportunities are socially determined, Figure 18.2 shows social mobility in relation to income inequality.

The figure shows income of offspring in relation to income of parents. The greater the degree of income inequality, the more the income of children resemble that of their parents; that is, the less the social mobility or, in other language, the less their meaningful opportunity.

If one accepts that health is the outcome, the consequence, of what happens in other sectors, then one cannot be concerned only with processes—dead suitors matter, not only whether they had a free choice to gamble for Turandot's hand. It is precisely the concern with outcomes that leads to the concern with the social determinants of health. Does that make me a nasty consequentialist?

Improving Health for Everyone or Reducing the Social Gradient?

When we began the English Review of Health Inequalities, we articulated two goals: to improve health for everybody and to reduce health inequalities.

Figure 18.3 shows what has been happening to life expectancy in England. It is very similar to a stylized graph that I drew earlier illustrating this potential dilemma (Marmot 2004).

The figure shows that, over a 10-year period in England, life expectancy improved. There three key features of this graph:

- Health improved for all social groups.
- Health improved for the spearhead group, the most deprived quarter of the population, by a dramatic 2.9 years in only 10 years.
- The average improved slightly more, so the gap did not narrow.

It is alleged that I would be happy to see health for everybody be worse if health inequalities would be less. This is not a position that I have ever articulated nor, I hope, implied. There is no question in my mind that the later life expectancy figures in Figure 18.3 are preferable to the earlier ones, for two reasons: health improved for everyone, and the worst off improved. Therefore, our first goal has been fulfilled, in a utilitarian way. But although the worst off have improved and, if I understand Rawls's difference principle, the later position is fairer than the earlier, I do not think we should stop there. The reason we conducted the English Review of Health Inequalities was not to make anybody's health worse—not to compromise the first goal: it was to work toward our second goal of reducing health inequalities while continuing progress on the first.

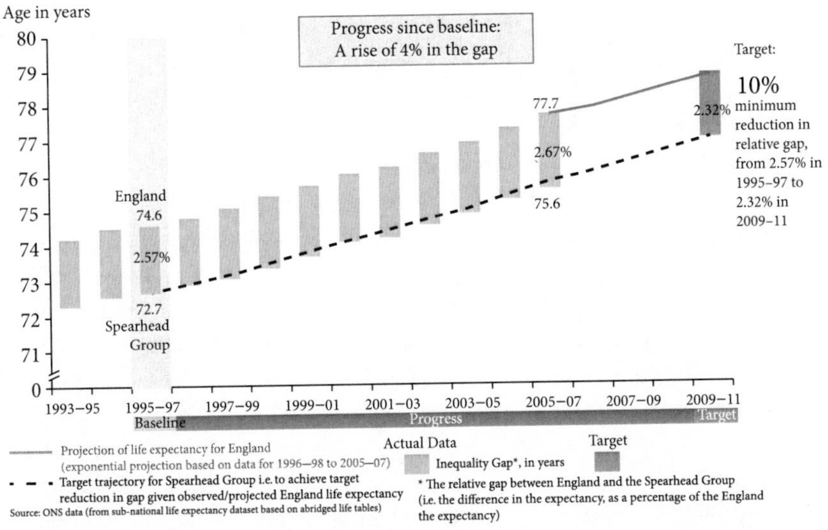

FIGURE 18.3 Male life expectancy at birth, inequality gap, England 1993–2007 and target for the year 2010.

Source: Department of Health.

When articulating these two separate goals, I was told there had to be a tradeoff between them. But why? We are not discussing the distribution of scarce health care resources but whether we want the general distribution of social and economic conditions to be done in a fairer way. One does not have to be an egalitarian to think that income inequalities have gone too far. In the United States, between 2002 and 2007, for every dollar of economic growth, 65 cents were captured by families in the top 1 percent of incomes. Suppose, as has been suggested, that reducing that extremely skewed income distribution improved health (Wilkinson and Pickett 2009): would that not be a gain worth having? Certainly, taking a little from the top 1 percent will not damage their health. Addressing the social conditions that give rise to poorer health for those lower down will improve their health. This is an old-fashioned argument for progressive taxation. How quaint!

Given the importance of the social determinants of health, I do not think we should accept the tradeoff argument. I do not think this is the standard moral problem of runaway trains and levers and fat people. In my view, it leads to fundamental questions of the kind of society we want for ourselves.

The Prince and Pauper

I have made plain that I think that avoidable health inequalities are unfair. What if the distribution went the other way, and the rich had poorer health? Indeed, it used to be thought that the more affluent suffered more from stress (the poor dears) and diseases of affluence as a result. It is true that I do feel sympathy for the 8-year-old offspring of the British upper classes who, traditionally, were shipped off to boarding school. The parents were emotionally stunted by such deprivation; why should their children not be, too. (A New Yorker cartoon had one woman explaining: "We adopted a Chinese child... and we're having her raised in China.")

Ramazzini, the founder of occupational medicine, and hence a particular hero of mine, wrote his seminal work *De Morbis Artificum Diatriba* (*Diseases of Workers*) in 1700. By pointing to how working conditions lead to ill health (he did not think that ill health led to working conditions), he made a potentially major contribution to understanding one of the sources of social inequalities in health. He also wrote a book on the health of princes. My first reaction, when discovering this book, was that I was more interested in the health of paupers than of princes. But I read it nevertheless. It was a revelation. Ramazzini understood how rich diet and overindulgence could lead to ill health in princes. I would not in any way describe such ill health as unjust, but it requires attention nevertheless. It is part of the first goal—improving health for everybody.

To take a more contemporary example: breast cancer is a major cause of death in women. In most countries where it has been studied, it is more common in women of higher social status—perhaps linked to later age at birth of the first child. I would not describe this distribution as unjust, but I would most certainly conclude that breast cancer is a priority. If improvements in management of this distressing cancer lead to improvements in survival, we should go for them. What would I give up to pay for them? Would I give up action on the social determinants of health? Certainly not. I would argue for both. My argument is that I am not the minister of finance—I am an advocate, based on evidence, for a fairer distribution of the social determinants of health. I would not give up improvements in treatment of breast cancer to pay for them. I could suggest other ways of raising the money— progressive taxation for example, or not paying for things that don't work—but that is the finance minister's job, not mine. He wouldn't listen to me anyway.

References

Adler, N., and Ostrove, J. (1999). Socioeconomic status and health: What we know and what we don't. In N. Adler, M. Marmot, B. McEwen, and J. Stewart (Eds.), *Socioeconomic status and health in industrial nations* (pp. 3–15). New York: New York Academy of Sciences.

Black, D. (1980). *Inequalities in health: Report of a research working group.* London: DHSS. Ref Type: Report

Canning, D., and Bowser, D. (2010). Investing in health to improve the wellbeing of the disadvantaged: Reversing the argument of the Marmot reports. *Social Science and Medicine, 71*, 1223–1226.

Case, A., Paxson, C., and Vogl, T. (2007). Socioeconomic status and health in childhood: A comment on Chen, Martin and Matthews, G Socioeconomic status and health: Do gradients differ within childhood and adolescence? *Social Science & Medicine, 64*(4), 757–761.

Chandra, A., and Vogl, T. S. (2010). Rising up with shoe leather? A comment on *Fair society, healthy lives* [Marmot Review]. *Social Science & Medicine, 71*(7), 1227–1230.

CSDH. (2008). *Closing the gap in a generation: Health equity through action on the social determinants of health.* Final Report of the Commission on Social Determinants of Health. *Geneva: World Health* Organization. Ref Type: Report

Deaton, A. (2013). What does the empirical evidence on SES and health tell us about inequity and about policy? In N. Eyal, S. A. Hurst, O. F. Norheim, and D. Wikler (Eds.), *Inequalities in health: Concepts, measures, and ethics* (Chapter 17). New York: Oxford University Press.

Fox, A. J., and Collier, P. F. (1976). Low mortality rates in industrial cohort studies due to selection for work and survival in the industry. *British Journal of Preventive and Social Medicine, 30*, 225–230.

Fox, A. J., and Goldblatt, P. O. (1982). *Socio-demographic mortality differentials: Longitudinal study 1971–5.* London: HMSO Series LS No 1.

Goldblatt, P. (1988). Changes in social class between 1971 and 1981: Could these affect mortality among men of working age? *Population Trends, 51*, 9–17.

———. (1989). Mortality by social class, 1971-85. *Population Trends, 56*, 6–15.

Goldsmith, J. R. (1975). What do we expect from an occupational cohort? *Journal of Occupational Medicine, 17*, 126–127.

Marmot Review. (2010). *Fair society, healthy lives: Strategic review of health inequalities in England post 2010*. London: Author. Ref Type: Report

Marmot, M. (2000). Social causes of social inequalities in health. In S. Anand, F. Peter, and A. Sen (Eds.), *Health, ethics and equity*. New York: Oxford University Press.

———. (2004). *The status syndrome*. New York: Henry Holt.

———. (2008). Health in a just society. *Lancet, 372*(9642), 881–882.

———. (2009). A continued affair with science and judgements. *International Journal Epidemiology, 38*(4), 908–910.

Marmot, M., Allen, J., and Goldblatt, P. (2010). A social movement, based on evidence, to reduce inequalities in health. *Social Science & Medicine, 71*, 1254–1258.

Marmot, M. G., Shipley, M. J., Hemingway, H., Head, J., and Brunner, E. J. (2008). Biological and behavioural explanations of social inequalities in coronary heart disease: The Whitehall II Study. *Diabetologia, 51*, 1980–1988.

Marmot, M. G., Shipley, M. J., and Rose, G. (1984). Inequalities in death—specific explanations of a general pattern. *Lancet, 323*, 1003–1006.

Murphy, K. M. (2006). The value of health and longevity. *The Journal of Political Economy, 114*(5), 871.

National Equity Panel. (2010). *An anatomy of economic inequality in the UK*. London: Centre for Analysis of Social Exclusion and Government Equalities Office.

Segall, S. (2013). Equality of opportunity for health. In N. Eyal, S. A. Hurst, O. F. Norheim, and D. Wikler (Eds.), *Inequalities in health: Concepts, measures, and ethics* (Chapter 10). New York: Oxford University Press.

Sen A. (1992). *Inequality reexamined*. Oxford: Oxford University Press.

———. (1999). *Development as freedom*. New York: Alfred A. Knopf, Inc.

Smith, J. P. (2007). The impact of socioeconomic status on health over the life-course. *Journal of Human Resources, 42*(4), 739–764.

Stringhini, S., Dugravot, A., Shipley, M., Goldberg, M., Zins, M., Kivimaki, M., et al. (2011). Health behaviours, socioeconomic status, and mortality: Further analyses of the British Whitehall II and the French GAZEL prospective cohorts. *PLoS Medicine, 8*(2), e1000419.

Stringhini, S., Sabia, S., Shipley, M., Brunner, E., Nabi, H., Kivimaki, M., et al. (2010). Association of socioeconomic position with health behaviors and mortality. *Journal of the American Medical Association, 303*(12), 1159–1166.

Wilkinson, R. G., and Pickett, K. E. (2009). *The spirit level: Why more equal societies almost always do better*. London: Allen Lane.

19 }

Individual Responsibility, Health, and Health Care

Julian Le Grand

Should individuals be held responsible for their own state of health? If they should be (or indeed if they should not be), should they be responsible for their own health care? What are the implications of the answers to these questions for the role of the state or, more generally, of the wider community? Should the state intervene to save people from the unhealthy consequences of their own actions? Should the state, or the wider community, pay for the health care of those who, through their own behavior, have contributed to their state of ill health? This chapter attempts to address these questions.

Responsibility and Control

In the context of discussions concerning interpretations of equity or social justice, I have argued that judgments about the inequity or injustice of the situation that an individual find his- or herself in depends crucially on the extent to which his or her situation is the result of factors within or beyond his or her control (Le Grand 1984, 1991), a position taken up by other philosophers and now known as luck-egalitarianism (Arneson 1989; Cohen 1989). If the factors determining an individual's situation are entirely beyond his or her control, the situation may be judged inequitable; if they are completely under his or her control, then it can be judged equitable.

Although these arguments are phrased in terms of equity or social justice, similar ones can be made using the language of responsibility. Specifically, judgments about the extent of responsibility that an individual has for his or her situation depend on the extent to which his or her situation is the result of factors within or beyond his or her control. If the factors determining his

I am grateful for helpful comments from Harald Schmidt, the participants in a seminar held at Centre for the Study of Mind in Nature, Oslo, October 14–15, 2010, and a referee for this chapter.

or her situation are entirely beyond his or her control, then he or she is not responsible for that situation; if they are completely under his or her control, then she is completely responsible; if they are partly under his or her control, then he or she is responsible to the extent that they are under control.

If this conception of responsibility is accepted, then, applied to the question of health and, more specifically, to the question of paying for health care, it would imply the following. If an individual's health state depends on factors entirely within his or her control, then he or she is responsible for that state and hence for (paying for) any health care that she might need. The health care should be financed either through the taking out private insurance or through paying directly out of pocket. If, on the other hand, his or her health state has arisen entirely from factors beyond his or her control (an inherited disease, say), then he or she is not responsible, and there is a prima facie argument for his or her health care to be financed by the state or the wider community, funded through taxation or some form of social insurance scheme. If his or her health state has arisen partly from factors within her control and partly from factors beyond his or her control, then the answer is a mix of public and private insurance.

These arguments may be relatively straightforward in theory but present distinct problems for their application in practice. For that will depend on how easy it is to identify how much control the individual has over the factors that contribute to his or her health state. And this is actually far from easy.

The factors determining (or affecting) individuals' health states are often divided into five categories: genetic, social, environmental, behavioral, and (errors from) health care. So, for instance, a much-quoted estimate has put the proportional contribution of each of these to premature mortality (one measure of ill health) as: genetic 30 percent, social 15 percent, environment 5 percent, health care errors 10 percent, and behavior 40 percent (McGinnis, Williams-Russo, and Knickman 2002). Now, for some of these factors, the extent or lack of control that individuals have over them can be specified relatively easily. Individuals have no control over their genes; so, if an illness is entirely genetic in origin, the individual can in no way be held responsible for that. Similarly, there seems to be little argument for holding individuals responsible for ill health that arises from (the surprisingly large) proportion due to errors in their health care. Once in the hands of the health system, individuals usually have little control over the care they receive, and they certainly have little capacity to avoid any actual errors their medical practitioners may make. So, for at least two of the factors listed above—amounting to 40 percent of the contribution to premature mortality, if the figures above are accepted—the individual has no responsibility for the ill health that may derive from them.

It might seem at first as though similar arguments could be made about the social and environmental factors, especially for the less well off. Poor individuals and families have fewer choices open to them than the better off. Many, perhaps most, poor individuals live in unhealthy environments, suffering from air and water pollution of various kinds; they also face high costs of, and have limited opportunity for, engaging in healthy activities, including good nutrition and exercise. If, as a consequence of these restricted choices, they fall ill, it would be hard to hold them responsible for that state.

However, things are not quite so simple. Are the restricted choices faced by the poor completely beyond their control? To what extent are the poor responsible for their very poverty? To what extent does their poverty arise from factors within their control or beyond their control? Not all the poor are victims of circumstance; some are in poverty as a result of their own choices and actions. Also, not all the poor are unhealthy: some manage to escape the constraints of their situation and engage in, for instance, good nutrition and exercise.

Which brings us to the vexed question of behavior. That certain behaviors do contribute to ill health is beyond dispute. For instance, it is well established that behavior involving the excessive consumption of tobacco, calories, salt, fat, and alcohol contribute not only to the principal fatal illnesses such as heart disease, malignant neoplasms, and cerebrovascular diseases, but also to many illnesses associated with high morbidity, such as diabetes and liver and kidney diseases (Detels et al. 2002). But is behavior of this kind—or of the other kinds that affect health or ill health—under individual control? And can we conclude from the indisputable fact that behavior matters for health that all individuals who, say, drink, smoke, or eat too much are wholly responsible for their health states, and—by implication—responsible for (and therefore responsible for paying for) their health care?

I think not. This is for a number of reasons. Two are fairly obvious. First, it is clear from the preceding discussion that not all the factors that contribute to this behavior are under the control of the individuals concerned. Some obesity is undoubtedly genetic. Even a tendency to addictive behavior of the kind involved in excessive smoking, alcohol use, or drug consumption has been identified as possibly having genetic roots. Second, some of the behaviors concerned arise from social and environmental factors that are indeed beyond individual control. A preference for fattening food may come from dietary patterns established in childhood. More important, as we have seen, many of the poor face environmental constraints on their behavior over which they have little power, and, moreover, many (probably most) of the poor are actually poor for reasons that are largely beyond their control.

But there are two other, perhaps more subtle, reasons why individuals should not be held completely (or even largely) responsible for their health states even when these arise from their own "unhealthy" behavior. The first concerns the role of luck, the second, the possibility of misjudgments. These require more attention.

Luck

First, the role of luck. Take the case of habitual smokers. Suppose that there is a 50 percent chance of heavy smokers developing lung cancer over their lifetimes from their habit. In that case, not every smoker will develop lung cancer; indeed, half will not. The half who do are the victims, not only of their own choices but also, at least in one sense, of bad luck. Their health in this situation is in part the outcome of a lottery and thus beyond their control—except in so far as they chose to enter that lottery in the first place. Thus, it would not seem fair to hold them *fully* responsible for their health state and hence for their health care—especially since half the smoking population will have made the same choices as them, but will face no cost at all: no ill health cost (at least not for that reason) and no cost of consequent health care.

Of course, the fact remains that the smokers concerned did choose to enter the lottery in the first place. So there does seem to be a case for their bearing some of the responsibility for their actions. But, in that case, perhaps there is also an argument for allocating a certain amount of responsibility to those who did not get lung cancer; for the (fortunate) outcome for them was also a matter of luck and thus beyond their control.[1] How might this be achieved?

One way is to consider the *ex ante* situation at the point at which the smoking "lottery" is entered and to invoke the concept of *annual expected value*. The annual expected value of an uncertain outcome is the value of the outcome itself multiplied by the probability of it actually occurring in the year concerned. So, if, for instance, the expected costs of treatment for lung cancer are £50,000 and the chances of a smoker acquiring it in any one year is 5 percent, the expected value of those costs is £2,500. Now it seems reasonable to hold people responsible for the expected value of an uncertain outcome, whether or not the outcome actually occurs. In this situation, this could be achieved by compelling all smokers to take out an appropriate amount of private health insurance (in the—unlikely—event that the private health insurance market were perfectly competitive, the annual premium would actually be equal to the expected value: £2,500). Alternatively, a tax could be levied on the activity itself (a tax on tobacco), and the proceeds of the tax devoted to paying the treatment costs involved. In either case, smokers would bear a measure of responsibility for their actions—and the responsibility would be borne regardless of whether those actions had adverse consequences for their own health.

More generally, for activities in which health risks can be clearly identified, everyone who undertakes the relevant activities should bear the costs of the associated health care, either through compulsory private insurance or some form of hypthecated tax on the activity concerned.

---

[1] Earlier versions of this argument can be found in Le Grand (1991, chapter 7).

Misjudgments

What of individuals who make misjudgments in their behavioral decisions and, as a result, end up in an unhealthy state? People can make misjudgments with respect to healthy and unhealthy behaviors for a number of reasons, including poor information, myopia, and what Aristotle termed *akrasia* or modern philosophers "weakness of the will" (Dworkin 1981).

The problem of poor information arises when individuals do not know or misperceive the health risks involved in their behaviors. In such cases, it would not seem appropriate to hold them fully responsible for their behavior, and it would therefore be appropriate to require some state intervention. However, in this case, it would seem that the appropriate role for the state in such cases is not to pay for the health care consequent on the individual undertaking risky behavior but simply to provide the individuals concerned with the correct information; then they would then become responsible for their actions.

Myopia and akrasia provide a stronger case for state involvement in paying for health care. Myopia or short-sightedness arises because the costs of most unhealthy activities impact in the future, whereas the benefits from them occur in the present. So, for a 20-year-old, the smoking of a cigarette or the playing of a computer game now, instead of, say, taking exercise, has an immediate pay-off in terms of pleasurable sensations or relaxation, whereas the cancer or heart disease that may follow is probably at least 30 years away. Given that the future is uncertain, it is then perfectly rational for the individual concerned to "discount" those costs: that is, to place a lower weight on them than if they were to occur in the present.

There are a variety of sources of this uncertainty and thus of discounting. He or she may die of something else in the meantime; there may be medical advances that mean that cancer or heart disease will not be the killers that they are now. Moreover, as we have seen, there is the question of his or her own physiognomy: many smokers or heavy eaters do not contract lung or heart disease, and the individual concerned may be one of the lucky ones.

Another reason for discounting the future is the phenomenon that, even in a world where there is certainty, people often seem to prefer pleasure now to that in the future. As David Hume says, "There is no quality in human nature which causes more fatal errors in our conduct than that which leads us to prefer whatever is present to the distant and remote (Hume n.d.)."

Now, even if the phenomenon of myopia is regarded as leading to "fatal errors" or mistakes, it is understandable. Most individuals find it difficult to conceive of being 30 years older than their current age: 20-year-olds may perceive themselves as being different people from their 50-year-old selves, in so far as they think about them at all, and hence thus may not weight these "other," rather alien, people's interests as much as their own immediate ones.

Indeed, there may be a form of "external cost" here, in which an individual engages in an action in which a third party (her older self) is affected adversely, but in which that third party is in no position to influence the activity or avoid its effects. In this case, the individual concerned, in deciding on her actions, does not give the consequences for her older self the same weight as that older self would if she were present. Hence, she may engage in actions that will damage that older self, creating what economist call an *externality*, a form of market failure that is often used to make a prima facie case for state intervention (Le Grand 2006, pp. 88–91).

Then there is akrasia or weakness of the will. Anecdotally, people undertaking unhealthy activities often acknowledge they are not necessarily acting in their own best long-run interest. The individual's "long-run self"—the person looking months in advance or reflecting on the experience in retrospect—admits to foolishness. And there is broader evidence for this phenomenon from public surveys. For instance, the desire to give up smoking is perhaps the most commonly reported anecdote supporting a long-run preference being unrealized as a result of weakness of the will at the point at which having another cigarette must be resisted. And surveys conducted by the U.K. Office of National Statistics have consistently reported that around 70 percent of current smokers in Great Britain wish to give up smoking (Taylor et al. 2006).

Telling evidence on the overall prevalence of misjudgment in smoking behavior comes for a study on smokers' reported levels of welfare. This measured the effect of various levels of cigarette taxes, using demographic and survey data. It examined whether increasing the price of cigarettes, and thus making them less attractive, led people whose demographic factors predicted them to be smokers to be any happier than comparable people in areas where excise duties were lower. The results showed significant and quite substantially higher rates of happiness following tax increases, in two quite independent datasets from the United States and Canada (Gruber and Mullainathan 2005). This suggests that smokers making a decision to smoke are misjudging what brings them a higher level of well-being; that they would have greater happiness if they were forced or in some way encouraged to restrict their smoking.

So where does this leave us with respect to responsibility, especially with respect to paying for health care? Since it is apparent that individuals do make misjudgments over decisions with respect to their longer run selves, and these misjudgments are understandable and indeed not necessarily avoidable by a reasonable person, it seems inappropriate to hold them fully responsible for the outcomes of the misjudgment. Again, therefore, we are pushed in the direction of the state, not the individual, meeting the relevant costs.

Conclusion

It may seem surprising that, starting from what might be thought of as an individualistic or desert-based notion of responsibility, we have developed a number of arguments that support a collectivist notion of financing health care, with the state meeting much of the relevant costs of ill health or intervening in other ways to save people from the consequences of their unhealthy decisions. So it is worth recapitulating the relevant arguments.

We started from the position that the degree of responsibility that individuals have for their health depends on the extent to which they have control over the factors that affect their health. We pointed out that many of those factors are actually beyond most individuals' span of control and that, for other factors, it is not easy to identify what is under their control and what is not. Moreover, even when an element of control can be identified, there are still health outcomes that arise from bad luck or from the understandable, and not easily avoidable, misjudgments that individuals make. Hence it is difficult, indeed impossible, to claim that individuals can be demonstrated to be wholly or even largely responsible for their health and therefore for paying for their own health care. Hence this suggests that a largely collectivist health care system is appropriate—at least in terms of finance.

Of course, issues concerning individual responsibility are not the only arguments concerning the appropriate role of the state with respect to health and health care. In particular, there are a number of well-known reasons why private markets in the area can fail to achieve social efficiency, including the presence of externalities, asymmetric information between patient and medical provider, and, in private health care insurance markets, the problems of moral hazard and adverse selection. Such arguments usually point in the direction of the desirability of some form of state intervention in that area. What the arguments of this chapter suggest is that this conclusion can be buttressed by arguments concerning the extent of individual responsibility.

References

Arneson R. (1989). Equality and equality of opportunity for welfare. *Philosophical Studies, 56*, 77–93.

Cohen G. (1989). On the currency for egalitarian justice. *Ethics, 99*. 906–944.

Detels, R., McEwan, J., Beaglehole, R., and Tanake, H. (Eds.). (2002). *Oxford textbook of public health* (4th ed.). Oxford: Oxford University Press.

Dworkin, G. (1981). Paternalism and welfare policy. In P. Brown, C. Johnson, and P. Vernier (Eds.), *Income support: Conceptual and policy issues*. Totowa, NJ: Rowman and Littlefield.

Gruber, J., and Mullainathan, S. (2005). Do cigarette taxes make smokers happier? *Advances in Economic Analysis and Policy, 5*(1), Article 4. Retrieved from http://www.bepress.com/bejeap/advances/2005

Hume, David. (n.d.) *Treatise on human nature* (Book III, part II, Section V11). Retrieved from http://www.philosophy-index.com/hume/treatise-human-nature/3-ii-vii.php

Le Grand, J. (1984). Equity as an economic objective. *Journal of Applied Philosophy, 1*, 39–51.

———. (1991). *Equity and choice: An essay in economics and applied philosophy.* London: HarperCollins.

———. (2006) *Motivation, agency and public policy: Of knights and knaves, pawns and queens.* Oxford: Oxford University Press.

McGinnis, J., Williams-Russo, P., and Knickman, J. (2002). The case for more active policy attention to health promotion. *Health Affairs, 21*, 71–93.

Taylor, T., et al. (2006). *Smoking-related behaviour and attitudes, 2005.* London: Office of National Statistics.

20 }

Reflections on Global Monitoring of Social Determinants of Health and Health Equity

Ritu Sadana

A Call for Greater Social Justice

WIDENING HEALTH INEQUITIES REFLECT SOCIAL DETERMINANTS OF HEALTH AND WARRANT ACTION

Inequalities in health imply a difference or a disparity either in the access to health-promoting opportunities and services or in the distribution of disease burden (e.g., morbidity, disability, and mortality) or in positive measures of health that reflect social and mental well-being. Differences in health can reflect biologic or genetic factors that do not reflect discrimination per se. However, health inequities are differences in health that are "unnecessary, avoidable, unfair and unjust," citing Margaret Whitehead's 1992 classic definition (Whitehead 1992): these should be avoided and, at the same time, often reflect social inequities. This is so because the factors that drive health inequities are systematic and not distributed randomly. Moreover, evidence shows that health inequalities are growing between the rich and poor, privileged and marginalized, and across different countries and regions, despite increases in public and private budgets for health, international aid for health, and global consensus on overall development goals that aim to improve health and the many other factors that contribute to better health. Making the connection between social inequities and health inequities, however, needs to be documented explicitly in different contexts and over time, in order to contribute to ongoing policy-making processes, implementation, and monitoring of progress toward improving health equity.

That being noted, the understanding that social inequities drive health inequities is not new. In fact, more than 60 years ago, the Constitution of

---

Disclaimer: The author is a staff member of the World Health Organization (WHO). The author alone is responsible for the views expressed in this publication, and they do not necessarily represent the decisions, policy or views of the WHO.

the World Health Organization (WHO) (1948) recognized "the enjoyment of the highest attainable standard of health" as "one of the fundamental rights of every human being without distinction of race, religion, political belief, economic or social condition." It also clearly noted that "[g]overnments have a responsibility for the health of their peoples which can be fulfilled only by the provision of adequate health and social measures." Given these and other principles, the constitution sets out 22 functions (a-v) for the Organization, with function (i) setting the stage explicitly for a social determinants' perspective as one means to achieve health, "to promote, in co-operation with other specialized agencies where necessary, the improvement of nutrition, housing, sanitation, recreation, economic or working conditions and other aspects of environmental hygiene" (WHO 1948). Around the same time, the Universal Human Rights declaration (1948) set out human rights that are indivisible, interrelated, and inseparable. The preamble and 30 articles of the Universal Declaration of Human Rights also establishes the foundation for a social determinants' perspective. Article 25 states, "Everyone has the right to a standard of living adequate for the health and well-being of himself and of his family, including food, clothing, housing and medical care and necessary social services, and the right to security in the event of unemployment, sickness, disability, widowhood, old age or other lack of livelihood in circumstances beyond his control (United Nations [UN] 1948)." Moreover, Article 28 points out that "[e]veryone is entitled to a social and international order in which the rights and freedoms set forth in this Declaration can be fully realized" (UN 1948). As discussed elsewhere (Sadana et al. 2011) these two fundamental documents underline that (1) the path to "the highest attainable standard of health" reflects inputs that are neither confined to medical treatment nor only under the jurisdiction of health systems; (2) that every individual's health matters, not simply national or population averages; and (3) that governments and institutions that represent governments have the responsibility to act and redress discriminatory practices and unfair differences.

More recently, many health practitioners and researchers who focus on inequities in health have articulated similar concepts in more operational terms, such as Paula Braveman and Sofia Gruskin (2003) who define equity in health as "the absence of systematic disparities in health, or in the major social determinants of health, between groups with different levels of underlying social advantage/disadvantage—that is, wealth, power, or prestige." Equity in legal settings is frequently used to refer to a type of decision making that remedies the injustice. Perfect health equity implies that everyone in society can attain their full health potential regardless of social position or other social circumstances and that health inequalities should be evenly distributed across socioeconomic groups. Much of the health literature points out that, although national averages for population health provide an indicator of health across populations or countries, indicators aggregated at the national level mask the distribution of health within national boundaries (World Health Organization [WHO] 2008*b*). Numerous studies conclude that some of the variations in health (inequalities) across different subpopulations can be identified as health inequities. Many of these differences are not only due to genetic variation, but also increasingly due to social factors that are amenable to policy. The underlying causes are complex, often reflecting systematic social, political, historical, economic, and environmental factors that interface with biological factors, that are accumulated during a lifetime, and that often are transferred across multiple generations. The term "social determinants" is often used as shorthand for all of these factors; distributions that show a systematic pattern across the entire population (akin to a dose–response gradient) are referred to as the "social gradient" (see Box 20.1) or whole of the gradient approach to illustrating systematic patterns.

BOX 20.1 } **Whole of the Gradient Approach to Monitoring Social Determinants and Health Equity**

Figure 1 shows that very different patterns of access to health services exist. The example here is for births attended by a trained health worker, by household wealth quintile, but similar systematic patterns can also be observed by many characteristics (such as place of residence, educational level, or occupational group) and across many different services or for health outcomes such as mortality due to specific causes. A *whole of the gradient* approach means that the entire population is monitored, including quintiles 2-3-4, and not only the poorest (quintile 1), in comparison to the least poor or richest (quintile 5) subgroups of the population.

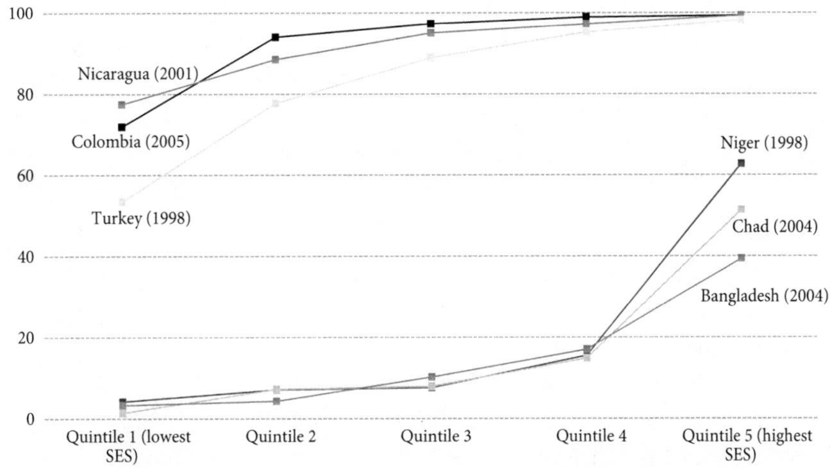

FIGURE 1 Percentage of births attended by trained personnel by household wealth (World Health Report 2008)

These observations show the importance of accurately measuring the pattern of inequality as an input to policy formation. When only the poorest do not have access to a service (three upper lines), policies will probably need to focus on expanding provision to particular groups that are excluded or marginalized. When almost everyone does not have access to a service (three lower lines), more universal strategies are usually required. In many settings, the pattern will fall somewhere between the two extremes and a combination of strategies will be required, with specific policies taking into account each national context, the factors contributing to the patterns observed, and interventions that can advance increasing fair, more equitable access or outcomes.

Global evidence suggests that at least one-fourth of health inequalities (differences found within a country's population) are due to a lack of access to effective health services. These include preventive, promotive, curative, or palliative services, and they often include essential services that have been defined by WHO, such as access to essential medicines or antenatal care. This percentage increases when adding in basic public health interventions, such as access to safe water. Social determinants of health contribute to about another half of the total health inequalities documented and are considered potentially avoidable (WHO 2008*b*; WHO Regional Office for Africa 2010; WHO 2011*a*). The WHO Commission agreed that health inequities mostly point to policy failure, reflecting unfair or unjust disparities in daily living conditions and in access to power, resources, and participation in society. Action to reduce health inequities therefore includes (1) action within the health sector or health system and (2) action on the social determinants of health—for the latter, these are actions that often lay outside of the health sector or health system. The dividing line between the two areas can vary in each country depending on the boundary of the health sector and health system.

One question that the WHO—governed by its 194 Member States—has been grappling with, is to what extent, as a specialized technical agency on health matters, should it act on a wider set of social determinants of health, such as taxation schemes or international trade agreements. Clearly, the organization has exercised a global leadership role in some areas that are considered as social determinants of health, for example, legislation and regulation addressing access to essential medicines, strengthening tobacco control, and, more recently, financing of health systems. Other social determinants of health might not seem to deal directly with health or medical issues, yet nevertheless are part of the larger causal pathway that can lead to health inequities. As an independent body, the Commission on Social Determinants of Health made some 56 recommendations, including several to the WHO, to address social determinants of health where the evidence is strongest both in terms of the causes of health inequities and in terms of actions that can be successful in reducing health inequities (WHO 2008*b*). Subsequently, in 2009, a landmark resolution was passed by the World Health Assembly that called on different global and national stakeholders, including the WHO, to work together and act on social determinants of health in order to reduce health inequities (WHO 2009), a topic further discussed in the section on sustaining interest in global monitoring.

RELATIONSHIP WITH SOCIAL JUSTICE

Others have instigated eloquent and rigorous investigations of the contemporary ethical issues underlying the relationship between health equity and social justice (see Anand, Peter, and Sen 2004) and the priority or tradeoffs to be given to those who are worse off in relation to the overall population (see others in this volume, including Norman Daniels [2013, Chapter 12, this volume] and Larry Temkin [2013, Chapter 1, this volume]). Issues described and debated include the intrinsic and instrumental justifications to be concerned about health equity and its relationship to equity in general, including non-discrimination and equal opportunity. Building on Amartya Sen's work (e.g., Sen 2000), the social determinants can be considered as those conditions that together provide the freedom people need to live the lives they value (Fox and Meier 2009).

Once accepted that certain inequalities in health indicate the degree of social justice, then these are considered as inequities in health. Following, a legitimate question is: who has the responsibility or obligation to take action and reduce these inequities in health as part of an overall drive for greater social justice? Over time, discourses concerning the production of disease and the subsequent redress provide insight on situating the responsibility to act. For example, Anne-Emanuelle Brin (2010) reviews the boundaries of public health action and stylizes three approaches on what to do, reflecting an interpretation of the underlying factors producing inequalities in health as follows: Louis-René Villermé notes that poverty and vice cause illness and disease, with the response being that individuals need "moral improvement"; Edwin Chadwick highlights that filth and immorality cause disease and poverty, and the solution is "sanitary reform"; and Freidrich Engles calls out that capitalism and class exploitation produce poverty, disease, and death, and that society needs to be "radically restructured." Interpretations and approaches moving across the Villermé, Chadwick, and Engles spectrum each represents an enlarged appreciation of the social causes of health inequalities, an increasing acknowledgment that these differences are unfair and hence inequitable, and the systemic nature in which these underlying causes are produced and reproduced. Importantly, these three approaches associating health and wealth are still reflected in contemporary debates, among other perhaps more nuanced influences, for example, that consider exclusionary processes that contribute to injustice (see Popay et al. 2008).

To know whether progress is being made toward greater social justice, a large and growing literature considers approaches to evaluate health, inequalities in health, what contributes to these inequalities, how to consider whether these are unfair (and hence inequities), and the distribution of inequities in health. One key message is that measurement approaches reflect values that are not fixed in time, and these values need to be made explicit prior to measures being used as inputs to policy formation, monitoring, or evaluation. Another is that measures should include a broad range of social determinants of health that are amenable or should be amenable to policy, beyond those factors that are only considered within the responsibility of the health sector or health system. Academics, practitioners, and advocates alike contend that data, analysis and evidence on unfair differences in health, the values underlying judgments on what is fair or unfair, and options for reducing unfair differences should be made known to policy and decision makers in government and nongovernmental sectors and in a format that can stimulate deliberation and action (see, in this volume, Michael Marmot [2013, Chapter 18] and Yukiko Asada [2013, Chapter 3]).

These discourses are entering international policy dialogues. For example, at the international level, a major United Nations (UN) report on *Social Justice in an Open World* (2006) notes that, in the contemporary context, social justice is typically taken to mean distributive justice. To guide the role and responsibility of the UN, the report proposes that striving toward *social justice* offers a basis to reconcile the distributive and redistributive effects of social and economic policies, with regard to the issues of rights. The report identifies three critical domains of equality and equity as central to fair distribution: equality of rights, equality of opportunities, and equity in living conditions. Going a step further, the report identifies areas of distributive inequality that should be evaluated as markers of social justice. Unsurprisingly, health is one of these, as "inequalities in the distribution of health services, social security and the provision of a safe environment" feature as one of six bundles identified. The report argues that improving the distribution of health within and across populations moves us (Member States and internationally) closer toward social justice. The relationship between health inequities and social inequities is bidirectional. The report also concedes that further conceptual effort is required to examine the extent to which the priority areas of equality/equity and areas of inequality identified actually lend operational content to "the notion of social justice" and contribute to the development of international justice.

To what degree such discourses are guiding policies and their implementation across the UN is beyond the scope of this chapter. Nevertheless, the WHO's definition of health—a state of complete physical, mental, and social well-being and not merely the absence of disease or infirmity (WHO 1948)—provides another entry point for discussions on the relationship of health, well-being, and social justice. In this volume, Larry Temkin (2013, Chapter 1, this volume) discusses this in much greater depth, noting that "good health isn't everything, but it is a lot" and that health constitutes "a large part of what makes a human life worth living." Elements of well-being also include people's living conditions and their opportunities to realize their potential, opportunities that, in principle, should be equally distributed across all people, without discrimination on any basis. In operational terms, one approach to well-being has been framed as a composite of different building blocks. For example, to come up with a broader approach with which to measure the progress of societies beyond their gross domestic product (GDP), the Stiglitz-Sen-Fitoussi (Commission on the Measurement of Economic Performance 2009) Commission's recommendations to assess "functioning and capabilities" draw on an objective epistemology using objective measurement tools and indicators, such as income, educational level, or mortality rates. Within this approach, health is seen as a key component of overall well-being. In practice, the Organization for Economic Cooperation and Development (OECD) has used this approach to measure and report on well-being using 11 different components, including health, in more than 30 countries (OECD 2011).

Overall, there is a growing understanding within international discourses that equity is an ethical concept that reflects distributive or social justice, that greater attention is being given to the importance of health inequities within this conversation, and that it is legitimate and important to do something about reducing health inequities.

However, over time and in different contexts, different sets of interests, values, and policy objectives guide what is considered an inequity versus an inequality and who has the responsibility for action. Public health practitioners who work to reduce health inequities—rather than to eliminate all health inequalities—act on the idea that improving equity in health, in practice, means using evidence to reduce unequal opportunities to be healthy and eliminate differences that are systematically associated with, for example, underlying social disadvantage. This, in practice, might be considered as a practical compromise between maximizing and egalitarian approaches. Addressing underlying social disadvantage in a systematic way, however, cannot be done without policy and decision makers in a wide range of sectors, as well as civil society organizations or similar entities, that promote and demand social justice. Practical experiences evaluated and synthesized illustrate that actions to reduce health inequities can be implemented within communities, national boundaries, or across countries, and all seem to be more successful within supportive policy environments. The desire to increase supportive policy environments and provide evidence on how to "scale up" or at least replicate successful interventions to reduce health inequities certainly contributed to the setting up of an independent, global WHO Commission on Social Determinants of Health (the Commission).

WHO COMMISSION ON SOCIAL DETERMINANTS OF HEALTH IDENTIFIES THE NEED TO IMPROVE MEASUREMENT AND ACCOUNTABILITY

In March 2005, the Commission, chaired by Sir Professor Michael Marmot, was launched to spearhead political action on the social causes behind ill health (WHO 2006*a*). The stated goal of the Commissioners was to leverage policy change by turning existing public health knowledge into actionable policy agendas. During its tenure, the Commission met in 11 countries and benefited from three streams of work: country action, including supporting and working with National Commissions (set up by a few countries, including Brazil) on the same topic; engagement with international and national civil society organizations addressing health and equitable development, including the Peoples' Health Movement; and knowledge synthesis through nine global networks addressing different themes (e.g., social exclusion, employment conditions, early child development, and women and gender, among others), including a dedicated network addressing measurement and evidence challenges co-led by the National Institute for Clinical Excellence in the United Kingdom and the Universida del Desarrolla (University for Development) in Chile.

During the May 2005 meeting of the Commission in Cairo, the WHO secretariat prepared a discussion paper outlining the development of a conceptual framework (Solar and Irwin 2005) largely synthesizing those proposed by Finn Diderichsen and others (Diderichsen 1998; Anand et al. 2001; Diderichsen, Evans, and Whitehead 2001). During the Commission's seventh meeting, in January 2007, in Geneva, the Commissioners agreed that it is of great importance to establish a systematic framework for the monitoring of social determinants of health and health inequities globally, along with regional and national efforts (Commission on Social Determinants of Health [CSDH] 2007*a*). A revised framework was further discussed during the Commission's seventh meeting in Geneva. Even if only a heuristic to illuminate areas where deeper analysis was needed, it was agreed that the framework should support debate and investigation clarifying a few questions germane to reducing health inequities, including (Solar and Irwin 2007):

1. Where do health differences among social groups originate, if we trace them back to their deepest roots?
2. What pathways lead from root causes to the stark differences in health status observed at the population level?
3. Where and how should we intervene to reduce health inequities?

With slight modifications, this was eventually adopted by the Commission in its Final Report, released in August 2008 (Figure 20.1). The framework serves to illustrate the pathways by which key social determinants of health influence the distribution of health outcomes, makes explicit the linkages

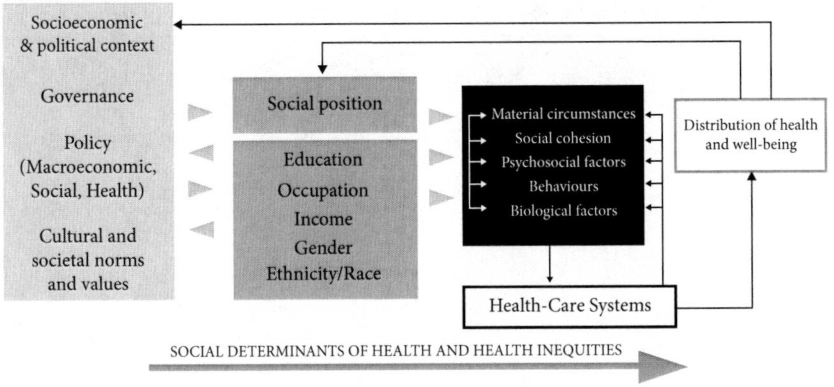

FIGURE 20.1 Commission on Social Determinants of Health (CSDH) framework linking social determinants of health and distribution of health.
Source: WHO (2008*b*, p. 43)

among different types of determinants, and makes visible the ways social determinants contribute to health inequities among groups in society.

The framework is based on Solar and Irwin's extensive literature reviews (Solar and Irwin, 2005, 2007) and the Commissioners' deliberations incorporating knowledge synthesized from country studies (Valentine et al. 2007) and from global knowledge networks (see WHO [2011*a*] for an overview). It illustrates that the socioeconomic and political context includes the entire range of structural aspects of a society that together define the scale of social, political, and economic stratification within a population and together are the "causes of the causes" of health inequities. This overall context generates hierarchies of social position, and this stratification within a population generates differential exposures, vulnerability, and effects in health according to the place in the social hierarchy that individuals and groups occupy. Health inequities flow from these patterns of social stratification—that is, from the systematically unequal distribution of power, prestige, and resources among groups in society. The unequal distribution of these intermediary factors constitutes the primary mechanism through which different social positions generate health inequities. The framework also designates the health system as a social determinant of health, given that the way health systems are organized can either amplify or mitigate intermediary factors, social position, or the overall context (see Box 20.2 for further details). Although based on evidence, other frameworks exist.

To summarize the framework and production of health inequities, the Commission repeatedly stated that inequities in health are "avoidable health inequalities" and that they arise because of the circumstances in which "people grow, live, work and age," including the social systems put in place to prevent and deal with illness.

BOX 20.2 } Explaining the Commission's Conceptual Framework, from Solar and Irwin (2007)

1. The social determinants framework adopted by the Commission differs from some others in the importance attributed to the *socioeconomic-political context*. Sir Professor Michael Marmot repeatedly noted during his tenure as Chair that these conditions in which people live and die are, in turn, shaped by the "causes of the causes"; that is, by underlying political, social, and economic forces.
2. "*Social position*" is at the center of the Diderichsen model because "within each society, material and other resources are unequally distributed. This inequality can be portrayed as a system of social stratification or social hierarchy" (p. 24). People attain different positions in the social hierarchy according mainly to their social class, with the most important stratifiers and their proxy makers including occupational status, educational achievement, income level, social class, gender, and ethnicity/race. These socioeconomic positions then translate into specific determinants of individual health status reflecting the individual's social location. This is described by mechanisms that play a role in stratifying health outcomes (p. 20), such as:
   - *Social contexts* create social stratification and assign individuals to different social positions.
   - *Social stratification* in turn engenders *differential exposure* to health-damaging conditions and *differential vulnerability*, in terms of health conditions and material resource availability.
   - Social stratification likewise determines *differential consequences* of ill health for more and less advantaged groups (including economic and social consequences, as well differential health outcomes per se).
3. The framework identifies a collection of intermediary factors covering "*differential exposures, vulnerabilities, and consequences*" as playing an important part in the explanation of health inequalities, further described as follows (pp. 12–13):
   - *Material factors* are linked to conditions of economic hardship, as well as to health-damaging conditions in the physical environment (e.g., housing, physical working conditions, etc.).
   - *Social cohesion* reflects the closeness (or distance) between social strata and the level of solidarity and community spirit.
   - *Psychosocial factors* include stressors (e.g., negative life events), stressful living circumstances, lack of social support, etc.
   - *Behavioral factors* include smoking, diet, alcohol consumption, and physical exercise, and are certainly important determinants of health.
   - The *health system* itself constitutes an additional relevant intermediary factor and serves as an important entry way for action.
4. The final block (far right side of the framework figure) represents "*differential health outcomes,*" described as "the outcomes that emerge at the end of the social 'production chain' of health inequities and are the measurable impacts of social factors upon comparative health status and outcomes among different population groups, i.e., health equity" (p. 42).

Moreover, deliberating on a briefing note prepared by the WHO and the University College London Secretariat (Sadana et al. 2007*a*), the Commission, in January 2007, specifically recommended that the conceptual framework should guide the selection of a minimum set of indicators and that these should build on the WHO's core indicators and other internationally agreed upon indicators, such as those included within the Millennium Development Goals (MDGs), in order to package and communicate efficiently existing data and not impose additional work on already overstretched national health information systems and global monitoring mechanisms (see CSDH 2007*a*).

During the same year, the WHO's strategic directions and objectives explicitly linked gaps in social justice to widening health inequities, as noted in its medium-term strategic plan for 2008–2013, found in the public domain (WHO 2008*a*). The plan pinpoints four major unrealized potentials for improving health, particularly the health of the poor, with the missing elements summarized as gaps in social justice, responsibility, implementation, and knowledge. The introduction notes that "future progress requires strong political will, integrated policies and broad participation" and acknowledges that "many important determinants of health fall outside of the direct sphere of influence of the health sector." Moreover, it presents 13 strategic objectives for the Organization, with one of these specifically addressing the underlying social and economic determinants of health. The plan was approved by the 60th World Health Assembly, in May 2007, with Resolution 60.11, with the preamble "[w]elcoming the cross-cutting nature of the strategic objectives that create synergies and promote collaboration between different programmes by capturing the multiple links among determinants of health, health outcomes, health policies, systems and technologies" (WHO 2007). Around the same time, the director-general of the WHO, Dr. Margaret Chan (Chan 2007), repeatedly called for greater accountability in addressing the distribution of health within countries and proposed that "[p]rogress in reaching the Millennium Development Goals will not be measured by national averages. It will be measured by improvements in life for society's most miserable and least visible communities."[1]

These high-level discourses and mandates, among others, supported the Commission and its work in advocating for the monitoring of social determinants and health inequities and searching for meaningful and policy-relevant indicators to do so. For example, a major peer review meeting of the findings of the global knowledge networks supporting the Commission was held in September 2007, in Rio De Janeiro (CSDH 2007*b*). Based on its deliberations, academic, government, and civil society peer reviewers recommended

---

[1] This theme was repeated during Dr. Chan's addresses to the WHO's regional committees during 2007, as well as many in other speeches around the same time in the public domain (see http://www.who.int/dg/speeches/2007/en/index.html).

that global monitoring would also strengthen resource mobilization efforts to address social determinants of health. Participants reiterated that global monitoring should build on existing international monitoring systems in the short term and pointed out several fundamental questions to be addressed in the mid term to support developing norms and standards in this area:

- What social determinants and health indicators to measure
- What criteria should be used for monitoring
- What social group categories should be considered
- How the magnitude of health inequality should be measured
- How the results should be communicated
- Where we should be in 2015 and 2020

As an initial step, participants recommended that a new global monitoring mechanism could focus on existing data sources that are already publicly accessible—such as the WHO, UN, and other multilateral agency databases used for monitoring progress, priority setting, or development assistance—and that the Commission could propose a small set of indicators that many countries already measure and report. As a follow-up, participants recommended that a measurement advisory group should be convened by the WHO to further review data collection, analysis, and reporting mechanisms and to recommend specific methods and measures that would describe inequities and develop innovations to advance this agenda, in consultation with Member States.

Addressing the first recommendation, in October 2007, during the Commission's ninth meeting in Beijing, Commissioners deliberated on a core set of indicators to support global monitoring of health inequalities requiring data disaggregated at the subnational level and social determinants of health, and it confirmed that it would be desirable to formulate recommendations to advance monitoring within its Final Report (CSDH 2007*c*). Together, this information could be discussed and health inequities clearly identified. Reflecting a collaborative effort to guide an operational approach (see Box 20.3), a briefing note prepared by the WHO and the University College London secretariat members proposed a small set of indicators (Sadana et al. 2007*b*). During the Commission's ninth meeting in Beijing, a short list was presented, debated, and agreed on, and 25 core indicators were proposed from existing data sources, as shown in Table 20.1. The second recommendation is addressed in the next section.

That being noted, improved global monitoring of social determinants of health and health inequities will not automatically dictate what policy options or interventions should be developed and implemented to address social determinants and reduce health inequities, even if monitoring could provide some insights. The next section highlights some approaches and recent efforts to situate global monitoring within different policy processes.

BOX 20.3 } Explaining the Process to Identify Potential Global Indicators to Monitor Social Determinants of Health

Key questions: Step one focused on clarifying the key questions that should be addressed in relation to each of the four "blocks" of the conceptual framework; for example "What are the key dimensions of social position?," "What is the extent of differential vulnerabilities?" and "What are the main resulting health inequities that emerge in a given society?"

Subthemes: Step two focused on identifying subthemes for each block, in which substantial literature from different parts of the world existed and highlighted the importance and contribution of each subtheme to health equity.

Long list of potential indicators: Step three focused on identifying and proposing a large set of indicators for each subtheme, primarily through a detailed review of existing data sources. About 180 existing indicators were identified, distributed across each of the framework's four blocks.

Short list of potential indicators: Step four proposed a short list based on agreed upon criteria privileging existing and valid data sources with multiple country data to monitor social determinants of health and health inequalities.

Source: Sadana et al. (2007*a*, 2007*b*)

Sustaining Interest in Global Monitoring and Its Use Within Policy Processes

STRENGTHENED MANDATES AND MECHANISMS FOR INTERNATIONAL COLLABORATION

In August 2008, the Commission's Final Report was released with the aspirational title "Closing the Gap Within a Generation" (WHO 2008*b*). The Report clarifies the Commission's definition of health inequity (p. 26): "Where systematic differences in health are judged to be avoidable by reasonable action, they are quite simply, unfair. It is this that we label health inequity." A major thread running through the Report is that progress toward closing the gap requires a narrowing of the gap between the worst off and the best off—and those in between—over time, through "reasonable action." To unpack and give direction on what reasonable actions should be pursued, the Report sets out detailed action areas, recommendations, and milestones—to governments, the WHO, other UN agencies, civil society, donors, multilaterals—in three overarching areas: (1) improve people's daily living conditions; (2) tackle the inequitable distribution of power, money, and resources; and (3) measure and understand the problem and assess the impact of action. For the third point, key areas addressing routine monitoring systems, new evidence on what works, and increased training are expressed through eight recommendations for action. Many of these recommendations do not require extreme or

TABLE 20.1 } **Proposed short list of indicators for global monitoring, October 2007**

Indicator	Data source
1. Sociopolitical Context—unit of analysis: country	
(1) Total debt service as % of gross national income (GNI)	WB
(2) The extent to which a country's citizens are able to participate in selecting their government, as well as freedom of expression, freedom of association, and free media	WB
(3) Total government expenditure on health and education as percent of total government expenditure	WHO, UNESCO
(4) Ratio of wages to corporate profits	WB
(5) Proportion of young people not in school or employment, by age and gender	OECD
(6) Proportion of employment in informal sector (%)	ILO
2. Social Stratification—unit of analysis: country or individual	
(7) Gini coefficient (income distribution)	WB
(8) Adult literacy rate (%) for the population over 15 years of age	UNDP; UNESCO
(9) Ratio of highest and lowest paid workers	ILO
(10) Net primary enrolment ratio of females to males	UNDP; UNESCO
(11) Completion of primary/secondary education by ethnic/race group in a country	WHO
3. Differential exposures and vulnerabilities—unit of analysis: individual	
(12) Prevalence of smoking (% adults)	UNDP
(13) Access to improved water (%)	WHO
(14) Proportion of population who rarely or never spend time with friends, colleagues, or others (%)	OECD
(15) Suicide rate (%)	WHO
(16) Children aged <5 years with diarrhea receiving ORT (%)	WHO
(17) Births attended by skilled health personnel	WHO, UNDP
(18) Measles immunization coverage among 1-year-olds (%)	WHO
4. Differential health outcomes—unit of analysis: individual	
(19) Healthy life expectancy (male, female)	WHO
(20) Under-5 mortality (UFMR) (rural, urban)	WHO
(21) Infant mortality ratio (IMR) (by wealth quintiles)	WHO
(22) Newborns with low birth weight (by mother's education)	WHO
(23) Children aged <5 years with moderate or extreme small weight and height (rural, urban)	WHO
(24) Prevalence of obesity in adults (15 years and older) (by wealth quintiles)	WHO
(25) HIV prevalence among adults aged 15–49 (male, female)	WHO

WB, World Bank; WHO, World Health Organization; UNESCO, United Nations Economic and Social Council; OECD, Organization for Economic Co-operation and Development; ILO, International Labour Organization; UNDP, United Nations Development Programme. *Source*: Sadana et al. (2007*a*, 2007*b*)

excessive action—they are thus "reasonable action"—yet they do require commitment, coordination, and some resources. It is not surprising that several recommendations concerning international collaboration and global monitoring are aimed at the WHO (see Box 20.4).

BOX 20.4 } The Commission's Recommendations to the WHO Addressing Indicators, Assessment, and Monitoring

12.1 WHO, in collaboration with other relevant multilateral agencies, supporting Member States, institutionalize health equity impact assessment, globally and nationally, of major global, regional and bilateral economic agreements.

15.1. By 2010, the Economic and Social Council, supported by WHO, should prepare for consideration by the UN the adoption of health equity as a core global development goal, with appropriate indicators to monitor progress both within and between countries.

16.3. WHO stewards the creation of a global health equity surveillance system as part of a wider global governance structure.

Source: The Commission's Final Report (WHO 2008*b*)

In October 2008, just months after the release of the Commission's Final Report, WHO Director-General Margaret Chan's remarks at the UN General Assembly in New York included a clear statement on the production of health inequities when she noted that "[p]olitical decisions ultimately determine how economies are managed, how societies are structured, and whether vulnerable and deprived groups receive social protection. Gaps in health outcomes are not matters of fate. They are markers of policy failure" (Chan 2008). The director-general of the WHO highlighted important issues in terms of responsibility and accountability; namely, that these policy failures need to be identified and addressed and that successful policies are not limited to those within the health sector. Less than a year later, during the UN Secretary-General's Forum in June 2009, Dr. Chan (2009) further described that "[o]ur world is dangerously out of balance, also in matters of health. Differences, within and between countries, in income levels, opportunities and health status are greater today than at any time in recent history. I further believe that a failure to make fairness an explicit objective, in policies, in the systems that govern the way nations and their populations interact, is one reason why the world is in such a great big mess." She repeated her call for fairness and greater accountability and stated that "[g]reater equity in the health status of populations, within and between countries, should be regarded as a key measure of how we, as a civilized society, are making progress."

As noted in this chapter's opening section, the WHO's governing bodies and the World Health Assembly further strengthened the Organization's mandate to stimulate international collaboration in this area by subsequently passing a resolution (WHA 62.14) during the 62nd World Health Assembly, in May 2009, that requests the WHO (comprised of its Member States and secretariat) to develop objective indicators, strengthen existing efforts, and monitor targets on health equity and its underlying causes (WHO 2009). It was further agreed that this task requires multiple sectors to work together in response to the overwhelming evidence that documents the inequitable distribution of health within and across countries (see Box 20.5). This resolution adds to the WHO constitutional mandate to monitor health trends, report on other important development indicators, and guide the work of its secretariat in each of the Organization's so-called core functions (e.g., addressing roles in leadership, research, norms and standards, policy options, technical support, and monitoring health situation and trends).

Addressing the second recommendation of the September 2007 Rio De Janeiro meeting, and mandated by WHA 62.14, the WHO launched a new scientific resource group on equity analysis and research in January 2010, composed of five subgroups to work on measurement challenges and to build consensus toward norms and standards. Areas of initial work included (1) measures of inequalities that can be used to identify and monitor within-country inequities, in a comparable fashion across countries and over time; (2) set of indicators that can monitor progress within countries toward health equity and universal coverage; (3) type of targets that can incorporate equity concerns, that would lend themselves to be monitored, benchmarked, and communicated, between now and 2025; and (4) the research priorities in this area that warrant global support (Ostlin et al. 2011).

Along with social justice and social determinants of health, the call to incorporate health equity "as a core global development goal, with appropriate indicators to monitor progress both within and between countries," as recommended by the Commission, had been clearly made. It is not surprising that, in this context, several UN policy and technical reports have incorporated analysis of health equity and social determinants within countries as an input to guide policies and actions. Two very different examples include the UN Department of Economic and Social Affairs' Committee for Development Policy's note "Implementing the Millennium Development Goals: Health

BOX 20.5 } Extracts Addressing Monitoring and Evaluation of Health Inequities from World Health Assembly Resolution 62.14 (May 2009) on "Reducing health inequities through the social determinants of health"

The WHO activities arising from resolution 62.14 mandates many stakeholders to work together to:

- "develop objective indicators for the monitoring of social determinants of health"
- "strengthen existing efforts on measurement and evaluation"
- "[develop and monitor] targets on health equity"
- "advocate for [the] topic to be high on global development and research agendas"
- "support research on effective policies and interventions"
- "strengthen research capacities and collaborations"

Inequality and the Role of Global Health Partnerships," published in 2009, and UNICEF's ninth edition of *Progress for Children*, subtitled "Achieving the MDGs with equity" that highlights the need to address variations within and across countries as a measure of progress toward the MDGs. Both documents (UN 2009; UNICEF 2010) ask why addressing health inequities within countries matters for achieving internationally agreed upon goals and both provide significant evidence on the contributions of social determinants to the health inequities documented.

The Commission's agenda has also synergized with regional policies related to monitoring and evaluation. For example, under the leadership of the Spanish presidency of the European Union (EU) in 2009, an independent expert report (Ministry of Health and Social Policy of Spain [MHSPS] 2010) on "Moving forward equity in health: Monitoring social determinants of health and the reduction of Health Inequalities" was issued with involvement of the WHO, in particular its Regional Office for Europe. Based on a detailed analysis and review of evidence involving regional experts, the report emphasized the need to make a shift in the European Union's (EU) approach to data collection, analysis, and application to monitor the distribution of health and contribution of social factors across society. In April 2010, an informal meeting of health ministers of the EU was organized in Madrid. The need to keep social determinants and health equity high on the EU agenda, as well as the role that monitoring plays in the process to reduce health inequalities, was documented and discussed. During this high-level meeting, WHO's director-general stated:

> Public health provides a good platform for looking at equity and how it is influenced by the way societies are organized and power and resources are distributed. In the health sector, equitable access to quality care makes a clear-cut life-and-death difference. This difference can be measured. It is often shocking. It violates our sense of fairness and justice. And it compels us to act.... The Commission [on Social Determinants of Health] found abundant evidence that the true upstream drivers of health inequities reside in the social, economic, and political environments. In the final analysis, the distribution of health within a population is a matter of fairness in the way economic and social policies are designed." (Chan 2010)

This clear message reiterated the essential values and interest that many public health practitioners champion; that unfair health differences, whether in access or outcomes, are health inequities; and that these inequities reflect and contribute to social injustice.

In the European region, during 2010, several actions were agreed upon including: (1) the need to go beyond marginally or incrementally improving existing data sources to routinely monitor across the whole population and (2) the need to create incentives to strengthen norms and capacity in monitoring and analysis, as part of mainstream health governance processes. Moreover, colleagues from the WHO Regional Office for Europe conveyed that, subsequently, more than 30 of its 53 Member States requested technical support in the area of social determinants and health. Very much in line, the European Parliament (2011) passed a resolution in March 2011 on reducing health inequalities in the EU and agreed in its preamble that the EU needs to "(1) make a more equitable distribution of health part of our overall goals for social and economic development; (2) improve the data and knowledge bases (including measuring, monitoring, evaluation, and reporting); (3) build commitment across society for reducing health inequalities; (4) meet the needs of vulnerable groups; and (5) develop the contribution of EU policies to the reduction of health inequalities." The legislation calls on "the Commission and [EU] Member States to press ahead with their efforts to tackle socio-economic inequalities, which would ultimately make it possible to reduce some of the inequalities relating to healthcare." It will be important to see how this and other regional efforts support national actions, as well as contribute to national and global monitoring and dissemination of learning.

BUILDING UP A GLOBAL PUBLIC GOOD

Monitoring global health inequities and social determinants of health for just about all countries on a periodic basis could yield an international public good—a new global knowledge base likely to motivate international and national agencies and civil society groups to enhance policy initiatives that address social determinants of health and aim to reduce health inequities. The Commission and other partners have noted that the absence of methods and international mechanisms to fulfil this monitoring role have hampered systematic efforts to monitor and evaluate progress on improving the social determinants of health globally, as well as to document the successful impact of past global or national actions toward improving health equity. More specifically, norms and standards, along with datasets, could be considered as nonrival goods that are made nonexclusive and remain within the public domain (Kaul and Mendoza 2003).

The policy discourses and mandates around the time of the Commission have provided a strong vision to promote the monitoring of social determinants of health and identify health inequities as a global public good—with an agenda that deserves to be supported by the institutional mechanisms that produce these goods, particularly if data are already being collected and widely shared across countries. The agenda also could emphasize that the approach supports applying analysis, evidence, and learning within local or national settings, so that actions to reduce health inequities have the potential to be informed by a growing global knowledge base—and eventually contribute to a global knowledge base.

Local policy makers could ask: "How do I know if health inequities are getting better or worse? What can I do? Who can I influence or empower?" Synthesizing the information and evaluated experiences addressing these practical and action-oriented questions and communicating these to different policy audiences clearly supports deliberations. Such evidence and its communication constitutes part of an international public good to move this agenda forward. The Commission makes clear, in its Final Report, that a policy maker would know that health inequities are getting better over time if there is documented evidence of a progressive flattening of the health gradient, meaning that the health of all social groups are improving toward a level closer to that of the most advantaged social group. A national policy maker could also ask: "Why should I care about inequities as I need to reach an MDG target (aggregated at the national level)?" Appropriate ways to visualize data through graphs and charts deserves more thought to illustrate progress (or decline), in addition to other evidence: for example, the WHO Regional Office for Africa reanalyzed existing household data in some 30 countries, including over time, and communicated both the changes in national averages and the changes in inequalities on a range of health indicators, including MDG indicators (see Box 20.6).

From an operational perspective, an approach to improve health equity can address what the health sector can do and what other sectors can do. In terms of what can be done, there is a growing evidence base on what actions work (Gribbin and Sadana 2010; WHO 2011*a*): translating these to different settings that support national governments or local communities to update policies and improve practices requires ongoing efforts, driven by home-grown policies (WHO 2013).

Certainly, the health system can implement more "equity-enhancing" policies. The Final Report of the Health Systems Knowledge Network (Gilson et al. 2007) and the Priority Public Health Conditions Knowledge Network (Blas and Kurup 2010) provide further global evidence of the capacity of the health system and public health programs to influence the production of health inequities. These reports document that it is a social system that can either improve equity, such as through progressive financing of health services and progress toward universal coverage, or reduce equity, such as through discriminatory practices when individuals seek care. The vast literature on health in all policies also demonstrates that governments can more broadly influence "equity-enhancing" actions in individual sectors or through intersectoral actions. Even if policies and actions reflect specific contexts, common elements of successful approaches can be identified, such as enabling nongovernmental actors to be full participants in the process toward greater social justice (Blas et al. 2008).

The WHO has contributed extensively to what the health sector can do to reduce health inequities, for instance through strengthening public health interventions; developing condition-specific programs, such as those addressing

BOX 20.6 } Visualizing Changes in National Averages and Inequalities in Health over Time

The WHO Regional Office for Africa published a report in 2010 on health inequities covering 30 countries in the region, in order to document the links among health inequalities, health inequities, health policy, and overall development. The report targets ministers of health and provides short, country-specific profiles that summarize "equity" analysis based on existing data, including upstream determinants and differential access to health services. The report also provides a regional perspective in light of within-country and across-country differential patterns, with the aim of encouraging the sharing of data and information, strategies, contextual knowledge, and further discussion on regional strategies and in-depth country collaborations, and to further refine the Regional Office's work plan on social and economic determinants, health equity, and priority public health programs.

The report attempts to communicate complex information on the range of within-country health inequalities through more than 20 indicators; through different social stratifications, such as by wealth, education, and geographic location; and by communicating absolute and relative changes in national averages and within-country inequalities side by side. This information was found to be an important input to deliberations, including processes to update health policy and evaluate interventions over time. For example, Figure 2 shows that relative changes in both within-country inequality and average infant mortality rates improved over time in a number of countries (in the lower left box), whereas, based on the data available, some countries documented higher average rates and increasing inequalities between the lowest and highest household wealth quintiles (in the upper right box).

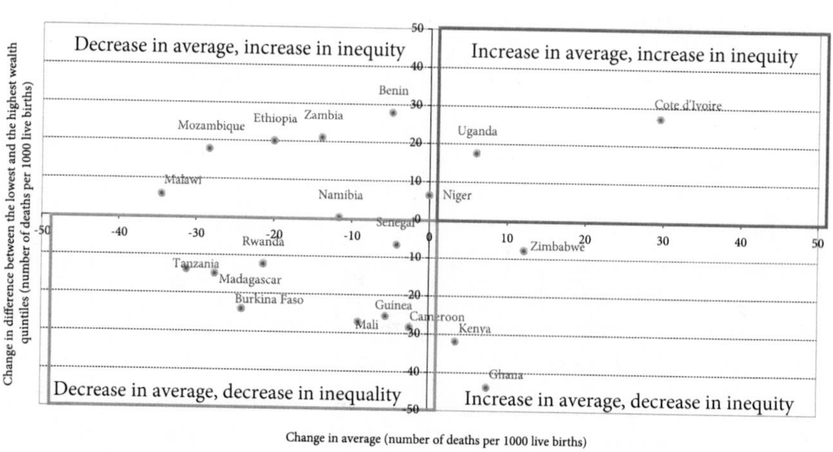

FIGURE 2 Change in infant mortality rates, within-country inequality versus national Average, 19 African countries, around 2000–2006

Source: Health Inequities in the African Region of the World Health Organization (2010, p. 190)

infectious disease outbreaks, malaria, or vaccines; and working with Member States to refine health policies and strengthen health systems. The WHO has provided policy support, normative guidance, monitoring and analysis, and technical assistance informed by global evidence on how to reduce health inequities in different contexts; for example, on the way that health systems are organized, financed, and staffed and the way that health programs are delivered (WHO, 2000; WHO 2006*b*; WHO 2008*c*; WHO 2010). Yet public health is not only concerned about health services. There are also programs undertaken in other sectors where evidence is strong that these programs are "health equity enhancing." These include early child development, halting violence against women, and participatory urban governance, areas in which the WHO has contributed to and, in different ways, supported monitoring and evaluation.

Vast experience also exists at the national and local level that links monitoring efforts with improved policies and practices across diverse settings, and these deserve to be documented and shared. One "ahead of the curve" example is the Basket of Health Inequality Indicators developed and compiled by the London Health Observatory (LHO, one of a network of local health observatories across the United Kingdom—see www.lho.org.uk). The LHO has implemented an operational approach that supports local analysis, policy formulation, action, continuous monitoring, and updating. It has negotiated access to individual and small area, disaggregated data from different sectors, and it includes a significant number of measures of social determinants of health, of access to health and other social services, and of health outcomes. It has linked these data together to analysis, program recommendations, and ongoing reporting relevant to different audiences at the local level, including municipal government, general practitioners, and other local social workers.

Conclusion

To conclude this albeit truncated and illustrative reflection on the policy discourses and recommendations guiding ways to enhance global monitoring of social determinants of health and health equity undertaken around the time of the Commission on Social Determinants of Health, one cannot overemphasize that health inequities often reflect failed policy (including no policy), and these are increasingly caused by social factors that are amenable to policy. This increased understanding that health inequities both reflect social inequities and contribute to social injustice has added to local, national, regional, and global deliberations on who has the responsibility or obligation to take action (and what type of action) to reduce health inequities. Increasing consensus among a wide range of stakeholders on frameworks for action and global public goods that can inform that action will further strengthen policies to incorporate approaches to address health inequities and their underlying causes, the social determinants of health. Likewise, concerted actions at global, regional, and national levels, drawing on multiple disciplines and stakeholders, are needed to maintain the momentum of the Commission's recommendations and the mandate provided by the World Health Assembly's 2009 Resolution 62.14 and the more recent Rio Political Declaration on Social Determinants of Health in 2011, which names five priority actions, including monitoring progress and increasing accountability (WHO 2011*b*), that was also endorsed by the World Health Assembly in 2012.

Acknowledgments

Many thanks to the Harvard Program in Ethics and Health; the University of Geneva; the Foundation Brocher; David Evans, director, Department of Health Systems Financing, WHO; and especially Dan Wikler, professor of population ethics and professor of ethics and population health, Department of Global Health and Population, Harvard School of Public Health, for the invitation and opportunity to present nontechnical reflections on how the Commission on Social Determinants of Health settled on its definitions and measures of health inequality and social determinants of health, and to highlight some of the contributing discourses that advanced thinking on monitoring in this area. This chapter's brief and personal reflections benefitted from discussions during the Brocher Summer Academy in Global Population on "Measurement and Ethical Evaluation of Health Inequalities," held in July 2010.

With a few minor updates since the summer academy, this chapter provides only one perspective and is not intended to be representative of the very complex, rich, and important overall efforts of the Commission on Social Determinants of Health or of the WHO on the topic of monitoring equity and health. The contributions of all Commissioners and others involved in the Commission's work streams have been extremely valuable to advance efforts toward global monitoring of social determinants of health. Commissioners Michael Marmot (Chair), Amartya Sen, Hoda Rashad, David Satcher, and Frances Baum, as well as the co-leads of the Knowledge Network on Measurement and Evidence, Mike Kelly and Josiane Bonnefoy, have especially championed and informed efforts addressing monitoring and evaluation. The efforts of the WHO and University of London secretariats that supported the Commission advanced operational thinking and analysis in this area and supported the Commission's deliberations specifically on monitoring challenges and options, particularly during its meetings in January 2007, in Geneva, and October 2007, in Beijing. The efforts cited (Sadana et al. 2007*a*, 2007*b*) that this chapter draws on include collaborative work with Ahmad Reza Hosseinpoor, Amit Prasad, Frank Pega, Tanja Houweling, Jeanette Vega, Orielle Solar, Nicole Valentine, and Tim Evans.

References

Anand, S., Diderichsen, F., Evans, T., et al. (2001). Measuring disparities in health: Methods and indicators. In T. Evans, M. Whitehead, F. Diderichsen, A. Bhuiya, M. Wirth (Eds.), *Challenging inequities in health: From ethics to action*. New York: Oxford University Press.

Anand, S., Peter, F., Sen, A. (Eds.). (2004). *Public health, ethics, and equity*. New York: Oxford University Press.

Blas, E., Gilson, L., Kelly, M. P., et al. (2008). Addressing social determinants of health inequities: What can the state and civil society do? *The Lancet, 372*(9650), 1684–1689.

Blas, E., Sivasankara, Kurup A. (Eds.). (2010). *Equity, social determinants and public health programmes*. Final report of the Priority Public Health Conditions Knowledge Network of the Commission on Social Determinants of Health. Geneva: World Health Organization.

Braveman, P., and Gruskin, S. (2003). Defining equity in health. *Journal of Epidemiological Community Health, 57*, 254–259.

Brin, A. E. (2010). Historicising, politicising and futurising closing the gap in a generation: Health equity through action on the social determinants of health. pp. 76–113. In S. Bhattacharya, S. Messenger, and C. Overy (Eds.), *Social determinants of health: Assessing theory, policy and practice* (pp. 76–113). New Delhi: Orient BlackSwan.

Chan, M. (2007). *Address to the Regional Committee for the Americas*. Fifty-ninth session, Washington, DC, October. Retrieved from http://www.who.int/dg/speeches/2007/20071001_washington/en/index.html

———. (2008). *Globalization and health*. Remarks at the United Nations General Assembly, October. Retrieved from http://www.who.int/dg/speeches/2008/20081024/en/index.html

———. (2009). *Greater equity in health should be a progress indicator*. Address at the United Nations Secretary-General's Forum on Advancing Global Health in the Face of Crisis, New York City, June. Retrieved from http://www.who.int/dg/speeches/2009/global_health_20090615/en/index.html

———. (2010). Keynote speech at an informal meeting of the health ministers of the European Union, Madrid, April. Retrieved from http://www.who.int/dg/speeches/2010/ihr_20100422/en/index.html

Commission on the Measurement of Economic Performance and Social Progress. (2009). Final report on the measurement of economic performance and social progress. Retrieved from (http://www.stiglitz-sen-fitoussi.fr/en/index.htm

Commission on Social Determinants of Health (CSDH). (2007*a*). Report of the seventh meeting of the Commission on Social Determinants of Health, January 17-19 2007, Geneva, Switzerland.

———. (2007*b*). Summary report. Symposium on social determinants of health, September 26-28, 2007, Rio de Janeiro, Brazil.

———. (2007*c*). Report of the ninth meeting of the Commission on Social Determinants of Health, October 24-26, 2007, Beijing, China.

Diderichsen, F. (1998). Understanding health equity in populations. In B. Avre-Pares (Ed.), *Promoting research on inequality in health* (pp. 99–114). Stockholm: Swedish Council for Social Research.

Diderichsen, F., Evans, T., and Whitehead, M. (2001). The social basis of disparities in health. In T. Evans, M. Whitehead, F. Diderichsen, A. Bhuiya, and M. Wirth (Eds.), *Challenging inequities in health: From ethics to action*. New York: Oxford University Press.

Kaul, I., and R. U. Mendoza. (2003). Advancing the concept of public goods. In I. Kaul, et al. (Eds.), *Providing global public goods: Managing globalization*. The United Nations Development Programme. New York: Oxford University Press.

European Parliament. (2011). Reducing health inequalities in the EU. INI/2010/2089. March 8, Strasbourg. Retrieved from http://www.europarl.europa.eu/oeil/FindByProcnum.do?lang=en&procnum=INI/2010/2089

Gilson, L., Doherty, J., Loewenson, R., and Francis, V. (2007). *Final report of the Health Systems Knowledge Network of the Commission on Social Determinants of Health*. Geneva: World Health Organization.

Gribbin, R., and Sadana, R. (2010). A summary of key policy actions to address the social determinants of health. Pp 24–37. In S. Bhattacharya, S. Messenger, and C. Overy (Eds.), *Social determinants of health: Assessing theory, policy and practice* (pp. 24–37). New Delhi: Orient BlackSwan.

London Health Observatory (LHO). www.lho.org.uk Accessed September 23, 2010.

Fox, A. M., and Meier, B. M. (2009). Health as freedom: Addressing social determinants of global health inequities through the human right to development. *Bioethics, 23*(2), 112–122.

Ministry of Health and Social Policy of Spain (MHSPS). (2010). *Moving forward equity in health: Monitoring social determinants of health and the reduction of health inequalities*. General Directorate of Public Health and Foreign Health, Ministry of Health and Social Policy, Government of Spain. Retrieved from http://www.msps.es/profesionales/saludPublica/prevPromocion/promocion/desigualdadSalud/PresidenciaUE_2010/conferenciaExpertos/docs/haciaLaEquidadEnSalud_en.pdf

OECD. (2011). *How's life? Measuring well-being*. Paris: OECD Publishing. Retrieved from http://www.oecd.org/statistics/howslifemeasuringwell-being.htm

Östlin, P., Schrecker, T., Sadana, R., Bonnefoy, J., Gilson, L., Hertzman, C., et al. (2011). Priorities on research for equity and health: Towards an equity-focused health research agenda. *PLoS Med, 8*(11), e1001115. doi:10.1371/journal.pmed.1001115.

Popay, J., et al. (2008). *Understanding and tackling social exclusion*. Final Report of the Social Exclusion Knowledge Network of the Commission on Social Determinants of Health. Geneva: World Health Organization.

Sadana, R., Hosseinpoor, A., Prasad, A., Solar, O., Vega, J., and Evans, T. (2007*a*). *WHO briefing note: Proposed operational approach and indicators to measure social determinants of health equity*. Seventh meeting of the Commission on Social Determinants of Health, January 17-19, 2007, Geneva, Switzerland, pp.1–24. Geneva: World Health Organization.

Sadana, R., Hosseinpoor, A., Prasad, A., Pega, F., Houweling, T., Solar, O., et al. (2007*b*). *WHO briefing note: Monitoring global health inequities*. Ninth meeting of the Commission on Social Determinants of Health, October 24-26, 2007, Beijing, China, pp.1–33. Geneva: World Health Organization.

Sadana, R., Simpson, S., Popay, J., Albrecht, D., Hosseinpoor, A., and Kjellstrom, T. (2011). Introduction—strengthening efforts to improve health equity. In Commission on Social Determinants of Health Knowledge Networks, Jennifer H. Lee, and

Ritu Sadana (Eds.), *Improving equity in health by addressing social determinants.* Geneva: World Health Organization. Retrieved from http://whqlibdoc.who.int/publications/2011/9789241503037_eng.pdf

Sen, A. (2000). *Development as freedom*, Oxford: Oxford University Press.

Solar, O., and Irwin, A. (2005). *Towards a conceptual framework for analysis and action on the social determinants of health.* Draft, WHO discussion paper for the Commission on Social Determinants of Health, Geneva: World Health Organization. Retrieved from http://www.acphd.org/healthequity/healthequity/documents/WHOConceptualFrame-1.pdf

———. (2007). *Towards a Conceptual Framework for Analysis and Action on the Social Determinants of Health,* WHO discussion paper for the Commission on Social Determinants of Health, Geneva: World Health Organization. Retrieved from http://www.who.int/social_determinants/resources/csdh_framework_action_05_07.pdf

United Nations (UN). (1948). *The universal declaration of human rights.* New York: Author

———. (2006). *Social justice in an open world.* New York: United Nations. Retrieved from http://www.un.org/esa/socdev/documents/ifsd/SocialJustice.pdf

———. (2009). *Implementing the millennium development goals: Health inequality and the role of global health partnerships.* New York: UN Department of Economic and Social Affairs (DESA), Committee for Development Policy.

UNICEF. (2010). *Progress for children: Achieving the MDGs with equity* (Number 9). New York: Author.

Valentine, N., Irwin, A., Bambas, L., Solar, O., and Prasad, A. (2007). *Health equity at the country level: Lessons from the CSDH on translating a complex agenda into action* (Based on the Commission on Social Determinants of Health Country report). Geneva: World Health Organization. Retrieved from http://www.who.int/social_determinants/EN_health_equity_country_level_lessons_from_csdh.pdf

Whitehead, M. (1992). The concepts and principles of equity and health. *International Journal of Health Services, 22*,429–445.

World Health Organization (WHO) (1948). *Constitution of the World Health Organization.* Geneva: Author.

———. (2000). *World health report: Health systems: Improving performance.* Geneva: Author.

———. (2006*a*). Commission on social determinants of health. Ref. WHO/EIP/EQH/01/2006, Geneva, Switzerland. Retrieved fromhttp://www.who.int/social_determinants/resources/csdh_brochure.pdf

———. (2006*b*). *World health report: Working together for health.* Geneva: Author.

———. (2007). World health assembly resolution 60.11: Medium-term strategic plan 2008–2013 (p. 50). Retrieved from http://apps.who.int/gb/ebwha/pdf_files/WHASSA_WHA60-Rec1/E/reso-60-en.pdf

———. (2008*a*). Medium term strategic plan 2008-2013 and programme budget 2008-2009. Retrieved from http://apps.who.int/gb/e/e_amtsp.html

———. (2008*b*). *Commission on Social Determinants of Health final report.* Geneva: Author. Retrieved from http://www.who.int/social_determinants/thecommission/finalreport/en/index.html

———. (2008*c*). *World health report: Primary health care: Now more than ever.* Geneva: Author.

———. (2009). World health assembly resolution 62.14: Reducing health inequities through action on the social determinants of health (p. 21). Retrieved from http://apps.who.int/gb/ebwha/pdf_files/WHA62-REC1/WHA62_REC1-en-P2.pdf

———. (2010). *World health report: Health systems financing: The path to universal coverage.* Geneva: Author.

———. (2011*a*). *Improving equity in health by addressing social determinants.* Edited by the Commission on Social Determinants of Health Knowledge Networks, Jennifer H. Lee, and Ritu Sadana. Geneva: Author. Retrieved from http://whqlibdoc.who.int/publications/2011/9789241503037_eng.pdf

———. (2011*b*). *Rio political declaration on social determinants of health.* Rio de Janeiro, Brazil, October 21.

________.WHO (2013). *Closing the Health Equity Gap: Policy Options and Opportunities for Action.* Geneva: Author. Retrieved from http://www.who.int/iris/bitstream/10665/78335/1/9789241505178_eng.pdf

WHO Regional office for Africa (2010). *Health inequities in the African region of the World Health Organization: Magnitude, trends and sources.* Brazzaville, Congo: Author.

INDEX